Advance Praise for *The Global 200 Executive Recruiters*

"Like no one else, Nancy Garrison-Jenn has her finger on the pulse of global executive search. Her insider knowledge, shared here freely, allows both the neophyte and the seasoned recruiter to better navigate in the world of international search."

> —J. STEVEN HILL, vice president
> International Human Resources, Viacom Inc.

"Nancy Garrison-Jenn has done it again, and in an even more useful fashion. Her book provides a global review of the executive search practice and details on the top search consultants. As the editor of the Worldwide Executive Tax and Immigration Guides for the world's human resource directors, I have a good understanding of their needs, and I recommend this book as an essential tool for helping them meet the executive human capital crisis of the year 2000+."

> —JACK B. ANDERSON, senior partner
> HSD Ernst & Young

THE GLOBAL 200

THE GLOBAL 200

EXECUTIVE RECRUITERS

*An Essential Guide to the Best Recruiters in the
United States, Europe, Asia, and Latin America*

NANCY GARRISON-JENN

Jossey-Bass Publishers • San Francisco

Jossey-Bass books and products are available through most bookstores. To contact Jossey-Bass directly, call (888) 376-2537, fax to (800) 605-2665, or visit our website at www.josseybass.com.

Substantial discounts on bulk quantities of Jossey-Bass books are available to corporations, professional associations, and other organizations. For details and discount information, contact the special sales department at Jossey-Bass Inc., Publishers: (415) 433–1740; Fax (415) 605-2665.

For sales outside the United States, please contact your local Simon & Schuster International Office.

Manufactured in the United States of America.

Library of Congress Cataloging-in-Publication Data

Garrison-Jenn, Nancy., Date.
    The global 200 executive recruiters / Nancy Garrison-Jenn — 1st edition
       p. cm.
    ISBN 0–7879–4139-5
      1. Executives—Recruiting.   2. Business consultants.   3. Executives—Recruiting—Directories.   4. Business consultants—Directories.   I. Title.
HF5549.5.R44J462 1998
658.4'07111—dc21   ·   98-11588

FIRST EDITION
HB Printing 10 9 8 7 6 5 4 3 2 1

CONTENTS

PREFACE

Several commercially successful books have been written about the leading executive search consultants in the U.S.A. These books are well done and quite popular. Yet their scope is insufficient for a variety of reasons. Certainly the U.S.A. is not the only place in the world where outstanding search professionals reside. Nor is it the only place in the world where outstanding search professionals reach in finding candidates.

Most of the books written to date about the headhunting profession are U.S.A. dominated. Those that attempt to go beyond its borders also include Canada and sometimes Mexico. It is time, past time, to recognize that there are outstanding search professionals working around the globe. They are everywhere, from Brazil to China to India and beyond. By recognizing that, and by presenting the personal voices of the consultants, *The Global 200* brings something new to the field.

The Need for The Global 200

Increasingly, global firms are looking outside the U.S.A. for senior management talent, especially in the fast developing markets of Asia, Eastern Europe, India, and Latin America. I feel that it is indeed time to pay tribute to some of the most respected global players. By listing and describing what I consider to be the top 200 outstanding professionals on a worldwide basis, this book provides a much needed service to clients and candidates alike. Surely companies searching for talent and the individuals who are that talent can benefit by broadening their horizons, by acknowledging the global marketplace that exists today.

The 200 individuals whose biographies are included in this book are truly outstanding search professionals, doing excellent work on a worldwide basis. Between these individuals and additional consultants who are cited and discussed, but whose individual biographies are not included here, the book covers a wealth highly regarded individuals. Given the breadth and depth of these individual consultants and the firms they represent, the reader is sure to find the right consultant and the right firm for the job.

How I Came to Write This Book

During a twenty-year career in international marketing with consumer goods firms (Revlon, Gillette, Atari, Moet Vuitton), I came into contact with and hired many of the global search firms. The good consultants fascinated me—and the interest stuck. In 1988, in Paris, I founded a consulting firm that focuses exclusively on the executive search profession. Today, I split my time between writing books on executive search and consulting. In my consulting to multinational firms—firms such as Coca-Cola, Diageo, LVMH, Viacom—and to many of the search firms themselves, I advise on the selection of search consultants on a regional and global basis.

When researching this book, I asked the senior management of the leading global search firms and several hundred senior human resource and line executives of major multinationals around the world—over and over again in numerous interviews—who they felt were outstanding individual search consultants. The consultants they named fall into a number of categories, including:

- *Leading high-end generalists.* These are the well-known consultants who work at very senior, board level positions. They include such individuals as Gerry Roche and Tom Neff in the U.S.A. and Miles Broadbent, David Kimbell, Ana Mann, and Jürgen Mülder in Europe. These consultants are constantly cited in the *Wall Street Journal*, the *New York Times*, *Financial Times*, and other international papers. Such consultants increasingly do nonexecutive director board assignments.

- *Outstanding, highly visible sector and industry specialists.* Many search consultants are retained for their in-depth knowledge of a sector or field. Increasingly, specialization is the name of the game and these individuals are well equipped to capitalize on that.

- *Consultants with significant global, multi-country experience and vision* These consultants typically work on an international basis.

To limit the list to the top 200 respected professionals, I have of necessity been highly selective; surely, one could mention more than 200 stars in the United States alone. However, as an American lucky enough to have lived in Brazil, Kenya, Sweden, France, and now England, I know how critical it is to consider the rest of the world—and how much is gained from a more global perspective. Indeed, it is becoming increasingly important to have well respected consultants in local offices on a global basis—especially in the newer, developing economies such as Brazil,

China, India, Poland, Russia, and the emerging Asian markets. This book, then, is my attempt to profile the shining stars and the rising stars of the executive search world. These are the ones to watch—and to have on your team. The information provided in the text and the profiles was confirmed before the book went to press. It is important to note, however, that the executive search market is in a state of profound change. Due to a sharp increase in consolidations, mergers, acquisitions and public offerings, affiliations, both of firms and individual consultants, change rapidly.

Who Should Use The Global 200?

My bias is clear: you needn't consider yourself a global player to benefit from *The Global 200*. If your firm is reaching into broader markets, or if it's attempting to do so and finding itself stalled, you may need to be expanding the scope of your searches. If you are a job seeker yourself, taking the broader perspective can only help. Use the text and the listings of *The Global 200* to find the right firm and the right consultant for the next step of your career.

I want to stress the importance of global or international vision and breadth of expertise. Multi-country sensitivity and the ability to work on assignments cross border is becoming increasingly important for clients who need to search in several markets at one time and who increasingly need to look outside their own industry sectors and geographic areas for talent. The consultants included here fully understand that.

How to Use This Book

In Chapter One, I provide a brief overview of the field and an introduction to how the profession got started and developed around the world. I also expand upon the global nature of the search profession today and I share insights into the debate between choosing a firm or choosing a consultant.

In Chapter Two, I pursue the question of making the right match, of finding the recruiter best suited for the job. How do you know whether to rely on the consultant or the firm? The two are intertwined: the individual is vitally important—as is the executive search firm. Even the most outstanding individual consultants need a strong, supportive, and globally minded firm behind them. This chapter provides guidance for both the company and the individual on selecting the right person and the right firm for a search. Throughout, I emphasize that the match—the mesh of personalities and purpose—is important. This connection is critical, both in choosing the consultant and firm, and then in getting the right client-to-candidate (and candidate-to-client) match.

Chapter Three provides advice to companies using a search firm to help them locate talent and bring it on board. It gives advice on managing the client-consultant relationship, the search process, and choosing a candidate.

Chapter Four is directed to job seekers. It covers such topics as why and how to cultivate a long-term relationship with a headhunter, how to get noticed, negotiating with prospective employers, and managing a career over time.

Chapters One through Four each include a brief executive summary of key points.

The discussion in Chapter Five serves as a gateway to the Directories, the part of the book most likely help with the specific search needs of those with global requirements and perspectives.

The Directories

Directory One, The Global 200 Profiles, offers thorough profiles of the top 200 consultants. These consultants have provided relevant information such as their addresses and telephone numbers, descriptions of their practices, and more personalized information, including photographs and their answers to my questions about consulting in today's marketplace.

In Directory Two, the Top Global Firms, I provide a brief explanation of the ownership and organization of each of the top firms. I also name the key players and give a quick assessment of each firm's current direction.

Directory Three, Consultants by Industry/Sector, provides ready cross reference by the consultants' stated areas of expertise. Since specialization is increasing in today's world, this directory should prove to be a particularly useful way to find a consultant to match your needs.

Directory Four sets forth the top 200 consultants by firm name.

Directory Five provides references to the top 200 by country.

If I have met my goals in writing this book, the text and each of the directories will serve useful purpose. Readers will find the best consultant and the best firm for their needs, with a minimum of time spent in the process.

Acknowledgments

In acknowledging those who contributed to this book, I must first credit The Top 200 themselves. These consultants created time in their full schedules to provide a wealth of information—both personal and professional; it is their contributions that distinguish this book. Special thanks to Richard Ferry for providing the Foreword to the book as well as much information and valuable global perspective along the way. Others helped by sharing their insights as headhunters and strategists in this exciting and fast moving profession. Thanks are due to headhunters Paul Buchanan-Barrow, Richard Buschman, Dennis Carey, Gerard Clery-Melin, Roddy Gow, Nicholas Gardiner, Richard King, Baldwin Klep, Herbert Mines, Jürgen Mülder, Hermann Sendele, Peter Van de Velde, and Tim Vignoles, to name a few. In addition, Kate Bryant and Kay Kennedy, heads of corporate communications, deserve particular thanks. I also owe much to the Human Resource directors who provided valuable insights and sound judgment on the profession despite all its turbulence. Special thanks to John de Leeuw, whose brilliant success first as a headhunter, then as head of human resources at Phillips and, more recently, Diageo (the combined Guinness-GrandMet) has taught me a lot about the profession. Thanks also to Lawrence DeMonaco (GE Capital), Austin Gillis (United Technologies), Steven Hill (Viacom), Concetta Lanciaux (LVMH), Abby Rudolph (Estee Lauder), and John Steele (BT). As great clients and colleagues, they have helped me understand the search process from the client side.

Thanks to Cedric Crocker, senior editor at Jossey-Bass Publishers, Inc., who brought together a terrific editorial and production team, including Molly Ahearn, editorial assistant; Cheryl Greenway, assistant editor; and Judith Hibbard, senior production editor. Together with Jon Peck of Dovetail Publishing Services, they handled the many challenges this book presented and made San Francisco seem "just around the corner" from London. My special thanks to Janet Hunter who, as developmental editor, kept the process constantly moving and maintained a sense of balance (and humor) despite the constant changes to the field and the book. She provided superb guidance on this, my first trade book.

And, most importantly, thanks to my three children—Alexandre, Stephan, and Gabrielle—and to my husband, Jean Hervé. They have talked, around the clock—in English, French, Portuguese, and Japanese—to many of the professionals included here. My husband offered sound advice, whenever and wherever it was called for, even amid the World Cup finals. My thanks to all of you.

London, England NANCY GARRISON-JENN
July 1998

ABOUT
THE AUTHOR

Nancy Garrison-Jenn has been closely tracking the executive search world for multinational firms since 1988, when she started her own firm in Paris.

She went out on her own after a twenty-year career in international consumer marketing management with Gillette, Revlon, Atari, and LVMH/Moet Vuitton. During her consumer marketing career, she was responsible for product launches in over 40 markets worldwide. During these years, she lived in Brazil, South Africa, and Kenya exercised subsidiary responsibility. Subsequent to these assignments, she was based in Los Angeles as a management consultant, specializing in the fields of entertainment, media, and communications. Clients included Warner Communications, Polygram, Disney, and leading consumer software firms.

Garrison-Jenn has written eight authoritative books for the *Economist* on executive search in Western Europe, Eastern Europe, Latin America, and most recently, on the Asia Pacific region. She also consults to many firms, including IAG, Coca-Cola, Diageo (formerly Grand Met-Guinness), LVMH, Sanofi, United Technologies, and Viacom. In her books and her consulting, she identifies outstanding consultants and firms on a regional or global basis. Her Executive Search reports (by region) for the Economist Intelligence Unit/EIU are considered the benchmark of the industry. In them, she summarizes key trends and provides candid personal assessments of each firm.

A graduate of the Yale University School of Management, she is part of the Yale Alumni Council and does interviewing for the University in Europe. She is fluent in English, French, Spanish, and Brazilian Portuguese.

Nancy Garrison-Jenn has dual American-French nationality and is married to a Frenchman. Together with their three children, they live in London.

FOREWORD

Leadership is paramount as we move into the twenty-first century, where intellectual capital will replace bricks and mortar as a company's most important asset. Original thinking, nontraditional decision making and the ability to instill a global vision and culture within an organization are just a few of the qualities that will be essential for the successful leader of tomorrow.

How are these global leaders to be found? Some will rise to the top through their organizations, which will spend considerable time and resources in developing a senior cadre of managers through rotation programs, overseas assignments and fast-tracking. Many other leaders will be identified, sought out, evaluated and placed in senior positions by executive recruiting consultants.

Who are these consultants who wield such power in the global marketplace? Just 30 years ago, they were members of a fledgling profession that was little known outside the world's largest corporations. Today they are routinely consulted by companies of all sizes, and by academic and nonprofit institutions around the world in developing markets as well as in highly industrialized nations.

With our fast-paced world constantly rewriting the script for players on the global stage, more and more organizations are turning to executive search professionals to identify their leaders for the future. Now *The Global 200 Executive Recruiters* will help make the job that much easier. My congratulations to Nancy Garrison-Jenn on her hard work and dedication, which have resulted in a valuable resource for organizations throughout the world.

RICHARD M. FERRY
Chairman, Korn/Ferry International

Executive Recruiters

Specialists in Human Capital, Brokers of the Knowledge Revolution

Executive search is a fast-growing, dynamic field that surpassed $6.5 billion in worldwide revenues in 1997, an 18 percent increase from the year before. This growth reflects a five-year boom cycle that has seen consistent double-digit growth and has nearly doubled the industry from its $3.5 billion level in 1993. If growth rates continue, worldwide search revenues should exceed $10 billion by the year 2000.

About half this revenue is currently earned in the United States and one-third in Europe (Western and Eastern Europe combined); the percentage of business outside the United States is steadily increasing. The industry is healthy and growing at an impressive rate, with no slowdown in sight. The top fifteen global firms had net revenue of almost $2 billion in 1997 and grew at a rate in excess of 19 percent over 1996 as they opened new offices throughout Europe, Asia, and Latin America and added staff around the world. The fastest-growing region in 1997 was Asia, especially Greater China, Malaysia, Taiwan, Korea, and India. Despite difficult economic conditions in Asia now, its search market is still growing. The former Soviet Union is also a quickly developing area for search, as are the Mideast and East European regions, including Greece, Turkey, Saudi Arabia, Poland, Slovenia, Slovakia, and the former Baltics. Latin America is also a booming region, especially Brazil and Chile.

The search world is extremely fragmented, with a natural concentration of small firms at the lower end of the revenue spectrum. More than half of all retainer firms fall below $1 million in revenues; at the other end of the spectrum, fewer than 1 percent of firms have revenues over $5 million. Five or six serious global players dominate the market at the high end, and they are becoming a good deal more professional and client focused. Most had between 20 and 30 percent revenue growth in 1997.

The search profession is going through turbulent times. Just the first half of 1998 has seen a significant number of mergers, acquisitions, and consolidations. Many of the loosely structured networks are disbanding because they can no longer compete effectively. Ed Kelley, Senior Vice President of Korn/Ferry International in Europe recently reflected on this, saying: "There will be fewer global players in the search profession as we know it today. There will be perhaps two to three global firms, several strong, well-positioned boutiques, and many new entrants. These new entrants may come from other fields; it is likely many will come from the technology industry since search today is very much technology and systems driven."

The top two global firms are Korn/Ferry International and Heidrick & Struggles. Korn/Ferry has been ranked first in net revenue for many years; however, Heidrick's recent acquisition of Mülder & Partner in Germany and many other strategic hires propels it to a leading position. Both firms had over $275 million in net revenues in 1997. Spencer Stuart, the third-largest firm, dominates the search market at CEO and board levels, along with the other firms in the top five. Russell Reynolds, the fourth largest firm worldwide, is a leader in financial services and telecommunications. It is doing extremely well, especially in Europe and Latin America. In 1997, its revenues were $184 million, up 25 percent from the previous year. Amrop International, the fifth-largest global firm, is the only one that is an independent association of firms (not wholly owned); it has had a series of public offerings in the United States, United Kingdom, and Canada to raise additional funds for expansion. LAI, its U.S. partner, acquired the U.S. branch of Ward Howell International (ranked number eight in the United States) in 1997. It is possible that, if these trials are successful, some of the other global firms will also make public offerings soon. Rounding out the top six global firms is Egon Zehnder International (EZI), with net revenue around $180 million in 1997. The only Swiss firm in the top ten, EZI is well respected for its integrated, one-firm organization and compensation structure and for the high number of McKinsey consultants on board.

This book has much to say about the top firms and the top individuals in executive recruiting worldwide. But first, some background on the field of executive search.

WHAT IS EXECUTIVE SEARCH?

Started in the United States more than fifty years ago, executive search is defined as the recruitment of senior executives and specialists with an average compensation level over $100,000. Regardless of actual pay (in certain developing markets, overall compensation may be lower than $100,000), those individuals targeted by executive search work at senior levels with regional, country, or international responsibility. This definition and the field itself have evolved as explained more thoroughly in the boxed section, "A Brief History of Executive Search." Both continue to evolve as international work becomes the norm.

TODAY'S GLOBAL SEARCHES

There's no denying it: boundaries are merging and the world is evolving quickly into one international marketplace. In executive search as in business, it's true: firms must cover the globe or at least acknowledge the interconnectedness of their markets. Outstanding search professionals can be found everywhere—as can outstanding candidates. Increasingly, global firms are looking outside the United States for senior management talent, especially in the fast developing markets of Asia, Eastern Europe, India, and Latin America.

Baldwin Klep (of Heidrick & Struggles in Brussels) once recommended an eastern European national working in Brazil to become the general manager of a fast moving consumer goods food conglomerate in Prague. If this seems an unlikely combination, consider the reasons. The consultant had already succeeded amid the "wild west" mentality in a startup operation in a small town in the northeast of Brazil. Different as the industries were, the attitude was transferable and, as predicted, most helpful for a start-up position in what was then the "wild east" of Prague. The candidate's experience in an emerging market where he had to literally roll up his sleeves and transport products in a canoe helped him survive—and thrive—in the pioneering lifestyle in Prague.

This is but one example. As reflected in the scope of this book, global or international vision and breadth of expertise are critical. Multicountry sensitivity and the ability to work on assignments across borders are becoming increasingly important. Companies need recruiters who can search in several markets at one time. Increasingly, they also need to look outside their own industry sectors and geographic areas for talent. Fortunately, a growing number of search consultants do outstanding work. And an increasing percentage of these consultants can be found outside the United States, both in large multinationals and in smaller boutique and specialized firms. How do I know this?

A BRIEF HISTORY OF EXECUTIVE SEARCH

For those with an interest in how executive search has evolved, here is a quick description.

Executive Search in the United States

In building the management consultancy Booz·Allen & Hamilton during the years following World War II, Edwin Booz said, "Often the best solution to a management problem is the right person." He thus defined an important aspect of the executive search profession that had grown out of the management consulting firms a few years earlier. Yet, strictly speaking, the pioneer of search predated Booz by decades. In 1926, an executive named Thorndike Deland launched a business that charged a $200 retainer to find expert buyers for New York department stores and an eventual fee of 5 percent of salary for those he placed. After the war, with Booz's influence, executive search grew steadily as part of the rapidly growing management consultancy business.

But it soon became evident to executive search practitioners at McKinsey and Booz·Allen that search might best be provided as an entirely separate business. There was a clear conflict of interest between recommending management changes and then offering, for an additional fee, to fill the positions created. Also, as client rosters grew at the larger management consultancies, too many organizations became off-limits hunting grounds.

Because executive search was only a small part of management consulting, these difficulties persuaded McKinsey to leave the sector in 1951. Ward Howell, head of the McKinsey search practice at that time, left to found the search firm that bears his name and that is among the world's largest. He was not alone. Handy Associates also broke away from McKinsey, and Booz·Allen, which maintained its search service until the late seventies before pulling out, developed many more of today's top search consultants. Among firms launched by former Booz·Allen consultants were Boyden (in 1946), Heidrick & Struggles (1953), Spencer Stuart (1956), and Amrop International Lamalie (1967).

The large accountancy firms also built search practices, but eventually these too could not be sustained amid potential conflicts with their audit practices and lengthy off-limits lists. For example, Lester Korn and Richard Ferry left what is now KPMG to set up Korn/Ferry and Russell Reynolds evolved from Price Waterhouse via William H. Clark. Although some of the accountancy firms continue to offer recruitment in offices outside the United States, most do middle or upper middle management work for existing clients. A.T. Kearney, acquired by EDS in 1996, was then one of the only strategy consulting firms left with a search practice.

Executive Search in Europe

Search in Europe began fifteen or twenty years later than in the United States. The first American executive search firm to arrive in Europe was Spencer Stuart, which opened an office in London in 1961 and in Paris three years later. Spencer Stuart is often called the "grandfather of search" in Europe, as it played the same important role as McKinsey and Booz·Allen in the United States. Dr. Egon Zehnder left Spencer Stuart to found the first distinctly European executive search firm in Zurich in 1964, adding offices in Brussels, Paris, and London by the end of that decade.

London was an important starting point for many American search firms that were attracted by the large number of U.S. firms with subsidiary offices there. Boyden, Korn/Ferry, Heidrick & Struggles, Russell Reynolds, and Spencer Stuart all opened offices in London by the end of the 1960s, targeting the high end of the British market. At the same time, a sizable number of recruitment firms—accustomed to reaching the middle management sector—also began to emerge. These were mainly British firms such as MSL, PA Consulting Group, and Tyzack. The selection market grew strongly in London in the late fifties and sixties because, unlike in the United States, effective national coverage of the potential market was offered by quality newspapers such as the Telegraph and the Times.

The first British executive search firms began in the 1970s with GKR (founded by Roy Goddard, David Kay, and Fred Rogers), John Stork (now merged with Korn/Ferry) and Whitehead Mann (part of Amrop International). Norman Broadbent emerged later with two successful partners from the Russell Reynolds office in London. Many of these strictly British firms have continued to prosper and to work at senior management levels, with most joining forces with a global firm or network.

The Swiss firm Egon Zehnder continues to be the first-ranked search firm in Europe, especially at senior management levels, although Heidrick & Struggle's recent merger with the number one German firm, Mülder & Partner, now makes Heidrick a leading contender for the dominant firm in Europe. Korn/Ferry, Spencer Stuart, Amrop International, and Russell Reynolds are also in the top five in Europe.

Executive Search in Central and Eastern Europe

Central and Eastern Europe are important growth regions for search, especially Poland, Hungary, and the Czech Republic, where most of the global firms now have local offices. Leading firms in this region are H. Neuman International, Korn/Ferry, Amrop, Egon Zehnder, and Ward Howell. H. Neuman was the pioneer in the region. Key development areas for the future are the Baltics, the former Soviet Union, and the Mideast, particularly Saudi Arabia, Israel, and Turkey.

Executive Search in Latin America

Boyden Associates, a pioneering firm in early global expansion, opened the first permanent search office in Mexico City in 1966 with a former ITT executive, Robert Taylor. He promptly opened another office in São Paulo.. The offices continued to grow but disagreements with the founder, Sid Boyden, led to Robert Taylor leaving the firm in 1970 to form TASA (Taylor Associates SA). Many outstanding TASA Latin America consultants joined Heidrick & Struggles in 1996. Today the most highly visible executive search firms in Latin America are Korn/Ferry, Egon Zehnder, Spencer Stuart, and, more recently, Heidrick & Struggles and Russell Reynolds.

Executive Search in Asia

Boyden opened an office in Hong Kong in 1965 and in Australia in 1966, both staffed by westerners. Theirs were the first firms in the Asia-Pacific region. The first Asian search consultant was Paul Cheng (then chairman of Inchscape Pacific and now of SC Rothschild in Hong Kong), earning him the title of "grandfather of search" in Asia. Cheng played an important role in building Spencer Stuart's business after setting up its Hong Kong office in 1976. Egon Zehnder and Korn/Ferry were quick to open multiple offices in the Asian region starting with Australia, Japan, and Hong Kong. In the late 1970s many of the firms then expanded into Singapore, making it an important center in its own right for the region including Malaysia, Indonesia, and Thailand.

Asia is an active region in the world of executive search, especially in Greater China, India, Malaysia, and South Korea, where many firms have recently opened local offices. Despite the recent economic downturn in Southeast Asia, the need for expert senior management is now more crucial than ever, especially for the large family-run Chinese conglomerate firms. Korn/Ferry, Egon Zehnder, and Russell Reynolds are the largest firms in Asia, with Heidrick & Struggles making aggressive advances in the information technology and telecommunications fields.

DETERMINING THE BEST

I have analyzed the executive search profession since the late 1980s, writing a series of benchmarking studies for The Economist (the Economist Intelligence Unit/EIU). These competitive market studies provide in-depth views on the major firms by geographic region as well as industry trends. I have always focused my work on the global and high-end niche firms themselves and not the individual consultants, because I have always believed that the firm is paramount. I agree with and respect the opinion of Egon P. Zehnder, founder and chairman of Egon Zehnder International, that it is indeed the firm (that is, the partnership) that matters and not the individual consultants themselves because, ultimately, highly efficient and well-integrated partnerships of consultants make the difference to the client.

David Kimbell, chairman of Spencer Stuart International and highly respected in senior-level search, certainly agrees with Zehnder's philosophy that the firm is key. His firm maintains a low profile in the media, unlike many other highly visible firms. So I was in good company in thinking of the firm as being primary. However, headhunter Nicholas P. Gardiner (of Gardiner Townsend & Associates, New York) recently made me stop and think twice about my viewpoint when he said: "Good search consultants do search as if their life depended upon it. Yours does, so look carefully for that characteristic when selecting one and check references."

Certainly, many of the top firms were built and continue to flourish based upon the reputations of outstanding individuals and charismatic leaders such as Egon Zehnder, Tom Neff and David Kimbell (Spencer Stuart), Russell Reynolds (Russell Reynolds), and Richard Ferry (Korn/Ferry International). Consultants at these firms (for example, Gerry Roche, John Thompson, and now Jürgen Mülder at Heidrick & Struggles; and Windle Priem at Korn/Ferry) have enriched the visibility and presence of the firms.

Through my constant evaluation of the field, I have come to believe that the individual and personal chemistry matter a great deal. Therefore, clients and candidates alike need to evaluate both the consultant and the firm together. That a firm is paramount, or is a market leader, will not necessarily get a particular job done.

Outstanding candidates will be discovered and wooed by respected search consultants who are supported by highly integrated, efficiently run global firms. The client must carefully select both the individual who will carry out the assignment and the firm that will provide support on a global basis. In recognition that the individual chosen does matter a great deal, this is my first book about individual consultants.

Certainly the debate will continue. But in practice, no matter how good the firm, if the personal chemistry between the client, the consultant, and the candidate is wrong then the relationship will not work and no one—neither client, candidate, nor consultant—will get what they desire.

SUMMARY

In this chapter, we defined executive search as the recruitment of senior executives and specialists with an average compensation level of over $100,000. Individuals targeted by executive search are employed at senior levels with regional, country, or international responsibility.

But this definition is changing even as the range of search reaches a global range. For example, in certain developing markets overall compensation may be lower than $100,000. Regardless of actual pay, however, the responsibilities of the executives and specialists are increasing. And the importance of individual consultants is rising.

In Chapter Two we take up the debate concerning whether to choose an individual or a firm, and we look at the selection criteria for those consultants profiled in *The Global 200*.

How to Select a Recruiter

Evaluating Individual Consultants and Firms

Human resource (HR) directors and other senior executives are constantly bombarded by executive search firms, many of which seem to offer the same services and advice. Job seekers are faced with an enormous number of consultants and firms, any one of which might find them that ideal position. How does one select the ideal consultant in the ideal firm?

As mentioned in Chapter One, Egon Zehnder, founder of Egon Zehnder International, believes that in executive search the firm and its culture are paramount, and that one must first choose a firm—rather than an individual—because there are only effective team players in a well-managed firm, not stars. Other experienced search consultants and HR directors disagree. They believe that the individual consultant matters most.

I believe that both the individual consultant and the firm are important, and an increasing number of HR directors agree. No matter what the credentials of the firm, if the consultant and the client are not well suited for each other, if their personal chemistry doesn't work, there is potential for disaster. Similarly, if the various offices of the search firm do not work well together in a highly integrated manner, or if there is bickering and unpleasant discussion over fee splitting between offices, completing a cross-border search may be extremely difficult. Therefore, as a practical matter one must have ways to evaluate both the individual consultant and that consultant's firm.

EVALUATING THE CONSULTANT

Given the need to evaluate both the individual consultant and the firm because neither can be completely independent of the other, how then do you begin the selection process? *The Global 200* should simplify your search. The individuals cited in this book are leading professionals in their field, they actively work with clients (in contrast to having primarily a senior management or administrative role in their firm), and they are enthusiastically supported by their colleagues and HR counterparts as outstanding players. Thus all the individuals cited in this book are worth your serious consideration.

> *Good search consultants do search as if their life depended upon it. Yours does, so look carefully for that characteristic when selecting one and check references.*
>
> —Nicholas P. Gardiner (Gardiner, Townsend & Associates, New York)

The chairman of Amrop International, Daniel Gauchat, said that "an outstanding consultant has an understanding of what drives a business as well as sound judgment on the professional and personal characteristics of successful candidates, which requires hands-on experience in a senior management role, and preferably in an international environment. It is also important to acquire effective consulting skills to deal with both conceptual as well as practical issues." This rings true for me, for I firmly believe that previous sector or industry experience provides invaluable benefits in assessing candidates.

As I selected consultants for inclusion in *The Global 200*, I looked at the following:

- Sector and industry visibility.
- Recommendations by HR professionals, firms, and colleagues.
- Mention by candidates who have used the consultants (and their firms) in recent job searches.
- Attention to global or international vision and expertise.

These criteria should also be of use to you in honing down the field.

Visibility

A senior consultant with high visibility in a specific market sector or industry inspires confidence—and ensures action. When Gerry Roche (Heidrick & Struggles) or Tom Neff (Spencer Stuart) call a CEO in the United States, the CEO takes the call; similarly for Jürgen Mülder (Heidrick & Struggles) in Germany or David Kimbell (Spencer Stuart) in the United Kingdom. In industry specialties, the same rule applies. For example, when Steven Potter (Highland Group), Win Priem (Korn/Ferry), Matthew Wright (Russell Reynolds), or Brian Sullivan (Sullivan & Company), all well known in financial services in New York City or London, call candidates, the candidates respond immediately. Anyone in the field knows it would be crazy not to. Cultivating an ongoing relationship with any of these headhunters is worthwhile. The well-known industry specialist (or generalist at the highest level) will get the targeted candidate to respond.

In my opinion, at the very senior levels the best search consultants are typically generalists, because senior executives at the highest levels usually need to have had previous experience in dealing with several industries, sectors, functions, markets, and so on. As will be discussed further, the generalist continues to be important for high-level CEO and board assignments.

In competing for major CEO and board positions, experience in the broadest sense offers the best solution. The team approach is vital and the team is often made up of a mixture of generalists with high personal standing and industry or functional specialists with respective deep-rooted backgrounds. In practice, clients are best served if the search firm can blend specialist experience with a generalist's approach.

—Jürgen Mülder
(Heidrick & Struggles, Frankfurt)

Recommendations

Recommendations are the key to choosing a consultant. This book consolidates the results of recommendations from many sources, including HR professionals, firms, colleagues, consultants, and candidates. In the preparation of my market intelligence reports for the EIU/Economist in London, I have, since 1990, conducted ongoing quantitative and qualitative market research studies in which I ask clients in a given market to name and assess individual consultants they have worked with. Search consultants are evaluated on the following criteria:

• Quality of candidates presented
• Sector/industry knowledge
• Speed of completion of assignments
• Overall service
• Value added

This information is then broken down by sector and industry and updated on an annual basis.

Praised by human resource professionals. The Executive Search Information Exchange, a group of HR professionals, meets regularly in New York to network and discuss issues relating to search. I have been a guest speaker for this group, discussing search in the international marketplace. I have also started a similar networking group of senior HR professionals in London, all with either global or European HR responsibility, to discuss executive search for the most senior management and nonexecutive positions. Similarly, in the past few years I have consulted to (and shared notes with) senior HR professionals from firms such as

Coca-Cola, Diageo, LVMH, and Viacom—firms with significant hiring needs worldwide. From these discussions, I have learned a great deal about the hiring of search firms on a global basis. I have used what I have gleaned from these meetings and discussion in selecting the Global 200.

Michael Boxberger (Korn/Ferry) puts it well in saying that to be a successful recruiter "you definitely have to immerse yourself in your client's business. You must be able to have a full understanding of the client company's culture, management structure and major issues in order to advise your client on what type of people they need to move the company forward. A good executive recruiter also needs to be a great listener, know how to read between the lines, be able to act as an extension of the client to effectively articulate the opportunity to the candidate and be experienced in high-level negotiating. Most important is sound judgment—about how the client and candidate will ultimately fit."

Chosen by firms and colleagues. Also as part of my EIU research, every local office of every executive search firm is systematically asked to cite the top five consultants in each of the major market sectors and industries as part of a quantitative questionnaire. In my ongoing dialogue with clients, I constantly ask, "Who is best at what—and why?" The answers I hear have shaped my selections.

Preferred by candidates. I am frequently asked by candidates (who are being courted by the search firms) who are the best consultants in a particular field. I am also asked by the search firms to talk to individuals they are trying to hire for their own firms. These interviews provide invaluable sources of input, for individuals have their own distinct impressions that they are often willing to share. It is important to remember that candidates become clients (and vice versa). The search market is dynamic and constantly changing; therefore, it's well worth the effort to constantly talk to all sides. A great recruiter is there in every way for the client. This includes understanding and anticipating the client's needs and providing added value.

> *Persistence, resilience, the ability to ask the right questions and then really listen to the answers, these are the characteristics that make for an outstanding search consultant.*
> —Roderick C. Gow (Amrop International)

International Vision and Expertise

For the system to work smoothly, individual consultants must be supported by their firms worldwide. If consultants have to spend time arguing over the splitting of fees between consultants or offices, then precious time will be wasted. The firm should function fluidly across borders. It is for these reasons that, as part of *The Global 200* directory, I include information on the organization of the top fifteen global firms—and that I encourage you to research the organization of any other firm you consider.

Baldwin Klep (Heidrick & Struggles, Brussels) suggests focusing on the following key criteria in the selection of a search firm for an international assignment:

- Is there truly an international partnership?
- Are there international obstacles (local profit centers, local bonus calculation) to cross-border cooperation?
- Is an international or regional team of consultants being presented?
- Do they know your sector well on a global or regional basis?

To supplement this, I have a quick way to determine if the consultants in a firm work well across borders. Ask a consultant you are considering hiring to name the firm's outstanding individuals in his or her sector or practice group around the world. If the consultant says "I'll get back to you" and can't name them immediately, continue your search for the right consultant. A confident answer doesn't guarantee that the consultants work well across borders, but it is a promising beginning.

What then are the characteristics of an outstanding search consultant, whether for locally based or international assignment? Egon Zehnder suggests that to be outstanding a consultant must possess the following:

- An impeccable sense of integrity and strong personal values.
- A solid, outstanding record of accomplishment wherever one worked before entering the executive search profession.
- A high level of competence reflecting a person's education, continuing learning practices, range and variety of personal experiences, and level of personal growth.

To this I add that an outstanding search consultant understands the client culture, sector, and industry as well as the client, if not better. Global or cross-cultural awareness is growing in importance and is an important value-added trait. The ability to think strategically falls in this category as well. Because the ideal candidate may or may not come from the given sector, a really good consultant will be able to search efficiently and creatively within his own sector or industry and understand where else to look, across both industries and cultures. Together, these make for a demanding set of personal criteria. They mark the traits I looked for in choosing the Global 200 consultants—and they are traits that can be useful to you. These traits must also be supported by the consultant's firm.

EVALUATING THE FIRM

According to Zehnder, the ideal firm should do the following:

- Provide situational leadership. A firm must fit its style to the needs of those who ask for the firm's advice. A solution for one client may be totally wrong for another.
- Make executive search consulting excellence exciting.
- Have consultants with exceptional intellectual qualifications. The consultants must be pragmatic, active, alert, disciplined, positive thinkers, good listeners, exceptional in their human contacts and skills, creative thinkers, and hardworking.
- Have an environment in which the consultants hold each other in high mutual respect, trust each other, foster teamwork, and excel in communication. The firm must be cohesive as a single firm with global resources, not individual stars. It must be one firm to assure that the consultants trust each other's goals and ambitions, each other's potential capabilities and ethics.

Zehnder's criteria are quite demanding. As an outsider, how can you fully evaluate the firm? There are a number of considerations to keep in mind.

Specialized Teams Versus Generalists

A primary benefit of using executive recruiters is being able to tap into their market intelligence. Therefore, be sure that the consultant and firm bring added-value and essential market intelligence. According to Tim Vignoles (formerly Korn/Ferry, now Garner International), to be successful, consultants must speak the language of the sector. Choose one that knows your sector or industry as well as, if not better than, you do.

Search firms are becoming increasingly specialized. Industry practice groups are emerging by sector and industry function on a global basis. These groups are composed of individual consultants with vital experience and contacts in the sector or industry. They serve a vital function: they are the most efficient way to find the best potential candidates on a worldwide basis. Therefore, you should question using individuals who do not have previous experience in your sector. They will probably not be in touch with the marketplace.

Specialty practice groups or specialist boutique firms now exist for every imaginable sector including financial services, real estate and insurance, consumer-retail, luxury goods, IT, telecommunications, health care, pharmaceutical, biotech, media and entertainment, foundations and nonprofit, and sports management. Heidrick & Struggles's Menlo Park IT group is well established in its field and the firm has managed to grow this practice worldwide. Russell Reynolds enjoys the same reputation in financial services, as does Korn/Ferry in financial services and, more recently, in media and entertainment and health care with its dedicated Princeton office. Egon Zehnder International is particularly well known in the pharmaceutical, health care, and fast moving consumer goods fields—and it is becoming more visible in financial services and technology.

But specialists are not always the answer. A firm that is based in a smaller market (for example, J. Peebles in New Zealand) cannot necessarily have dedicated specialists, for the marketplace is too small. And at the very highest levels of search—finding board directors and nonexecutive directors—one will typically find highly visible generalists (for example, Gerry Roche and Tom Neff) who can easily search across industries.

But beyond the highest-level searches, the future of generalists is often debated. According to Neal Maslan (LAI Ward Howell, Los Angeles), the day of the generalist is limited: "Clients demand specialization for industry knowledge; they want knowledge-based consultants to represent them." Dick Buschmann (Korn/Ferry, Netherlands) agrees: "We do not need generalists, provided the marketplace is large enough to have specialists in the different practice areas. I see a role for generalists in smaller markets (for example, Chile, New Zealand) and in emerging markets (for example, Malaysia, Thailand), but only there."

Jonathan Holman (Holman Group, San Francisco) believes we still need generalists, but decreasingly. For certain searches, he says, "It is enormously helpful to be a generalist and to work in a large firm with tentacles into many industries. A good generalist can do most searches well. However, the marketplace for top-quality executives has become so competitive that specialization is helpful in establishing credibility with candidates (and clients)."

Paul Buchanan-Barrow of Korn/Ferry International says: "The role of a generalist is to be able to think laterally and to help cross-fertilize one industry with another. Chief executives have moved successfully from one industry to another; good HR or marketing disciplines are equally applicable across many industries. Therefore, the ability to search across a wide range of industries is essential for a good recruiter. Generalists will remain, especially at the most senior levels."

The debate continues, but the short answer seems to be that the nature of the assignment has an influence. And for an ongoing, long-term relationship, a search firm that offers a dedicated specialty practice group generally has an advantage.

Organization of the Firm

How a search firm is organized is increasingly important in providing quality service, including global, multicountry research and the ability to have consultants work simultaneously on assignments from different offices around the world. Thus a firm's organization is becoming more and more of an issue. There are three basic ways to organize a search firm:

- By local office (geographic)
- By specialty practice group (industry expertise)
- By account management (by client)

Making the matrix work, having the proper balance devoted to each aspect, is very difficult. It seems, though, that the ideal solution would be a careful balance of all three.

Another aspect of organization to consider is the impact of local offices versus headquarters dominance. Among the top ten global firms, Amrop International and Korn/Ferry have the largest number of local offices worldwide (eighty-four and seventy-one, respectively), Russell Reynolds has the fewest (thirty-three), and Egon Zehnder, Heidrick & Struggles, and Spencer Stuart are somewhere in between (forty-eight, fifty, and forty-two, respectively). Are the numbers important?

What about geographic balance? Korn/Ferry, Egon Zehnder, and Spencer Stuart have extremely well-balanced and well-established practices across the continents, including the U.S. and Latin America, Europe, and Asia; Heidrick & Stuggles and Russell Reynolds are quickly joining their ranks. Certainly it appears to be a trend in the top firms, but does the search firm need a local office in every market to function effectively there? If understanding the local culture and being able to network there are important, you do need a local office. If, however, you are searching for a senior executive only once, perhaps this can effectively be handled from headquarters.

> *If the client is a global player, it is increasingly important for the organization to focus on account management and specialty practice group. The individual country management becomes much less important because consultants must constantly search cross-border to find the best candidates.*
>
> —John de Leeuw (Group HR Director of Diageo, London)

A balance needs to be achieved between the local office and global or regional headquarters. If the headquarters is too controlling, it will diminish the entrepreneurial spirit of the consultants in the field. But if the local partners are too autonomous, they will have difficulty working together across borders. To determine the balance in a specific firm, ask a consultant to assess his partners in the offices worldwide—and listen carefully to what he says.

Ownership: Structure and Compensation

The ownership structure of firms is becoming increasingly important to ever-demanding and increasingly sophisticated clients. The two main types of ownership are integrated (wholly owned), and independent networks. Many clients feel that integrated firms provide better global coverage and that the consultants work more closely together as partners. Egon Zehnder and Richard Ferry would both agree strongly. Others prefer the entrepreneurial spirit of the nonintegrated firms. These two main forms of ownership can be further divided into four basic types:

- Integrated (wholly owned).
- Nonintegrated close associations of locally owned firms with equity.
- Nonintegrated associations of locally owned firms without equity.
- Combinations (that is, strategic alliances and joint-venture associations).

Table 2.1 shows the ownership structure of the firms I rank as the top fifteen, in order. (For more information on these firms, see Directory Two.)

I provide this information on the top firms to emphasize the fact that in selecting a search firm, it is important to consider the firm's ownership structure. To make a fully informed decision you may need to know how the consultants are

Table 2.1   Ownership of the top 20 executive search firms

Firm Name	Wholly owned	Association with equity	Association without equity	Combination
Korn/Ferry Int'l	X			
Heidrick & Struggles	X			
Spencer Stuart	X			
Russell Reynolds	X			
Amrop Int'l		X		
Egon Zehnder Int'l	X			
Ray Berndtson				X
Ward Howell Int'l		X		
H. Neumann Int'l				X
Transearch			X	
A. T. Kearney				X
Hever Group			X	
Norman Broadbent				X
Horton Int'l				X
Boyden		X		

compensated for a multicountry search. If the ability to search across borders in several markets at a time is important to the search process, it may be better to work with an integrated, wholly owned firm (that is, Egon Zehnder, Spencer Stuart, Heidrick & Struggles, Russell Reynolds, or Korn/Ferry) where it is easier to delegate and the partners tend to have the same value system and emphasis on quality. In an integrated firm, partners are more accustomed to working together; the firm's structure facilitates this.

An independent affiliation of firms will find it harder than an integrated firm to get agreement and to move forward as a team. Experience shows that it is typically more difficult to get close, seamless cross-border cooperation in a noninte-grated group because of haggling over fee splitting and how the consultants are compensated.

Compensation systems of the leading search firms are quite varied. Egon Zehnder compensates consultants on a global, one-firm seniority-based system that encourages fluid, cross-border activity; Heidrick & Struggles includes performance in the specialty practice group as an important variable; Spencer Stuart and Korn/Ferry evaluate the performance of the local office as a profit center. Korn/Ferry has a new bonus pool that rewards cross-border performance.

Make sure that the consultant you choose is highly motivated to carry out the assignment and that his or her colleagues in other offices will be similarly motivated, especially if the project requires searching across borders. Ask how partners are compensated in the firm and how the system rewards and encourages cross-border work. A local office profit center (in which consultants are rewarded based upon local office profits only) does not encourage a partner in Paris to help a partner in Frankfurt. Ideally, search consultants should be well compensated for assisting their colleagues worldwide and they should be rewarded for excellent leadership (whether of an office, a practice group, or a client account).

Value-added Versus Filling the Spec

For a nonexecutive director or senior-level assignment, for example, a background in senior management and broad industry experience may be preferred. But as search assignments become more complicated and cross borders (especially in emerging markets), the ability to think strategically becomes of utmost importance. For this reason, some search firms offer a consulting team that is strategically oriented. For example, Egon Zehnder has a large number of consultants with previous experience at McKinsey, a firm that requires the consultants to work well in teams and to be able to work at the same senior-management level. Zehnder offers a service, called management appraisal, which is the assessment of senior management talent. This is a growing business for them now accounting for 20 percent of their business in Germany. Egon Zehnder devotes a great deal of its time and resources to the training of its consultants to provide true added value. Its consultants have all undergone an extensive training program in the United States on interviewing, candidate and client assessment, interpersonal skills, and the like. And it has an additional training program for management appraisal. Every partner and consultant goes through a training course on "competency-based interviewing" and another on interpersonal skills training. This training is part of a mind-set that Zehnder tries to develop in all of its people worldwide.

Few executive search firms devote as much time, effort, and resources to training as does Egon Zehnder, but there is a good deal of interest in making this happen. Zehnder comes closest to growing its own people, much the way that Anderson Consulting, McKinsey, and J. P. Morgan do in their own industries.

Expectations on Communication and Work Load

Frequency of communication, timing, and methods are of critical importance to a search. The client needs to confirm up front that the search firm is used to working in the manner most efficient for his needs and that the vehicles for interoffice communication are modern and up-to-date. In evaluating the firm, determine the following:

- When will the first review of candidates be? In three weeks? Six weeks?
- Is the communication among the consultant team in the field to be consistent or more haphazard?
- How many searches is the consultant working on at one time?
- Can the consultant devote the time needed for the successful completion of your project?

What would be reasonable guidelines? According to Jürgen Mülder, "The outstanding consultant is able to produce two to four exciting candidates in four to six weeks after the initiation of the search. He presents clients of such caliber that the client has a problem of choosing. If the consultant succeeds in another two to four weeks to close the search, I would consider this outstanding."

According to Neal Maslan (LAI Ward Howell, Los Angeles), the importance of workload depends on the quantity and quality of research support and on where the searches are in the cycle of the search process. Obviously, initiation, launch, candidate identification interview, and final referencing stages each demand varying amounts of time. In general, a consultant can handle from seven to nine active engagements while giving clients excellent service within a reasonable cycle time. Most consultants would agree with this estimate. For consultants with extensive support teams dedicated exclusively to their clients, this number might be even higher.

Advanced Technology

In choosing a firm, you should feel convinced that the search firm is constantly investing in technology to ensure that the search process has maximum efficiency. In determining whether the search firm has the most advanced technology in the fields of communication and database technology and has made a long-term investment in technology, you might ask the whether the firm uses the following:

- Voice mail
- Internet access and a website
- Videoconferencing

How global is its database and does it enhance cross-border communication on projects?

Korn/Ferry and Heidrick & Struggles are leaders in technology; this is evident in the smooth functioning of many of their specialty practice groups. Clearly, the efficient management of information is a key criterion for the success of a search firm.

Several global firms are now using the Internet as a way to advertise middle and upper middle management positions for their clients. Korn/Ferry recently went one step further: it announced a new joint venture to create the first on-line recruitment firm (Korn/Ferry–FutureStep) to target mid-level executives via the Internet. FutureStep is creating a powerful database that matches potential applicants with job positions, supported by the Korn/Ferry filtering process and brand name. It should leverage the power of the Internet and provide a valuable data service for the client. Although it is too soon to tell if the service will be successful, it is certainly an interesting venture. (For more information, see Korn/Ferry's website at http://www.kornferry.com.) Other firms, Heidrick & Struggles among them, are watching Korn/Ferry's launch with real interest and may provide similar services in the future.

Off-Limits Restrictions

Where can the firm's consultants go? And, often more importantly, where can't they go? It is very simple to determine which companies are off limits: just ask. Sit down early in the process with the search consultant and determine up front which are the ideal target companies and which of those, if any, are off limits to the headhunter's firm. If all your target companies are off limits because of previous client relationships, then this is not the right firm. If only one company is off limits and you want very much to work with that firm, perhaps a second search firm needs to be called in. But the situation should be made very clear early in the process.

Who Will Do the Work?

One final piece of advice in evaluating the firm brings us full circle. As Jonathan Holman says: "Select your search firm based on the consultant who will do the work and make sure that he or she will actually be doing it. Do not fall prey to large firms who send in their top talker to sell you and then delegate the real work to junior people." If the senior partner does the initial client presentation and then quietly disappears to another large client after a few months, you are not getting what you paid for.

SUMMARY

In evaluating a consultant, take note of the following:

- Sector or industry visibility. Bear in mind that the well-known consultant (whether an industry specialist or a generalist at the highest level) will get the targeted candidate to respond.
- Recommendations by HR professionals, firms, and colleagues. This is how you find the inside story and get a better sense of a match.
- Mentions by candidates. Those who have used the consultants and their firms in recent job searches are well qualified to speak.
- Attention to global or international vision and expertise. There is no denying it: the world's markets are blending together.

In evaluating the firm, take note of the following:

- Specialized teams versus generalists. The nature of the assignment has an influence on which is more appropriate for a particular search. For an ongoing long-term relationship, a search firm that offers a dedicated specialty practice group generally has an advantage. But for the highest-level nonexecutive and board positions, generalists take the lead.
- Organization. The organization of the firm, whether by geographic location, industry expertise, or client, plays a role as does the status of the local office versus headquarters.
- Ownership. The ownership of the firm has a direct effect on how the members work together. In choosing a firm, be aware of whether it is integrated or affiliated.
- Value-added versus filling the spec. Look for consultants with the strategic skills that provide significant added value.

- Expectations on communication and work load. Understand your expectations and be sure to discuss them up front.
- Advanced technology. Determine whether the search firm has the most advanced communication and database technology and has made a long-term investment in it. Such technology is important if the firm is to stay current and be strong in the future.
- Off-limits restrictions. Know which, if any, firms are off limits. Consider that in your decisions.

One final tip in choosing your search firm: choose based on the individual consultant who will do the work. Bottom line: whether a company is seeking talent or an individual is searching for the ideal position, the contact is the executive consultant and the chemistry must be right.

As a follow up to this chapter, Chapter Three presents advice to companies seeking talent. It covers how to best make use of the consultant and firm chosen.

Advice to Companies Seeking Talent

Once you have selected the ideal consultant and firm for your needs, how do you then make the best use of their expertise and capabilities? This chapter presents some advice on managing the relationship and evaluating and selecting candidates.

MANAGING THE RELATIONSHIP

With the search firm and the consultant chosen, the hard part begins: actively managing the process and making the relationship work. In speaking with experienced search consultants and their HR counterparts, I asked them to describe the characteristics of great clients and how to best manage the client-consultant relationship. Distilled down, here is their advice.

Form a Partnership with Your Consultant

Robert Benson (Spencer Stuart, Frankfurt), having had years of experience with difficult clients on both sides of the Atlantic, summarizes this point nicely: "Partner with your consultant . . . treat the person as an insider. Share all dimensions of your problem, including the political aspects. If you cannot trust the headhunter with this type of information, you are probably working with the wrong individual." Together, you can actively manage the search process.

Michael Boxberger, president and CEO of Korn/Ferry, also emphasizes the importance of partnership, noting that "a great client is willing to participate in the recruiting process, both providing and seeking input, and is willing to listen to a recruiter's advice, even if it differs from the client's own viewpoint. The best clients trust your advice and treat you as a partner in the process."

Roderick C. Gow of Amrop International says that "above all, a search is a partnership of the consultant and the client. Frequently, clients are not sure of exactly what they want and need to be helped by the consultant to reach the right sort of conclusion. Where a chief executive or product head is recruited, the individual who is satisfied will turn to the consultant to assist in the subsequent building process. This is search work at its best."

The idea of partnership received constant mention. Jürgen Mülder states that "a great client involves you in all major questions as far as corporate governance and top management compensation are concerned as well as all major concerns. It is a relationship of mutual trust and candid openness."

A number of consultants confirmed that great clients are like great friends in that there is a mutual bond of trust and respect. Indeed, very often great clients do become good friends. Richard King of Cordiner King Hever in Melbourne confirmed this, adding, "I do my best work with clients who have become good friends. I will go to any length not to let them down."

Emphasize Your Expectations

A number of consultants stressed the importance of being clear and direct about expectations of work by the consultant and the firm. As Jonathan Holman says, "Good search firms have more work than they can handle. You should manage them as you manage any outside supplier in a partnership effort. Do not presume that there is some magical process taking place from which you can absent yourself. Set up a specific timetable and make sure the firm lives up to it."

Robert Benson agrees: "Be direct and firm in stating your expectations regarding the frequency of communications, scope of information desired, timing, etc. Without verbalizing them, consultants will manage those elements to match their needs and not yours. Demanding clients are great clients but unrealistic clients. Set out your needs clearly but expect them to be challenged."

John de Leeuw, currently group HR director for Diageo (which resulted from the merger of Guinness and Grand Met), agrees: "The client must be absolutely clear on specific expectations up front regarding the services required, individual consultants to be part of the team, fee structure, ideal target firms, etc. I want to be involved at all stages of the process. Most important are the regional links. Also, close and regular communication is essential: I want to be informed of all communication between the client and consultants globally on a weekly basis."

This outlook is especially notable and de Leeuw's tactical and strategic understanding of how HR people can get the best out of search is impressive. This may be partly because de Leeuw was a headhunter in the early stages of his career in the Netherlands. This helped him understand the dynamics of search and gave him a tactical and strategic understanding of the search profession. As Paul Buchanan-Barrow, managing partner of Korn/Ferry, said, De Leeuw's history "contrasts very markedly with some other HR people who have never been recruiters and who think that the job is easy!"

Communication about needs and expectations is critical. According to Richard King, "Some of the best appointments are lateral solutions. These require a fair degree of confidence that the consultant really understands the client's need and can persuade the client accordingly. At the CEO level, this usually has to do with leadership skills and not specific industry experience. Search consultants love such solutions, but sadly they are difficult to achieve."

Make the Search a Top Priority

Because everyone loses when a search languishes, do whatever you can to sustain the momentum in the recruiting process. As Andy Hunter (Pendleton James, Boston) states, "So often the client will complain that the search takes too long. However, when it comes to actually interviewing the candidates, it is often the senior management team of the client that is traveling across the globe and is unavailable for interviews. Many wonderful candidates are lost because the client couldn't react quickly enough. Instead, make the hiring a priority."

Paul Buchanan-Barrow underscores the need for making the search a top priority: "A great client must be demanding, understanding, and have a sense of urgency."

The client should retain an ongoing interest in the search as it progresses and make it clear to everyone that the appointment is absolutely critical to the success of the organization. In practice, this is typified by frequent communication, weekly progress reports, and a constant pervading sense of urgency. It is making sure that every key executive on the client side makes the time in their busy schedules to see candidates sooner rather than later. It is making sure that all client-consultant communication is open and timely.

Remember: Candidates Are Not Applicants

Matthew Wright, head of Russell Reynolds (Europe), confirms that candidates have to be sold on the prospective role and career opportunity. They should be sold both by the client and by the individual search consultant. The ideal candidate might be perfectly happy in his current job, with no desire to move. The headhunter must convince the candidate that the prospective assignment is an exciting one and an essential next step.

ADVICE ON THE SELECTION OF CANDIDATES

The professionals I interviewed also had some advice on selecting candidates, choosing the one person from those they present.

Understand Your Needs

As a first step in being clear on expectations for candidates, determine the traits leading to successful performance in the firm. Work with the consultant to be sure these traits are appropriate and fully understood. Some firms will take these further than others. For example, according to Phil Vivian (a London-based Egon Zehnder consultant who helps develop training courses on interpersonal skills for the firm), Zehnder develops critical competencies for every assignment. For example, a candidate for an IT director position must be able to demonstrate the following:

- Ability to establish a vision statement for the firm.
- Knowledge of the latest technology developments.
- Ability to provide high-level customer service.

Consultant Herbert Mines (New York) summarizes the need to be clear about expectations nicely: "Think carefully in advance about what you really want to know [about the candidate]. Have a clear idea of the traits which produce successful performance in your company and focus your questions in these areas. There is no magic bullet to an interview: only persistence and careful listening."

Go Beyond the Comfort Zone

In many cases, even at nonCEO levels, success is determined by a candidate's relevant skills rather than industry knowledge. Neal Maslan recently had a client who initially insisted that the CFO come from the managed care field. The client felt this background was necessary to fully understand the technical issues. In successfully recruiting an "off-spec" candidate out of G.E., it became readily apparent to the client that the real requirements were the ability to learn a new industry quickly, superb operational finance experience, and an ability to take a company through an initial public offering process. In fact, the industry experience was not crucial.

Often the comfort zone equates to a certain image, whether it reflects the CEO or a dominant pattern in the firm. Indeed, according to veteran consultant John Johnson (Amrop International, Cleveland), clients tend to be most comfortable hiring in their own image. Candidates are often embraced or rejected upon initial "feel." Johnson counsels clients to go beyond this: if they fall madly in love with a candidate right on the spot, they should work hard to find the weaker points.

Likewise, if the tendency is to dismiss an individual on initial reaction, he would advise the client to look deeper.

Johnson remembers a search for a well-known consumer packaged firm in which three outstanding candidates were all rejected outright by the president. He asked the head of human resources why. The response was clear: "Look around you. The president is six five and everyone else on the senior management team is over six feet. The president doesn't like to look down." And of course each of Johnson's three candidates was under six feet.

> A great client tends to accept creative solutions to senior recruitment, leaving the traditional patterns of narrow function or specific sector preferences by the wayside.
>
> —Jürgen Mülder
> (Heidrick & Struggles, Frankfurt)

Clients do tend to hire in their own image. But it is not enough to hire someone merely because you are comfortable with them. You must go beyond this point, for the ideal candidate may not fit the corporate mold. The client must therefore determine beforehand what is and is not acceptable to top management and communicate this clearly to the search consultant. Without this step, valuable time on both sides will invariably be wasted.

Choose Confident Candidates

A self-confident executive is a better team member, is willing to complement others, and is happy to see others succeed. According to Andy Hunter, "He or she will possess exceptional influencing skills, which means an ability to market ideas and communicate effectively through various management layers. Confident executives can be identified by straightforwardness, the ability to admit mistakes, and flexibility in solving problems."

Look for the Global Perspective

Increasingly, everywhere in the world, senior executives need a global perspective to be most effective. As many industries consolidate and merge across borders around the world, the successful candidate needs to be cross-culturally sensitive and experienced in more than one industry sector and geographic market. To be successful in an emerging market, one needs to have worked in another one. A search consultant that belongs to one of the major global firms with dynamic specialty practice groups supported by a strong research team will be most efficient at finding the best candidates.

Neal Maslan advises clients to look for global executives who understand the competition, who can manage complexity and teams with cultural diversity, and who can deal with uncertainty. As he says, "Screen/evaluate against core competencies required and hire the star athlete."

Michael Boxberger emphasizes the importance of a global perspective, given that the world is quickly evolving into one international marketplace: "The ability to act swiftly and intelligently across geographic lines is key to survival and success of any business."

SUMMARY

The consultants contacted for this book offered advice on managing the client-consultant relationship. They suggest that it pays to take the following steps.

- Form a partnership with your consultant to actively manage the search process. In time, great clients often become great friends with their consultants, thus strengthening the client-consultant relationship and increasing the chances of future success.
- Emphasize your expectations of work by the consultant and firm. Communicate your needs clearly.
- Make the search a top priority. Demonstrate how important the search is by being available and making sure that those necessary to the interview process are available as well. Also, be sure to keep communication open and timely.
- Remember that candidates are not applicants and may well need to be sold on the company.

In selecting from the candidates that the consultant brings to your attention, keep the following points in mind.

- Understand your needs and expectations. What competencies are required and where is there flexibility?
- Go beyond the comfort zone. Avoid the trap of hiring in your own image.
- Choose confident candidates.
- Look for candidates with global perspective.

In Chapter Four we will shift perspective and provide tips for the candidates in a search.

Advice to Job Seekers

As an executive, you need to take charge of your own career. No one today can assume that a promising career track awaits at any one firm. The steady wave of mergers and acquisitions and new technology renders many jobs obsolete. And you cannot assume that because you are doing an outstanding job in your current assignment a headhunter will approach you with a splendid career opportunity on a silver platter. You might be lucky, but why leave your career to chance? Instead, you can work with an executive recruiter and take steps to actively manage your career.

WHY AN EXECUTIVE RECRUITER?

A headhunter is often a useful partner for a capable and promising executive, for a variety of reasons. The headhunter can do the following:

- Serve as market intelligence, a personalized barometer on what you are worth in your marketplace.
- Provide a powerful assessment of where you stand compared to others in your field.
- Help pinpoint your strengths and weaknesses, priorities, and motivations.
- Help you focus on your career aspirations, a critical step that many people find nearly impossible to make the time to do on their own.

Even if on a particular search you are not selected as a candidate or decide not to accept a position, by cultivating a relationship with a headhunter you will have a clearer picture of where you stand on the job market. You'll have a better notion of what direction your career might take. You'll also have a candid assessment of what you're worth outside. All of these pieces of information are extremely valuable.

Meeting with a recruiter will be most productive when everything is going well and you are not actively looking for another job. Rather than being on the defensive, you are then in a position of strength. This is the ideal time to get a step ahead, size up your present situation, and think clearly about longer-term opportunities. In fact, Georges Holzberger (Highland Group, New York) has said that 90 percent of the candidates his company recruits are not looking for a job. So always have an up-to-date résumé on hand, and take the time to meet headhunters when they call.

You never know when you will need a headhunter. The odds are that someday you will, whether for a specific assignment or expert advice. Remember that a headhunter's valuable personal assessment can help you carefully assess your next step and ultimate career path.

HOW TO CULTIVATE A RELATIONSHIP WITH AN EXECUTIVE RECRUITER

A headhunter is always on the lookout for new talent and will naturally look closely at you if your profile makes you a candidate on a current search or if you may be of interest to a future client.

To increase your chances, you must convey that you have something special to offer. Cultivating a relationship with a headhunter has many parallels to cultivating the press. Take advantage of the opportunities in the entrees that present themselves. If a headhunter contacts you unsolicited asking for a few minutes of your time to assess a colleague, be friendly and cooperative. You needn't offer a lot of time, but with the attitude that this is an opportunity rather than an intrusion you may benefit later.

If you intend to initiate contact with a headhunter, effort in preparing for your initial contact can be well worth the time. Here are some tips on selecting and cultivating a headhunter.

Be Selective

Limit the number of headhunters you contact and actively cultivate. It is not wise to send your résumé to every headhunter in town. Instead, carefully select one or two with whom you wish to cultivate a relationship. How do you narrow the field?

You have in your hands a timesaving tool: use the listings. Ideal headhunters are well known and respected in their fields, offer excellent market intelligence (by being tuned in to all the right players), display personal integrity and honesty (critical because you are entrusting the chosen headhunter with your future), and, most important, are on the same wavelength with you. A really good headhunter is hard to find. The excellent ones are highly visible and frequently approached. That being the case, you need to distinguish yourself to make yourself interesting to that ideal headhunter.

Connect with a Particular Headhunter

Once you've decided on a headhunter or two, personalize your initial contact with a well-known referral. Victor Loewenstein (Egon Zehnder, New York) advises candidates to use a personal reference from a client or a valued opinion leader to network and attract the attention of the search consultant. Don't just make a cold phone call or send an impersonal letter. Instead, invest the time to find out who in your network already knows the headhunter. Try to personalize both the contact and the initial referral.

Make a personal impression. If at all possible, sit across the table from the consultant for that initial contact and then maintain an easy relationship where you are available as an expert source, if needed.

Look for Mutual Interests

If you're looking to cultivate a particular headhunter, find some interest that the two of you share. Whether it's an interest in the derivatives market, East Asian art, or motorcycle racing, such a connection is a great start. If you find no common hobbies or interests, consider joining a charity or arts committee in which the headhunter is also involved.

NEGOTIATING WITH A PROSPECTIVE NEW EMPLOYER

Before setting you up with an interview with a prospective employer, a headhunter will be reasonably sure of a good match. But you also need to take steps both before and during the interview to improve your chances.

Before the Interview

Before even accepting the interview, be sure that you have demanded honest communication from the recruiter and willingly provided the same yourself. Be candid and don't role play. It's your future that will be hurt if the new situation does not work.

Do your homework thoroughly before walking in the door. Research the company, understand market perceptions about it, and think about what you might do to enhance the company's or the department's performance. This research will stand you in good stead during the interview and beyond.

At the Interview

The adage is that you never get a second chance to make a first impression. Keep it in mind. Look the interviewer in the eye and project your self-confidence.

Be straightforward, candid, and honest. Never lie about anything. Be discreet; never give away confidential information or even give the appearance of doing so. Emphasize the positive reasons for any changes in your career.

Be sure to present yourself as having researched the company thoroughly. Robert Benson confirms this: "Do not go in and expect to be educated. Enhance your knowledge by asking probing questions based on what you have learned before going."

Most importantly, sell yourself but do not oversell. Make them love you before you start making demands. Try to convey your knowledge of the market and your position in it. Practically all employers today value international experience; if you have it, emphasize your strengths in that area. Don't come across as desperate; instead let them assume you have many irons in the fire. Consider your job in the interview as that of demonstrating that you are a team builder, that you have cultural mobility and insight, and a track record of creating change. Let the headhunter sell you.

Before you start negotiating, make sure that you are in a position to negotiate; that is, the client really wants to hire you.

—Robert Benson
(Spencer Stuart, Frankfurt)

References are usually called at the end of the negotiation process when you're being offered the job. Make sure you know that your references will say good things about you. If you can, test a reference beforehand in another position that you don't care about. By doing so, you can find out what is said.

Jonathan Holman advises, "We are in an era when references are as important as track record. Make sure you know what your references are going to say. Ask them for permission to be provided as references and if there are any issues they will raise that they feel you should know about." If you or your references say that you left employment because of a mutual agreement, only the most dense of potential employers will interpret this to mean anything other than that you were fired. Sophisticated employers will judge you at least as much by the quality of your questions as by the quality of your answers.

Maximize your strengths; minimize your weaknesses. It makes sense: always maximize what you are good at and enjoy. Dennis McDonald (formerly of Russell Reynolds, Sydney) also suggests, "minimize what you have difficulty with or less knowledge of."

MANAGING YOUR CAREER

Entire books have been written on managing careers. Here, I offer just two bits of advice: maintain your relationships and build your strengths in the international arena.

Maintain Your Relationships

Never say goodbye to an executive recruiter. Perhaps after interviewing for a new job you are not selected. Or perhaps you decide the job is not for you. Neither is a reason to bring your relationship with a headhunter to an end. Instead, keep the headhunter informed of what is happening in your career. Communicate. Keep the headhunter's file on you up-to-date; make it an accurate picture of who you are—and who you are becoming. Let the headhunter know of any promotions or changes. This way, the day that the right opportunity comes along you will be among the first people the headhunter contacts.

Josette Sayers (Jouve & Associes, Paris) underscores the importance of maintaining a relationship and communicating: "An executive recruiter is not a trophy hunter (merely interested in adding another well-known name to his list) but a committed professional who does his best to evaluate candidates fairly and satisfy his clients' needs. I have worked as a headhunter for almost twenty years, meeting an average of twenty executives a week. And yet among all the individuals I see, there are some I remember more vividly than others. They are not necessarily the most brilliant, but they are the most self-aware, who by virtue of the total commitment of excellence reap the benefits of success and share the success with the people around them. In addition to being committed and competent, they know how to communicate." Sayers's experience translates into some very concrete advice: be committed, competent, and communicative.

Build Your International Strengths

Boundaries have changed. Companies are looking for top executives who can operate comfortably not just in the United States but also in Europe, the Far East, and Latin America—and all of the above.

Baldwin Klep (Heidrick & Struggles, Brussels) offers this advice, applicable to all executives whether expressly international or not:

- Evaluate each proposed (internal or external) job as a potential building block toward accomplishing your ultimate career goal.
- Create your own opportunities to make a measurable impact in your job; do not get confused by a complex international matrix structure about taking on a clear responsibility.

- Build your own professional network on an ongoing basis; keep track of internal and external contacts that you respect.
- Insist on thorough periodic evaluations from your boss; listen to the weaknesses and learn from them.
- Look for an internal mentor.
- Be a mentor for others: this adds to your learning and to the field.

And listen to your instincts. If what you find out about the job environment beforehand and in the interview does not feel right, don't take the job. As Andy Hunter (Pendleton James, Boston) says: "Chemistry, culture, environment, whatever name you choose, is a prime ingredient for a successful career."

In summary, Neal Maslan adds, "View your career as a marathon, not a sprint. Be willing to take chances and remember that you cannot cross a giant chasm in small steps. Be bold and know when to make the leap."

SUMMARY

As an individual, you have numerous reasons to cultivate a relationship with an executive recruiter. An executive recruiter can help you by doing the following:

- Letting you know what you are worth in your marketplace.
- Assessing where you stand compared to others in your field.
- Pinpointing your strengths and weaknesses, priorities, and motivations.
- Helping you focus on your career aspirations.

How can you best cultivate a relationship with an executive recruiter? First and foremost, if a headhunter contacts you, be helpful. A small bit of time spent talking when a headhunter calls to use you as a source of information can be a powerful investment. If you contact a headhunter, be selective. Focus your time and energy—and the headhunter's. If you have a particular headhunter in mind, look for mutual interests.

Good as they are, you shouldn't rely solely on a headhunter. Be careful to network yourself as well: become famous, work on your career.

To best present yourself in an interview and through negotiations with a prospective new employer, prepare before the interview by being sure your communication with the headhunter is completely forthcoming. Research the company, culture, and environment thoroughly.

In the interview, keep in mind the importance of first impressions and make them count for you:

- Be honest
- Ask good questions
- Sell yourself but do not oversell
- Check your references
- Maximize your strengths; minimize your weaknesses

Create the time in your schedule to actively manage your career, both independently and with the headhunter of your choice. Throughout, maintain your relationships with care. And, given the global nature of business today, be sure to build and emphasize your strengths in the international area.

With this as background, in Chapter Five and *The Global 200* directories that follow we delve more deeply into the outstanding executive recruiters and search firms.

Outstanding
Consultants and Firms

In the directories that follow this chapter, the top consultants and their firms are presented in a variety of ways to help you find them. This chapter serves as a guide to those directories.

Directory One sets forth the profiles of the two hundred top consultants, alphabetically by last name. Many of the names are exceptionally well-known and respected founders or leaders of great firms and of highly visible senior partners well known for their senior-level work. Included are such people as Richard Ferry (Korn/Ferry), Tom Neff (Spencer Stuart), Gerry Roche (Heidrick & Struggles), and John Johnson (LAI Ward Howell) in the United States and Miles Broadbent (the Miles Partnership) and Jürgen Mülder (Heidrick & Struggles) in Europe. All of these individuals are actively involved in major client relationships in search today.

Other individuals were selected for inclusion here because they are sector or industry specialists of particular repute. These consultants, many of them in their thirties and forties, have developed a loyal client following and are greatly admired by their peers. They include Matthew Wright (Russell Reynolds), Windle Priem (Korn/Ferry), Jonathan Baines (Baines Gwinner), Philippa Rose (Rose Partnership), and Steven Potter (the Highland Group) in financial services. In the information technology and telecommunications field, they include John Thompson and Tom Friel (Heidrick & Struggles), Charles Polachi (Fenwick Partners/Heidrick & Struggles), and Akira Arai (Korn/Ferry) in Tokyo. Specialists also include include Bill Simon and Michele James (both of Korn/Ferry) and Tim Vignoles (Garner International) in media and entertainment.

The profiles contain a lot of information. To help the reader access the appropriate consultant more readily, the next two directories provide additional ways to pinpoint both the right individual and the right firm for the job.

Acknowledging that the individual consultant and the firm must be looked at together, I discuss in Directory Two what I consider to be the top fifteen global firms. I present a brief history and explanation of the ownership, organization, and structure of each. I include this information because how the search firm is owned and organized is today more and more of an issue, for it can influence how well the members work across borders. I also identify the key players in each firm and offer my take on each firm's current direction.

Because specialization and practice group allegiance are key to providing efficient service to a client, in Directory Three, the Global 200 Consultants by Sector and Industry, I list those profiled in this book by their stated sector or industry expertise. For each sector and industry included, I provide a brief description of the field in today's marketplace.

I emphasize this directory because, as discussed earlier in the book, the most predominant and powerful trend in the executive search field today is the emergence of specialty practice groups or the clustering of consultants by sector or industry within their firms on a global basis. Search consultants often become totally absorbed in (and loyal to) their practice groups, which often transcend country borders. An increasing number of global search firms have organized their consultant teams according to sector and industry as well as functional expertise. This allows a regional or global team of consultants to work together on an ongoing, long-term, close-knit basis to provide powerful market intelligence and dedicated service to the client.

The listings by sector and industry provide ready access to the outstanding, highly visible sector and industry specialists. These listings include categories for the following:

- CEO/Board of Directors
- Automotive
- Consulting and Professional Services
- Consumer Financial Services
- Education, Nonprofit Organizations, Associations and Foundations
- Fashion, Luxury, and Retail
- Fast Moving Consumer Goods
- Financial Services
- General Management

- Industry, Manufacturing, and Construction
- Information Technology
- Insurance
- International, Cross-Border Specialists
- Investment Banking and Trading
- Media, Entertainment, and Publishing
- Natural Resources
- Pharmaceutical/Health Care
- Real Estate
- Sports, Recreation, Leisure, and Hospitality
- Telecommunications
- Venture Capital and Start up Companies

One of these categories warrants specific mention here. Consultants with significant global, multicountry experience and vision are listed in Directory Three under International, Cross-Border Specialists. One example is Eric Salmon (Salmon & Partners) with expertise in France and Italy. Josette Sayers (Jouve & Associes) and Henry de Montebello (Russell Reynolds) are both based in Paris and focus on clients in France and the United States. It is becoming increasingly important for the global firms to be able to offer seamless cross-border service to their clients including global, multicountry research and the ability to have consultants work simultaneously on assignments from different offices around the world. I expect this section to expand in subsequent editions of this book.

These three directories provide key information on and cross references to the top consultants and top firms. Two additional directories—Consultants by Firm and Consultants by Country—complete the cross-references and assure that the reader can locate a particular consultant. In Directory Four, Consultants by Firm, I also include several outstanding consultants from Egon Zehnder International and Spencer Stuart whose profiles are not part of this book because of their firm's policy. Much as I respect these firms, I do believe that the selection of a search firm should be based on a combination of the individual consultant and the firm; these consultants are highly qualified. I hope to include more of these outstanding consultants in the next edition of *The Global 200*.

In this first attempt to portray the field's most outstanding leaders, I have strived to obtain a sort of regional and global balance. Thus, I have included several individuals from quickly developing markets such as Brazil, the Czech Republic, China, Hungary, Indonesia, Malaysia, and Russia, many of whom work at lower average fee levels than their New York, London or Tokyo counterparts and have less industry visibility. Many fine consultants also exist in other developing markets such as India (notably the Egon Zehnder team) and Poland (Russell Reynolds); this, however, is the subject of another book.

To limit this book to 200 profiles, I have omitted the majority of the search consultants, thousands of whom are outstanding, well-respected individuals. I acknowledge in advance the limitations inherent in confining the listing to the top 200 and challenge other consultants to make me aware of who you are, as there will surely be subsequent editions of this book.

THE GLOBAL 200

EXECUTIVE DIRECTORIES

The Global 200
Executive Recruiter Profiles

GEORGE L. ABDUSHELISHVILI

Ward Howell International Holdings Ltd.
15 Bolshoy Tryokhgorny per.
123022 Moscow
Russia

Telephone: 7 (095) 956-68-45
Fax: 7 (095) 252-19-82
E-mail: info@whru.com
Company Website: http://www.laix.com

DATE OF BIRTH: March 5, 1962

NATIONALITY: Russian—Grew up in St. Petersburg, Russia

EDUCATIONAL BACKGROUND:

St. Petersburg State University—Economics, 1985
St. Petersburg Technical University—Postgraduate studies, Economics, 1989

LANGUAGES SPOKEN: Russian, English

CAREER HIGHLIGHTS: Creation and management of Baltic Consulting Group (local recruitment company) conducting assignments for western clients in Russia, Ukraine, and Baltic countries. Joined Ward Howell, Russia, in 1993

SPECIAL INTERESTS/HOBBIES: Classical literature, swimming

GEOGRAPHIC SCOPE OF RECRUITING: Russia and the CIS countries

SECTOR/INDUSTRY SPECIALIZATION: Commercial Banking, FMCG, Pharmaceutical, Entertainment industries

FAVORITE HISTORICAL FIGURE/MODEL/MENTOR: Peter the Great/Andrei Sakharov

SINGLE MOST IMPORTANT ISSUE IN CONDUCTING A HIGH LEVEL SEARCH: To be at or above the level of professionalism of those for whom you hunt and of those being hunted.

MOST SIGNIFICANT OTHER ASPECT OF PERSONAL OR PROFESSIONAL LIFE: Everlasting challenge in the new growing market.

WHAT IS THE BEST PREPARATION FOR BEING A SUCCESSFUL RECRUITER? An excellent educational background is important, and should equip the person with the ability to think strategically. In terms of experience, it is necessary to have a background of success, a winner's psychology, which may have been obtained in a number of different fields, such as business, politics, or sport. To complement these things, recruiters need leadership and entrepreneurial skills to allow them to manage any given project through to its completion.

WHAT WOULD YOU BE DOING IF YOU WERE NOT AN EXECUTIVE RECRUITER? I think I would probably be a manager/partner of some other firm, most likely in the professional services industry.

WHAT ARE THE CHARACTERISTICS OF A GREAT CLIENT? A great client is one who combines the expertise to recognize a good candidate with the strength, power, ability and willingness to hire him.

WHAT CHALLENGES DO YOU SEE AHEAD IN THE GLOBAL MARKETPLACE? I see fundamental changes taking place in the structure of our industry's organizations and an end to loosely affiliated networks. People within the industry will have to adapt to these changes. A further challenge, especially for emerging markets, is the question of attracting and hiring truly world-class professionals in the face of competition from other markets.

JUHA-PEKKA AHTIKARI

Stålberg & Ahtikari Oy/Amrop International
Bulevardi 2 A
00120 Helsinki
Finland

Telephone: 358 9 660 466
Fax: 358 9 611 910
E-mail: juha-pekka.ahtikari@amrop.com
Company Website: http://www.amrop.com

DATE OF BIRTH: March 20, 1956

NATIONALITY: Finnish—Grew up in Finland

EDUCATIONAL BACKGROUND:
Master of Laws, University of Helsinki

LANGUAGES SPOKEN: Finnish, Swedish, English, German

CAREER HIGHLIGHTS: Being able to build up international preferred supplier relationships with large multinational companies

SPECIAL INTERESTS/HOBBIES: Skiing, motorcycling, farming, literature

GEOGRAPHIC SCOPE OF RECRUITING: Serve clients nationally and internationally specialising in Baltic States, Russia, and CIS

SECTOR/INDUSTRY SPECIALIZATION: Consumer goods, information technology, telecom and service industry

FAVORITE HISTORICAL FIGURE/MODEL/MENTOR: Gustavus Adolphus

SINGLE MOST IMPORTANT ISSUE IN CONDUCTING A HIGH LEVEL SEARCH: To genuinely understand my client's business and culture and specific requirements of the position. Especially in the developing markets, cultural fit of the candidates to the immediate and long term needs of the local and international organisation of the client is key success factor.

WHAT IS THE BEST PREPARATION FOR BEING A SUCCESSFUL RECRUITER? There is no optimal preparation for this business. Personal characteristics are the critical success factor.

WHAT WOULD YOU BE DOING IF YOU WERE NOT AN EXECUTIVE RECRUITER? Attorney at Law

WHAT ARE THE CHARACTERISTICS OF A GREAT CLIENT? Client is seeking for and is maintaining a partnership with the search consultant. Open and creative dialogue with the search consultant in order to develop the partnership and to solve problems.

WHAT CHALLENGES DO YOU SEE AHEAD IN THE GLOBAL MARKETPLACE? Executive search consultant's capability to solve long term problems with their clients' executive recruitments in diversified global markets.

JEAN-LOUIS ALPEYRIE

Heidrick and Struggles
245 Park Avenue
New York, NY 10167
U.S.A.

Telephone: 1 (212) 867-9876
Fax: 1 (212) 370-9035
Company Website: http://www.h-s.com

DATE OF BIRTH: January 17, 1943

NATIONALITY: French—Grew up in Paris

EDUCATIONAL BACKGROUND:
HEC, 1967, major: marketing
University of California, Berkeley, 1969, M.B.A., major: operation research

LANGUAGES SPOKEN: French, English, Spanish

CAREER HIGHLIGHTS:
1984–present Heidrick & Struggles
1977–1984 Booz·Allen
1969–1971 McKinsey

SPECIAL INTERESTS/HOBBIES: Theology

GEOGRAPHIC SCOPE OF RECRUITING: North America, Europe, Asia

SECTOR/INDUSTRY SPECIALIZATION: Information technology, media and entertainment

FAVORITE HISTORICAL FIGURE/MODEL/MENTOR: Franklin D. Roosevelt

SINGLE MOST IMPORTANT ISSUE IN CONDUCTING A HIGH LEVEL SEARCH: Easy access to the board/CEO

MOST SIGNIFICANT OTHER ASPECT OF PERSONAL OR PROFESSIONAL LIFE: Proven ability and track record at conducting searches in all key markets on three continents. Supportive wife and children (most of the time).

WHAT IS THE BEST PREPARATION FOR BEING A SUCCESSFUL RECRUITER? Having had a management position within a well-managed company. Alternatively, management consulting.

WHAT WOULD YOU BE DOING IF YOU WERE NOT AN EXECUTIVE RECRUITER? I would be a history teacher in a first-class university.

WHAT ARE THE CHARACTERISTICS OF A GREAT CLIENT? A great client tells you the way it is; wants the good news and the bad news; openly lets you know where you stand.

WHAT CHALLENGES DO YOU SEE AHEAD IN THE GLOBAL MARKETPLACE? The main challenge is to identify and get the best candidates to be interested in the client's job. Companies need the best people we can find and there are no more of them than there were 10 years ago.

DAVID C. ANDERSON

Heidrick & Struggles, Inc.
2200 Ross Avenue, Suite 4700E
Dallas, TX 75201
U.S.A.

Telephone: 1 (214) 220-3950
Fax: 1 (214) 220-1029
E-mail: dca@h-s.com
Company Website: http://www.h-s.com

DATE OF BIRTH: March 18, 1942

NATIONALITY: American—Grew up in Corpus Christi, Texas

EDUCATIONAL BACKGROUND:
B.S., aerospace engineering, Texas A&M University

LANGUAGES SPOKEN: English, limited Spanish

CAREER HIGHLIGHTS:

1967–1980	IBM Corporation
1980–1984	Paul R. Ray & Company
1884–1992	Spencer Stuart
1992–present	Heidrick & Struggles 1992-present

SPECIAL INTERESTS/HOBBIES: Texas Nature Conservancy Board; fishing, hunting, and golf

GEOGRAPHIC SCOPE OF RECRUITING: Global

SECTOR/INDUSTRY SPECIALIZATION: International Technology Practice with emphasis on telecommunications, information technology and information services

FAVORITE HISTORICAL FIGURE/MODEL/MENTOR: Thomas Jefferson

SINGLE MOST IMPORTANT ISSUE IN CONDUCTING A HIGH LEVEL SEARCH: Knowledge of the client's business

MOST SIGNIFICANT OTHER ASPECT OF PERSONAL OR PROFESSIONAL LIFE: Achieving a balance of professional responsibilities with family and personal commitments is important.

WHAT IS THE BEST PREPARATION FOR BEING A SUCCESSFUL RECRUITER? Possess deep knowledge of an industry or industries experiencing change and/or significant growth challenges, preferably global in scope. A thorough knowledge of the client company and the company's industry is critical to success.

WHAT WOULD YOU BE DOING IF YOU WERE NOT AN EXECUTIVE RECRUITER? Serving in a key management role within an entrepreneurial, high growth technology company.

WHAT ARE THE CHARACTERISTICS OF A GREAT CLIENT? A client that values the experience, industry knowledge and judgment that the search consultant can provide as an added value extension of the company's management team. This level of commitment often results in multiple assignments over a long period of time.

WHAT CHALLENGES DO YOU SEE AHEAD IN THE GLOBAL MARKETPLACE? Clients expanding into new, global markets are experiencing common challenges associated with building new management teams who can effectively operate and are capable of achieving growth and profitability objectives within very different culture and business environments.

JACQUES P. ANDRÉ

Ray & Berndtson
101 Park Avenue
New York, NY 10167
U.S.A.

Telephone: 1 (212) 370-1316
Fax: 1 (212) 370-1462
E-mail: jandre@rayberndtson.com
Company Website: http://www.rayberndtson.com

DATE OF BIRTH: August 29, 1937

NATIONALITY: U.S.A.—Grew up in Davenport, Iowa

EDUCATIONAL BACKGROUND:
  B.B.A., University of Miami

LANGUAGES SPOKEN: English

CAREER HIGHLIGHTS: 32 years in executive search. Board of Directors of Ray & Berndtson, Association of Executive Search Consultants, and Alliance Gaming Corporation

SPECIAL INTERESTS/HOBBIES: Golf, gardening, travel, scuba diving, furniture refinishing

GEOGRAPHIC SCOPE OF RECRUITING: Global

SECTOR/INDUSTRY SPECIALIZATION: Financial services

FAVORITE HISTORICAL FIGURE/MODEL/MENTOR: Winston Churchill

SINGLE MOST IMPORTANT ISSUE IN CONDUCTING A HIGH LEVEL SEARCH: Managing the selection and negotiating processes.

MOST SIGNIFICANT OTHER ASPECT OF PERSONAL OR PROFESSIONAL LIFE: Home and professional relationships.

WHAT IS THE BEST PREPARATION FOR BEING A SUCCESSFUL RECRUITER? Historically, sales and general management were the preferred routes. As the industry has matured, human resources has gained greater acceptance. In reality, it is more a matter of the person's personal traits. Drive, determination, a reasonable level of intelligence, and salesmanship are essential traits.

WHAT WOULD YOU BE DOING IF YOU WERE NOT AN EXECUTIVE RECRUITER? Hopefully, playing golf or traveling. However, if I had to work (I could never survive on my golf skills), I would be in human resources or another phase of consulting.

WHAT ARE THE CHARACTERISTICS OF A GREAT CLIENT? The ideal client is looking for a "partnership" with his/her search consultant. Unfortunately, some clients fail to gain the full value from the relationship because they think of the search consultant as only a tool to identify candidates. That is only one aspect of the service we provide.

WHAT CHALLENGES DO YOU SEE AHEAD IN THE GLOBAL MARKETPLACE? Consistently providing the same, high level of service. This requires a high degree of coordination and cooperation and each consultant approaching the relationship with the same commitment.

JAVIER ANITUA

Russell Reynolds Associates
Castellana, 51
28046 Madrid, Spain

Telephone: 34 (1) 319-7100
Fax: 34 (1) 310-4470
E-mail: janitua@russreyn.com
Company Website: http://www.russreyn.com

DATE OF BIRTH: June 22, 1951

NATIONALITY: Spanish citizen—Grew up in Spain

EDUCATIONAL BACKGROUND:
S.A. Degree in Civil Engineering, University of Madrid. INSIDE Program, U.C. Deusto, Bilbao. Advanced Management Program, The Wharton School, University of Pennsylvania.

LANGUAGES SPOKEN: Spanish, Basque, English, French

CAREER HIGHLIGHTS: Prior to joining Russell Reynolds Associates in 1986, served as Office Manager of the multinational law firm Baker & McKenzie in Madrid. Earlier was a Senior Consultant at Arthur Andersen & Co., a Project Planner for The Austin Company and Project Manager for Nex Ingenieros.

SPECIAL INTERESTS/HOBBIES: Family, Music, Gastronomy

GEOGRAPHIC SCOPE OF RECRUITING: Europe

SECTOR/INDUSTRY SPECIALIZATION: CEO and senior management assignments across a range of industries, both for local Spanish companies and multinational companies with operations in Spain.

FAVORITE HISTORICAL FIGURE/MODEL/MENTOR: Fernando el Católico

SINGLE MOST IMPORTANT ISSUE IN CONDUCTING A HIGH LEVEL SEARCH: A mutual commitment on the part of client and executive recruiting firm to sharing information and open communication.

WHAT IS THE BEST PREPARATION FOR BEING A SUCCESSFUL RECRUITER? Executive recruiting is a knowledge business; in order to provide clients with the best service, a recruiter must have a superior understanding of clients and markets. We must understand the business environment in which our clients operate, recognize the key factors for success, and what defines outstanding performance. This type of perspective often is founded in industry experience prior to becoming an executive recruiter. This knowledge, paired with skill in assessing an individual's leadership and potential within an organization, leads our clients to the best talent in the marketplace.

WHAT WOULD YOU BE DOING IF YOU WERE NOT AN EXECUTIVE RECRUITER? I love this work and have not considered doing anything else.

WHAT ARE THE CHARACTERISTICS OF A GREAT CLIENT? A global, diversified organization whose CEO has a clear vision of the strategy to be implemented and is strongly committed to carrying out that strategy.

WHAT CHALLENGES DO YOU SEE AHEAD IN THE GLOBAL MARKETPLACE? At the most senior corporate level, the evolution of the global marketplace has created an unprecedented demand for executives with international experience—a demand which far outstrips the available supply of talent. Companies are looking for business leaders with an operating background in a given country or region, as well as local experience in at least one country other than his or her own. Finding the right balance of local and international talent will be an ongoing challenge for companies as they move into geographic areas where they have little prior experience.

AKIRA ARAI

Korn/Ferry International-Japan
AIG Bldg.
1-1-3 Marunouchi, Chiyoda-ku
Tokyo, 100 Japan
Telephone: 81-3-3211-6851
Fax: 81-3-3216-1300
E-mail: akira.arai@kornferry.com
Company Website: http://www.kornferry.com

DATE OF BIRTH: July 7, 1937

NATIONALITY: Japanese—Grew up in Japan

EDUCATIONAL BACKGROUND:
Matto Agricultural College/BS degree Agricultural Administration
Sopia University English Communication School

LANGUAGES SPOKEN: Japanese, English

CAREER HIGHLIGHTS: Chairman & CEO of Korn/Ferry International-Japan. 24 years experience of senior level search since the Japan Office opened in 1973. Successfully recruited top management positions including Compaq, DEC, Nortel.

SPECIAL INTERESTS/HOBBIES: Photography

GEOGRAPHIC SCOPE OF RECRUITING: Mainly Japan

SECTOR/INDUSTRY SPECIALIZATION: Advanced Technology Industry

SINGLE MOST IMPORTANT ISSUE IN CONDUCTING A HIGH LEVEL SEARCH: To understand clients' needs clearly and correctly, and educate clients on local market's characteristics.

BIGGEST COMPETITOR: Egon Zehnder in Japan

MOST SIGNIFICANT OTHER ASPECT OF PERSONAL OR PROFESSIONAL LIFE: Family (Hiroko Arai and two daughters, one in Honolulu and one in Tokyo)

WHAT IS THE BEST PREPARATION FOR BEING A SUCCESSFUL RECRUITER?
- To have product knowledge and market familiarity with the Advanced Technology Industry, globally and locally.
- To have the ability to help clients understand the Japan Market with appropriate and timely information.
- To be result-oriented and present excellent candidates with high caliber through keen observations.

WHAT WOULD YOU BE DOING IF YOU WERE NOT AN EXECUTIVE RECRUITER? I would be involved in consulting services for foreign affiliated companies in Japan, related to HR functions; consultation on compensation, appraisal guideline, and/or work rules/benefits.

WHAT ARE THE CHARACTERISTICS OF A GREAT CLIENT? A great client has strong technology, a business strategy or company policy which can be accepted by local market, understands Japanese business practice and business culture, and can convey authority, autonomy, and responsibilities for operations to the local head.

WHAT CHALLENGES DO YOU SEE AHEAD IN THE GLOBAL MARKETPLACE? Executive Recruiters must develop and maintain global services for the increasing number of multi-national firms.

AYSEGÜL AYDIN

Amrop International
Ebulula Caddesi Caglayan Sitesi
26/9 Levent Istanbul 80630
Turkey
Telephone: 90-212-270-51-55
Fax: 90-212-270-51-56
E-mail: amrop@superonline.com
Company Website: http://www.amrop.com

DATE OF BIRTH: July 11, 1964

NATIONALITY: U.S. and Turkish—Grew up in U.S. and Turkey

EDUCATIONAL BACKGROUND:
- Portage Northern High School, Michigan, U.S.A
- Middle East Technical University, Ankara, Turkey-BS in Business Administration
- Michigan State University, Michigan, U.S.A.-Double major in Marketing and Advertising

LANGUAGES SPOKEN: English and Turkish

CAREER HIGHLIGHTS:
- Have held managerial positions since age 24.
- Offered regional trade marketing director position at British American Tobacco Co. for Middle East, CIS countries, Turkey, Eastern Europe, and North Africa in 1996. Instead, I established my own business.

SPECIAL INTERESTS/HOBBIES: Travel, learning about cultures

GEOGRAPHIC SCOPE OF RECRUITING: Turkey, CIS countries, and European countries

SECTOR/INDUSTRY SPECIALIZATION: FMCG, retail, tobacco, service, finance, advertising, amusement and recreation

FAVORITE HISTORICAL FIGURE/MODEL/MENTOR: Ataturk, founder of the modern Turkish Republic.

MOST IMPORTANT ISSUES IN CONDUCTING A HIGH LEVEL SEARCH: Ethics and competency assessment.

BIGGEST COMPETITOR: None in the Turkish market

WHAT IS THE BEST PREPARATION FOR BEING A SUCCESSFUL RECRUITER? Extensive experience in real business world. Must have performed both operational and managerial tasks—preferably in multicultured settings.

WHAT WOULD YOU BE DOING IF YOU WERE NOT AN EXECUTIVE RECRUITER? I would be assuming an executive role in a multinational FMCG company.

WHAT ARE THE CHARACTERISTICS OF A GREAT CLIENT?
- Willingness to cooperate and openness
- Time investment and reachability
- Partnership understanding

WHAT CHALLENGES DO YOU SEE AHEAD IN THE GLOBAL MARKETPLACE? The impact of globalization overshadowing the importance of local concerns.

JONATHAN F. T. BAINES

Baines Gwinner Limited
30 Eastcheap
London, EC3M 1HD, U.K.

Telephone: 44 171 623 1414
Fax: 44 171 623 1100
E-mail: JFTB@baines.co.uk
Company Website: http://www.baines.co.uk

DATE OF BIRTH: November 12, 1949

NATIONALITY: British—Grew up in U.K. and Germany

EDUCATIONAL BACKGROUND:
University College, London University
BSc Economics 2:1

LANGUAGES SPOKEN: English, French

CAREER HIGHLIGHTS:
- Establishing Baines Gwinner in 1986
- First successful search for a Chief Executive of an Investment Bank in Europe

SPECIAL INTERESTS/HOBBIES: Skiing, fox-hunting

GEOGRAPHIC SCOPE OF RECRUITING: Global

SECTOR/INDUSTRY SPECIALIZATION: Financial Services with a focus on investment banking

FAVORITE HISTORICAL FIGURE/MODEL/MENTOR: Warren Beatty

SINGLE MOST IMPORTANT ISSUE IN CONDUCTING A HIGH LEVEL SEARCH: Commitment

BIGGEST COMPETITOR: Constantly changing

MOST SIGNIFICANT OTHER ASPECT OF PERSONAL OR PROFESSIONAL LIFE: Achievement

WHAT IS THE BEST PREPARATION FOR BEING A SUCCESSFUL RECRUITER? Detailed industry experience.
Thorough training in all aspects of search. Marketing and negotiating skills.

WHAT WOULD YOU BE DOING IF YOU WERE NOT AN EXECUTIVE RECRUITER? Running a successful West
End Club

WHAT ARE THE CHARACTERISTICS OF A GREAT CLIENT? Communication and commitment

WHAT CHALLENGES DO YOU SEE AHEAD IN THE GLOBAL MARKETPLACE? Rationalization, competition from
the Internet

STEPHEN BAMPFYLDE

Saxton Bampfylde
35 Old Queen Street
London SW1H 9JA

Telephone: 44 0171 799 1433
Fax: 44 0171 222 0489

DATE OF BIRTH: March 31, 1952

NATIONALITY: British—Grew up in Portsmouth

EDUCATIONAL BACKGROUND:
First Class Degree in Economics and Social and Political Science, Jesus College, Cambridge University

LANGUAGES SPOKEN: English and French (basic)

SPECIAL INTERESTS/HOBBIES: Skiing, family, the Church of England

GEOGRAPHIC SCOPE OF RECRUITING: International

SECTOR/INDUSTRY SPECIALIZATION: Media/Government/FTSE Top 100 Companies/Board Level Appointments

FAVORITE HISTORICAL FIGURE/MODEL/MENTOR: Sir Thomas More and Benedict of Nursia. Both of these combined a deep faith and commitment to quiet contemplation alongside a highly active role in the world (More in Henry VIII's government and Benedict in founding a monastic order). I also particularly like the fact that Benedict was unsuccessful in his first monastery and had to learn some hard lessons about the nature of humanity before founding a second and more successful one. The concept of balance may have become a late 20th century jargon phrase but it has significant historical origins!

SINGLE MOST IMPORTANT ISSUE IN CONDUCTING A HIGH LEVEL SEARCH: Understanding a client's brief

MOST SIGNIFICANT OTHER ASPECT OF PERSONAL OR PROFESSIONAL LIFE: Part-time Benedictine monk at Acton Abbey

WHAT IS THE BEST PREPARATION FOR BEING A SUCCESSFUL RECRUITER? A lifelong study of "people in process in organisations." There is an academic literature to be mastered (often overlooked) as well as life experience to be gained.

WHAT WOULD YOU BE DOING IF YOU WERE NOT AN EXECUTIVE RECRUITER? University Professor, Media Chief Executive, Priest

WHAT ARE THE CHARACTERISTICS OF A GREAT CLIENT? Thoughtful, committed, patient, trusting, team-player

WHAT CHALLENGES DO YOU SEE AHEAD IN THE GLOBAL MARKETPLACE? To continue to build a global search grouping that goes beyond the ego-needs of any single professional within it which delivers the highest quality service to clients across a range of cultures and geographies without being a prisoner of the culture of a head office, whether that be California, Switzerland, or anywhere else.

BRUNO-LUC BANTON

Russell Reynolds Associates
7 Place Vendôme
75001 Paris, France

Telephone: 33 1 49 26 13 90
Fax: 33 1 42 60 03 85
E-mail: bbanton@russreyn.com
Company Website: http://www.russreyn.com

DATE OF BIRTH: February 24, 1956

NATIONALITY: French citizen—Grew up in Africa, Spain, France

EDUCATIONAL BACKGROUND:
Master's in Law, Postgraduate Degree in Intellectual Property and Patent Law, University of Paris.

LANGUAGES SPOKEN: French, English, Spanish, German

CAREER HIGHLIGHTS: 13 years of experience in executive recruiting. Served as Vice President, Corporate Alliances and Special Projects at EuroDisney. Previously was Director of the Classical Music Department, Deutsche Grammophon and Archiv Produktion with Polygram France/Philips Group.

SPECIAL INTERESTS/HOBBIES: Literature, philosophy, classical music, fine art

GEOGRAPHIC SCOPE OF RECRUITING: Greater Europe

SECTOR/INDUSTRY SPECIALIZATION: Consumer Markets (i.e., consumer products and consumer services, apparel/textile and luxury products, retail, leisure and hospitality, media/communication and entertainment). Focus on pan-European, global and worldwide searches.

MOST SIGNIFICANT OTHER ASPECT OF PERSONAL OR PROFESSIONAL LIFE: In our business, there is no clear distinction between personal and professional life. The good executive recruiting consultant relies on all facets of his or her personality to do what they have to do.

WHAT IS THE BEST PREPARATION FOR BEING A SUCCESSFUL RECRUITER? First of all, an executive recruiter must forget the idea of a classical career (climbing the ladder) but focus their entire energy on bringing added value to clients and candidates/individuals. They should develop a set of professional skills through numerous and diversified business achievements in a given industry stream (in order to have an industry focus recruitment knowledge), in different geographic locales (in order to get a broad geographical and multicultural grasp).
A great recruiter should also develop a set of personal and individual skills including perception, analysis, and assertiveness—and reinforce personal identity.

WHAT WOULD YOU BE DOING IF YOU WERE NOT AN EXECUTIVE RECRUITER? Something dealing with people development.

WHAT ARE THE CHARACTERISTICS OF A GREAT CLIENT? A great client considers recruitment as an element of strategic management; considers search consultants as real business partners and advisers; understands the value a well-established and long lasting relationship with an executive recruiter can bring.

WHAT CHALLENGES DO YOU SEE AHEAD IN THE GLOBAL MARKETPLACE?
Do companies understand precisely the kind of profile they will increasingly need?
Does the market generate today the kind of profile companies will strongly need in the near future?

PETER BASSETT

Korn/Ferry International
252 Regent St.
London W1R 5DA
U.K.

Telephone: 44 171-312-3100
Fax: 44 171 414-0544
E-mail: peter.bassett@kornferry.com
Company Website: http://www.kornferry.com

DATE OF BIRTH: December 23, 1946

NATIONALITY: British—Grew up in Coventry, Warks

EDUCATIONAL BACKGROUND:
Bablake School, Coventry
Bushey G.S., Watford
1964–70 Birmingham University, BSC 1967 (Chemistry), PhD 1970
1970–73 Royal Society Post-Doctoral Fellow at University of York, Physics Dept.

LANGUAGES SPOKEN: English (mother tongue), French

CAREER HIGHLIGHTS:
1982–87   Board Member, PA Technology
1992–date   Managing Partner at Korn/Ferry

SPECIAL INTERESTS/HOBBIES: Music

GEOGRAPHIC SCOPE OF RECRUITING: Worldwide

SECTOR/INDUSTRY SPECIALIZATION: Health Care and Pharmaceuticals

FAVORITE HISTORICAL FIGURE/MODEL/MENTOR: Carl Sagan

SINGLE MOST IMPORTANT ISSUE IN CONDUCTING A HIGH LEVEL SEARCH: Being regarded as a member of the high level cadre of people and having credibility as a Discussion Partner.

MOST SIGNIFICANT OTHER ASPECT OF PERSONAL OR PROFESSIONAL LIFE: The privilege of working with the very best professionals.

WHAT IS THE BEST PREPARATION FOR BEING A SUCCESSFUL RECRUITER? General Management, after working through a key corporate function such as sales or marketing. This gives a good, focused training in business followed by the broad overview in which the crucial role of people can be fully appreciated.

WHAT WOULD YOU BE DOING IF YOU WERE NOT AN EXECUTIVE RECRUITER? Running my own business in high-technology or value-added professional services.

WHAT ARE THE CHARACTERISTICS OF A GREAT CLIENT? One with whom one has a close rapport so that a trusting relationship can be built. It is helpful if the client is significant in business terms so that its relationship carries real value.

WHAT CHALLENGES DO YOU SEE AHEAD IN THE GLOBAL MARKETPLACE? Marrying the diversity of markets, culture and language to a unified corporate mission.

HERBERT BECHTEL

Heidrick & Struggles—Mülder & Partner
Frankfurt Airport Center 1, Hugo-Eckener-Ring,
60549 Frankfurt
Germany

Telephone: 49 (069) 69 70 02-0
Fax: 49 (069) 69 70 02-97
Company Website: http://www.h-s.com

DATE OF BIRTH: February 22, 1947

NATIONALITY: German—Grew up in Germany

EDUCATIONAL BACKGROUND:
Bachelor of Science degree in Mechanical Engineering, University-Gesamthochschule Siegen

LANGUAGES SPOKEN: German, English

CAREER HIGHLIGHTS:
- Sales Manager, Wang Laboratories Germany and U.K.
- General Manager, Prime Computer, Germany
- Vice President and Regional Director, National Advanced Systems, Germany
- Partner/Director, SUP, Frankfurt
- Heidrick & Struggles since 1989
  Partner Technology Practice, Frankfurt
  1993 Managing Partner Technology Practice Europe
  1994 Practice Leader Technology Practice Germany
  1997 Managing Partner Germany

SPECIAL INTERESTS/HOBBIES: Reading, Modern Art

GEOGRAPHIC SCOPE OF RECRUITING: Europe with focus on Germany

SECTOR/INDUSTRY SPECIALIZATION: Information Technology, Professional Services

SINGLE MOST IMPORTANT ISSUE IN CONDUCTING A HIGH LEVEL SEARCH: Integrity

MOST SIGNIFICANT OTHER ASPECT OF PERSONAL OR PROFESSIONAL LIFE: Good health

WHAT IS THE BEST PREPARATION FOR BEING A SUCCESSFUL RECRUITER? Good industry knowledge combined with exceptional listening skills and services orientation

WHAT ARE THE CHARACTERISTICS OF A GREAT CLIENT? Open and precise communication, timeliness

WHAT CHALLENGES DO YOU SEE AHEAD IN THE GLOBAL MARKETPLACE? Flexibility and mobility of top talents, cultural and language differences, balanced and frequent u.s.a.ge of state of the art technology

MICHAEL D. BEKINS

Korn/Ferry International
1900 Century Park East
Los Angeles, CA 90067
U.S.A.

Telephone: 1 (310) 552-1834
Fax: 1 (310) 553-6452
E-mail: mike.bekins@kornferry.com
Company Website: http://www.kornferry.com

NATIONALITY: American—Grew up in California

EDUCATIONAL BACKGROUND:

BA from Pepperdine University; MBA from University of Southern California

LANGUAGES SPOKEN: English

CAREER HIGHLIGHTS: Korn/Ferry International since 1980, mostly in Asia/Pacific; lived and worked in Australia (three years); Japan (four years); Singapore (two years); Malaysia (two years). Also, covered Korea on a part-time basis for five years, focusing on Korean conglomerates.

SPECIAL INTERESTS/HOBBIES: Travel, Asian culture, Chinese and Japanese art, reading.

GEOGRAPHIC SCOPE OF RECRUITING: Currently based in Los Angeles, with management responsibility for all markets in Asia/Pacific—especially senior-level regional searches for multinational companies.

Experienced with Japanese and Korean multinationals. Serves as a bridge between North American/Australian clients and Asian markets, focusing on cross-border and region-wide recruiting.

SECTOR/INDUSTRY SPECIALIZATION: Industry generalist, with primary experience in consumer products, technology, professional service firms; regional general management searches across markets; domestic Japanese and Korean conglomerates operating globally.

MOST IMPORTANT ISSUES IN CONDUCTING A HIGH LEVEL SEARCH: In the global firms, achieving the balance between serving local markets using local search consultants on one hand, and serving the global needs of large clients on the other. Serving clients through teamwork and spirited cooperation.

MOST SIGNIFICANT OTHER ASPECT OF PERSONAL OR PROFESSIONAL LIFE: Primary residence in California; second residence in Australia. Splits professional and personal life between California and Asia/Pacific.

WHAT IS THE BEST PREPARATION TO BEING A SUCCESSFUL RECRUITER? In the past, the recruiter was a good networker with good contacts—a good salesperson. Today, the best recruiter, especially in the larger firms, is experienced in leading senior-level project teams across geographies—using influence to get things done through other people, with the help of information technology. In the not-too-distant future, no firm or search professional will survive without the ability to operate seamlessly across markets, using information and communication technology to deliver, in short order, the best candidates, wherever those candidates happen to be.

WHAT WOULD YOU BE DOING IF YOU WERE NOT AN EXECUTIVE RECRUITER? An entrepreneur or writer.

WHAT ARE THE CHARACTERISTICS OF A GREAT CLIENT? A company, large or small, with aspirations to lead an industry or niche.

WHAT CHALLENGES DO YOU SEE AHEAD IN THE GLOBAL MARKETPLACE? Large global organizations need not be homogeneous. The challenge is to build diversity and local initiative into the fabric of a cohesive global organization—knowing when to be local and when to be global, when to use the larger resources of the company and when to implement local strategies. Dealing with these issues, with speed and flexibility, through the matrix, and across cultures, is the biggest internal challenge facing large companies.

DAVID WESLEY BENN

Korn/Ferry International
Level 18, Gold Fields House
1 Alfred Street
Sydney, NSW 2000
Australia

Telephone: 61 (02) 9247 7941
Fax: 61 (02) 9251 2043
E-mail: david.benn@kornferry.com
Company Website: http://www.kornferry.com

DATE OF BIRTH: August 22, 1940

NATIONALITY: Dual citizenship: Australian/American—Grew up in East Coast U.S.A. (Virginia)

EDUCATIONAL BACKGROUND:
MBA (International Finance), New York University Graduate Business School, 1969
BA (Economics), Washington & Lee University, 1962

LANGUAGES SPOKEN: English

CAREER HIGHLIGHTS:

1986–Present	Korn/Ferry
1983–1986	Trans-City International
1980–1983	Wells Fargo Bank
1962–1980	Chemical Bank

SPECIAL INTERESTS/HOBBIES: Backpacking; reading; wine appreciation

GEOGRAPHIC SCOPE OF RECRUITING: Australasia/cross regional

SECTOR/INDUSTRY SPECIALIZATION: Financial Services

FAVORITE HISTORICAL FIGURE/MODEL/MENTOR: Winston Churchill

SINGLE MOST IMPORTANT ISSUE IN CONDUCTING A HIGH LEVEL SEARCH: Integrity

MOST SIGNIFICANT OTHER ASPECT OF PERSONAL OR PROFESSIONAL LIFE: Wife and family

WHAT IS THE BEST PREPARATION FOR BEING A SUCCESSFUL RECRUITER? At the top end of search, you need a strong empathy with both the personal circumstances and business pressures faced by candidates based on senior management experience of your own. This argues for it being a second career, best undertaken in your 40s. Industry background is not as important as orientation and energy, but I believe service industry backgrounds have the easiest transitions to the conflicting demands of business development and execution.

WHAT WOULD YOU BE DOING IF YOU WERE NOT AN EXECUTIVE RECRUITER? At this stage of my career, after a number of years in international banking, a principal in a work out/corporate reconstruction financial boutique.

WHAT ARE THE CHARACTERISTICS OF A GREAT CLIENT? Work openly and honestly to an agreed timetable; available regularly for short, focused reviews of developments; decisive and realistic on closure issues.

WHAT CHALLENGES DO YOU SEE AHEAD IN THE GLOBAL MARKETPLACE? Search is a mature industry in most developed countries, and pressure for growth is often driving marginal revenue down market. It will increasingly be important for the larger search companies to diversify into the selection business/technology driven applications to service clients in a more solution driven, cost effective basis, but with the same quality standards. The search business will, by definition, go up market as a result, but volume will increase at a decreasing rate.

ROBERT L. BENSON

Spencer Stuart
Schaumainkai 69
60596 Frankfurt
Germany

695 East Main St.
Stamford, CT 06901
U.S.A.

Telephone: 49 69 610 927 16
Fax: 49 69 610 927 60
E-mail: bbenson@spencerstuart.com
Company Website: http://www.spencerstuart.com

1 (203) 326-3790
1 (203) 326-3737

DATE OF BIRTH: December 23, 1942

NATIONALITY: American—Grew up in U.S.A.

EDUCATIONAL BACKGROUND:
B.S. Business Administration, Quinnipiac College

LANGUAGES SPOKEN: English; some French and some German

CAREER HIGHLIGHTS: CIGNA Corporation—General Management & Human Resources

SPECIAL INTERESTS/HOBBIES: Skiing, boating, golf, computing and travel

GEOGRAPHIC SCOPE OF RECRUITING: United States and Europe

SECTOR/INDUSTRY SPECIALIZATION: Industrial and Financial Services

FAVORITE HISTORICAL FIGURE/MODEL/MENTOR: Father

MOST IMPORTANT ISSUES IN CONDUCTING A HIGH LEVEL SEARCH: Trust: building credibility by delivering quality results through client orientation, professionalism, due diligence, honesty, quality of communications and bringing insights to client problems to create a reputation of value, reliability and trust.

MOST SIGNIFICANT OTHER ASPECT OF PERSONAL OR PROFESSIONAL LIFE: The opportunity to experience a multi-cultural business and personal lifestyle.

WHAT IS THE BEST PREPARATION FOR BEING A SUCCESSFUL RECRUITER?
- General management experience
- International perspective and experience
- Strong industry and functional expertise
- Heavy involvement in change and restructuring
- Multiple company and/or industry experience

WHAT WOULD YOU BE DOING IF YOU WERE NOT AN EXECUTIVE RECRUITER? Consulting with organizations in high state of change or teaching.

WHAT ARE THE CHARACTERISTICS OF A GREAT CLIENT? Knowledgeable in the process but not driven by it. An honest, open, direct and demanding partner who is available. Provides quality feedback both positive and negative.

WHAT CHALLENGES DO YOU SEE AHEAD IN THE GLOBAL MARKETPLACE?
- Lack of supply of top quality international managers
- Increasing demands for speed and availability of consultant regardless of "clock"!
- Increasing use of technology by "people-people"—a contradiction and conflict

BRUCE CLAY BERINGER

Heidrick & Struggles
100 Piccadilly
London W1U 9FN

Telephone: 44-171-491-3124
Fax: 44-171-495-3720
E-mail: BBE@h-s.com
Company Website: http://www.h-s.com

DATE OF BIRTH: November 14, 1947

NATIONALITY: American—Grew up in United States and Europe

EDUCATIONAL BACKGROUND:
  1970–73   J.D., Syracuse University College of Law
  1966–70   B.A., College of William & Mary, Major-Political Science

LANGUAGES SPOKEN: English/French

CAREER HIGHLIGHTS:
  1993–present   Managing Director of London office; H&S Managing Partner, Emerging Markets.
  1984–93   Resident in Kuwait for Russell Reynolds
  1975–83   Haight Gardner Poor & Havens; worked in international corporate-commercial law, 1978–80

SPECIAL INTERESTS/HOBBIES: Foreign affairs, travel, water sports, mountain biking, theater

GEOGRAPHIC SCOPE OF RECRUITING: Western, Central & Eastern Europe, Middle East and Africa

SECTOR/INDUSTRY SPECIALIZATION: Emerging Markets including FMCG, Financial Services, Law

FAVORITE HISTORICAL FIGURE/MODEL/MENTOR: Winston Churchill, Jack Welch

SINGLE MOST IMPORTANT ISSUE IN CONDUCTING A HIGH LEVEL SEARCH: Melding client expectation with market reality through comprehensive "quality" communication

BIGGEST COMPETITOR: Egon Zehnder

MOST SIGNIFICANT OTHER ASPECT OF PERSONAL OR PROFESSIONAL LIFE: Adaptability to environments of change

WHAT IS THE BEST PREPARATION FOR BEING A SUCCESSFUL RECRUITER? Strong research, preparation, listening and patience.

WHAT WOULD YOU BE DOING IF YOU WERE NOT AN EXECUTIVE RECRUITER? Management consulting

WHAT ARE THE CHARACTERISTICS OF A GREAT CLIENT?
  • Great name
  • Great communication
  • Great growth/change

WHAT CHALLENGES DO YOU SEE AHEAD IN THE GLOBAL MARKETPLACE? The need to assimilate cultural differences in a homogenizing global client base

LINDA BIALECKI

Bialecki Inc.
780 Third Avenue, #4203
New York, NY 10017
U.S.A.

Telephone: 1 (212) 755-1090
Fax: 1 (212) 755-1130
Company Website: http://www.bailecki.com

DATE OF BIRTH: March 28, 1947

NATIONALITY: American—Grew up in U.S.A.

EDUCATIONAL BACKGROUND:
   1979, MBA, Stanford University
   1969, BA, University of California, Berkeley

LANGUAGES SPOKEN: English

SPECIAL INTERESTS/HOBBIES: Scuba diving, cooking, traveling

GEOGRAPHIC SCOPE OF RECRUITING: Worldwide

SECTOR/INDUSTRY SPECIALIZATION: Investment banking clients: capital markets, sales, trading, research, investment banking

FAVORITE HISTORICAL FIGURE/MODEL/MENTOR: Eleanor Roosevelt

SINGLE MOST IMPORTANT ISSUE IN CONDUCTING A HIGH LEVEL SEARCH: Integrity

MOST SIGNIFICANT OTHER ASPECT OF PERSONAL OR PROFESSIONAL LIFE: Technology; extensive database of qualitative candidate information

WHAT IS THE BEST PREPARATION FOR BEING A SUCCESSFUL RECRUITER? Psychologist or investigative reporter

WHAT WOULD YOU BE DOING IF YOU WERE NOT AN EXECUTIVE RECRUITER? CIA agent

WHAT ARE THE CHARACTERISTICS OF A GREAT CLIENT? Vision. Courage. Willingness, indeed interest in hiring great talent that might be an out-of-the-box solution.

WHAT CHALLENGES DO YOU SEE AHEAD IN THE GLOBAL MARKETPLACE? Finding individuals and organizations that work seamlessly globally.

MICHAEL D. BOXBERGER

Korn/Ferry International
1800 Century Park East
Suite 900
Los Angeles, CA 90067
U.S.A.

Telephone: (310) 552-1834
Fax: (310) 553-8640
Company Website: http://www.kornferry.com

DATE OF BIRTH: August 19, 1946

NATIONALITY: American—Grew up in Elgin, IL

EDUCATIONAL BACKGROUND:
1972, University of Texas at Austin, M.B.A., finance,
1968, University of Denver, B.A. , biological sciences

LANGUAGES SPOKEN: English

SPECIAL INTERESTS/HOBBIES: Bird shooting, fishing, running, reading

GEOGRAPHIC SCOPE OF RECRUITING: Worldwide

SECTOR/INDUSTRY SPECIALIZATION: CEOs, COOs, Board of Directors

FAVORITE HISTORICAL FIGURE/MODEL/MENTOR: Dwight Eisenhower

SINGLE MOST IMPORTANT ISSUE IN CONDUCTING A HIGH LEVEL SEARCH: Identify candidates who, through leadership by example, have a history of truly "making a difference" regardless of circumstances and a proven ability to succeed in complex, difficult situations and to bounce back from adversity and to win in the end.

MOST SIGNIFICANT OTHER ASPECT OF PERSONAL OR PROFESSIONAL LIFE: Family

WHAT IS THE BEST PREPARATION FOR BEING A SUCCESSFUL RECRUITER? Immerse yourself in your client's business. You must have a full understanding of the client company's culture, management structure and major issues in order to advise on what type of people they need to move the company forward. A good executive recruiter also needs to be a great listener, know how to read between the lines, be able to act as an extension of the client to effectively articulate the opportunity to the candidate, and be experienced in high-level negotiating. Most important is sound judgment about how the client and candidate will ultimately fit. A recruiter who throws a number of candidates against the wall and hopes one will stick will never be a great search professional.

WHAT WOULD YOU BE DOING IF YOU WERE NOT AN EXECUTIVE RECRUITER? I find the very close interaction with clients that characterizes executive search very appealing to me. It's hard for me to envision anything that I would enjoy more than running the most successful global firm in the business.

WHAT ARE THE CHARACTERISTICS OF A GREAT CLIENT? A great client is willing to participate in the recruiting process—both providing and seeking input—and who is willing to listen to a recruiter's advice, even if it differs from the client's own viewpoint. The best clients trust your advice and treat you as a partner in the process.

WHAT CHALLENGES DO YOU SEE AHEAD IN THE GLOBAL MARKETPLACE? The world is quickly evolving into one international marketplace, which means the ability to act swiftly and intelligently across geographic lines is key to the survival and success of any business. For example, take information technology: It transforms the way businesses operate across the globe—and it's still changing rapidly. Companies must be able to catch up with the techno-wave and modify their approaches to maintain their leadership. At Korn/Ferry, we're constantly developing new and expedient approaches (most recently, our on-line Korn/Ferry: FutureStep division) to help our clients build and maximize their leadership capital.

IRENA BRICHTA

Heidrick & Struggles s.r.o.
Lazarská 5, 110 00 Prague 1
Czech Republic/Slovakia

Telephone: 42-2-24946565
Fax: 42-2-24946567
E-mail: bri@h-s.com
Company Website: http://www.h-s.com/prague.htm

DATE OF BIRTH: September 2, 1950

NATIONALITY: British + Czech—Grew up in U.K.

EDUCATIONAL BACKGROUND:
1975–76: Strathclyde Business School—M.B.A.
1970–75: University of Glasgow-Honours Degree—M.A. (Czech & Archeology)
1961–70: Northampton Girls Grammar School

LANGUAGES SPOKEN: English, Czech, intermediate German, good French, spoken Polish, basic Hungarian

CAREER HIGHLIGHTS:
Country Manager, Czech Republic
13 yrs., East Europe Export Sales/Marketing Manager: Ethicon Ltd., Johnson & Johnson
Marketing Director, Johnson & Johnson, Budapest
Sales Director, Kraft Jacobs Suchard, Budapest
Consultant, Egon Zehnder International., Prague

SPECIAL INTERESTS/HOBBIES: Board Member both of American Chamber, Prague and of British Chamber, Prague; Chairman, Business Leaders' Forum; Horseriding, skiing, running, reading, traveling

GEOGRAPHIC SCOPE OF RECRUITING: Czech and Slovak Republics

SECTOR/INDUSTRY SPECIALIZATION: FMCG, Pharma, Financial Services, Professional Services

FAVORITE HISTORICAL FIGURE/MODEL/MENTOR: Karel IV (Charles IV, King of Bohemia, who was also Charles I, Holy Roman Emperor)

SINGLE MOST IMPORTANT ISSUE IN CONDUCTING A HIGH LEVEL SEARCH: To exceed client's' expectations and to fully satisfy client's needs.

MOST SIGNIFICANT OTHER ASPECT OF PERSONAL OR PROFESSIONAL LIFE: Enthusiasm and commitment are most important in anything one does.

WHAT IS THE BEST PREPARATION FOR BEING A SUCCESSFUL RECRUITER? Having business experience at management level, at least 5–8 years, or consulting experience. Also practice being a good listener! And practice developing business relationships and networking.

WHAT WOULD YOU BE DOING IF YOU WERE NOT AN EXECUTIVE RECRUITER? A senior management executive or having a holiday!

WHAT ARE THE CHARACTERISTICS OF A GREAT CLIENT? A client who desires to work closely with an executive search consultant, as a "partnership," in an open, friendly, and professional manner.

WHAT CHALLENGES DO YOU SEE AHEAD IN THE GLOBAL MARKETPLACE? The same as at present—identifying suitably qualified and experienced senior executives who meet a client's expectations both prior to and post hiring.

MILES BROADBENT

The Miles Partnership
Bennet House
54 St. James's Street
London WW1A 1JT

Telephone: 44 171-495-7772
Fax: 44 171-495-7773
Company Website: http://www.miles-partnership.com

DATE OF BIRTH: February 22, 1936

NATIONALITY: British—Grew up in England

EDUCATIONAL BACKGROUND:
M.A. Magdalene College, Cambridge University
MBA Harvard Business School

LANGUAGES SPOKEN: French and German

CAREER HIGHLIGHTS: Joined the executive search industry in 1979 with the London office of Russell Reynolds Associates. Became Managing Director of the RRA London office in 1981, and was immediately appointed to the RRA Worldwide Executive Committee.

Left RRA in 1983 and was a founder of Norman Broadbent International Ltd. Formally appointed Chief Executive in December 1987, and ran its worldwide business for eight years during its most spectacular period of growth, until December 1995. Formed The Miles Partnership, which is expanding internationally.

Involved in the appointment of Ian McGregor as Chairman of British Steel, and was personally responsible for the recruitment of Colin Marshall as Chief Executive of British Airways. These two high profile and successful appointments led to assignments to recruit many other major public company Chief Executives. Recruited an average of six Chief Executives a year since 1983. Among the more high profile recent appointments have been the Chief Executive of Glaxo Wellcome, Sir Richard Sykes (the Chief Executive of Granada), Gerry Robinson; and the Chief Executive of Rentokil Initial, Sir Clive Thompson. Responsible for the recruitment of the Chief Executives of Hong Kong Telecom, the Kowloon Canton Railway Company and China Light and Power. The Chairmen I have recruited include the Chairman of Glaxo Wellcome Plc, Sir Colin Corness; the Chairman of Scottish & Newcastle Plc, Sir Alistair Grant; the Chairman of Railtrack Plc, Sir Robert Horton; the Chairman of Redland Plc, Rudolph Agnew; the Chairman of Blue Circle Industries, Lord Tugendhat; and the Joint Chairman of Reed Elsevier, Nigel Stapleton. Outside the purely industrial company sector, I was responsible for the recruitment of George Bain as Principal of the London Business School, and more recently advised the Government on the appointment of Sir Christopher Bland as Chairman of the Board of Governors of the BBC.

I have appointed over 20 Non-Executive Directors per annum to major British public companies over the past three or four years. Perhaps one of the more interesting group of board appointments has been to the board of Guinness where I recruited Dominic Cadbury, Chairman of Cadbury Schweppes to the board of Guinness together with Keith Oates, Deputy Chairman of Marks & Spencer and the distinguished German Chief Executive, Dr. Helmut Sihler, formerly Chief Executive of Henkel.

SPECIAL INTERESTS/HOBBIES: Tennis and golf

GEOGRAPHIC SCOPE OF RECRUITING: Worldwide

SECTOR/INDUSTRY SPECIALIZATION: All industries—Chairmen, CEOs, CFOs, and outside directors

continues ▶

FAVORITE HISTORICAL FIGURE/MODEL/MENTOR: Colin Marshall remains the most successful recruitment. Not only did he turn around British Airways from a lame duck to the most profitable airline in the world, but he has gone on to become Chairman of British Airways, Deputy Chairman of BT, Chairman of Inchcape, a Director of HSBC and Chairman of the CBI. He is an upfront leader who leads by example, a real workaholic, and a man who gets into the detail as well as directing the big picture and strategy.

SINGLE MOST IMPORTANT ISSUE IN CONDUCTING A HIGH LEVEL SEARCH: The single most important issue in conducting a high level search is that I must produce a candidate who is better than the client was expecting. It is all too easy to produce an average or reasonable candidate, but you really only do the job well if you push yourself beyond the OK candidate to the outstanding candidate who will really make a difference to your client's business. Colin Marshall, Richard Sykes, Gerry Robinson, and Clive Thompson are good examples of what I mean. There are many more who have equally made their mark on less high profile companies. I am only really satisfied if I produce a top quality result for my client.

BIGGEST COMPETITOR: I am not sure that size is important. What matters is top quality, not size.

MOST SIGNIFICANT OTHER ASPECT OF PERSONAL OR PROFESSIONAL LIFE: I do not believe it is necessary or appropriate to spend very long hours in the office. I believe that one should achieve a good balance between professional and personal life. I think the headhunting business is ideal to achieve this balance, because one can think about assignments at home just as well as in the office. I have found that time spent quietly thinking about assignments is probably as productive, if not more productive, than time spent looking at names on a computer screen or similar. The way to find good candidates is not by looking at a lot of names, but by talking to the people in industry who can recommend you in a rifle shot way to the best two or three candidates. The key is to talk to those people who know who are the best candidates.

JOHN R. BROCK

Korn/Ferry International
1100 Louisiana
Suite 2850
Houston, TX 77002
U.S.A.

Telephone: (713) 651-1834
Fax: (713) 650-1139
E-mail: brockj@kornferry.com
Company Website: http://kornferry.com

DATE OF BIRTH: August 14, 1947

NATIONALITY: American—Grew up in Houston, Texas

EDUCATIONAL BACKGROUND:
Certified Public Accountant
M.B.A., Finance, University of Texas, 1970
B.B.A., Accounting, University of Texas, 1969

LANGUAGES SPOKEN: English

CAREER HIGHLIGHTS:
7 years Public Accounting—KPMG Peat Marwick
5 years Investment Banking—Paine Webber
4 years President Houston Economic Development Council
Managing Director—Korn/Ferry International's Global Energy

SPECIAL INTERESTS/HOBBIES: Golf, hunting, fishing

GEOGRAPHIC SCOPE OF RECRUITING: Global

SECTOR/INDUSTRY SPECIALIZATION: Energy, Automotive

SINGLE MOST IMPORTANT ISSUE IN CONDUCTING A HIGH LEVEL SEARCH: Understanding client's professional and personal needs.

MOST SIGNIFICANT OTHER ASPECT OF PERSONAL OR PROFESSIONAL LIFE: Balancing professional and personal life.

WHAT IS THE BEST PREPARATION FOR BEING A SUCCESSFUL RECRUITER? A tenure in public accounting to better understand business needs.

WHAT WOULD YOU BE DOING IF YOU WERE NOT AN EXECUTIVE RECRUITER? I'd be on the senior golf tour.

WHAT ARE THE CHARACTERISTICS OF A GREAT CLIENT? All my clients are great.

WHAT CHALLENGES DO YOU SEE AHEAD IN THE GLOBAL MARKETPLACE? Delivering a locally focused service on global basis.

HOBSON BROWN, JR.

Russell Reynolds Associates
200 Park Avenue, Suite 2300
New York, NY 10166-0002
U.S.A.

Telephone: 1 (212) 351-2000
Fax: 1 (212) 370-0896
E-mail: hbrown@russreyn.com
Company Website: http://www.russreyn.com

DATE OF BIRTH: January 2, 1942

NATIONALITY: American—Grew up in North Carolina

EDUCATIONAL BACKGROUND:
M.B.A. in Finance, The Wharton School, University of Pennsylvania, 1969
B.A. in Economics, University of North Carolina, 1964

LANGUAGES SPOKEN: English

CAREER HIGHLIGHTS: Commercial banker with J. P. Morgan before joining Russell Reynolds Associates in 1977

SPECIAL INTERESTS/HOBBIES: Fly fishing, pheasant/grouse/quail shooting, hunting

GEOGRAPHIC SCOPE OF RECRUITING: Worldwide

SECTOR/INDUSTRY SPECIALIZATION: CEO and Directors' assignments

FAVORITE HISTORICAL FIGURE/MODEL/MENTOR: General George Patton

SINGLE MOST IMPORTANT ISSUE IN CONDUCTING A HIGH LEVEL SEARCH: Exceeding expectations—of the client and lead candidate. Conducting assignments at the CEO and Director levels requires a unique mix of strategic thinking, creativity, persistence, diplomacy . . . and a healthy sense of humor.

MOST SIGNIFICANT OTHER ASPECT OF PERSONAL OR PROFESSIONAL LIFE: At the top level, business opportunities—as well as potential candidates—present themselves in virtually every aspect of our professional as well as personal lives. Candidates are making significant decisions that involve not just themselves but their families. These issues combine to make ours a 24-hour-a-day, 7-day-a-week business.

WHAT IS THE BEST PREPARATION FOR BEING A SUCCESSFUL RECRUITER? Successful recruiters have deep industry knowledge—often from first-hand experience in the industries serve. They are focused on the market— experts in their clients' businesses, on top of the issues they face, and able to consult with them on the business challenges they face.

WHAT WOULD YOU BE DOING IF YOU WERE NOT AN EXECUTIVE RECRUITER? Working with clients to help solve business challenges through identifying and retaining people who add real value to the organization is a fascinating business—I can't imagine doing anything else.

WHAT ARE THE CHARACTERISTICS OF A GREAT CLIENT? Trust and honesty.

WHAT CHALLENGES DO YOU SEE AHEAD IN THE GLOBAL MARKETPLACE? In today's marketplace, the challenges facing the CEO—technological change, political and economic reform, workforce diversity, shareholder activism—have been magnified to a global scale. Business leaders are subjected to greater scrutiny and held to a higher performance standard by increasingly attentive boards of directors as well as institutional shareholders. These challenges place a high premium on leaders who have a reputation for excellence—in the business practices they implement, the products and services they create, and the talent they attract.

KURT BRUUSGAARD

Ray & Berndtson A/S
Nyhavn 63C, 1051 Copenhagen K
Denmark

Telephone: 45 33 14 36 36
Fax: 45 33 32 43 32
E-mail: kb@rbcph.dk
Company Website: http://www.rayberndtson.com

DATE OF BIRTH: February 14, 1942

NATIONALITY: Danish—Grew up in Copenhagen, Denmark

EDUCATIONAL BACKGROUND:
Bachelor's, 1972, Management & Organization, Copenhagen School of Business Administration
B.S., 1966, Mechanical Engineering, Technical College, Copenhagen

LANGUAGES SPOKEN: English, German, Italian

CAREER HIGHLIGHTS: Managing Director-industrial company; Assistant to CEO, Spies Leisure Group

SPECIAL INTERESTS/HOBBIES: Hunting, tennis, music, art, Italy, Rotary International, human potential movements

GEOGRAPHIC SCOPE OF RECRUITING: After having been active in the Scandinavian countries focus today is Denmark.

SECTOR/INDUSTRY SPECIALIZATION: Generalist—General Management, marketing/sales

FAVORITE HISTORICAL FIGURE/MODEL/MENTOR: Leonardo da Vinci

MOST IMPORTANT ISSUES IN CONDUCTING A HIGH LEVEL SEARCH: Creativity, timing, sense of urgency, ability to combine various information, see things as part of a greater whole, simplify them and make priorities.

MOST SIGNIFICANT OTHER ASPECT OF PERSONAL OR PROFESSIONAL LIFE: Extra mental capacity

WHAT IS THE BEST PREPARATION FOR BEING A SUCCESSFUL RECRUITER?
- General Management experience on a high level.
- Skills and interest within Human Resources.
- Sales and result-oriented personality plus sense of urgency and commitment to "walk the extra mile."
- Capable of focusing and making priorities.
- Sound judgment, obvious ability for matchmaking, and a "never-give-up" attitude.

WHAT WOULD YOU BE DOING IF YOU WERE NOT AN EXECUTIVE RECRUITER? I would probably be president of an industrial company or a service company, or maybe a lawyer working within the industrial field.

WHAT ARE THE CHARACTERISTICS OF A GREAT CLIENT? A "great client" is currently a front-runner in its field, It has a strong image and a clear strategy plus financial means to implement the strategy. It is growth- and development-oriented and has board and management members with recognized talents. The great client is ambitious, has vision and is thus committed to finding the best managerial talent. A close-knit relationship and cooperation follow naturally.

WHAT CHALLENGES DO YOU SEE AHEAD IN THE GLOBAL MARKETPLACE? The necessity of being global and local worldwide—"The one firm" concept. Speed and the extensive use of computer technology; the scarcity of star performers; extensive competition in keeping and getting top talents increasing number of cross-border searches.

PAUL BUCHANAN-BARROW

Korn/Ferry International
252 Regent St.
London W1R 5DA
U.K.

Telephone: 44 171-312-3100
Fax: 44 171-414-0525
E-mail: paul.buchananbarrow@kornferry.com (office)
　　　 buchanan-barrow@msn.com (home)
Company Website: http://www.kornferry.com

DATE OF BIRTH: April 23, 1945

NATIONALITY: British—Grew up in U.K.

EDUCATIONAL BACKGROUND:
　University of St. Andrews-M.A.

LANGUAGES SPOKEN: English and excruciating French

CAREER HIGHLIGHTS: Director-County Bank; Managing Director-GKR

SPECIAL INTERESTS/HOBBIES: Music, keeping fit and walking

GEOGRAPHIC SCOPE OF RECRUITING: Worldwide, especially U.K./U.S.A.

SECTOR/INDUSTRY SPECIALIZATION: Generalist specialising in board work-chairman, nonexecutive directors, CEOs

FAVORITE HISTORICAL FIGURE/MODEL/MENTOR: Nelson Mandela

SINGLE MOST IMPORTANT ISSUE IN CONDUCTING A HIGH LEVEL SEARCH: Attention to detail (and good luck)

WHAT IS THE BEST PREPARATION FOR BEING A SUCCESSFUL RECRUITER? A thorough grounding in business, preferably with line management experience in a very fast moving, customer orientated environment.

WHAT WOULD YOU BE DOING IF YOU WERE NOT AN EXECUTIVE RECRUITER? Looking for a job.

WHAT ARE THE CHARACTERISTICS OF A GREAT CLIENT? Urgency and consistency and an understanding of the realities of life.

WHAT CHALLENGES DO YOU SEE AHEAD IN THE GLOBAL MARKETPLACE? A major challenge is for each "global search firm" to make its network work more efficiently on behalf of its clients. Another potential challenge is the impact of recruiting via the Internet, i.e. Korn/Ferry FutureStep

SKOTT B. BURKLAND

Skott/Edwards Consultants
1776 On the Green
Morristown, NJ 07960
U.S.A.

Telephone: 1 (973) 644-0900
Fax: 1 (973) 644-0991
E-mail: search@skottedwards.com
Company Website: http://www.skottedwards.com

DATE OF BIRTH: May 25, 1942

NATIONALITY: American—Grew up in Philadelphia, Pennsylvania

EDUCATIONAL BACKGROUND:
Dickinson College, Carlisle, PA, B.A. Degree
Drexel University, postgraduate work
Rutgers University, postgraduate work

LANGUAGES SPOKEN: English

CAREER HIGHLIGHTS: President, Skott/Edwards Consultants

MOST SIGNIFICANT ACCOMPLISHMENT: Received AESC Gardner W. Heidrick Award

SPECIAL INTERESTS/HOBBIES: Porsche GT-3 race car driver

GEOGRAPHIC SCOPE OF RECRUITING: North America and Western Europe

SECTOR/INDUSTRY SPECIALIZATION: General Management, Board of Directors. Heavy emphasis in Pharmaceuticals and Information Technology.

FAVORITE HISTORICAL FIGURE/MODEL/MENTOR: My paternal grandfather

SINGLE MOST IMPORTANT ISSUE IN CONDUCTING A HIGH LEVEL SEARCH: Integrity. To have the strength to do a complete and comprehensive search, to have the integrity to point out strengths and weaknesses of a client organization, and of a potential candidate. To have the integrity to negotiate a fair and honest arrangement. To have the integrity to not deviate from the practice or the professionalism and the standards of our ethics.

MOST SIGNIFICANT OTHER ASPECT OF PERSONAL OR PROFESSIONAL LIFE: I believe it is important to recognize that as an executive search consultant we have an integral role in the third most important part of a person's life. The first is faith, the second is family, and the third is career. Because we play a major role in a person's life, we must conduct ourselves with the highest standards of integrity and ethics.

WHAT IS THE BEST PREPARATION FOR BEING A SUCCESSFUL RECRUITER? The best preparation is a well-rounded business background with strong technical experience coupled with general management. In addition, a studied understanding of human behavior is essential.

WHAT WOULD YOU BE DOING IF YOU WERE NOT AN EXECUTIVE RECRUITER? A race car driver, an attorney, or a physician

WHAT ARE THE CHARACTERISTICS OF A GREAT CLIENT? A great client receives an executive search consultant as a partner. A client trusts, shares and embraces an executive search consultant.

WHAT CHALLENGES DO YOU SEE AHEAD IN THE GLOBAL MARKETPLACE? As the marketplace shrinks and information becomes available more quickly, clients tend to feel that search should be completed faster. There should be an emphasis on the quality of search, not the quantity of candidates or the speed of search completion.

RICHARD BUSCHMAN

Korn/Ferry International
World Trade Centre Strawinskylaan 545
1077XX Amsterdam
The Netherlands

Telephone: 31 20 664 1301
Fax: 31 20 675 0205
E-mail: amsterdam@kornferry.com
Company Website: http://www.kornferry.com

DATE OF BIRTH: September 21, 1951

NATIONALITY: Dutch—Grew up in The Netherlands

EDUCATIONAL BACKGROUND:
Masters Degree in Management Science
Harvard; IMD

LANGUAGES SPOKEN: Dutch, English, French, German

CAREER HIGHLIGHTS:
Senior Vice President Human Resources, KNP BT (Royal Dutch Paper Mills/Bührmann Tetterode)
Senior Vice President Human Resources, Sara Lee/DE

SPECIAL INTERESTS/HOBBIES: Golf, sailing

GEOGRAPHIC SCOPE OF RECRUITING: Global

SECTOR/INDUSTRY SPECIALIZATION: Fast moving consumer goods, manufacturing, finance

SINGLE MOST IMPORTANT ISSUE IN CONDUCTING A HIGH LEVEL SEARCH: To have had personal business and managerial experience at a high level

MOST SIGNIFICANT OTHER ASPECT OF PERSONAL OR PROFESSIONAL LIFE: My family

WHAT IS THE BEST PREPARATION FOR BEING A SUCCESSFUL RECRUITER? Through experience, we know that there is no one best way. However, successful recruiters have some common characteristics, including being an industry specialist and therefore, have an in-depth know-how about his clients and their competition, is execution and quality driven, and able and willing to take an independent point of view versus clients and candidates.

WHAT WOULD YOU BE DOING IF YOU WERE NOT AN EXECUTIVE RECRUITER? I would still or again be the VP of HR for a Fortune 100 multinational company.

WHAT ARE THE CHARACTERISTICS OF A GREAT CLIENT? To me, all clients are great, and if they are not, it is the recruiter's job to make them great clients. If the recruiter does not believe he/she can turn them into great clients, he/she should not be working for them.

WHAT CHALLENGES DO YOU SEE AHEAD IN THE GLOBAL MARKETPLACE? Our clients are challenged by the further globalization, consolidation, specialization and use of technology; it is our challenge to have the people, technology, organization and leadership in place in order to serve our clients in meeting these challenges.

LUIZ CARLOS DE QUEIRÓS CABRERA

PMC Amrop International
Rua do Rocio 220, 8ª andar
04552-000 São Paulo, SP
Brazil

Telephone: 55 (11) 822-9077
Fax: 55 (11) 822-0781
E-mail: pmcamrop@amcham.com.br
Company Website: http://www.amrop.com

DATE OF BIRTH: March 5, 1944

NATIONALITY: Brazilian—Grew up in Brazil

EDUCATIONAL BACKGROUND:

Metallurgical Engineer, Mauá Institute of Engineering, 1967
Graduate course in Business Administration, São Paulo Graduate School of Business Administration, 1977
Extension course, Graduate School of Business, University of Southern California, 1976

LANGUAGES SPOKEN: Portuguese, English, Spanish, working knowledge of French and Italian

CAREER HIGHLIGHTS: Founding partner of PMC Amrop International, in 1975; Board Member of Amrop International from 1991 to 1995

SPECIAL INTERESTS/HOBBIES: Teaching, reading, soccer, and volleyball

GEOGRAPHIC SCOPE OF RECRUITING: Brazil

SECTOR/INDUSTRY SPECIALIZATION: Top level searches-all sectors

FAVORITE HISTORICAL FIGURE/MODEL/MENTOR: Albert Einstein, Peter Drucker

SINGLE MOST IMPORTANT ISSUE IN CONDUCTING A HIGH LEVEL SEARCH: To know and understand the client's culture, management style, and the business itself

BIGGEST COMPETITOR: Mr. Guilherme Dale, Spencer Stuart

MOST SIGNIFICANT OTHER ASPECT OF PERSONAL OR PROFESSIONAL LIFE:

Personal: strongly oriented to the family.
Professional: Assist executives in career development (improvement) in two ways—lecturing and moving them to a challenging position.

DENNIS C. CAREY

Spencer Stuart
2005 Market St., Suite 2350
Philadelphia, PA 19103
U.S.A.

Telephone: 1 (215) 851-6201
Fax: 1 (215) 963-0182
Company Website: http://www.spencerstuart.com

DATE OF BIRTH: October 27, 1949

NATIONALITY: American—Grew up in California and New Jersey

EDUCATIONAL BACKGROUND:
PhD, University of Maryland
Post-doctoral, Harvard University-Fellow
Fellow, European Common Market
Fellow, Princeton University Theological Seminary

LANGUAGES SPOKEN: Spanish, English

CAREER HIGHLIGHTS:
- Currently Managing Director at Spencer Stuart
- Placed CEO of AT&T and others. Placed corporate directors at over 60 of America's leading corporations.

SPECIAL INTERESTS/HOBBIES: Swam English Channel, 1980; triathlons; "Top 20 Swimmers in World," WSF 1981

GEOGRAPHIC SCOPE OF RECRUITING: Global

SECTOR/INDUSTRY SPECIALIZATION: Head of board recruiting for SSI

FAVORITE HISTORICAL FIGURE/MODEL/MENTOR: Winston Churchill; former governor Pete duPont is role model and mentor (was my boss for 5 years)

SINGLE MOST IMPORTANT ISSUE IN CONDUCTING A HIGH LEVEL SEARCH: Confidentiality

MOST SIGNIFICANT OTHER ASPECT OF PERSONAL OR PROFESSIONAL LIFE:
- Married to Janet Lee Carey, Ph.D., and have two children, Maggie and Matt
- Serve on Board of Spencer Stuart
- Serve on Board of Closure Medical Corp. (NASDAQ)
- Founder and Chairman, Global Intelligence™ Corp.

MAGNUS CARLSSON

Amrop International
Oxtorget 3, S-111 57 Stockholm
Sweden

Telephone: 46 8 411 25 05
Fax: 46 8 411 32 32
E-mail: stockholm@amrop.se
Company Website: http://www.amrop.com

DATE OF BIRTH: January 22, 1951

NATIONALITY: Swedish—Grew up in Sweden

EDUCATIONAL BACKGROUND:
   University degree in Psychology and Economy

LANGUAGES SPOKEN: Swedish, English, German

CAREER HIGHLIGHTS: Yet to come

SPECIAL INTERESTS/HOBBIES: Art and book collecting

GEOGRAPHIC SCOPE OF RECRUITING: Scandinavia, mostly Sweden

SECTOR/INDUSTRY SPECIALIZATION: Finance, trading and manufacturing

FAVORITE HISTORICAL FIGURE/MODEL/MENTOR: Nelson Mandela; courage, integrity, reconciliation, leadership

SINGLE MOST IMPORTANT ISSUE IN CONDUCTING A HIGH LEVEL SEARCH: Understanding of culture and
   values in the organisation.

BIGGEST COMPETITOR: Egon Zehnder

MOST SIGNIFICANT OTHER ASPECT OF PERSONAL OR PROFESSIONAL LIFE:

WHAT IS THE BEST PREPARATION FOR BEING A SUCCESSFUL RECRUITER? A good basic education in
   behavioral sciences and business administration. Experience from management is of course almost a must.

WHAT WOULD YOU BE DOING IF YOU WERE NOT AN EXECUTIVE RECRUITER? I would probably be an
   industrial psychologist.

WHAT ARE THE CHARACTERISTICS OF A GREAT CLIENT?
   - Larger group of companies
   - Attractive culture and values
   - Modern management style
   - Interesting business
   - Open for creative solutions

WHAT CHALLENGES DO YOU SEE AHEAD IN THE GLOBAL MARKETPLACE?
   - The IT revolution
   - Globalisation
   - The more project-like management positions

JAMES J. CARPENTER

Russell Reynolds Associates
200 Park Avenue
New York, NY 10166
U.S.A.

Telephone: 1 (212) 351-2008
Fax: 1 (212) 370-0896
E-mail: jcarpenter@russreyn.com
Company Website: http://www.russreyn.com

DATE OF BIRTH: June 5, 1956

NATIONALITY: American—Grew up in Upstate New York and Central Maine

EDUCATIONAL BACKGROUND:

M.B.A., Columbia University, 1981.
B.S., Government, St. Lawrence University, 1978.

LANGUAGES SPOKEN: English

CAREER HIGHLIGHTS: Prior to joining Russell Reynolds Associates, I worked for eight years in consumer products, consulting, and strategic marketing. My most recent position was with PepsiCo where I was involved in acquisition and divestitures, strategic marketing analysis, and new business development activities. Prior to this, I was with the Strategy Consulting firm of Cresap, McCormick and Paget, conducting a broad range of consulting studies both domestically and abroad.

SPECIAL INTERESTS/HOBBIES: I am an avid skier and have participated in that sport in both Europe and the United States. I am also a collector of antiques.

GEOGRAPHIC SCOPE OF RECRUITING: Global. Have conducted CEO search both in Europe and the United States.

SECTOR/INDUSTRY SPECIALIZATION: I head RRA's Consumer Sector and have developed a specialty in recruiting senior general management and marketing executives to a broad range of businesses in consumer and industrial products. Recent senior level assignments include: Chief Executive Officers of Dial Corporation, Lenox, and Playtex, and the recruitment of Ron Zarrella to General Motors as Executive Vice President and General Manager of Marketing, Sales, and Services for the North American Automotive Operation.

FAVORITE HISTORICAL FIGURE/MODEL/MENTOR: Stephen Covey, author of *Seven Habits of Highly Effective People.*

SINGLE MOST IMPORTANT ISSUE IN CONDUCTING A HIGH LEVEL SEARCH: An in-depth understanding of the key leverage points of the client's business so as to identify candidates from within their industry and outside, who have familiarity with those key leverage points and are able to optimize the company's performance against those criteria.

BIGGEST COMPETITOR: Tom Neff/Tom Hardy, Spencer Stuart

MOST SIGNIFICANT OTHER ASPECT OF PERSONAL OR PROFESSIONAL LIFE: Having recently married for the first time at the age of 40, my relationship with my wife and my daughter are the single biggest focus in my life at this time.

WHAT IS THE BEST PREPARATION FOR BEING A SUCCESSFUL RECRUITER? Most successful recruiters have a broad base of experience, not necessarily a deep base of experience, across different businesses before joining the industry. Personal characteristics that seem to distinguish the highly successful from the moderately successful include: an exceptional sense of urgency, a need to persuade or convince people of their position, and an exceptional empathy to both clients and candidates in the course of the process.

WHAT WOULD YOU BE DOING IF YOU WERE NOT AN EXECUTIVE RECRUITER? As compared to other professional experiences I had before recruiting, executive recruiting fits me like a glove and it is hard to imagine doing anything else in my career. However, if I had not ended up in this business I probably would have gone to Wall Street either in Mergers and Acquisitions or Equity Sales. A long-term personal interest of mine is to be involved in the Winter Olympics, or more modestly, a ski instructor at a major resort.

WHAT ARE THE CHARACTERISTICS OF A GREAT CLIENT? A great client clearly understands the key leverage points of their business and is willing to consider candidates from outside of their industry who can bring to bear experience on similar leverage points. A clear vision of the future opportunity in the company is of great benefit as is decisiveness.

WHAT CHALLENGES DO YOU SEE AHEAD IN THE GLOBAL MARKETPLACE? The biggest challenge that multi-national companies face now is establishing a global brand while, at the same time, acknowledging distinctions between local markets. Balancing flexibility (to change direction or compete in new opportunities) with long-term capital investment (required to be a leader in any industry) is a source of considerable anxiety among executives. Additionally, given the different styles of business around the world, taking a strong culture from any domestic market and keeping it consistent across national boundaries has been a huge challenge for even the biggest and best of corporations.

CHOON SOO CHEW

Russell Reynolds Associates
6 Battery Road, #16-08
Singapore 0104

Telephone: 65-225-1811
Fax: 65-224-4058
E-mail: cchew@russreyn.com
Company Website: http://www.russreyn.com

NATIONALITY: Singapore citizen—Grew up in Singapore

EDUCATIONAL BACKGROUND:
M.B.A., The Wharton School, University of Pennsylvania, 1983
B.S. (Honours) in Economics and Accounting, Bristol College, U.K., 1981

LANGUAGES SPOKEN: English, Chinese

CAREER HIGHLIGHTS: Before joining Russell Reynolds Associates, eight years of commercial and merchant banking experience.

SPECIAL INTERESTS/HOBBIES: Golf

GEOGRAPHIC SCOPE OF RECRUITING: Asia

SECTOR/INDUSTRY SPECIALIZATION: Financial Services/Global Banking

WHAT IS THE BEST PREPARATION FOR BEING A SUCCESSFUL RECRUITER? Experience in a service industry. Also, a continuing interest in helping clients build successful organizations by identifying the business leaders they need, and providing talented executives with opportunities to demonstrate their full potential.

WHAT WOULD YOU BE DOING IF YOU WERE NOT AN EXECUTIVE RECRUITER? Managing my own investments.

WHAT ARE THE CHARACTERISTICS OF A GREAT CLIENT? Someone with whom I can build a relationship based on mutual trust, respect and shared advice.

WHAT CHALLENGES DO YOU SEE AHEAD IN THE GLOBAL MARKETPLACE? The need for talented executives with a global perspective, who can function effectively in multiple cultures and are capable of coping with change. This need comes from the dynamic, at times volatile, nature of world markets due to the immediacy of changes in capital flow.

ALAN CHOI

Korn/Ferry International (HK) Ltd.
2104-2106 Gloucester Tower
The Landmark
Hong Kong

Telephone: 1 (852) 2521-5457
Fax: 1 (852) 2810-1632
E-mail: Intranet-alan.choi@kornferry.com
        Internet-alanchoi@hk.net
Company Website: http://www.kornferry.com

DATE OF BIRTH: February 13, 1953

NATIONALITY: British—Grew up in Hong Kong

EDUCATIONAL BACKGROUND:

M.A., Mass Communications, Syracuse University, New York
Baccalaureate Diploma, Journalism, Hong Kong Baptist College, Hong Kong

LANGUAGES SPOKEN: English, Chinese (Cantonese and Mandarin)

CAREER HIGHLIGHTS: Korn/Ferry Trent-Rossler Award

SPECIAL INTERESTS/HOBBIES: Wine tasting

GEOGRAPHIC SCOPE OF RECRUITING: Greater China

SECTOR/INDUSTRY SPECIALIZATION: High-tech

FAVORITE HISTORICAL FIGURE/MODEL/MENTOR: Mao Zedong

SINGLE MOST IMPORTANT ISSUE IN CONDUCTING A HIGH LEVEL SEARCH: Rapport with client

WHAT IS THE BEST PREPARATION FOR BEING A SUCCESSFUL RECRUITER? Prior experience in the business
world before joining the search industry.

WHAT WOULD YOU BE DOING IF YOU WERE NOT AN EXECUTIVE RECRUITER? Owner of a winery, or an
Enologist.

WHAT ARE THE CHARACTERISTICS OF A GREAT CLIENT? Respect. The search consultant can only be as good as
the input he receives from the client.

WHAT CHALLENGES DO YOU SEE AHEAD IN THE GLOBAL MARKETPLACE? Emergence of a global talent pool,
which will pose major threat to local boutique firms which thrive on having clients and candidates in the same
market.

JEFFREY E. CHRISTIAN

Christian & Timbers
25825 Science Park Drive, Suite 400
Cleveland, Ohio 44122
U.S.A.

Telephone: 1 (216) 464-8710
Fax: 1 (216) 464-6160
E-mail: jchristian@ctnet.com
Company Website: http://www.ctnet.com

DATE OF BIRTH: January 10, 1956

NATIONALITY: US Citizen—Grew up in Ohio

CAREER HIGHLIGHTS:
- Founded Christian & Timbers in 1979.
- Created the first high-tech search firm.
- Became one of the leaders in CEO searches.

SPECIAL INTERESTS/HOBBIES: Skiing, boating, competitive sports

GEOGRAPHIC SCOPE OF RECRUITING: Global

SECTOR/INDUSTRY SPECIALIZATION: CEO and Board Member searches

FAVORITE HISTORICAL FIGURE/MODEL/MENTOR: Dr. Martin Luther King

SINGLE MOST IMPORTANT ISSUE IN CONDUCTING A HIGH LEVEL SEARCH: Perseverance and the unwillingness to accept mediocrity

MOST SIGNIFICANT OTHER ASPECT OF PERSONAL OR PROFESSIONAL LIFE: Learning to be a good father while also enhancing my leadership skills in my business life

WHAT IS THE BEST PREPARATION FOR BEING A SUCCESSFUL RECRUITER? It is more fundamental than preparation. Being a successful recruiter is mainly about genetics. As I have watched individuals who we have hired become great search consultants, I have noticed that those who succeed are those that have the basic raw skills of high intellectual capacity, curiosity, intuition, incredible energy and perseverance. They are simply born with these characteristics. In addition, before entering into the search business they have had experience interacting with high-level executives in a professional relationship building environment.

WHAT WOULD YOU BE DOING IF YOU WERE NOT AN EXECUTIVE RECRUITER? I often ask myself this question. As I love building new products and creating new solutions for the marketplace, I could imagine myself starting as a product marketing manager and moving up towards a vice president of marketing role. I would hope that by now in my career I would be a general manager of an information technology business or a consumer product business, or possibly even the CEO of a company.

WHAT ARE THE CHARACTERISTICS OF A GREAT CLIENT? A great client is a board of directors that is in agreement regarding the succession plan of their company in bringing in a new CEO. A great client recognizes what they need to do to attract a new CEO into their company. They must promote someone from a smaller job to a bigger job and provide the necessary enticements with a larger compensation package. For the bigger CEO assignments, they also have to provide a significant hire-on bonus to attract the right person.

Ultimately, a great client is someone with whom we partner on the project. They will take new information, absorb it and be willing to be flexible in the search strategy. Great clients work together with us in crafting and articulating the overall search strategy.

WHAT CHALLENGES DO YOU SEE AHEAD IN THE GLOBAL MARKETPLACE? The biggest challenge in the global marketplace is being able to provide a high level of service while growing a major search firm. Today it's important that Christian & Timbers be in multiple geographies but at the same time maintain a very high level of quality in our search execution with efficient methods of communication. Some of the issues involve the utilization of the Internet and intranets to solve some of the internal language barriers in connecting multiple office locations.

MICHAEL T. CHRISTY

Heidrick & Struggles
8000 Towers Crescent Drive, Suite 555
Vienna, VA 22182
U.S.A.

Telephone: 1 (703) 761-4830
Fax: 1 (703) 761-4846
E-mail: mtc@h-s.com
Company Website: http://www.h-s.com

DATE OF BIRTH: June 27, 1941

NATIONALITY: American—Grew up all over the world, U.S. Air Force family

LANGUAGES SPOKEN: English, some Russian

CAREER HIGHLIGHTS:
- 20 year career as U.S. Air Force Officer
- Joined Heidrick & Struggles in 1988
- Elected Director, 1991
- Named Managing Partner, Technology Practice in 1995

SPECIAL INTERESTS/HOBBIES: Golf, tennis, Corvette

GEOGRAPHIC SCOPE OF RECRUITING: Worldwide

SECTOR/INDUSTRY SPECIALIZATION: Information Technology

FAVORITE HISTORICAL FIGURE/MODEL/MENTOR: Bobby R. Inman, Admiral, U.S. Air Force (retired)

SINGLE MOST IMPORTANT ISSUE IN CONDUCTING A HIGH LEVEL SEARCH: Establishing a relationship of mutual trust and confidence with the client

MOST SIGNIFICANT OTHER ASPECT OF PERSONAL OR PROFESSIONAL LIFE: Wife, Carmen; daughter, Krista; son-in-law, Ken

WHAT IS THE BEST PREPARATION FOR BEING A SUCCESSFUL RECRUITER? Line management experience; having successfully faced the leadership challenges of growing and developing a successful organization.

WHAT WOULD YOU BE DOING IF YOU WERE NOT AN EXECUTIVE RECRUITER? Playing golf, tennis, and skiing.

WHAT ARE THE CHARACTERISTICS OF A GREAT CLIENT? Honesty, clarity of vision, decisiveness, and superb leadership skills.

WHAT CHALLENGES DO YOU SEE AHEAD IN THE GLOBAL MARKETPLACE? Particularly in the IT industry, the availability of enough senior executive talent to meet the demand.

ALEX CIRONE

Korn/Ferry International
Av. Quintana 585, 6th Floor
(1129) Buenos Aires, Argentina
Telephone: 54 (1) 804-0046
Fax: 54 (1) 804-7568
E-mail: cirone@kferryar.datamar.com.ar
Company Website: http://www.kornferry.com

DATE OF BIRTH: June 6, 1953

NATIONALITY: Argentine—Grew up in Argentina and lived three years in the United States

EDUCATIONAL BACKGROUND:
Degree in Clinical Psychology from the University of Buenos Aires.
Completed doctoral studies in Industrial Sociology at the UADE (Argentine Business University).
Attended the "Senior Marketing Program" at the Columbia University and the "Advanced Human Resources Program" at the University of Michigan.

LANGUAGES SPOKEN: Spanish, English, and Portuguese

CAREER HIGHLIGHTS: Successful opening of the Korn/Ferry's Buenos Aires office during a period of political instability and economic turmoil.

SPECIAL INTERESTS/HOBBIES: Gourmet cooking, farming, and flying airplanes.

GEOGRAPHIC SCOPE OF RECRUITING: Regional Vice President/Partner, West Latin America, heading the Buenos Aires and Santiago de Chile offices, and supervising the operations in Uruguay, Colombia, Ecuador and Peru.

SECTOR/INDUSTRY SPECIALIZATION: Consumer goods and general management, HR

FAVORITE HISTORICAL FIGURE/MODEL/MENTOR: Jorge Newberry (pioneer pilot of the Argentine aviation)

SINGLE MOST IMPORTANT ISSUE IN CONDUCTING A HIGH LEVEL SEARCH: Understanding the client's vision and values, and company's strategy in order to identify candidates with high potential and leadership as well as cultural fit with the company.

BIGGEST COMPETITOR: Egon Zehnder

MOST SIGNIFICANT OTHER ASPECT OF PERSONAL OR PROFESSIONAL LIFE: Quality family life, continuous improvement as professional, and active community member.

WHAT IS THE BEST PREPARATION FOR BEING A SUCCESSFUL RECRUITER? A thorough understanding of human behaviour and people management skills combined with fully proven line experience in a multinational/global corporation.

WHAT WOULD YOU BE DOING IF YOU WERE NOT AN EXECUTIVE RECRUITER? Either an international gourmet chef or manager of an M&A venture capital fund.

WHAT ARE THE CHARACTERISTICS OF A GREAT CLIENT? Professional honesty, trust in his/her organizational values, business wit and clear strategic thinking with a good leadership vision to help the business community to grow in a healthy environment.

WHAT CHALLENGES DO YOU SEE AHEAD IN THE GLOBAL MARKETPLACE? Being truly global with sustained development and long-term vision.

GERARD CLERY-MELIN

Heidrick & Struggles
112 Av. Kleber
Paris 75784 France

Telephone: 33 1 44 34 17 08
Fax: 331 44 34 17 75
Company Website: http://www.h-s.com

DATE OF BIRTH: October 2, 1945

NATIONALITY: French—Grew up in France

EDUCATIONAL BACKGROUND:
- Graduate of H.E.C. (Hautes Etudes Commerciales 1967)
- Former student of I.E.P. Paris (Institut d'Etudes Politique)

LANGUAGES SPOKEN: English, French

CAREER HIGHLIGHTS:

1984–present	President-CEO, H&S International Inc.
1982–84	President, Heidrick & Struggles Europe
1978–82	Manager, Heidrick & Struggles Paris office
1974–78	Spencer Stuart & Ass., Paris, France, Consultant then Vice President
1970–74	W.R. Grace & Co. Industrial Chemical Group, Product Manager then Marketing Manager then Product Line Manager for Graphic Arts-Europe

SPECIAL INTERESTS/HOBBIES: Reading, golf

GEOGRAPHIC SCOPE OF RECRUITING: Global

SECTOR/INDUSTRY SPECIALIZATION: No

FAVORITE HISTORICAL FIGURE/MODEL/MENTOR: Louis XI

SINGLE MOST IMPORTANT ISSUE IN CONDUCTING A HIGH LEVEL SEARCH: Know your candidates and your client as much as possible, have their trust.

BIGGEST COMPETITOR: Egon Zehnder

MOST SIGNIFICANT OTHER ASPECT OF PERSONAL OR PROFESSIONAL LIFE: High geographic mobility, round-the-clock availability

WHAT IS THE BEST PREPARATION FOR BEING A SUCCESSFUL RECRUITER? No particular preparation except good knowledge of corporate life and business/economics.

WHAT WOULD YOU BE DOING IF YOU WERE NOT AN EXECUTIVE RECRUITER? I would build an entertainment business.

WHAT ARE THE CHARACTERISTICS OF A GREAT CLIENT? Global, increasing shareholder value, CEO/Board seeking best mgt. talents, strong HR infrastructure

WHAT CHALLENGES DO YOU SEE AHEAD IN THE GLOBAL MARKETPLACE? Homogeneous level of global service quality, common knowledge base, speed of delivery

BRUNO COLOMBO

Spencer Stuart
Corso Monforte, 36
20122 Milano
Italy

Telephone: 39 2 796441
Fax: 39 2 782452
E-mail: bcolombo@spencerstuart.com
Company Website: http://www.spencerstuart.com

DATE OF BIRTH: May 31, 1932

NATIONALITY: Italian—Grew up in Italy; worked in U.S.A. and France

EDUCATIONAL BACKGROUND:
Degree in Economics, Milan
PMD Harvard Business School, Cambridge, Mass.

LANGUAGES SPOKEN: Italian, English, French

CAREER HIGHLIGHTS: Partner, Pietro Gennaro Associati-WW Marketing Manager, Olivetti-General Manager, Rinascente-Regional Manager Europe, Spencer Stuart

SPECIAL INTERESTS/HOBBIES: Golf

GEOGRAPHIC SCOPE OF RECRUITING: Italy and other countries

SECTOR/INDUSTRY SPECIALIZATION: Consumer, Service Business, Board Member

MOST SIGNIFICANT OTHER ASPECT OF PERSONAL OR PROFESSIONAL LIFE: Extensive managerial experience in the search business from 1982.

WHAT IS THE BEST PREPARATION FOR BEING A SUCCESSFUL RECRUITER? Having developed a successful career as a manager certainly helps in dealing with clients at top level. The most important thing is to really understand client needs and to become the client's advisor.

WHAT WOULD YOU BE DOING IF YOU WERE NOT AN EXECUTIVE RECRUITER? Most likely I would have continued to be a business manager.

WHAT ARE THE CHARACTERISTICS OF A GREAT CLIENT? Vision and clear ideas, a good balance between flexibility and the point of no compromise.

WHAT CHALLENGES DO YOU SEE AHEAD IN THE GLOBAL MARKETPLACE? Larger growth possibilities on audacious and creative strategies. Also greater speed of change on all fronts (market, technology, finance, competition, social and political environment). These are the reason why mamagers have become the determining factor in corporate success.

LUIS CONDÉ MOLLER

Seeliger y Condé/Amrop International
Calle Provenza, no. 267 Pral.
08008 Barcelona
Spain

Telephone: 34 (3) 215.28.00
Fax: 34 (3) 215.28.10
E-mail: luis.conde@syc.es
Company Website: http://www.amrop.com

DATE OF BIRTH: March 27, 1950

NATIONALITY: Spanish—Grew up in Barcelona

EDUCATIONAL BACKGROUND:
Economics degree, University of Barcelona

LANGUAGES SPOKEN: Spanish, Catalan, French, and English

CAREER HIGHLIGHTS:
- Founder and president of the Financial Executives Association in Barcelona
- Executive VP of Banco Consolidado de Venezuela
- Co-founder of Seelige y Condé in 1990

SPECIAL INTERESTS/HOBBIES: Water and snow skiing, sailing, and classical music

GEOGRAPHIC SCOPE OF RECRUITING: Spain and Latin America

SECTOR/INDUSTRY SPECIALIZATION: Finance, consumer goods, family-owned business

FAVORITE HISTORICAL FIGURE/MODEL/MENTOR: King Alfonso XII and Henry Kissinger

SINGLE MOST IMPORTANT ISSUE IN CONDUCTING A HIGH LEVEL SEARCH: Building up and enlarging the Deutsche Bank professional team and the professionalization of the top family-owned businesses.

BIGGEST COMPETITOR: Egon Zehnder

MOST SIGNIFICANT OTHER ASPECT OF PERSONAL OR PROFESSIONAL LIFE: Entrepreneur, imaginative and hard worker.

WHAT IS THE BEST PREPARATION FOR BEING A SUCCESSFUL RECRUITER? Having worked in the service sector (re: banking), being a good communicator and having the ability to penetrate into the client's business thus giving him the best assessment it may require. Knowing how to listen.

WHAT WOULD YOU BE DOING IF YOU WERE NOT AN EXECUTIVE RECRUITER? I would probably be an investment banker based in U.S.A.

WHAT ARE THE CHARACTERISTICS OF A GREAT CLIENT? Someone who understands what a partnership with the executive recruiter means and someone that believes in the possibilities of candidate more than in his background.

WHAT CHALLENGES DO YOU SEE AHEAD IN THE GLOBAL MARKETPLACE? A larger sectoral specialization, a better understanding and increasing knowledge of the companies, larger quality standards and higher expectancies on behalf of the client, less players in the market and a large growth of activities.

IAN DOUGLAS CORDINER

Cordiner King Hever
44/525 Collins Street
Melbourne, Vic. 3000
Australia

28/2 Chifley Square
Sydney, NSW 2000
Australia

Telephone: 61 (03) 9629 4862   61 (02) 9233-4244
Fax: 61(03) 9614 6484   61 (02) 9233 3727

E-mail: ckhmelb@onaustralia.com.au
Company Website: http://www.sbpsearch.com

DATE OF BIRTH: January 8, 1940

NATIONALITY: Australian—Grew up in South Africa

EDUCATIONAL BACKGROUND:
Matriculation at Hilton College, Natal
BSc (Eng) at University of Witwatersrand
Chartered Engineer trained in operational research and systems analysis

LANGUAGES SPOKEN: English, Afrikaans

CAREER HIGHLIGHTS: General Manager of a diversified manufacturing business at age 33. Co-founder of Cordiner King Hever in 1985.

SPECIAL INTERESTS/HOBBIES: Grape growing, forestry, golf, fly fishing

GEOGRAPHIC SCOPE OF RECRUITING: Australia and New Zealand

SECTOR/INDUSTRY SPECIALIZATION: General Managers and Nonexecutive Directors

FAVORITE HISTORICAL FIGURE/MODEL/MENTOR: Dr. Livingstone—A 19th century Scottish explorer of Africa who demonstrated creativity, persistence, and courage in the face of great adversity. A person of high moral standing and dignity, who was able to relate to people of vastly different cultural backgrounds and did not seek to impose his values on others.

SINGLE MOST IMPORTANT ISSUE IN CONDUCTING A HIGH LEVEL SEARCH: Fundamental grasp of client requirements, business issues and organisational culture which is continually developed and tested as the consulting relationship grows with key decision-makers.

MOST SIGNIFICANT OTHER ASPECT OF PERSONAL OR PROFESSIONAL LIFE: Six formative years with McKinsey & Co.

WHAT IS THE BEST PREPARATION FOR BEING A SUCCESSFUL RECRUITER? Academic training in the humanities, commerce or law. An early career with direct responsibility for managing people. Consulting on strategic issues with a qualitative focus. Good mentorship provided by a very senior executive. Project tasks with complex inter-relationships and clear end results. Diversity of organisation experience.

WHAT WOULD YOU BE DOING IF YOU WERE NOT AN EXECUTIVE RECRUITER? Growing the best wine grapes in the world. Advising Boards and Councils on governance issues. Completing a Doctorate in Business.

WHAT ARE THE CHARACTERISTICS OF A GREAT CLIENT? Open about core issues. Clear about needs. Quick to seek advice or counsel. Ready to share views. Responsive to creative solutions. Firm in decision making.

WHAT CHALLENGES DO YOU SEE AHEAD IN THE GLOBAL MARKETPLACE? Working in a business environment that does not differentiate between time zones or seasons. Balancing technical communications wizardry with the human aspect of face-to-face meetings. Identifying corporate leaders who can put a compassionate slant on the driving forces of economic rationalism and financial globalization.

MICHAEL J. COREY

LAI Ward Howell
401 East Host Drive
Lake Geneva, WI 53147
U.S.A.

Telephone: 1 (414) 249-5200
Fax: 1 (414) 249-5210
E-mail: mcorey@lai.usa.com
Company Website: http://www.laix.com

DATE OF BIRTH: July 18, 1939

NATIONALITY: American—Grew up in Southern and Midwestern United States

EDUCATIONAL BACKGROUND:
Bachelor of Science degree in Business, Northern Illinois University, DeKalb, Illinois, U.S.A.

LANGUAGES SPOKEN: English

CAREER HIGHLIGHTS: Chief Executive Officer of own firm for 25 years

SPECIAL INTERESTS/HOBBIES: Music, golf, skiing, cooking

GEOGRAPHIC SCOPE OF RECRUITING: Global

SECTOR/INDUSTRY SPECIALIZATION: Insurance, Benefits, Healthcare

FAVORITE HISTORICAL FIGURE/MODEL/MENTOR: Ray Kroc

SINGLE MOST IMPORTANT ISSUE IN CONDUCTING A HIGH LEVEL SEARCH: Creative, value added identification capabilities, providing "off the screen" solutions on a timely basis with integrity and a complete and clean assessment of both the prospect and the opportunity

MOST SIGNIFICANT OTHER ASPECT OF PERSONAL OR PROFESSIONAL LIFE: Family

WHAT IS THE BEST PREPARATION FOR BEING A SUCCESSFUL RECRUITER? The best preparation starts early in your career. It is imperative that the process of search be fully understood and mastered. As an individual's skills develop, it is essential that relationship building be foremost in one's mind. I have found that extensive exposure to client industry meetings, seminar participation and writing articles can be very important. Finally, the ability to develop attention to detail and follow-up is critical.

WHAT WOULD YOU BE DOING IF YOU WERE NOT AN EXECUTIVE RECRUITER? I would be involved in some sort of entrepreneurial endeavor that involved bringing people together. This might include networking my relationships into some type of deal making.

WHAT ARE THE CHARACTERISTICS OF A GREAT CLIENT? Someone who trusts you implicitly, communicates and has excellent follow through. Also, a great client is one who will go beyond the search to create an intense relationship.

WHAT CHALLENGES DO YOU SEE AHEAD IN THE GLOBAL MARKETPLACE? The ability to translate our results oriented philosophy to business cultures around the world.

PETER D. CRIST

Crist Partners, Ltd.
Suite 2650
303 W. Madison
Chicago, IL 60606
U.S.A.

Telephone: 1 (312) 920-0609
Fax: 1 (312) 920-0608
E-mail: pcrist@cristpartners.com
Company Website: http://www.cristpartners.com

DATE OF BIRTH: March 8, 1952

NATIONALITY: American—Grew up in Ohio

EDUCATIONAL BACKGROUND:
A.B., Brown University, political science, 1974

LANGUAGES SPOKEN: English

CAREER HIGHLIGHTS:
- 18 years with Russell Reynolds
- Member of Global Executive Committee and Co-Head of North America for Russell Reynolds Associates
- Launched Crist Partners in early 1995; now 13 people

GEOGRAPHIC SCOPE OF RECRUITING: North America

SECTOR/INDUSTRY SPECIALIZATION: CEO, COO, and CFO searches, focus on succession related projects and board searches. We have a minimum fee of $100,000. Average search is for positions with $500,000+ compensation.

FAVORITE HISTORICAL FIGURE/MODEL/MENTOR: A. Lincoln

SINGLE MOST IMPORTANT ISSUE IN CONDUCTING A HIGH LEVEL SEARCH: Remaining focused on the mutual needs of the client and the candidates

MOST SIGNIFICANT OTHER ASPECT OF PERSONAL OR PROFESSIONAL LIFE: Wife and 4 boys

WHAT IS THE BEST PREPARATION FOR BEING A SUCCESSFUL RECRUITER? Learn the fundamentals (start at a young age). If you master the fundamentals and build upon the basics, (rather than business development emphasis), you will become a successful recruiter. This takes patience and the appreciation that it is a career, not a job.

WHAT WOULD YOU BE DOING IF YOU WERE NOT AN EXECUTIVE RECRUITER? Congressman/political office

WHAT ARE THE CHARACTERISTICS OF A GREAT CLIENT?
- A company with a great platform from which to work
- A person within that company who has the alacrity and leadership skills to attract outstanding people.

WHAT CHALLENGES DO YOU SEE AHEAD IN THE GLOBAL MARKETPLACE? The velocity of the market suggests most global companies will have difficulty adjusting to the dynamic nature of change. There will be an unprecedented demand cycle for senior level talent in all major markets of the world.

GUILHERME DE NORONHA DALE

Spencer Stuart
Alameda Santos, 1787 - 19th Floor
01419-010 São Paulo, SP
Brazil

Telephone: 55 (11) 284-0349
Fax: 55 (11) 289-1159
E-mail: gdale@spencerstuart.com.br
Company Website: http://www.spencerstuart.com

DATE OF BIRTH: January 26, 1943

NATIONALITY: Brazilian—Grew up in Rio de Janeiro

EDUCATIONAL BACKGROUND:
Harvard, MBA, 1970
University of Brazil, Chemical Engineer, 1966

LANGUAGES SPOKEN: Portuguese (mother tongue), English, Spanish, some French

CAREER HIGHLIGHTS: Started Spencer Stuart office in Brazil in 1977, built to leadership position

SPECIAL INTERESTS/HOBBIES: Sports in general, international travel

GEOGRAPHIC SCOPE OF RECRUITING: Brazil and South America

SECTOR/INDUSTRY SPECIALIZATION: Boards, CEOs, Energy. Also Consumer Goods, Retail, Industrial

FAVORITE HISTORICAL FIGURE/MODEL/MENTOR: Arnold Tempel, ex-CEO Spencer Stuart

SINGLE MOST IMPORTANT ISSUE IN CONDUCTING A HIGH LEVEL SEARCH: Right perception of client business and needs plus talent to develop candidate to match these

MOST SIGNIFICANT OTHER ASPECT OF PERSONAL OR PROFESSIONAL LIFE: Family life

WHAT IS THE BEST PREPARATION FOR BEING A SUCCESSFUL RECRUITER? MBA or equivalent, plus over 10 years career with a multinational company, and/or international management consulting company. Multi-function and international exposure are a plus. Entrepreneurial ventures are well regarded.

WHAT WOULD YOU BE DOING IF YOU WERE NOT AN EXECUTIVE RECRUITER? I would probably be a management consultant or an M & A officer.

WHAT ARE THE CHARACTERISTICS OF A GREAT CLIENT? A great client uses the search consultant as a partner and a consultant for all matters related to people problems at the top. He/she develops a long-standing alliance with the search consultant, within a collaborative and trusting relationship.

WHAT CHALLENGES DO YOU SEE AHEAD IN THE GLOBAL MARKETPLACE? The need to form "best teams" made up of global practice specialists and local or regional geographic experts within a global search firm.

NESTOR OSVALDO D'ANGELO

Heidrick & Struggles
Avenida Tamanaco
Torre Extebandes
Piso 7
El Rosal
Caracas 1060, Venezuela

Poba International No. 709
P.O. Box 02-5255
Miami, FL 33102-5255
U.S.A.

Telephone: 58 2) 951.45.22-951.42.74
Fax: (58 2) 951.61.85
Company Website: http://www.h-s.com

DATE OF BIRTH: March 12, 1951

NATIONALITY: Venezuelan/Argentinian—Grew up in Buenos Aires, Argentina

EDUCATIONAL BACKGROUND:
Universidad de Buenos Aires, Argentina. Certified Public Accountant (1970).
Postgraduate studies in Business Administration (1971–1973).

LANGUAGES SPOKEN: Spanish, English

CAREER HIGHLIGHTS:
- President of Shulton de Venezuela (subsidiary of American Cyanamid)
- General Manager (Venezuela) and Controller Western Hemisphere/Far East (New York) of Helena Rubinstein (subsidiary of Colgate-Palmolive)
- Manager at Arthur Andersen & Co. in Argentina and Venezuela

SPECIAL INTERESTS/HOBBIES: Reading, Latin American art

GEOGRAPHIC SCOPE OF RECRUITING: Venezuela, Colombia, Brazil, Argentina, Mexico, and Puerto Rico

SECTOR/INDUSTRY SPECIALIZATION: Financial services, consumer and industrial

FAVORITE HISTORICAL FIGURE/MODEL/MENTOR: Pope John Paul II

SINGLE MOST IMPORTANT ISSUE IN CONDUCTING A HIGH LEVEL SEARCH: Obtain a clear understanding of the key skills the referred executive must possess in order to create and sustain competitive advantage

MOST SIGNIFICANT OTHER ASPECT OF PERSONAL OR PROFESSIONAL LIFE: Successful managerial career with two U.S. multinationals, achieving the position of country general manager at the age of 28. More than 10 years of search experience, being one of the leaders of his firm's expansion in Latin America.

GIANNI DELL'ORTO

Heidrick & Struggles International
Corso Venezia, 16
20121 Milan, Italy
Telephone: 39-3-76000393
Fax: 39-2-76000801
E-mail: gdo@h-s.com
Company Website: http://www.h-s.com

DATE OF BIRTH: January 9, 1940

NATIONALITY: Italian—Grew up in Italy

EDUCATIONAL BACKGROUND:
High school scientific
Electric Engineering degree
Polytechnic of Milan
PMD Harvard Business School

LANGUAGES SPOKEN: Italian (mother tongue), English, French, Spanish

SPECIAL INTERESTS/HOBBIES: Ski (instructor), karate (2 dan-instructor), chi kung-healing Tao (instructor)

GEOGRAPHIC SCOPE OF RECRUITING: Pan-European

SECTOR/INDUSTRY SPECIALIZATION: Health care, Consumer Goods, Board of Directors

FAVORITE HISTORICAL FIGURE/MODEL/MENTOR: John Welch

SINGLE MOST IMPORTANT ISSUE IN CONDUCTING A HIGH LEVEL SEARCH: High level network of proven successful top executives

BIGGEST COMPETITOR: Time pressure

MOST SIGNIFICANT OTHER ASPECT OF PERSONAL OR PROFESSIONAL LIFE: Always keeping peace deep inside when swimming in the hectic business environment

WHAT IS THE BEST PREPARATION FOR BEING A SUCCESSFUL RECRUITER?
- quickly obtain an academic degree and possibly a well-recognized MBA.
- get to the top of the management structure (Board of Management level) as quickly as possible in a multinational environment and before age 35.
- learn avidly, throughout whole life, everything concerning human nature, social interactions and all types of negotiations.

WHAT WOULD YOU BE DOING IF YOU WERE NOT AN EXECUTIVE RECRUITER? CEO of a big corporation in industry or services.

WHAT ARE THE CHARACTERISTICS OF A GREAT CLIENT? A great client is visionary, creative, in control of his/her organization, perfectly understands how to take advantage of executive search's know-how and networking, and always acts in strict partnership with executive search consultants especially when problems arise.

WHAT CHALLENGES DO YOU SEE AHEAD IN THE GLOBAL MARKETPLACE? Gigantic market opportunities, but difficult to be perceived in proper time and space. In other words, extremely difficult to steadily maintain a "helicopter" view with the incredibly rapid rate of change on all factors influencing businesses.

HENRY DE MONTEBELLO

Russell Reynolds Associates
7 Place Vendôme
75001 Paris, France
Telephone: 33.1.49.26.13.40
Fax: 33.1.42.60.03.85
E-mail: hdemontebello@russreyn.com
Company Website: http://www.russreyn.com

DATE OF BIRTH: March 20, 1946

NATIONALITY: Dual (American and French)—Grew up in Paris and New York

EDUCATIONAL BACKGROUND:
M.B.A., The Colgate Darden Graduate School of Business Administration, University of Virginia, 1976
A.B., (cum laude) Harvard University, 1968

LANGUAGES SPOKEN: French, English, Spanish

CAREER HIGHLIGHTS: Over 18 years experience in executive recruiting, all at Russell Reynolds Associates in Europe and the United States; previously strategy and organizational consultant in the U.K.

SPECIAL INTERESTS/HOBBIES: Chinese figurines (Han and Tang Dynasties), tennis, squash, scuba diving

GEOGRAPHIC SCOPE OF RECRUITING: Europe/North America

SECTOR/INDUSTRY SPECIALIZATION: General Industry; Consumer Products and Services; Sports Management

FAVORITE HISTORICAL FIGURE/MODEL/MENTOR: Role Model/Mentor: my father. Historical figure: Marshal Lannes (an ancestor from the Napoleonic Era).

SINGLE MOST IMPORTANT ISSUE IN CONDUCTING A HIGH LEVEL SEARCH: True partnership between consultant and client enabling frank communication and exchange of ideas

BIGGEST COMPETITOR: In France, large network of alumni of elite French schools; otherwise depends upon country and industry sector

MOST SIGNIFICANT OTHER ASPECT OF PERSONAL OR PROFESSIONAL LIFE: Family (married, with 4 children between the ages of 10 and 16); community service (serve on not-for-profit boards); cross-cultural management issues (follow regularly)

WHAT IS THE BEST PREPARATION FOR BEING A SUCCESSFUL RECRUITER? A solid education, cross-border business and/or consulting experience combined with the ability to listen and to communicate, to exhibit common sense, industry knowledge, empathy, a real sense of urgency and huge curiosity and a love for the hunt.

WHAT WOULD YOU BE DOING IF YOU WERE NOT AN EXECUTIVE RECRUITER? Consulting full time; running a foundation and a winery on the side.

WHAT ARE THE CHARACTERISTICS OF A GREAT CLIENT? A great client is a change agent, not afraid to make decisions. A great client exhibits loyalty and confidence in his recruiter and implicates the recruiter in his business planning and decision making process and partners with the recruiter in his strategic and organizational vision.

WHAT CHALLENGES DO YOU SEE AHEAD IN THE GLOBAL MARKETPLACE? The ability to anticipate and identify rapid change and those who make it happen, both this generation and the next. Keeping up with issues that are critical to the success of one's clients throughout the world. The ability to react quickly and anticipate client's needs. The necessity to continually improve the quality of service to make oneself and one's firm indispensable to top management.

FLORIANE DE SAINT PIERRE

F.S.P. SA
134, rue du Faubourg Saint Honoré
75008 Paris, France
Telephone: 33 (1) 45 61 24 89
Fax: 33 (1) 45 61 24 88
E-mail: fsp.sa@wanadoo.fr

DATE OF BIRTH: July 30, 1964

NATIONALITY: French—Grew up in France

EDUCATIONAL BACKGROUND:
1985: Graduate of ESSEC, Cergy-Pontoise (École des Sciences Économiques et Commerciales)

LANGUAGES SPOKEN: French, English (fluent)

CAREER HIGHLIGHTS:
Since 1990: F.S.P. SA-International Executive Search-President & CEO
1985–1990: Christian Dior (LVMH Group)-Controller

SPECIAL INTERESTS/HOBBIES: Contemporary art and photography, lifestyles (relating to restaurants, hotels, the art of cooking)

GEOGRAPHIC SCOPE OF RECRUITING: International and in particular Europe and U.S.A.

SECTOR/INDUSTRY SPECIALIZATION: Prestige brands with strong image: products for self (fashion and accessories, perfumes and cosmetics, . . .), products for the home, entertainment (hotels, media, travelling, . . .)

FAVORITE HISTORICAL FIGURE/MODEL/MENTOR: K'ang-hi (Emperor of China, 1654–1722), Sir Terence Conran

SINGLE MOST IMPORTANT ISSUE IN CONDUCTING A HIGH LEVEL SEARCH: Finding new managerial and creative talents for clients as a result of a completely qualitative process and thorough understanding of their needs.

MOST SIGNIFICANT OTHER ASPECT OF PERSONAL OR PROFESSIONAL LIFE: Contemporary art and photography collector. Fundraising activities for homeless children as a member of the "Comité d'Honneur d'Aide à l'Enfance: Rêve d'Enfants." Contribution to start-up companies

WHAT IS THE BEST PREPARATION FOR BEING A SUCCESSFUL RECRUITER?
- Professionally, to have worked as an executive for the business he/she recruits for
- Personally, to be cultivated, intuitive, global and exposed to international

WHAT WOULD YOU BE DOING IF YOU WERE NOT AN EXECUTIVE RECRUITER? I would still have my own company in brand and lifestyles, image and design consulting.

WHAT ARE THE CHARACTERISTICS OF A GREAT CLIENT?
- Has and can communicate a clear company vision and strategy.
- Is open to "new blood" on the team
- Makes decisions quickly

WHAT CHALLENGES DO YOU SEE AHEAD IN THE GLOBAL MARKETPLACE? To bring added value, innovative talents, visionary people, cultivated and global managers to clients

DAVID M. DEWILDE

LAI Chartwell Partners International, Inc.
275 Battery Street, Suite 2180
San Francisco, CA 94111
U.S.A.

Telephone: 1 (415) 296-0600
Fax: 1 (415) 296-7588
E-mail: dewildav@lai.usa.com
Company Website: http://www.laix.com

DATE OF BIRTH: August 11, 1940

NATIONALITY: American—Grew up in U.S.A.

EDUCATIONAL BACKGROUND:

1984, Stanford University, MS Management, Sloan Fellow
1967, University of Virginia, J.D.
1962, Dartmouth College, A.B., National Merit Scholar

LANGUAGES SPOKEN: English

CAREER HIGHLIGHTS: David M. deWilde, a former lawyer and investment banker who held senior financial posts in two Administrations, is the founder and Chief Executive Officer of Chartwell Partners International Inc.

Before forming Chartwell Partners, Mr. deWilde was a Managing Director of Boyden International Inc., where he headed the San Francisco office. He has conducted a wide variety of senior-level searches, primarily for clients in financial services: investment banking, investment management, depository institutions, mortgage finance, and real estate.

Mr. deWilde was Executive Vice President for Policy and Planning of the Federal National Mortgage Association (FNMA) from 1981 until 1983. In that position, he was responsible for developing Fannie Mae's mortgage-backed security, adjustable-rate mortgages and negotiated bulk purchase programs. In 1976, President Ford appointed Mr. deWilde President of the Government National Mortgage Association (GNMA). At Ginnie Mae he developed new techniques to handle a record-breaking volume of mortgage-backed security guarantees and mortgage sales.

Prior to joining GNMA, Mr. deWilde served as Deputy Commissioner of the Federal Housing Administration (FHA) and Deputy Assistant Secretary for Housing Production and Mortgage Credit. He also served as acting Assistant Secretary of the Department of Housing and Urban Development (HUD).

Mr. deWilde gained his private sector experience as a Managing Director of Lepercq de Neuflize & Co., an investment banking firm, and as an investment banker in the Washington Office of Lehman Brothers Inc. in the early 1970s. As a lawyer, he was associate general counsel of HUD and was associated with the Wall Street law firm of Curtis, Mallet-Prevost, Colt & Mosle.

Mr. deWilde is a Director of Berkshire Realty Company, Inc. a NYSE listed real estate investment firm, Fritzi California, a privately held apparel manufacturing firm, and Silicon Valley Bancshares. He is also a member of the Business Advisory Council of the University of Virginia School of Law.

SPECIAL INTERESTS/HOBBIES: Four children

GEOGRAPHIC SCOPE OF RECRUITING: Primarily U.S. Also, Europe, Asia, and elsewhere in North America.

SECTOR/INDUSTRY SPECIALIZATION: We specialize in recruiting CEOs and CFOs who build shareholder value in an environment of change. We are particularly experienced in financial services, airlines, and real estate.

continues ▶

FAVORITE HISTORICAL FIGURE/MODEL/MENTOR: Winston Churchill—The most important world leader during this century. He exemplifies the standards that we set for ourselves and for the executives we seek. The firm was named Chartwell Partners International in his honor.

SINGLE MOST IMPORTANT ISSUE IN CONDUCTING A HIGH LEVEL SEARCH: The single most important issue is FIT. Therefore, it is critical to understand the client's need, and to think clearly about the combination of skills and experience required to meet that need. It then becomes important to evaluate each candidate to determine whether she or he is best qualified to meet this particular challenge, and the type of environment that will maximize any candidate's prospects for success. A clear understanding of this fit, and the ability to communicate it to both the client and the executive, is the key to recruiting the right executive into a "win-win" situation.

MOST SIGNIFICANT OTHER ASPECT OF PERSONAL OR PROFESSIONAL LIFE: Integrity

WHAT IS THE BEST PREPARATION FOR BEING A SUCCESSFUL RECRUITER? In order to succeed in recruiting senior executives, it helps to have been one. An effective recruiter must thoroughly understand his clients' needs and be able to evaluate the experiences and abilities of the candidates. The ability to perform these functions is greatly enhanced by relevant personal experience.

WHAT WOULD YOU BE DOING IF YOU WERE NOT AN EXECUTIVE RECRUITER? Before I began in executive recruiting fifteen years ago, I had been a lawyer, an investment banker and a senior executive. Since I started in executive recruiting, I have never seen a position that suits me as well. If I were to give up my executive recruiting practice, I would want to be an investor who could back the best executives I found.

WHAT ARE THE CHARACTERISTICS OF A GREAT CLIENT? Great clients are strong leaders who attract other able executives and create opportunities for them to succeed. I also prefer clients who are thoroughly engaged in the search process and committed to its success.

WHAT CHALLENGES DO YOU SEE AHEAD IN THE GLOBAL MARKETPLACE? The demand for executive leadership in international business has far outstripped the supply. A search firm must therefore be able to identify international executives who fit the need wherever they are in the world. Search firms must also be proactive in recruiting such executives, in assisting clients in dealing with the difficult career and personal issues which impede such moves. We have recently joined Amrop, a global network of firms dedicated to this goal.

NANNO J. H. DE VRIES

Amrop International
Bergstrasse 109
8032 Zürich
Switzerland

Telephone: 41 1-267 60 10
Fax: 41 1-267 60 19
E-mail: nanno.de.vries@amrop.com
Company Website: http://www.amrop.com

DATE OF BIRTH: June 15, 1946

NATIONALITY: Swiss/Dutch—Grew up in the Netherlands

EDUCATIONAL BACKGROUND:
M.B.A., University of St. Gallen, Switzerland
Royal Dutch Military Academy, Captain Dutch Airforce

LANGUAGES SPOKEN: Dutch, German (Swiss German), English, French

CAREER HIGHLIGHTS: Founded my own executive search company in 1987; by early 1990s one of the market leaders in quality search; successful integration into AMROP

SPECIAL INTERESTS/HOBBIES: Skiing (carving)/mountain biking/old timers/internet

GEOGRAPHIC SCOPE OF RECRUITING: Key market is Switzerland, extensive experience in the other West. European markets

SECTOR/INDUSTRY SPECIALIZATION: Consumer goods industry/retail/wholesale/automotive

FAVORITE HISTORICAL FIGURE/MODEL/MENTOR: Copernicus (1473–1543); Jacques Cousteau (explorer)

SINGLE MOST IMPORTANT ISSUE IN CONDUCTING A HIGH LEVEL SEARCH: Catching the "chemistry" of the client company, their decision makers and the candidate, to make the "real match"

BIGGEST COMPETITOR: After 24 years in executive search, I don't have competitors, only "colleagues" and loyal clients (80% repeat business).

MOST SIGNIFICANT OTHER ASPECT OF PERSONAL OR PROFESSIONAL LIFE: For me executive search still is the most exciting and challenging profession and a lot of fun

WHAT IS THE BEST PREPARATION FOR BEING A SUCCESSFUL RECRUITER?
- Solid educational background (preferably academic) on MBA level or technical degree.
- 8–10 years professional experience of which at least 5 years in a line function

WHAT WOULD YOU BE DOING IF YOU WERE NOT AN EXECUTIVE RECRUITER? I would be the marketing/sales director or CEO of a medium-sized, international consumer goods company (including production).

WHAT ARE THE CHARACTERISTICS OF A GREAT CLIENT?
A great client accepts an executive search consultant as an equal partner—if necessary even as his own personal career counselor; is loyal, open, holds no secrets; and willing to invest in a long-term relationship

WHAT CHALLENGES DO YOU SEE AHEAD IN THE GLOBAL MARKETPLACE? Challenges include globalisation, transparency of markets, acceleration of product cycles, financial engineering, and international mobility of candidates and clients

H. BRUCE DINGMAN

Robert W. Dingman Company, Inc.
650 Hampshire Rd., #116
Westlake Village, CA 91361
U.S.A.

Telephone: 1 (805) 778-1777
Fax: 1 (805) 778-9288
E-mail: bruce@dingman.com
Company Website: http://www.dingman.com

DATE OF BIRTH: 1947

NATIONALITY: American—Grew up in Upstate New York, and Texas

EDUCATIONAL BACKGROUND:
B.S. Hotel Administration, Cornell University

LANGUAGES SPOKEN: English, Spanish, Portuguese

CAREER HIGHLIGHTS: Frequent ranking by Executive Recruiters News in the "Top 50 Retained Search Firms."

SPECIAL INTERESTS/HOBBIES: Cooking; caring for spouse with multiple sclerosis

GEOGRAPHIC SCOPE OF RECRUITING: U.S. primarily but also some international. Have personally worked/lived in four countries.

SECTOR/INDUSTRY SPECIALIZATION: President/CEO searches and next level down across a broad spectrum of business and nonprofits

FAVORITE HISTORICAL FIGURE/MODEL/MENTOR: Peter Drucker—no one has given better insights into people or business.

SINGLE MOST IMPORTANT ISSUE IN CONDUCTING A HIGH LEVEL SEARCH: Matching the values system of the candidate and client, including people values, ethical values, cultural values and leadership style, factors that go beyond the usual business competencies issues. Finding the best organizational/personal fit between the client and candidate.

MOST SIGNIFICANT OTHER ASPECT OF PERSONAL OR PROFESSIONAL LIFE: Co-founder of Christian Search Coalition, a group of retained search professionals devoting a portion of their time and resources to serving Christian groups seeking leadership.

WHAT IS THE BEST PREPARATION FOR BEING A SUCCESSFUL RECRUITER? Degree in psych w/ minor in business; 5–10 yrs. business experience; a project orientation; learned (5 yrs.) executive recruiting from one of the top recruiters.

WHAT WOULD YOU BE DOING IF YOU WERE NOT AN EXECUTIVE RECRUITER? President of startup companies or doing mergers & acquisitions

WHAT ARE THE CHARACTERISTICS OF A GREAT CLIENT? Has a vision, market niche, knows their personal & organizational strengths & weaknesses

WHAT CHALLENGES DO YOU SEE AHEAD IN THE GLOBAL MARKETPLACE? Being able to respond more quickly to both national and international marketplace changes

LAUREN M. DOLIVA

Heidrick & Struggles, Inc.
Four Embarcadero Center, Suite 3570
San Francisco, CA 94111
U.S.A.

Telephone: 1 (415) 981-2854
Fax: 1 (415) 982-0482
E-mail: lmd@h-s.com
Company Website: http://www.h-s.com

DATE OF BIRTH: September 18, 1947

NATIONALITY: American—Grew up in California, U.S.A.

EDUCATIONAL BACKGROUND:
Ph.D., University of California, Berkeley (Counseling Psychology)
M.A., Harvard University (Teaching)
B.A., University of California, Los Angeles

LANGUAGES SPOKEN: English and Spanish

CAREER HIGHLIGHTS: Elected to Executive Committee, Heidrick & Struggles, Inc.

SPECIAL INTERESTS/HOBBIES: Enjoying my two children; exploring the Internet; global travel; tending my roses and drawing.

GEOGRAPHIC SCOPE OF RECRUITING: Global

SECTOR/INDUSTRY SPECIALIZATION: Interactive consumer-based media and commerce business, fast growth consumer-oriented businesses

FAVORITE HISTORICAL FIGURE/MODEL/MENTOR: David Elliott—office Managing Partner who hired and mentored me—for his ability to identify and nurture the best in others. Lynn O'Donnell—-my friend, whose courage in losing to cancer taught me a new meaning for the word "brave."

SINGLE MOST IMPORTANT ISSUE IN CONDUCTING A HIGH LEVEL SEARCH: Anticipating the issues that surface in the recruitment and guiding both the client and the candidate to understand each other's competencies—and capability gaps.

BIGGEST COMPETITOR: Time

MOST SIGNIFICANT OTHER ASPECT OF PERSONAL OR PROFESSIONAL LIFE: Giving my children good memories

WHAT IS THE BEST PREPARATION FOR BEING A SUCCESSFUL RECRUITER? Personal drive, focus on the client's needs.

WHAT WOULD YOU BE DOING IF YOU WERE NOT AN EXECUTIVE RECRUITER? I love what I do, but if I were to do something else, I would likely start an organizational development counseling practice—or be an artist.

continues ▶

WHAT ARE THE CHARACTERISTICS OF A GREAT CLIENT? Clients who engage with you as a partner and collaborator become great clients. Accessibility and the willingness to share both personal and professional issues that might impact the search are important.

WHAT CHALLENGES DO YOU SEE AHEAD IN THE GLOBAL MARKETPLACE? First, I believe that the way search firms have divided the world into specific industries will change: broad definitions of technology, health care, financial services, etc. will not be as relevant. Second, the increased pace of communications due to technology puts pressure on time that we might use to allow ourselves to think and to consider. Third, we need to prepare talent to truly embrace the diversity of cultures and the differential impact on business.

JAMES J. DRURY III

Spencer Stuart
401 North Michigan Avenue, Suite 3400
Chicago, Illinois 60611
U.S.A.

Telephone: (312) 822-0080
Fax: (312) 822-0116
E-mail: jdrury@spencerstuart.com
Company Website: http://www.spencerstuart.com

DATE OF BIRTH: March 10, 1942

NATIONALITY: U.S.A.—Grew up in Chicago, Illinois; San Francisco, California; Charleston, West Virginia; and Indianapolis, Indiana

EDUCATIONAL BACKGROUND:

B.S., Aeronautical Engineering, The University of Notre Dame, Notre Dame, Indiana, 1964
M.B.A., Marketing and Finance, The University of Chicago Graduate School of Business, Chicago, Illinois, 1966

LANGUAGES SPOKEN: English

CAREER HIGHLIGHTS:

1984–Present	Spencer Stuart: Vice Chairman, Chairman Midwest Region; Member of the firm's Management Operating Committee; Member of the firm's Board of Directors; Head of North American Industrial Practice; Global oversight responsibility for the industrial, healthcare/pharmaceutical, and entertainment practices.
	Previously Managing Partner/Midwest and Southeast U.S. Regions; Managing Partner/Chicago Office and Midwest Region
1979–84	Nordeman Grimm, Inc., Partner
1974–79	Arthur Young & Co., Manager/Marketing Consulting Practice
1969–74	Donald R. Booz & Associates, Manager
1966–69	The Boeing Company, Manager/Strategic Planning

SPECIAL INTERESTS/HOBBIES: Member, United States Polo Association (since 1984); Captain, Pinecroft Farm polo team; Board Director, Music of the Baroque Orchestra and Chorus; Board Trustee, Citizens for Conservation

GEOGRAPHIC SCOPE OF RECRUITING: International

SECTOR/INDUSTRY SPECIALIZATION: Industrial, consumer products, retail and business services

FAVORITE HISTORICAL FIGURE/MODEL/MENTOR: Billy Hitchcock, finest American polo player in the 30's and 40's.

SINGLE MOST IMPORTANT ISSUE IN CONDUCTING A HIGH LEVEL SEARCH: Don't be too quick to take no for an answer.

BIGGEST COMPETITOR: No one in particular. None can be taken lightly.

MOST SIGNIFICANT OTHER ASPECT OF PERSONAL OR PROFESSIONAL LIFE: Love for the business and the incredibly rewarding professional and personal life that it has afforded me and my colleagues.

continues ▶

WHAT IS THE BEST PREPARATION FOR BEING A SUCCESSFUL RECRUITER? Combination of management consulting and industry management. Human resources is not necessarily good preparation.

WHAT WOULD YOU BE DOING IF YOU WERE NOT AN EXECUTIVE RECRUITER? Venture capital

WHAT ARE THE CHARACTERISTICS OF A GREAT CLIENT? Decisiveness and confidence in and partnership with the search consultant. More interested in the solution than bureaucratic control of the search process.

WHAT CHALLENGES DO YOU SEE AHEAD IN THE GLOBAL MARKETPLACE? I do not necessarily believe that serving clients on a global basis is possible, even though it sounds elegant. The large global companies tend to treat search firms like vendors rather than advisors and regional HR executives are fairly parochial in who they use, not necessarily interested in global relationships.

MAURICE C. ELLETT

Ward Howell International
P.O. Box 4046
Auckland 1
New Zealand

Telephone: 64-9-309 0886
Fax: 64-9-309 0885
E-mail: wardhowell@xtra.co.nz
Company Website: http://www.laix.com

DATE OF BIRTH: September 7, 1946

NATIONALITY: New Zealand—Grew up in Auckland

EDUCATIONAL BACKGROUND:
Auckland University-Bachelor of Science (Psychology)
Auckland University-Bachelor of Commerce (Management Science)

LANGUAGES SPOKEN: English

CAREER HIGHLIGHTS: Appointment of many Chief Executives of New Zealand's top corporations and boards

SPECIAL INTERESTS/HOBBIES: Diving, community interests

GEOGRAPHIC SCOPE OF RECRUITING: Australasia

SECTOR/INDUSTRY SPECIALIZATION: Primary, industrial, public

SINGLE MOST IMPORTANT ISSUE IN CONDUCTING A HIGH LEVEL SEARCH: Identifying suitable candidates compatible with New Zealand business ethos and systems from the international arena.

MOST SIGNIFICANT OTHER ASPECT OF PERSONAL OR PROFESSIONAL LIFE: 26+ years in executive recruitment.

WHAT IS THE BEST PREPARATION FOR BEING A SUCCESSFUL RECRUITER? A well-rounded business knowledge covering a diversity of functional areas and exposure to various cultures of business management. Also essential is the ability to be tactical as well as strategic in a hands-on methodology.

WHAT WOULD YOU BE DOING IF YOU WERE NOT AN EXECUTIVE RECRUITER? An HR Director, General Manager Human Resources or similar or a line manager associated with sales and marketing but involving people.

WHAT ARE THE CHARACTERISTICS OF A GREAT CLIENT? The organisation would be under strong leadership with vision, decisiveness and the empowerment of subordinate managers who themselves are decisive and assume accountability for the key outcomes appropriate to their commercial responsibility.

WHAT CHALLENGES DO YOU SEE AHEAD IN THE GLOBAL MARKETPLACE? The big challenge will be to continue to identify those who have a combination of strategic management, analysis and holistic corporate perspectives with the empathy and interpersonal skills to motivate large teams of people.

LEON FARLEY

Leon A. Farley Associates
468 Jackson Street
San Francisco, CA 94111
U.S.A.

Telephone: 1 (415) 989-0989
Fax: 1 (415) 989-5908
E-mail: FARLEYSF@aol.com

DATE OF BIRTH: May 6, 1935

NATIONALITY: American—Grew up in Southern California

EDUCATIONAL BACKGROUND:
Attended UCLA-J.D. and B.A. in English Literature

LANGUAGES SPOKEN: Spanish

CAREER HIGHLIGHTS:
Chair and three-time Board member of AESC
The AESC Gardner W. Heidrick Award for "Outstanding Contribution to the Profession," 1984

SPECIAL INTERESTS/HOBBIES: Adventure travel, theatre, rugby

GEOGRAPHIC SCOPE OF RECRUITING: Domestic and International combined with the resources of Penrhyn International, our global network.

SECTOR/INDUSTRY SPECIALIZATION: Emphasis on financial services, technology and board positions in all industries.

FAVORITE HISTORICAL FIGURE/MODEL/MENTOR: Winston Churchill, Gandhi, Martin Luther King

SINGLE MOST IMPORTANT ISSUE IN CONDUCTING A HIGH LEVEL SEARCH: Managing the client's expectations during the search process and assuring that the final candidate performs in a predictable manner to assure the desired results

MOST SIGNIFICANT OTHER ASPECT OF PERSONAL OR PROFESSIONAL LIFE: I am very proud of my four children and four grandchildren, their lives and their values. I cherish my work within the industry with so many fine professional colleagues.

WHAT IS THE BEST PREPARATION FOR BEING A SUCCESSFUL RECRUITER? A broad liberal arts education, ideally coupled with an MBA, reflected by superior writing and speaking skills. Extensive multi-cultural exposure. Business success, preferably including profit and loss experience, sufficient to afford an understanding of the major business functions. A deep understanding of human psychology, the mind of a novelist and the soul of a poet.

WHAT WOULD YOU BE DOING IF YOU WERE NOT AN EXECUTIVE RECRUITER? If I knew, I would be doing it! Fantasies from time-to-time have included being an explorer, movie director, and foreign correspondent.

WHAT ARE THE CHARACTERISTICS OF A GREAT CLIENT? A great client is one who is accessible, good-humored; able to fuse vision and reality, and willing to accept constructive guidance—and even criticism.

WHAT CHALLENGES DO YOU SEE AHEAD IN THE GLOBAL MARKETPLACE? The advent of technology and the pressure on search firms to grow is creating commercial imperatives that threaten to overwhelm professional excellence. Search consultants must differentiate themselves by maintaining a clear vision, producing excellence by limiting the assignments undertaken and resisting the temptation to engage in volume placements.

ANNE M. FAWCETT

The Caldwell Partners/Amrop International
64 Prince Arthur Avenue
Toronto, Ontario
M5R 1B4

Telephone: 1 (416) 920-7702
Fax: 1 (416) 922-8646
E-mail: leaders@caldwellpartners.com
       resumes@caldwellpartners.com
Company Website: http://www.caldwellpartners.com

DATE OF BIRTH: September 30, 1945

NATIONALITY: Canadian

EDUCATIONAL BACKGROUND:
B.Sc., The University of Western Ontario

LANGUAGES SPOKEN: English

SPECIAL INTERESTS/HOBBIES: Reading, travel, community service

GEOGRAPHIC SCOPE OF RECRUITING: North American and International

SINGLE MOST IMPORTANT ISSUE IN CONDUCTING A HIGH LEVEL SEARCH: Thorough knowledge of the circumstance, strengths, and weaknesses of the enterprise.

WHAT IS THE BEST PREPARATION FOR BEING A SUCCESSFUL RECRUITER? Highly developed listening, conceptual and process management skills.

WHAT WOULD YOU BE DOING IF YOU WERE NOT AN EXECUTIVE RECRUITER? Lawyer/Agent

WHAT ARE THE CHARACTERISTICS OF A GREAT CLIENT? High standards, full information sharing, and a "work with" attitude.

WHAT CHALLENGES DO YOU SEE AHEAD IN THE GLOBAL MARKETPLACE? The war for talent is only just beginning. The competition for great people will transform our profession and many of our client's businesses.

RICHARD M. FERRY

Korn/Ferry International
1800 Century Park East, Suite 900
Los Angeles, CA 90067
U.S.A.

Telephone: 1 (310) 843-4111
Fax: 1 (310) 553-8640
E-mail: ferryr@kornferry.com
Company Website: http://www.kornferry.com

DATE OF BIRTH: September 26, 1937

NATIONALITY: American—Born in Ohio, grew up in Midwest

EDUCATIONAL BACKGROUND:
B.S. Business Administration, Kent State University
Certified Public Accountant

LANGUAGES SPOKEN: English

CAREER HIGHLIGHTS:
Co-founding Korn/Ferry International in 1969 and leading the global expansion of the firm.
Establishing White House Task Force on executive manpower to recruit Presidential appointments.

SPECIAL INTERESTS/HOBBIES: Community service, education, golf

GEOGRAPHIC SCOPE OF RECRUITING: Worldwide

SECTOR/INDUSTRY SPECIALIZATION: Board of Directors and CEO/COO level assignments

FAVORITE HISTORICAL FIGURE/MODEL/MENTOR: Sir Winston Churchill

SINGLE MOST IMPORTANT ISSUE IN CONDUCTING A HIGH LEVEL SEARCH: Finding candidates who can provide the new direction that a corporation needs to prosper in the 21st Century's global environment. In short, finding executives who can think "out of the box" and transform a vision into reality.

MOST SIGNIFICANT OTHER ASPECT OF PERSONAL OR PROFESSIONAL LIFE: Serving on corporate boards of Avery Dennison, Dole Food Company, and Pacific Life Insurance Company. Forty-one year marriage with six children and six grandchildren.

WHAT IS THE BEST PREPARATION FOR BEING A SUCCESSFUL RECRUITER? Certainly, as clients demand more and more specialization, expertise in a specific industry is very important. I would add to that experience with general human resource issues such as compensation, hiring and personnel. Then there are the more intangible skills: excellent communications; a sincere interest in people and what motivates them; and an intuitive ability to evaluate executives and how they might fit within an organization's culture.

WHAT WOULD YOU BE DOING IF YOU WERE NOT AN EXECUTIVE RECRUITER? If I weren't Chairman of Korn/Ferry International, I would be definitely running another company. I find it very satisfying to be involved in a business that I have helped create—and to see it continue to expand and prosper.

WHAT ARE THE CHARACTERISTICS OF A GREAT CLIENT?   A great client is someone who considers the recruiter as a real partner-so the two can work closely together and build a strong and continuing relationship. The goal of any recruiter is to help an organization, over the long term, build the leadership capital that will leverage its financial, human and intellectual resources.

WHAT CHALLENGES DO YOU SEE AHEAD IN THE GLOBAL MARKETPLACE? Technology and the Internet are rapidly changing the face of business-certainly, Korn/Ferry is feeling the impact and is continuing to reinvent our approach to search as a result. Companies are consolidating, breaking down geographic barriers, looking for very different types of leaders. As a firm, we need to look globally for the leaders our clients are seeking-today, the right candidate-whether the company is a Silicon Valley start-up or a major European-based multinational-could be anywhere in the world.

MICHEL FLASAQUIER

Jouve & Associés
54, avenue Marceau
75008 Paris
France

Telephone: 33 1 40 70 90 00
Fax: 33 1 47 20 55 56

DATE OF BIRTH: July 1, 1945

NATIONALITY: French—Grew up in France

EDUCATIONAL BACKGROUND:
Engineering Degree, Ecole Centrale de Paris (ECP)
M.Sc. in Industrial Management, Sloan School, Massachusetts Institute of Technology (M.I.T.)

LANGUAGES SPOKEN: French (mother tongue), fluent English

CAREER HIGHLIGHTS:
- Director of the President's Office, Jacques Borel International (1972-1977)
- MIS Director Europe, Merck Sharp & Dohme (1977-1983)
- Russell Reynolds in Paris (1984-1988)
- Equity Partner, Jouve & Associés since 1988

SPECIAL INTERESTS/HOBBIES: Opera and Modern Music

GEOGRAPHIC SCOPE OF RECRUITING: France + pan European searches

SECTOR/INDUSTRY SPECIALIZATION:
- High technology, particularly IT, Telecommunications and Health and Biotechnology
- Financial Institutions and Venture Capital
- Industrial companies

FAVORITE HISTORICAL FIGURE/MODEL/MENTOR: The nice thing about executive recruiting is that there are very few people I don't learn from.

SINGLE MOST IMPORTANT ISSUE IN CONDUCTING A HIGH LEVEL SEARCH: In-depth understanding of client company. Ability to fully cooperate with client's representatives (work hand in hand with them) at all stages of the recruitment process.

WHAT IS THE BEST PREPARATION FOR BEING A SUCCESSFUL RECRUITER? There is no single preparation for being an executive recruiter. Experience acquired with a blue chip company, i.e., a leader in its industry, is probably a good start. Other prerequisites are a talent for interpersonal relationships as well as a strong motivation for project-type work.

WHAT WOULD YOU BE DOING IF YOU WERE NOT AN EXECUTIVE RECRUITER? I've been an executive recruiter too long to be in a position to think realistically about the other lives I could have led.

WHAT ARE THE CHARACTERISTICS OF A GREAT CLIENT? A great client is a client with whom we establish a relationship based on mutual trust so as to obtain results and attract outstanding candidates.

WHAT CHALLENGES DO YOU SEE AHEAD IN THE GLOBAL MARKETPLACE? Internationalization of executive recruiters skill set.

THOMAS J. FRIEL

Heidrick & Struggles
2740 Sand Hill Road
Menlo Park, CA 94025
U.S.A.

Telephone: 1 (650) 234-1500
Fax: 1 (650) 854-4191
E-mail: tjf@h-s.com
Company Website: http://www.h-s.com

DATE OF BIRTH: October 25, 1947

NATIONALITY: American—Grew up in St. Louis, Missouri

EDUCATIONAL BACKGROUND:
BS Industrial Engineering, Purdue University, 1969
MBA, Stanford University, 1973

LANGUAGES SPOKEN: English and French

CAREER HIGHLIGHTS: In executive search with Heidrick & Struggles since 1979, as Partner/Director since1982. Established the firm's Technology/Silicon Valley office in 1984. It is now the largest technology search office in the world. Built and headed Technology Search Practice from 1983 to 1995. Established and headed Heidrick & Struggles' Industry Practice Committee. Served as a member of the firm's Systems Committee, Management Committee, three-time elected member of the Executive Committee and Global Policy Committee. Managing Partner, Asia Pacific 1992 to present. Past President, California Executive Recruiters Association (CERA).

SPECIAL INTERESTS/HOBBIES: Coaching youth sports, travel, wine

GEOGRAPHIC SCOPE OF RECRUITING: Worldwide, but with emphasis on North America and Asia Pacific

SECTOR/INDUSTRY SPECIALIZATION: Information Technology-Majority of work is at CEO and Board level

FAVORITE HISTORICAL FIGURE/MODEL/MENTOR: Winston Churchill

SINGLE MOST IMPORTANT ISSUE IN CONDUCTING A HIGH LEVEL SEARCH: Establishing personal credibility as a peer with client and leading candidates enables performance as a valued partner and advisor.

MOST SIGNIFICANT OTHER ASPECT OF PERSONAL OR PROFESSIONAL LIFE: Success of those I have mentored and helped become successful in the search profession

WHAT IS THE BEST PREPARATION FOR BEING A SUCCESSFUL RECRUITER? The best recruiters combine a good education, solid work experience including some general management experience, and a history of doing things that are hard. I also believe it is enormously helpful to have sold something somewhere in a prior experience.

WHAT WOULD YOU BE DOING IF YOU WERE NOT AN EXECUTIVE RECRUITER? I would probably be involved in some other aspect of management consulting. Probably as a principle/owner in a small to mid-sized consulting or venture capital partnership.

WHAT ARE THE CHARACTERISTICS OF A GREAT CLIENT? The best clients combine a sense of urgency, a clear vision of what they want and a willingness to trust their search consultant. I always do my best work for clients who view me as a partner, not as a vendor.

WHAT CHALLENGES DO YOU SEE AHEAD IN THE GLOBAL MARKETPLACE? The biggest challenge facing corporations worldwide is the limited talent pool of qualified senior executives compared to business ideas and capital, which are in abundant supply. Management talent is in seriously short supply in the face of rising demand.

KOICHI (KRIS) FUKUDA

Heidrick & Struggles
Kasumigaseki Building 31F.
3-2-5 Kasumigaseki
Chiyoda-ku, Tokyo
Japan 100

Telephone: 81 (3) 3500-5310
Fax: 81 (3) 3500-5350
E-mail: KXF@h-s-japan.com
Company Website: http://www.h-s.com

DATE OF BIRTH: November 15, 1950

NATIONALITY: Japanese—Grew up in Japan and U.S.A.

EDUCATIONAL BACKGROUND:
Duke University, M.B.A.
Beloit College, B.A.

LANGUAGES SPOKEN: Japanese, English, German

CAREER HIGHLIGHTS:
President, Boston Scientific
President, Duke University Alumni Association

SPECIAL INTERESTS/HOBBIES: Flying a plane (FAA licensed pilot), playing flute

GEOGRAPHIC SCOPE OF RECRUITING: Asia-Pacific, especially Japan

SECTOR/INDUSTRY SPECIALIZATION: High-technology and Medical

FAVORITE HISTORICAL FIGURE/MODEL/MENTOR: Mr. Hideo Ishihara, Chairman of Goldman Sachs

SINGLE MOST IMPORTANT ISSUE IN CONDUCTING A HIGH LEVEL SEARCH: Quality

MOST SIGNIFICANT OTHER ASPECT OF PERSONAL OR PROFESSIONAL LIFE: Maintain quality of life

WHAT IS THE BEST PREPARATION FOR BEING A SUCCESSFUL RECRUITER? To have an executive position in a multi-national organization

WHAT WOULD YOU BE DOING IF YOU WERE NOT AN EXECUTIVE RECRUITER? Running my own strategic consulting company

WHAT ARE THE CHARACTERISTICS OF A GREAT CLIENT? Has a sense of urgency. Has a full understanding of the position in question. Knows what his requirements are. A long-term relationship develops.

WHAT CHALLENGES DO YOU SEE AHEAD IN THE GLOBAL MARKETPLACE? There is not much time to react and anticipating changes is becoming harder to do.

SAKIE T. FUKUSHIMA

Korn/Ferry International
AIG Building, 7th Floor
1-1-3 Marunouchi
Chiyoda-ku, Tokyo 100
Japan

Telephone: 81 (3) 3211-6851
Fax: 81 (3) 3216-1300
E-mail: sakie.fukushima@kornferry.com
Company Website: http://www.kornferry.com

DATE OF BIRTH: September 9, 1949

NATIONALITY: Japanese—Grew up in Japan

EDUCATIONAL BACKGROUND:
B.A., Seisen College, Tokyo
International Christian University, Tokyo (Graduate Studies)
Ed.M., Harvard Graduate School of Education
M.B.A., Stanford Business School

LANGUAGES SPOKEN: Japanese, English

CAREER HIGHLIGHTS:
- Currently Vice President, Partner, and Member of Korn/Ferry International Board of Directors
- Strategy Management Consultant, Brain & Company, Boston & Tokyo, 1987–1990
- Instructor, Harvard University, 1974–1980

SPECIAL INTERESTS/HOBBIES: Mystery novels, music, travel

GEOGRAPHIC SCOPE OF RECRUITING: Japan

SECTOR/INDUSTRY SPECIALIZATION: Consumer goods, retail, professional services

FAVORITE HISTORICAL FIGURE/MODEL/MENTOR: Richard Ferry

SINGLE MOST IMPORTANT ISSUE IN CONDUCTING A HIGH LEVEL SEARCH: Quality, integrity, professionalism

MOST SIGNIFICANT OTHER ASPECT OF PERSONAL OR PROFESSIONAL LIFE:

WHAT IS THE BEST PREPARATION FOR BEING A SUCCESSFUL RECRUITER? Working experience in a strategic management consulting firm.

WHAT WOULD YOU BE DOING IF YOU WERE NOT AN EXECUTIVE RECRUITER? Strategy management consultant with specialization in organization development

WHAT ARE THE CHARACTERISTICS OF A GREAT CLIENT? Willingness to listen

WHAT CHALLENGES DO YOU SEE AHEAD IN THE GLOBAL MARKETPLACE? Finding high quality candidates who can function effectively in a global setting.

R. WILLIAM (BILL) FUNK

Korn/Ferry International
3232 Lincoln Plaza
Dallas, Texas 75201
U.S.A.

Telephone: 1 (214) 954-1834
Fax: 1 (214) 954-1849
Company Website: http://www.kornferry.com

DATE OF BIRTH: June 2, 1948

NATIONALITY: American—Grew up in Uniontown, Pennsylvania

EDUCATIONAL BACKGROUND:

Purdue University, Master of Science degree in Industrial Relations, 1974

Ohio University, Master of Arts degree in Government, 1972

California State College, California, Pennsylvania, Bachelor of Arts degree in Political Science, 1970

LANGUAGES SPOKEN: English

CAREER HIGHLIGHTS: Currently serve as the Managing Director of the Dallas Office of Korn/Ferry International; Managing Director of the Education/Not-for-Profit Practice and the Utility Practice. Also serve on various management committees within the firm. Personally recruited to Korn/Ferry International in 1992 by CEO Michael Boxberger, who had hired me into the search business at Heidrick & Struggles twelve years earlier.

From 1980 until 1992, Heidrick & Struggles—Managing Partner of the Houston Office (1982 to 1988) and Managing Partner of the Southwest Region/Dallas and Houston (1988 to 1992). Member of the firm's Operating Committee (1982 to 1992), Board (1982 to 1992), and Executive Committee of the Board (1988 to 1991). In 1989, one of three individuals formally nominated by the Board Nominating Committee to stand as a candidate for the Presidency of the firm.

Began career with Exxon Company, U.S.A. in 1974. Progressed through five positions of increasing responsibility before entering the search field in 1980.

One of the most prolific recruiters of Presidents, CEOs, and Board members in the country. Have recruited these executives into a wide range of companies, industries, and education and not-for-profit organizations. Have placed over 100 Presidents and CEOs and nearly nearly thirty Directors on the Boards of New York Stock Exchange-listed companies.

Recognized recruiter of Presidents for major colleges and universities (over 50 placements to date). Have placed the sitting Presidents/Chancellors of the following universities and colleges, among many others: Ohio State University, Tulane University, University of Texas-Austin, University of Illinois, University of Utah, Worcester Polytechnic Institute, University of Minnesota, Babson College, University of Alabama, University of Wyoming, Indiana University, Clemson University, University of Iowa, University of Nebraska, and University of Missouri System

SPECIAL INTERESTS/HOBBIES: When not working, I place a premium on the time spent with my family. I enjoy running and fitness activities. I have served on various charitable and university boards and I am a frequent volunteer at St. Mark's School of Texas where my two sons attend lower school. I enjoy most spectator sports, theater, cross-country skiing, and beach vacations.

GEOGRAPHIC SCOPE OF RECRUITING: The nexus of my consulting is in North America, but I am frequently sought out by Partners in Europe, Australia, and Asia to assist on university and energy-related assignments.

SECTOR/INDUSTRY SPECIALIZATION: Education and not-for-profit; energy and utilities; and board placements. I also work in a number of other areas, including marine and industrial.

FAVORITE HISTORICAL FIGURE/MODEL/MENTOR: No single role model or historical figure comes to mind. I respect and admire honest and sincere individuals, and persons who have a sense of purpose and work hard. Those who have overcome some kind of adversity, or who have had to battle back from a personal tragedy or difficult situation seem to have a special strength.

SINGLE MOST IMPORTANT ISSUE IN CONDUCTING A HIGH LEVEL SEARCH: Maintaining a process of integrity—doing what you promise to do; demonstrating respect for the candidates by keeping them informed of developments on a timely basis.

MOST SIGNIFICANT OTHER ASPECT OF PERSONAL OR PROFESSIONAL LIFE: My wife and sons. Trying to balance the demands of a robust search practice with a desire to spend meaningful time with my family is a constant challenge.

WHAT IS THE BEST PREPARATION FOR BEING A SUCCESSFUL RECRUITER? I am not sure if there is any "best" preparation. It is important to have a high energy level; to be mentally "tough" in avoiding low lows and high highs; communicate well; have a genuine respect for people; know how organizations work; and possess an intuitive "feel" for the personality and character of candidates.

WHAT WOULD YOU BE DOING IF YOU WERE NOT AN EXECUTIVE RECRUITER? There are other callings that I find fascinating! The two that would be at the top of my list would be: (1) a trial attorney, arguing cases about which I might feel passionate; and/or (2) a high school or college basketball coach.

WHAT ARE THE CHARACTERISTICS OF A GREAT CLIENT? A "great" client is one who respects what I do and appreciates the work we perform. It is important for the client to commit the time necessary to talk about the project, meet with the candidates in a timely manner, and make fairly rapid decisions.

WHAT CHALLENGES DO YOU SEE AHEAD IN THE GLOBAL MARKETPLACE? There is obviously an increasing demand for industry and functional specialization on the part of clients. Technology has become an important ally of the search consultant. Capital expenditures to assure that the firm/consultant has these technological tools—and the ability to use them—will not be insignificant. However, those who are not able to access the most relevant data bases and communicate via email, Octel, voice mail, fax, teleconference, and Internet will fall back in the pack. The low- and middle-range recruiter will find her/himself increasingly in competition with new, lower cost, technology driven providers. The various job posting services provided on the Internet, the "Monster Board," for example, will become more sophisticated and will gain market-share.

It will be important to have worldwide capabilities. For those in large firms, it will be essential to serve multi-national clients in a uniform manner throughout the world. Independent practitioners and boutique firms will have to forge linkages and partnering arrangements to provide this service for their clients. Finding candidates who have true international capabilities and experiences for the positions which demand them will be challenging for the foreseeable future.

HIDEAKI FURUTA

Jomon Associates Inc.
Toranomoa Toyo Building, 8th Floor
1-4-2 Toranomoa, Minato-ku, Tokyo
105 Japan

Telephone: 81-3-3591-7281
Fax: 81-3-3591-7389
E-mail: furuta@jomon.co-jp
Company Website: http://www.jomon.co-jp

DATE OF BIRTH: January 2, 1953

NATIONALITY: Japanese—Grew up in Tokyo

EDUCATIONAL BACKGROUND:

1976 BA Tokyo University (Economics)

LANGUAGES SPOKEN: Japanese, English

CAREER HIGHLIGHTS: Before beginning acareer as a headhunter, I worked with Kobe Steel and Nomura Securities, two major Japanese companies. Serving mainly as staff for the sales and planning division, I obtained knowledge about management, including human resource management. I joined Russell Reynolds in 1993 and achieved a significant sales record in the Japanese market. I established my own firm in 1996.

SPECIAL INTERESTS/HOBBIES: Ancient history

GEOGRAPHIC SCOPE OF RECRUITING: Mainly Japan and Asia

SECTOR/INDUSTRY SPECIALIZATION: Start-up companies, multi-national companies

FAVORITE HISTORICAL FIGURE/MODEL/MENTOR: I respect corporate founders

SINGLE MOST IMPORTANT ISSUE IN CONDUCTING A HIGH LEVEL SEARCH: To find a person whose character can fit to the culture of the company, not to the job description.

MOST SIGNIFICANT OTHER ASPECT OF PERSONAL OR PROFESSIONAL LIFE: To reform the society where people can make the most of their abilities and enjoy their lives.

WHAT IS THE BEST PREPARATION FOR BEING A SUCCESSFUL RECRUITER? Sincerity

WHAT WOULD YOU BE DOING IF YOU WERE NOT AN EXECUTIVE RECRUITER? I believe this is my calling or my mission. I'm sure that I should be an executive recruiter whatever happens to me.

WHAT ARE THE CHARACTERISTICS OF A GREAT CLIENT? A great client organization helps their employees grow.

WHAT CHALLENGES DO YOU SEE AHEAD IN THE GLOBAL MARKETPLACE? To establish networks among head hunters based on reliance—not on capital

JAY GAINES

Jay Gaines & Company
450 Park Avenue
New York, NY 10022
U.S.A.

Telephone: 1 (212) 308-9222
Fax: 1 (212) 308-5146
E-mail: JGandCO@compuserve.com

DATE OF BIRTH: April 18, 1947

NATIONALITY: U.S. Citizen—Grew up in Oceanside, Long Island, New York

EDUCATIONAL BACKGROUND:
B.A. in Psychology from George Washington University
M.S. in Industrial Psychology from Columbia University

LANGUAGES SPOKEN: English

CAREER HIGHLIGHTS: Having achieved significant and measurable impact on such industry leaders as Morgan Stanley, McGraw-Hill, Fidelity, Reuters and others by building successful senior management teams and making the external recruiting process an exciting, winning proposition.

One highlight that led to the long-term building of our general management practice in the information industry was the 1990 landmark search for the CEO of EJV.

SPECIAL INTERESTS/HOBBIES: Boating, skiing, hiking, reading, and politics

GEOGRAPHIC SCOPE OF RECRUITING: U.S. and Europe (primarily U.K.)

SECTOR/INDUSTRY SPECIALIZATION: Financial Services, Information and Publishing, Information Technology, Software and Consulting

FAVORITE HISTORICAL FIGURE/MODEL/MENTOR: Abraham Lincoln-he held to a vision, was smart, had integrity and compassion, but acted unflinchingly on what he needed to do.

SINGLE MOST IMPORTANT ISSUE IN CONDUCTING A HIGH LEVEL SEARCH: Grasp!! Striving for long-term success and integration of the individual into the new culture. This often is an illusive, always difficult goal. It requires a deep understanding of what works from a cultural, psychological/attitudinal and experiential dimension. While there may be many benefits in hiring a key individual for the short-term, we believe striving for success beyond the three year mark is really the critical benchmark and a very tough one to achieve.

MOST SIGNIFICANT OTHER ASPECT OF PERSONAL OR PROFESSIONAL LIFE: Balancing family life which often is sacrificed in the intense pursuit of search. Additionally, I am organizing materials to write a book and speak out on careers and corporate life success and failure.

WHAT IS THE BEST PREPARATION FOR BEING A SUCCESSFUL RECRUITER? My view is that the recruiting profession both internally and externally is not as strong as it should be. Few people proactively plan their careers to be recruiters and there are many different paths individuals follow to become recruiters. The typical common denominators are people and relationship skills, selling skills, assessment skills, etc.

continues ▶

In our firm we value those skills but we value rigorous analytic thinking above all. The training and preparation may come from people in analytically intensive disciplines such as finance, consulting and portfolio management. Preparation begins with an education that is intellectually challenging and difficult; experience in a profession where selection and promotion is based on a rigorous, systematic and analytic approaches and performance ideally is tracked to some form of benchmark. We also strive to inculcate a global mindset and set of standards in the pursuit of most assignments. We pick individuals with some of those characteristics and develop them internally over a longstanding period of time.

WHAT WOULD YOU BE DOING IF YOU WERE NOT AN EXECUTIVE RECRUITER? The field of industrial psychology with particular emphasis in career counseling and management development has always been of tremendous interest. We consistently incorporate these themes into our executive recruiting program.

WHAT ARE THE CHARACTERISTICS OF A GREAT CLIENT? The characteristics of a great client are as follows:

- The client has a dream or vision which he or she is committed to and can effectively articulate and convey to all around.
- The client recognizes the criticality of the recruitment process. Beyond committing the necessary time and resources, puts a deep personal stake in making the effort successful.
- The individual understands the risks inherent in the recruiting and selection process, knows how to minimize them but at the end of the effort understands, accepts and manages the risks in bringing someone into a new organization.
- The individual creates a management climate that maximizes the chances for the individual's success. The environment stresses integrity, growth and development and minimizes counterproductive dynamics.

WHAT CHALLENGES DO YOU SEE AHEAD IN THE GLOBAL MARKETPLACE? Our world has been in rapid transition. Integrating a truly global point-of-view and keeping pace with a global set of demands has been an extremely demanding effort for those who have led the transition. The challenge for most sectors will be to develop and inculcate a truly global mind set (versus international). This will involve the ability to recognize potential in people of diverse nationalities and backgrounds who can be developed into global executives who are not limited in their effectiveness by local cultural outlooks. Parallel to this, truly global benchmarks relating to education, business models, and technology must be put in place.

E. NICHOLAS P. GARDINER

Gardiner, Townsend & Associates
101 East 52nd Street
New York, NY 10022
U.S.A.

Telephone: 1 (212) 230-1889
Fax: 1 (212) 838-0424

DATE OF BIRTH: June 19, 1939

NATIONALITY: American—Grew up in Asia and the United States

EDUCATIONAL BACKGROUND:
Yale University, B.A., 1961
Harvard Business School, PMD, 1971

LANGUAGES SPOKEN: English, French, German, Spanish

CAREER HIGHLIGHTS: Established the first U.S.-based cross-border specialty search firm

SPECIAL INTERESTS/HOBBIES: Published on the French Middle Ages, Triathlons

GEOGRAPHIC SCOPE OF RECRUITING: Cross-border executive search-Europe, North America, Latin America, and Asia

SECTOR/INDUSTRY SPECIALIZATION: Financial Services and Diversified Industries

FAVORITE HISTORICAL FIGURE/MODEL/MENTOR: Ferdinand Magellan (first person to circumnavigate the earth): intrepid navigator, courageous soldier and visionary.

SINGLE MOST IMPORTANT ISSUE IN CONDUCTING A HIGH LEVEL SEARCH: Assessing courage

MOST SIGNIFICANT OTHER ASPECT OF PERSONAL OR PROFESSIONAL LIFE: International Relations; President, Radio Free Europe Fund; Board Director, American Council on Germany; Board Director, French American Foundation; Japan Society; European Institute.

WHAT IS THE BEST PREPARATION FOR BEING A SUCCESSFUL RECRUITER? Listening.

WHAT WOULD YOU BE DOING IF YOU WERE NOT AN EXECUTIVE RECRUITER? I would build a national center for languages and cross-cultural studies in the United States.

WHAT ARE THE CHARACTERISTICS OF A GREAT CLIENT? Grace and integrity under pressure plus loyalty and trust for proven performance.

WHAT CHALLENGES DO YOU SEE AHEAD IN THE GLOBAL MARKETPLACE? The superficial perception of a global civilization which masks the deep cultural differences between nations and peoples.

JOHN T. GARDNER

Heidrick & Struggles
233 South Wacker Drive
Chicago, IL 60606
U.S.A.

Telephone: 1 (312) 496-1346
Fax: 1 (312) 496-1048
E-mail: jtg@h-s.com
Company Website: http://www.h-s.com

DATE OF BIRTH: June 21, 1943

NATIONALITY: American—Grew up in United States

EDUCATIONAL BACKGROUND:
Bachelor of Science, industrial management, Georgia Institute of Technology (Georgia Tech), Atlanta, Georgia
Masters in Business Administration, Harvard Business School, Boston, Massachusetts

LANGUAGES SPOKEN: English

CAREER HIGHLIGHTS: McKinsey; GE; currently Managing Partner, Industrial Practice of H & S

SPECIAL INTERESTS/HOBBIES: Tennis, sailing, golf

GEOGRAPHIC SCOPE OF RECRUITING: Global, with emphasis on North America

SECTOR/INDUSTRY SPECIALIZATION: Industrial, consumer durables

FAVORITE HISTORICAL FIGURE/MODEL/MENTOR: George Patton

SINGLE MOST IMPORTANT ISSUE IN CONDUCTING A HIGH LEVEL SEARCH: Matching the needs of the business with both the "soft" and technical skills/experience sets of potential candidates.

WHAT IS THE BEST PREPARATION FOR BEING A SUCCESSFUL RECRUITER? A successful business career which provides exposure to how business operates "at the top" and develops skills in leadership, communications, relationship building and assessment/development of people.

WHAT WOULD YOU BE DOING IF YOU WERE NOT AN EXECUTIVE RECRUITER? Running a traditional business, probably industrial.

WHAT ARE THE CHARACTERISTICS OF A GREAT CLIENT? High standards, vision, appreciation and desire for strong (and perhaps unusual) talent and a willingness to work in an equal partnership with the search consultant(s).

WHAT CHALLENGES DO YOU SEE AHEAD IN THE GLOBAL MARKETPLACE? The need for search firms to know and be able to recruit outstanding talent on a global basis and provide core clients with consistent, value-added service wherever their organizational needs exist.

ANDREW GARNER

Garner International Limited
6 Derby Street
Mayfair
London W1Y 7HD

Telephone: 44 171 629 8822
Fax: 44 171 629 8833
E-mail: garnerinternational@btinternet.com
Company Website: http://www.garnerinternational.co.uk

DATE OF BIRTH: August 9, 1944

NATIONALITY: British—Grew up in U.K.

EDUCATIONAL BACKGROUND:
University of Birmingham, B.Com (Honours)
Honorary Senior Visiting Fellow, Manchester Business School

LANGUAGES SPOKEN: English

CAREER HIGHLIGHTS:
1970–Youngest member of senior management in Mars Inc., worldwide
1990–Published *Smart Moves*
1990–Chariman of Boyden World Corp
1997–Founded Garner International

SPECIAL INTERESTS/HOBBIES: Motor racing, politics, teaching, public speaking

GEOGRAPHIC SCOPE OF RECRUITING: Worldwide

SECTOR/INDUSTRY SPECIALIZATION: Telecoms, Retail, FMCG

FAVORITE HISTORICAL FIGURE/MODEL/MENTOR: Winston Churchill/Noel Coward/Stirling Moss

SINGLE MOST IMPORTANT ISSUE IN CONDUCTING A HIGH LEVEL SEARCH: Candidate care

BIGGEST COMPETITOR: Spencer Stuart

WHAT IS THE BEST PREPARATION FOR BEING A SUCCESSFUL RECRUITER?
- Good formal education
- Post-graduate experience in a multi-national company
- Career development which includes cross-functional exposure
- General management-preferably board level-responsibility
- A wide range of non-work personal interests

WHAT WOULD YOU BE DOING IF YOU WERE NOT AN EXECUTIVE RECRUITER? Managing a substantial multi-national company or acting (stage and film)

WHAT ARE THE CHARACTERISTICS OF A GREAT CLIENT? A great client is available and exhibits trust, openness, inclusiveness, responsibility, and reasonableness.

WHAT CHALLENGES DO YOU SEE AHEAD IN THE GLOBAL MARKETPLACE?
Structural unemployment and job insecurity across the management class in OECD countries
Polarisation amongst recruitment firms between the very large and boutiques

FRANCISCO GASSET

Spencer Stuart
Oquendo 23
28006 Madrid
Spain

Telephone: 34 1 4112449
Fax: 34 1 5614275
E-mail: fgasset@spencerstuart.com
Company Website: http://www.spencerstuart.com

DATE OF BIRTH: April 18, 1951

NATIONALITY: Spanish—Grew up in Spain

EDUCATIONAL BACKGROUND:
- Degree in law
- MBA-IESE Barcelona

LANGUAGES SPOKEN: Spanish, English, French

CAREER HIGHLIGHTS:
- CEO, Williams & Humbert, 1977-79
- Senior partner, Spencer Stuart, 1979-present
  Managing Director Spain
  Member of International boards

SPECIAL INTERESTS/HOBBIES: Hunting

GEOGRAPHIC SCOPE OF RECRUITING: Spain, Portugal

SECTOR/INDUSTRY SPECIALIZATION: Boards, consumer, pharmaceuticals

FAVORITE HISTORICAL FIGURE/MODEL/MENTOR: King Juan Carlos

SINGLE MOST IMPORTANT ISSUE IN CONDUCTING A HIGH LEVEL SEARCH: Quality

WHAT IS THE BEST PREPARATION FOR BEING A SUCCESSFUL RECRUITER? CEO experience (search)

WHAT WOULD YOU BE DOING IF YOU WERE NOT AN EXECUTIVE RECRUITER? CEO of a consumer goods firm

WHAT ARE THE CHARACTERISTICS OF A GREAT CLIENT? Trust, long term planner

BOB GATTIE

Gattie Tan Soo Jin Management
   Consultants Pte Ltd./Amrop International
3 Shenton Way
#11-08 Shenton House
Singapore 068805

Telephone: 65 255 3188
Fax: 65 224 7585
E-mail: bg1512@mbox4.singnet.com.sg
Company Website: http://www.amrop.com

DATE OF BIRTH: December 15, 1943

NATIONALITY: British. Permanent resident of Singapore—Grew up in England and U.S.A.

EDUCATIONAL BACKGROUND:

B.A. (Econ/Pol), University of Leeds, England
Masters Degree (Econ Dev), University of Pittsburgh, U.S.A.

LANGUAGES SPOKEN: English, French

CAREER HIGHLIGHTS: Chairman, Asia Pacific Region Amrop International (1994-1996). Responsible for starting new Amrop International offices in South Korea, Tokyo, Bangkok, Manila, Jakarta, and New Delhi.

SPECIAL INTERESTS/HOBBIES: Squash, travel

GEOGRAPHIC SCOPE OF RECRUITING: Asia/Pacific

SECTOR/INDUSTRY SPECIALIZATION: Finance, Healthcare, Information Technology

FAVORITE HISTORICAL FIGURE/MODEL/MENTOR: Lee Kuan Yew

SINGLE MOST IMPORTANT ISSUE IN CONDUCTING A HIGH LEVEL SEARCH: Understanding client requirements and fully communicating that understanding to candidates

MOST SIGNIFICANT OTHER ASPECT OF PERSONAL OR PROFESSIONAL LIFE: Family.

WHAT IS THE BEST PREPARATION FOR BEING A SUCCESSFUL RECRUITER? Successful business experience in a profit and loss responsible position.

WHAT WOULD YOU BE DOING IF YOU WERE NOT AN EXECUTIVE RECRUITER? Starting an executive search company!

WHAT ARE THE CHARACTERISTICS OF A GREAT CLIENT? Decisiveness, openness, trust, pays on time.

WHAT CHALLENGES DO YOU SEE AHEAD IN THE GLOBAL MARKETPLACE? Balancing tensions.

DANIEL A. GAUCHAT

Amrop International
155 George Street
Sydney N.S.W. 2023
Australia

Telephone: 61 2 9252-3500
Fax: 61 2 9247-2757
E-mail: daniel.gauchat@amrop.com
Company Website: http://www.amrop.com

DATE OF BIRTH: October 2, 1943

NATIONALITY: Swiss and Australian—Grew up in Switzerland and Australia

EDUCATIONAL BACKGROUND:

Bachelor of Commerce (Marketing)-with Merit, University of New South Wales, Sydney, Australia
MBA, INSEAD, Fontainebleau, France
Company Directors Diploma-with Merit, Australian Institute of Company Directors

LANGUAGES SPOKEN: English, French, German, Spanish

CAREER HIGHLIGHTS: Top level management experience in Europe (9 years) and Asia (8 years). International Chairman Amrop International 1997/1998 during a time of rapid growth and considerable structural change.

SPECIAL INTERESTS/HOBBIES: International trade, business and history, sports, theatre, music

GEOGRAPHIC SCOPE OF RECRUITING: International with special emphasis on Asia

SECTOR/INDUSTRY SPECIALIZATION: Retail and multinational corporations, fast moving consumer goods, service organizations, hi-tech companies

FAVORITE HISTORICAL FIGURE/MODEL/MENTOR: William Shakespeare

SINGLE MOST IMPORTANT ISSUE IN CONDUCTING A HIGH LEVEL SEARCH: To have the ability to enjoy the complete confidence of the Chairman/Board/CEO as a knowledgeable business partner and professional consultant who can make a major impact on an organization through the successful recruitment of high caliber candidates.

MOST SIGNIFICANT OTHER ASPECT OF PERSONAL OR PROFESSIONAL LIFE: Family and extensive international network of business and personal contacts

WHAT IS THE BEST PREPARATION FOR BEING A SUCCESSFUL RECRUITER? Hands-on experience in a senior management role, preferably in an international environment, to develop an understanding of what drives a business and sound judgment on the professional and personal characteristics of successful candidates. It is also important to acquire effective consulting skills to deal with conceptual and practical issues.

WHAT WOULD YOU BE DOING IF YOU WERE NOT AN EXECUTIVE RECRUITER? After a very successful 25 year international business career prior to entering the search business nine years ago, I would focus on advising corporations on their international strategies and take on some non-executive directorships. It would also be fun to be involved in helping a start-up service business achieve its potential.

WHAT ARE THE CHARACTERISTICS OF A GREAT CLIENT? An organization which excels in its business and knows where it wants to go. A great client should be willing to share information, be receptive to lateral thinking and be fully involved and responsive during the search process.

WHAT CHALLENGES DO YOU SEE AHEAD IN THE GLOBAL MARKETPLACE? The challenges include the ability to service clients under greater time constraints, by the effective usage of technology and increased industry specialization. The search business,-like that of its clients,-must become increasingly international in its outlook and capability.

RICHARD GLYNN

Richard Glynn Consultants Pte Ltd
10 Collyer Quay #24-04B
Ocean Building
Singapore 049513
Republic of Singapore

Telephone: 65 538-3393
Fax: 65 532 7078
E-mail: rglynn@pacific.net.sg
Company Website: http://www.iicpartners-esw.com

DATE OF BIRTH: October 1, 1936

NATIONALITY: British—Grew up in the U.K. and for nearly 30 years in Singapore, Hong Kong and Thailand.

EDUCATIONAL BACKGROUND:

Entirely in the U.K.

LANGUAGES SPOKEN: English, fair Thai, some Indonesian and Malay

CAREER HIGHLIGHTS:

Senior Vice President, Boyden International 1981-87

CEO & Founder, Richard Glynn Consultants in Singapore, Thailand and Hong Kong, 1987

SPECIAL INTERESTS/HOBBIES: Classical music, jazz, the visual arts, travel, South-East Asian antiques, food and the cultures of the countries in South-East Asia where I live and work

GEOGRAPHIC SCOPE OF RECRUITING: South-East Asia—principally Singapore, Malaysia, Thailand, Indonesia where we have our own offices and where I divide my time. But also the Philippines, Hong Kong, China, and Taiwan.

SECTOR/INDUSTRY SPECIALIZATION: Generalist but particularly active in financial services, consumer goods and health care, entertainment and the media

SINGLE MOST IMPORTANT ISSUE IN CONDUCTING A HIGH LEVEL SEARCH: Absolutely integrity, quality of service, and international reach

MOST SIGNIFICANT OTHER ASPECT OF PERSONAL OR PROFESSIONAL LIFE: Dedication to the highest performance standards

WHAT IS THE BEST PREPARATION FOR BEING A SUCCESSFUL RECRUITER? A clear understanding of the client's requirement in terms of the position, the scope, the reporting lines, the career opportunity, and the ideal type of candidate. It is also very important to have a good understanding of the client's corporate culture, any recent senior management movement or reorganisation; the history of the client's business, including value, volume, growth, profit & loss, and domestic vs. international. And agreed parameters regarding compensation.

WHAT WOULD YOU BE DOING IF YOU WERE NOT AN EXECUTIVE RECRUITER? Probably active in another area of management consulting in relation to South East Asia.

WHAT ARE THE CHARACTERISTICS OF A GREAT CLIENT? Great communication. Quick response. Absolute openness to enable a close and frank working relationship. Flexibility and the ability to understand and appreciate any frustrations and problems of the search. A totally professional understanding of executive search and the right attitude towards the search firm.

WHAT CHALLENGES DO YOU SEE AHEAD IN THE GLOBAL MARKETPLACE? The shortage of the right type of local managers in some countries in East Asia with the highest growth potential, e.g., China, Indonesia, Thailand, Malaysia and the Philippines. The ability of governments, companies, and managers in East Asia to effectively handle slower or negative growth and cope with economic and business crises, after years of consistent rapid, double-digit growth.

MIKE GOLDSTONE

Heidrick & Struggles Hong Kong Ltd
54th Floor, Bank of China Tower
1 Garden Road
Hong Kong

Telephone: 852 2802 8887
Fax: 852 2519 8411
Company Website: http://www.h-s.com

DATE OF BIRTH: March 25, 1959

NATIONALITY: British—Grew up in England

EDUCATIONAL BACKGROUND:
 1988: Cranfield School of Management, MBA
 1980: University of Bristol, U.K., BA (Hons) in History, 2.1

LANGUAGES SPOKEN: English and French, some Mandarin and Cantonese

CAREER HIGHLIGHTS:
 1992 Partner, co-founder of Worldwide Telecommunications Practice
 1994 appointed as Managing Partner, Hong Kong and elected a Director of the Asia Pacific Board

SPECIAL INTERESTS/HOBBIES: Chinese and Vietnamese history/Thomas Pynchon/fly fishing/skiing

GEOGRAPHIC SCOPE OF RECRUITING: Asia-Pacific

SECTOR/INDUSTRY SPECIALIZATION: Information Technology/Telecommunications including the Chief Information Officer function

FAVORITE HISTORICAL FIGURE/MODEL/MENTOR: General Vo Nguyen Giap

SINGLE MOST IMPORTANT ISSUE IN CONDUCTING A HIGH LEVEL SEARCH: Understanding your client

BIGGEST COMPETITOR: Alan Tsui

MOST SIGNIFICANT OTHER ASPECT OF PERSONAL OR PROFESSIONAL LIFE: Jet lag

JEAN-PIERRE GOUIRAND

Heidrick & Struggles
112 avenue Kléber
75116 Paris, France

Telephone: 33 1 44 34 17 40
Fax: 33 1 44 34 17 17
E-mail: jpg@h-s.com
Company Website: http://www.h-s.com

DATE OF BIRTH: October 1, 1943

NATIONALITY: French—Grew up in France

EDUCATIONAL BACKGROUND:
ESCP, MBA (George Washington University)

LANGUAGES SPOKEN: French, English, some Spanish

CAREER HIGHLIGHTS: Putting Heidrick & Struggles on the map in France (and to a lesser extent, in Europe).

SPECIAL INTERESTS/HOBBIES: Aerospace industry, golf, sailing

GEOGRAPHIC SCOPE OF RECRUITING: Europe/North America

SECTOR/INDUSTRY SPECIALIZATION: Industry (Practice Manager) + Retail

FAVORITE HISTORICAL FIGURE/MODEL/MENTOR: Spencer Stuart "Spence"

SINGLE MOST IMPORTANT ISSUE IN CONDUCTING A HIGH LEVEL SEARCH: Getting the client's time and attention to meet candidates

BIGGEST COMPETITOR: Egon Zehnder

MOST SIGNIFICANT OTHER ASPECT OF PERSONAL OR PROFESSIONAL LIFE: I consider myself lucky to have "bumped" into Executive Search, totally by chance, when I was 29! Probably it's the most exciting business one can be in today, but extraordinarily demanding, challenging, captivating. It's important not to lose one's head (I have seen many do that in ES!). A good family life, well-balanced is a key.

WHAT IS THE BEST PREPARATION FOR BEING A SUCCESSFUL RECRUITER? I consider recruiting as a profession, which trains its best operators internally. In H&S, the best consultants are those who were brought up from inside (in Europe).

WHAT WOULD YOU BE DOING IF YOU WERE NOT AN EXECUTIVE RECRUITER? I have always been doing search and cannot imagine doing anything else, so the question is difficult . . . probably International Marketing.

WHAT ARE THE CHARACTERISTICS OF A GREAT CLIENT? A client where you have a long-standing relationship: you can look back and see your mark on the business. A client who understands the power of executive search, knows how to use you as a consultant rather than a provider of "bodies."

WHAT CHALLENGES DO YOU SEE AHEAD IN THE GLOBAL MARKETPLACE? Internationalization of the "executive's body" still not completed. Disenchantment with large organizations which do not use and develop their people well, when expectations keep growing in that respect.

WILLIAM E. GOULD

Gould, McCoy & Chadick
300 Park Avenue, 20th Floor
New York, NY 10022
U.S.A.

Telephone: 1 (212) 688-8671
Fax: 1 (212) 308-4510
E-mail: wegould@gouldmccoychadick.com
Company Website: http://www.gouldmccoychadick.com

DATE OF BIRTH: October 23, 1932

NATIONALITY: American—Grew up in U.S.A.

EDUCATIONAL BACKGROUND:
Harvard Business School, M.B.A., with distinction, 1965
Williams College, B.A., 1957

LANGUAGES SPOKEN: English, German

CAREER HIGHLIGHTS: AESC Gardner M. Heidrick Award for Outstanding Contribution to the Profession. Past Chair of AESC. Listed among the top 5 general management recruiters in John Sibbald's *The New Career Makers*.

SPECIAL INTERESTS/HOBBIES: Skiing, fly fishing, hiking, sailing; traveling to new cultures

GEOGRAPHIC SCOPE OF RECRUITING: North and South America, Western and Eastern Europe, North Africa, Middle East, Asia

SECTOR/INDUSTRY SPECIALIZATION: Consumer packaged goods, healthcare, industrial, high-tech, Board, international general management

FAVORITE HISTORICAL FIGURE/MODEL/MENTOR: L. K. Sillcox, my godfather, who retired at age 100

SINGLE MOST IMPORTANT ISSUE IN CONDUCTING A HIGH LEVEL SEARCH: A well-executed, high-level executive search is a balance of many issues, including open, candid and honest dialogue between client, candidates, and the executive recruiter. If a candidate fails after joining a client, the reason is generally because of a poor cultural fit. It is critical that there be a free flow of information, feelings, and intuition among all parties to minimize the risk of a cultural mismatch.

BIGGEST COMPETITOR: Egon Zehnder, Heidrick & Struggles, Korn/Ferry, Spencer Stuart, Russell Reynolds

MOST SIGNIFICANT OTHER ASPECT OF PERSONAL OR PROFESSIONAL LIFE: My personal interests are many and private, all involving my wife, family and a global network of close friends and activities.

WHAT IS THE BEST PREPARATION FOR BEING A SUCCESSFUL RECRUITER? Business exposure to different cultural environments and a history of promotion/success in each company. Continual personal development and the recognition of a person with a point of view, the ability to work with a diverse group of people/cultures, and a curiosity of what makes organizations work. A comfort level with people, a reputation for integrity, openness, honesty in one's assessment of people are essential.

WHAT WOULD YOU BE DOING IF YOU WERE NOT AN EXECUTIVE RECRUITER? I am still fulfilled and enthusiastic about the profession and can not think of a business I would rather be in. If I were doing something else it would be entrepreneurial, service-oriented, global and helping/coaching executives.

WHAT ARE THE CHARACTERISTICS OF A GREAT CLIENT? One that treats you as an equal partner. Our best clients are the ones that bring us in to help define the search specification by interviewing the key inside executives who will report to this person and the person to whom this position will be reporting-a 360° assessment of the position.

WHAT CHALLENGES DO YOU SEE AHEAD IN THE GLOBAL MARKETPLACE? To stay abreast of rapid technology changes which can aid the search process. To recruit the brightest people for our firm, offer them a career track and continue our reputation for excellence, integrity and identifying the best quality candidates.

MINA GOURAN

Korn/Ferry International
252 Regent St.
London W1R 5DA

Telephone: 44 171 312 3100
Fax: 44 171 312 3130
E-mail: mina.gouran@kornferry.com
Company Website: http://www.kornferry.com

NATIONALITY: British—Grew up in U.K. & U.S.A.

EDUCATIONAL BACKGROUND:
BA Economics, DePauw University, U.S.A.
MBA

LANGUAGES SPOKEN: English, Farsi

CAREER HIGHLIGHTS: First female and youngest General Manager at British Airways with responsibility for systems software/PC applications/tech support.

SPECIAL INTERESTS/HOBBIES: Walking/music/theatre

GEOGRAPHIC SCOPE OF RECRUITING: Primarily Europe but increasingly searching worldwide

SECTOR/INDUSTRY SPECIALIZATION: IT/Telecoms

FAVORITE HISTORICAL FIGURE/MODEL/MENTOR: Alexander the Great/my mother

SINGLE MOST IMPORTANT ISSUE IN CONDUCTING A HIGH LEVEL SEARCH: High level networking. Next most important: focus, creativity, communication (proactive).

MOST SIGNIFICANT OTHER ASPECT OF PERSONAL OR PROFESSIONAL LIFE: Energy and enthusiasm

WHAT IS THE BEST PREPARATION FOR BEING A SUCCESSFUL RECRUITER? Business knowledge; good listening and communication skills.

WHAT WOULD YOU BE DOING IF YOU WERE NOT AN EXECUTIVE RECRUITER? Leading a medium sized business.

WHAT ARE THE CHARACTERISTICS OF A GREAT CLIENT? Communicates, involves you in the business.

WHAT CHALLENGES DO YOU SEE AHEAD IN THE GLOBAL MARKETPLACE? Increasing competition among employers for limited supply of truly international minded executives able to operate effectively across regions/the globe.

RODERICK C. GOW

LAI Ward Howell
200 Park Avenue, 31st Floor
New York, NY 10166
U.S.A.

Telephone: 1 (212) 973-7600
Fax: 1 (212) 867-3535
Company Website: http://www.laix.com

DATE OF BIRTH: September 9, 1947

NATIONALITY: British: Born and educated in United Kingdom
with extensive international travel.

EDUCATIONAL BACKGROUND:

Winchester College, Winchester, England
Trinity College, Cambridge University, England, M.A.

LANGUAGES SPOKEN: English; fluent French; slight familiarity with German

CAREER HIGHLIGHTS:

- BA, MA Trinity College, Cambridge University
- Search Consultant, Russell Reynolds Associates Inc. and GKR Group
- Managing Parner of LAI since 1995

SPECIAL INTERESTS/HOBBIES: Hunting (as well as heads), sailing, painting, music, reading, and walking

GEOGRAPHIC SCOPE OF RECRUITING: Global, with particular emphasis on senior level cross-border assignments

SECTOR/INDUSTRY SPECIALIZATION: Global Financial Services including Investment & Retail Banking, Investment Management and Insurance. Major multi-national cross-border senior level search.

FAVORITE HISTORICAL FIGURE/MODEL/MENTOR: Field Marshall Lord Wavell

SINGLE MOST IMPORTANT ISSUE IN CONDUCTING A HIGH LEVEL SEARCH: The clearest possible understanding of the client's requirements, the most detailed and rigorous examination of skills and talents available in the market, and absolute dedication to exceed the client's expectations in an effective and timely manner.

BIGGEST COMPETITOR: The challenge of technology!

MOST SIGNIFICANT OTHER ASPECT OF PERSONAL OR PROFESSIONAL LIFE: An interest in the impact of people on organizations has been a theme throughout my life, whether in the military as a junior officer and later instructor at the Royal Military Academy, Sandhurst or in banking both in the U.K. and U.S.A. with the need to look beyond the balance sheet and at the caliber of the management running a company.

In all cases, organizations and corporations are constantly being impacted by the talents and leadership of outstanding managers and also damaged by indifferent leadership or lack of vision.
searches

WHAT ARE THE CHARACTERISTICS OF A GREAT CLIENT? "The desire to hire" is often key. Frequently clients are not sure of exactly what they want and need to be helped by the consultant to reach the right sort of conclusion. Above all, a search is a partnership of the consultant and the client. Relationships are based on success. On many occasions where a chief executive or product head is recruited, the individual who is satisfied will turn to the consultant and his or her firm to assist in the subsequent building process. This is search work at its best.

JOIE A. GREGOR

Heidrick & Struggles
245 Park Avenue, Suite 4300
New York, NY 10167-0152
U.S.A.

Telephone: 1 (212) 551-0542
Fax: 1 (212) 867-3219
E-mail: jag@h-s.com
Company Website: http://www.h-s.com

DATE OF BIRTH: February 1950

NATIONALITY: American—Grew up in Loudonville, Ohio

EDUCATIONAL BACKGROUND:
B.A.-University of Colorado
M.A.-Case Western Reserve University
M.S.-Stanford University (IBM Sloan Fellow)

LANGUAGES SPOKEN: English

CAREER HIGHLIGHTS: 13 years IBM headquarters (product marketing, strategy, etc.) and field sales management roles

SPECIAL INTERESTS/HOBBIES: Golf, gardening, anthropology (paleoanthropology and primate behavior)

GEOGRAPHIC SCOPE OF RECRUITING: U.S. with emphasis on major global relationships

SECTOR/INDUSTRY SPECIALIZATION: Industrial and Information Technology

FAVORITE HISTORICAL FIGURE/MODEL/MENTOR:
- Role model—my father
- Mentor—J. Richard Young, former senior IBM executive

SINGLE MOST IMPORTANT ISSUE IN CONDUCTING A HIGH LEVEL SEARCH: Understanding the client's business strategy and culture

MOST SIGNIFICANT OTHER ASPECT OF PERSONAL OR PROFESSIONAL LIFE: Involved in a number of educational initiatives at the secondary school level-in particular math and science and curriculum reform

WHAT IS THE BEST PREPARATION FOR BEING A SUCCESSFUL RECRUITER? A combination of line and staff positions with one or more companies in one or more industries.

WHAT WOULD YOU BE DOING IF YOU WERE NOT AN EXECUTIVE RECRUITER? I cannot imagine doing anything else but executive search.

WHAT ARE THE CHARACTERISTICS OF A GREAT CLIENT? Open, honest, realistic and pragmatic.

WHAT CHALLENGES DO YOU SEE AHEAD IN THE GLOBAL MARKETPLACE? Finding senior executives who truly understand how to lead and manage in a global economy.

JOSEPH E. GRIESEDIECK, JR.

Spencer Stuart
525 Market Street, Suite 3700
San Francisco, CA 94105
U.S.A.

Telephone: 1 (415) 495-4141
Fax: 1 (415) 495-1908
Company Website: http://www.spencerstuart.com

DATE OF BIRTH: July 3, 1944

NATIONALITY: American—Grew up in St. Louis, Missouri

EDUCATIONAL BACKGROUND:
Brown University

LANGUAGES SPOKEN: English, Spanish

CAREER HIGHLIGHTS: Chief Executive Officer of Spencer Stuart. I have a special focus on senior management recruiting in consumer products and services, retail, telecommunications and for boards of directors. Associated with the Firm since 1985. With 19 years in the executive search field, I was a Senior Vice President and Managing Director of another major executive search firm prior to joining Spencer Stuart, establishing that firm's offices in San Francisco and the Silicon Valley.

Prior to entering the executive search profession in 1979, I was Group Vice President with Alexander & Baldwin, Inc., and spent 12 years with the Falstaff Brewing Corporation, concluding that tenure as President and Chief Operating Officer. I also served as a Director of the company.

SPECIAL INTERESTS/HOBBIES: Former formula race car driver

GEOGRAPHIC SCOPE OF RECRUITING: International

SECTOR/INDUSTRY SPECIALIZATION: Board Services, Consumer Goods & Services

SINGLE MOST IMPORTANT ISSUE IN CONDUCTING A HIGH LEVEL SEARCH: Client satisfaction

MOST SIGNIFICANT OTHER ASPECT OF PERSONAL OR PROFESSIONAL LIFE: 5 children and 2 grandchildren

WHAT IS THE BEST PREPARATION FOR BEING A SUCCESSFUL RECRUITER?
- Ideally, business experience at a level integral to that of the clients whom you are advising.
- Having dealt successfully with adversity during your professional life.
- to be decisive; able to exercise your convictions, yet able to be a good listener.

WHAT WOULD YOU BE DOING IF YOU WERE NOT AN EXECUTIVE RECRUITER? Running a company

WHAT ARE THE CHARACTERISTICS OF A GREAT CLIENT?
- Responsiveness
- Decisiveness
- Ability to work with the recruiter as a business partner, not a vendor
- Integrity

WHAT CHALLENGES DO YOU SEE AHEAD IN THE GLOBAL MARKETPLACE? The biggest challenge of the global executive search firm is to be able to meet client needs on a consistent basis in market.

ANDERS GULLIKSSON

Korn/Ferry International AB
Jakobsbergssgatan 7
S-111 44 Stockholm

Telephone: 46-8-611 50 15
Fax: 46-8-611 50 35
E-mail: anders.gulliksson@kornferry.com
Company Website: http://www.kornferry.com

DATE OF BIRTH: June 13, 1944

NATIONALITY: Swedish—Grew up in Kristhinehamn, Sweden

EDUCATIONAL BACKGROUND:
Master of Arts, Uppsala University, Uppsala, Sweden

LANGUAGES SPOKEN: Swedish (mother tongue), English

CAREER HIGHLIGHTS: President and owner-Tiger Rang AB, Uddevalla, Sweden

SPECIAL INTERESTS/HOBBIES: Art, classic music, tennis, soccer, and traveling

GEOGRAPHIC SCOPE OF RECRUITING: Scandinavia

SECTOR/INDUSTRY SPECIALIZATION: General Industry, Service, Consumer Goods

FAVORITE HISTORICAL FIGURE/MODEL/MENTOR: Dag Hammarsköld

SINGLE MOST IMPORTANT ISSUE IN CONDUCTING A HIGH LEVEL SEARCH: Match candidates' personalities to clients business culture.

MOST SIGNIFICANT OTHER ASPECT OF PERSONAL OR PROFESSIONAL LIFE: High quality in professional and private life.

WHAT IS THE BEST PREPARATION FOR BEING A SUCCESSFUL RECRUITER? To get a really deep understanding of the client's situation I believe you also need to have own experience from Line Manager positions. Before I joined the search business I worked as a General Manager during nine years. Experience from different types of businesses is very valuable.

WHAT WOULD YOU BE DOING IF YOU WERE NOT AN EXECUTIVE RECRUITER? General Manager for a fairly large company and board member of a couple of interesting companies.

WHAT ARE THE CHARACTERISTICS OF A GREAT CLIENT? I want to be proud of my clients. It's much easier if you can strongly recommend your candidates to join the client's firm. Clients who allow people to grow and offer them great challenges are my favorites. I'm lucky to have some very attractive clients.

WHAT CHALLENGES DO YOU SEE AHEAD IN THE GLOBAL MARKETPLACE? The different alternatives for recruiting will increase. Positioning will be more important. Korn/Ferry will become like a brand name with a broader range of services within recruitment.

AXEL HAMPE

Delta Management Consultants GmbH
Bavariaring 44
D-80336 Munchen
Germany

Telephone: 49-89-767071-0
Fax: 49-89-767071-90
E-mail: hampe.delta@t-online.de

DATE OF BIRTH: 07-12-44

NATIONALITY: German—Grew up in Essen in the Ruhr

EDUCATIONAL BACKGROUND:
  Studies in London and Cologne
  Degree in Business Administration

LANGUAGES SPOKEN: German, English, French, Italian

CAREER HIGHLIGHTS: Director Marketing and Sales worldwide for Blaupunkt/Bosch

SPECIAL INTERESTS/HOBBIES: Sailing, snowboarding, antiques

GEOGRAPHIC SCOPE OF RECRUITING: Germany (and worldwide through Hever Group)

SECTOR/INDUSTRY SPECIALIZATION: Automotive, high-tech

FAVORITE HISTORICAL FIGURE/MODEL/MENTOR: Lord Dahrendorf

SINGLE MOST IMPORTANT ISSUE IN CONDUCTING A HIGH LEVEL SEARCH: Put yourself in the shoes of your client and present only candidates you would hire yourself.

BIGGEST COMPETITOR: Amrop/Korn/Ferry

MOST SIGNIFICANT OTHER ASPECT OF PERSONAL OR PROFESSIONAL LIFE: Interesting people

WHAT IS THE BEST PREPARATION FOR BEING A SUCCESSFUL RECRUITER? A career in industry in different environments.

WHAT WOULD YOU BE DOING IF YOU WERE NOT AN EXECUTIVE RECRUITER? Marketing in consumer goods, sailing, and writing.

WHAT ARE THE CHARACTERISTICS OF A GREAT CLIENT?
  • Growing
  • Cooperative
  • Quick

WHAT CHALLENGES DO YOU SEE AHEAD IN THE GLOBAL MARKETPLACE?
  • Finding international talent
  • Coordinating decentralized clients

JOHN T. W. HAWKINS

Russell Reynolds Associates, Inc.
1700 Pennsylvania Avenue, NW,
Suite 850
Washington, DC 20006
\U.S.A.

200 Park Avenue
New York, NY 10166
\U.S.A.

Telephones: 1 (202) 628-2150
Fax: 1 (202) 331-9348
E-mail: jhawkins@russreyn.com
Company Website: http://www.russreyn.com

1 (212) 351-2000

DATE OF BIRTH: June 11, 1954

NATIONALITY: American—Grew up in U.S.A.

EDUCATIONAL BACKGROUND:
B.A., University of Virginia
MBA, Dartmouth/Tuck

LANGUAGES SPOKEN: English

CAREER HIGHLIGHTS: Global Practice Leader, Directors Practice (1997); RRA Health Care Sector Head (1993); RRA Managing Director (1992). Taking a company public (1987).

SPECIAL INTERESTS/HOBBIES: Squash, duck hunting, golf, Asia-Pacific

GEOGRAPHIC SCOPE OF RECRUITING: Global

SECTOR/INDUSTRY SPECIALIZATION: Board Directors-All Sectors; Pharmaceuticals; General Managers; CEOs, COOs-All Sectors.

SINGLE MOST IMPORTANT ISSUE IN CONDUCTING A HIGH LEVEL SEARCH: Knowing when to push hard and when not to.

MOST SIGNIFICANT OTHER ASPECT OF PERSONAL OR PROFESSIONAL LIFE: Raising my three young children (8, 10, 12).

WHAT IS THE BEST PREPARATION FOR BEING A SUCCESSFUL RECRUITER?
- Strong written and verbal communication skill building and attendance at a first-rate business school.
- Prior work experience at a senior (ideally board) level.

WHAT WOULD YOU BE DOING IF YOU WERE NOT AN EXECUTIVE RECRUITER? I would probably be a senior executive in a corporate setting.

WHAT ARE THE CHARACTERISTICS OF A GREAT CLIENT? A great client respects and appreciates the work I perform, views me as a partner, listens well and is coachable.

WHAT CHALLENGES DO YOU SEE AHEAD IN THE GLOBAL MARKETPLACE?
- Database management-IS integration
- Reconciling business practices (i.e., corporate governance)
- Cross cultural understanding

FRIEDBERT HERBOLD

Hofmann Herbold & Partner/Amrop International
Altkönigstrasse 8, D-61462 Koenigstein
Germany
Telephone: 49/61462/2905-0
Fax: 49/61462/2905-189

DATE OF BIRTH: March 6, 1939

NATIONALITY: German—Grew up in Heidelberg

EDUCATIONAL BACKGROUND:
Dipl. Volkswirt, University Heidelberg
MBA, University Geneva

LANGUAGES SPOKEN: German, English, French

CAREER HIGHLIGHTS: General Manager Marketing and Sales Europe

SPECIAL INTERESTS/HOBBIES: Golf and modern history

GEOGRAPHIC SCOPE OF RECRUITING: Europe, U.S.A.

SECTOR/INDUSTRY SPECIALIZATION: Automotive, Packaging, Industry

SINGLE MOST IMPORTANT ISSUE IN CONDUCTING A HIGH LEVEL SEARCH: Listening and market knowledge

BIGGEST COMPETITOR: Heidrick & Struggles

MOST SIGNIFICANT OTHER ASPECT OF PERSONAL OR PROFESSIONAL LIFE: Calmness

WHAT IS THE BEST PREPARATION FOR BEING A SUCCESSFUL RECRUITER? Experience

WHAT WOULD YOU BE DOING IF YOU WERE NOT AN EXECUTIVE RECRUITER? General Manager

WHAT ARE THE CHARACTERISTICS OF BEING A GREAT CLIENT? Good briefing and flexibility

WHAT CHALLENGES DO YOU SEE AHEAD IN THE GLOBAL MARKETPLACE? Globalization of Executive Search

HENRY G. HIGDON

Higdon Prince
230 Park Avenue, Suite 1455
New York, NY 10169
U.S.A.

Telephone: 1 (212) 986-4662
Fax: 1 (212) 986-5002
E-mail: Higprin@aol.com

DATE OF BIRTH: June 1, 1941

NATIONALITY: American—Grew up in U.S.A. (East Coast, Midwest, and West Coast)

EDUCATIONAL BACKGROUND:

1959, Phillips Academy, Andover, Massachusetts
1964, B.A. Degree, Yale University, New Haven, Connecticut

LANGUAGES SPOKEN: English and working knowledge of French

CAREER HIGHLIGHTS:

1992–present: Chairman, Higdon Prince Inc. (New York)
1986–1992   Chairman, Higdon, Joys & Mingle, Inc. (New York)
1971–1986:   Executive Vice President and Member of the Executive Committee, Russell Reynolds Associates (New York, Houston, and Los Angeles)

SPECIAL INTERESTS/HOBBIES: Sports-rugby, squash; church activities-Moderator of Stanwich Congregational Church, former Senior Deacon; alumni affairs-former President of the Alumni Association and Trustee of Phillips Academy, Chairman of 25th Year Reunion (Yale), President of Yale Football Association, current Member of the Board, Yale Football Association.

GEOGRAPHIC SCOPE OF RECRUITING: North America and Europe

SECTOR/INDUSTRY SPECIALIZATION: Financial services with major expertise in all aspects of global investment management

FAVORITE HISTORICAL FIGURE/MODEL/MENTOR: Winston Churchill, as an inspirational leader and savior of a great nation in a crucial period in history, and for his scholarship and great communication skills.

SINGLE MOST IMPORTANT ISSUE IN CONDUCTING A HIGH LEVEL SEARCH: Ability to establish trust and confidence with both the client and with prospective candidates.

BIGGEST COMPETITOR: Spencer Stuart Associates

MOST SIGNIFICANT OTHER ASPECT OF PERSONAL OR PROFESSIONAL LIFE:

- Attaining balance in my life; constant struggle to be a top professional as well as a good father, a good husband, and good Christian.
- Following the fortunes of two daughters who have attended and graduated from Yale, and a son who is currently a Senior at Harvard.

WHAT IS THE BEST PREPARATION FOR BEING A SUCCESSFUL RECRUITER? There is no best preparation for being a successful recruiter. I believe that personal instincts and characteristics are more important than any specific experience. I would say, however, that a fine educational background, followed by association with any organization or institution noted for the excellence of its people and reputation would be important. It is important to have been associated with or surrounded by bright, motivated and competent people who have been involved in an organization with extremely high standards. Thus, early experience in an outstanding organization, in any service industry, would be helpful.

WHAT WOULD YOU BE DOING IF YOU WERE NOT AN EXECUTIVE RECRUITER? A head football coach or an athletic director at a major university.

WHAT ARE THE CHARACTERISTICS OF A GREAT CLIENT? A great client is responsive, decisive, operates with a sense of urgency, and understands what it is to recruit candidates as opposed to interview applicants. A great client is a good listener, takes advice and counsel well, and is engaged in and committed to completing search assignments. Loyalty is important, as is the ability to offer a compliment when a job is well done and the willingness to offer constructive criticism.

WHAT CHALLENGES DO YOU SEE AHEAD IN THE GLOBAL MARKETPLACE? The two most obvious challenges will be technical enhancements to make businesses more efficient and economical, as well as the globalization of challenges as different geographies become even more interdependent. Individual strategic and problem-solving skills will become increasingly in demand, as big businesses figure out how to operate a virtually global company, i.e., with strategic alliances and joint ventures, as opposed to operating, manufacturing and selling in all global markets, on a totally integrated basis. The bottom line is that there will be tremendous educational challenges in the future to prepare bright, ambitious and motivated students for operating in a single complex world economy.

JONATHAN S. HOLMAN

The Holman Group, Inc.
1592 Union Street, #239
San Francisco, CA 94123
U.S.A.

Telephone: 1 (415) 751-2700
Fax: 1 (415) 751-4897
E-mail: Holmanjon@aol.com

DATE OF BIRTH: May 26, 1945

NATIONALITY: American—Grew up in U.S.A. and Puerto Rico

EDUCATIONAL BACKGROUND:
Princeton University, bachelor's degree, 1966
Stanford University Graduate School of Business, MBA, 1968

LANGUAGES SPOKEN: English, Spanish

CAREER HIGHLIGHTS: Pfizer, Inc. 1968–71-Personnel Director, Central Research Laboratories; E. & J. Gallo Winery, 1971–78-Director of Human Resources; Bacci, Bennett, Gould & McCoy, 1978–81-Partner; The Holman Group, Inc., 1981–present-Founder and President

GEOGRAPHIC SCOPE OF RECRUITING: Primarily U.S.A., though on behalf of companies worldwide

SECTOR/INDUSTRY SPECIALIZATION: Focused almost exclusively on Presidential level searches for the electronics and information technology industries, including hardware, software, instruments, information services, data and telecommunications, venture capital. Have completed over 200 searches at the CEO and COO levels, for companies ranging from start-ups to multi-billion dollars in revenues.

FAVORITE HISTORICAL FIGURE/MODEL/MENTOR:[DELETE ME]

SINGLE MOST IMPORTANT ISSUE IN CONDUCTING A HIGH LEVEL SEARCH: A deep understanding of the specifics of the client and the client's needs before the search begins. Even the greatest of executives are not generically qualified for all companies, so screening candidates without careful analysis of the client is impossible.

WHAT IS THE BEST PREPARATION FOR BEING A SUCCESSFUL EXECUTIVE RECRUITER? The very broadest possible education and a diversity of successful and unsuccessful business experiences. Executive recruiting is not rocket science. It rewards hard work, a genuine interest in organizations and people, a bent to research and a thick skin. Anything which produces these characteristics will help.

WHAT WOULD YOU BE DOING IF YOU WERE NOT AN EXECUTIVE RECRUITER? Previously I was a human resources executive, which is what I most likely still would be if I had not gone into executive recruiting. At this point, however, I would most likely become a teacher if I were to stop my business activities.

WHAT ARE THE CHARACTERISTICS OF A GREAT CLIENT? I once asked this question of a colleague, who said, "Enormous people needs and indifference to spending money." However, I disagree. Great clients understand why they are initiating a search and are absolutely candid with candidates and recruiters as to the nature of the organization, the reason for conducting the search and the realistic opportunity going forward for the individual hired.

WHAT CHALLENGES DO YOU SEE AHEAD IN THE GLOBAL MARKETPLACE? In the high technology industries in which I specialize, an almost unbelievable shortage of skilled management is by far the largest problem. The rate of formation of new companies has been so high that there simply are not enough knowledgeable executives to populate them. This will have a meaningful dampening effect on company performance.

LAWRENCE (LARRY) J. HOLMES

Columbia Consulting Group
20 South Charles Street
Baltimore, MD 21201
U.S.A.

Telephone: 1 (410) 385-2525
Fax: 1 (410) 385-0044
E-mail: email: ccgbal@erols.com
Company Website: In progress

DATE OF BIRTH: December 19, 1941

NATIONALITY: American—Grew up in Virginia, U.S.A.

EDUCATIONAL BACKGROUND:
B.S., Science, 1964, Old Dominion University.
Attended Drake University on Graduate Scholarship in Physics for one year.

LANGUAGES SPOKEN: English

CAREER HIGHLIGHTS:
- Engineering Management at Aetna Life & Casualty and Maryland Casualty
- Human Resource Management at American General and Sun Life Insurance

SPECIAL INTERESTS/HOBBIES: Sports & Family

GEOGRAPHIC SCOPE OF RECRUITING: North America/Mexico/U.K.

SECTOR/INDUSTRY SPECIALIZATION: Financial Services/Technology

FAVORITE HISTORICAL FIGURE/MODEL/MENTOR: Leonardo da Vinci

MOST SIGNIFICANT OTHER ASPECT OF PERSONAL OR PROFESSIONAL LIFE: Personally, having two children and six grandchildren who are healthy and productive. Professionally, the time spent (25 years) in the search profession and enjoying its significant aspects.

WHAT IS THE BEST PREPARATION FOR BEING A SUCCESSFUL RECRUITER? If preparation means "professional work experience," then I do not feel that any specific training makes the best recruiter; understanding people and negotiations are the critical factors. If preparation means "search preparation," then prior planning for marketing and execution of a search are the key success factors.

WHAT WOULD YOU BE DOING IF YOU WERE NOT AN EXECUTIVE RECRUITER? I would be a physics teacher and a coach or counselor. If I had known professionals when young, I would be a deal maker.

WHAT ARE THE CHARACTERISTICS OF A GREAT CLIENT? A client who is participative in all phases of a search, trusting of your judgment, and pays a full fee on a timely basis.

WHAT CHALLENGES DO YOU SEE AHEAD IN THE GLOBAL MARKETPLACE? The challenges in the global marketplace will be:
- Validating a successful track record of a candidate in a nonsimilar environment.
- Use of communication (teleconference, video conferencing, Internet, e-mail, etc.) to increase productivity, identification, and contact.

GEORGES L. HOLZBERGER

Highland Search Group, L.L.C.
565 Fifth Avenue, 22nd Floor
New York, NY 10017
U.S.A.

Telephone: 1 (212) 328-1108
Fax: 1 (212) 328-1197
E-mail: georges.holzberger@searchers.com
Company Website: http://www.searchers.com

DATE OF BIRTH: July 2, 1956

NATIONALITY: U.S.A. and France (dual citizen)—Grew up in Aruba (Netherlands Antilles) first 6 years, then New York City, upstate New York, U.K., France

EDUCATIONAL BACKGROUND:
Lycee Français de New York and Pawling High School (Pawling, NY)
A-Levels Eton College, Windsor Berks, U.K
B.A. from Williams College in 1978
M.B.A. from New York University in 1981

LANGUAGES SPOKEN: English, fluent French, very rusty German and Portuguese

CAREER HIGHLIGHTS: Started Highland Search Group 9/95 with two other partners, Steve Potter and Jim Phillips. We have grown to six partners and 35+ people in two years, largely focused on financial services. Formerly at Russell Reynolds Associates: in New York 1984, Hong Kong 1985, Singapore 1986, and on Wall Street since 1987.

SPECIAL INTERESTS/HOBBIES: My children and, time permitting, reading, exercise (tennis, scuba), movies, outdoors.

GEOGRAPHIC SCOPE OF RECRUITING: Largely U.S.A., some Europe, limited Asia for now

SECTOR/INDUSTRY SPECIALIZATION: Investment banking, structured finance, capital markets, derivatives, sales and trading in equity/fixed income/FX

FAVORITE HISTORICAL FIGURE/MODEL/MENTOR: My maternal grandfather, who is a renaissance man. At 94, he is a living "historical figure"!

SINGLE MOST IMPORTANT ISSUE IN CONDUCTING A HIGH LEVEL SEARCH: Closing the search by actually getting the successful candidate through the resignation process. On Wall Street, this has become more of a challenge in the case of top candidates. Firms are counter-offering aggressively.

BIGGEST COMPETITOR: Too many good ones to list. Hopefully, this book missed most of them!

MOST SIGNIFICANT OTHER ASPECT OF PERSONAL OR PROFESSIONAL LIFE: Personal: family. Professional: My credo—Do better work, with greater integrity, and have more fun while making more money than the other guys.

WHAT IS THE BEST PREPARATION FOR BEING A SUCCESSFUL RECRUITER? A good liberal arts education and the "school of hard knocks."

WHAT WOULD YOU BE DOING IF YOU WERE NOT AN EXECUTIVE RECRUITER? Getting more sleep.

WHAT ARE THE CHARACTERISTICS OF A GREAT CLIENT? A great client truly needs our services (isn't window-shopping); is a realistic and informed consumer of search services; is a collaborative (not secretive or confrontational) partner in the process; and pays bills on time!

WHAT CHALLENGES DO YOU SEE AHEAD IN THE GLOBAL MARKETPLACE? Competitors who are smarter, faster and more adept technologically than before. Ditto for clients.

W. MICHAEL M. HONEY

Ray & Berndtson
400, 400 - 5th Avenue S.W.
Calgary, Alberta, Canada T2P 0L6

Telephone: 1 (403) 269-3277-main number;
        1 (403) 215-2556-private line
Fax: 1 (403) 262-9347
E-mail: oh@prbcan.com
Company Website: http://www.prbcan.com

DATE OF BIRTH: February 9, 1941

NATIONALITY: Canadian and British—Grew up in Zambabwe

EDUCATIONAL BACKGROUND: Bachelor and Master of Arts degrees in Law from Cambridge University, England, as well as a Master of Business Administration degree from the University of Cape Town, South Africa. Also qualified as a Barrister at Law, Lincoln's Inn, London, England.

LANGUAGES SPOKEN: English

CAREER HIGHLIGHTS: Co-founder (in 1988) and partner of O'Callaghan Honey/Ray & Berndtson, Inc. Entered the executive search business in 1985 joining The Caldwell Partners in Calgary. Vice President, The Resource Service Group which held controlling ownership in an oil and gas company and companies providing helicopters and other services and products to the oilfield, mining, and other resource industries from 1972 to 1985. Senior executive positions with Alcan Canada Products Ltd. and Alcan Wire and Cable in Montreal and Toronto from 1966 to 1972.

SPECIAL INTERESTS/HOBBIES: Outdoors and outdoor sports. Hiking, fishing, shooting, tennis, photography.

GEOGRAPHIC SCOPE OF RECRUITING: Worldwide

SECTOR/INDUSTRY SPECIALIZATION: Energy industry, particularly exploration and production oil and gas executives, and energy professionals for the financial services industry.

FAVORITE HISTORICAL FIGURE/MODEL/MENTOR: Winston Churchill

SINGLE MOST IMPORTANT ISSUE IN CONDUCTING A HIGH LEVEL SEARCH: Personal involvement in sourcing and proactive approach of potential candidates. Avoiding the temptation of too much leverage using researchers and associates to interact with very senior executives.

MOST SIGNIFICANT OTHER ASPECT OF PERSONAL OR PROFESSIONAL LIFE: Wife and five children.

WHAT IS THE BEST PREPARATION FOR BEING A SUCCESSFUL RECRUITER? As broad a business background as possible with exposure to different functional areas, with some experience in marketing, sales or business development.

WHAT WOULD YOU BE DOING IF YOU WERE NOT AN EXECUTIVE RECRUITER? Managing my own mid-size energy service business of some kind.

WHAT ARE THE CHARACTERISTICS OF A GREAT CLIENT? A great client is a good listener who respects the view of the recruiter, is decisive, has good intuition in choosing between candidates, and is an attractive individual for whom to recruit candidates.

WHAT CHALLENGES DO YOU SEE AHEAD IN THE GLOBAL MARKETPLACE?
- Increased availability and accessibility to clients of information on potential candidates through the Internet and other electronic sources.
- Continuing strengthening of large powerful global search firms.

ROBERT H. HORTON

Horton International Inc.
420 Lexington Avenue, Suite 810
New York, NY 10170
U.S.A.

Telephone: 1 (212) 973-3780
Fax: 1 (212) 973-3798
E-mail: horton@horton-intl.com
Company Website: http://www.horton-intl.com

DATE OF BIRTH: September 22, 1932

NATIONALITY: American—Grew up in Washington

EDUCATIONAL BACKGROUND: B.A. degree in Economics and Business Administration, Whitman College, 1954

LANGUAGES SPOKEN: English

CAREER HIGHLIGHTS: Held senior management positions with Hughes Aircraft Company and United Technologies Corporation. Directed projects in Europe and South America involving satellite communications, radar and computer equipment manufacturing. Founded an executive search firm in 1978 and developed it to become one of the top 15 in the world.

SPECIAL INTERESTS/HOBBIES: Study of the international markets with emphasis on emerging markets/democracies. Primary interest in the analysis of socioeconomic factors which influence the evolution of strong economies.

GEOGRAPHIC SCOPE OF RECRUITING: Global

SECTOR/INDUSTRY SPECIALIZATION: Aerospace and Communications

SINGLE MOST IMPORTANT ISSUE IN CONDUCTING A HIGH LEVEL SEARCH: Understanding and ability to articulate the challenge of the client's need in a way and to a degree that stimulates and motivates the candidate to seriously consider the opportunity.

MOST SIGNIFICANT OTHER ASPECT OF PERSONAL OR PROFESSIONAL LIFE: To have developed an international consulting practice with offices in 30 plus countries that has had zero defections internationally or domestically over a 20 year period.

WHAT IS THE BEST PREPARATION FOR BEING A SUCCESSFUL RECRUITER? An industry or commercial background that involved solving technical or operating problems, at a senior level, under a variety of business/geographic conditions. Essentially all executive search assignments are concerned with curing some type of operating problem. To have solved similar problems enables the search professional to be a consultant in assisting the client in defining solutions and, more importantly, conveying the essence of the challenge to the candidate. It is the challenge that motivates the best candidates to consider joining the client.

WHAT WOULD YOU BE DOING IF YOU WERE NOT AN EXECUTIVE RECRUITER? Working with companies to solve operating problems with an owner's concern about profitability, customer satisfaction and growth.

WHAT ARE THE CHARACTERISTICS OFA GOOD CLIENT? A good sense of the key criteria for successful candidates, a corporate vision and culture that attracts good candidates, an interview and assessment process that is both professional and timely, and executive assimilation and career development procedures that promote retention.

WHAT CHALLENGES DO YOU SEE AHEAD IN THE GLOBAL MARKETPLACE? For clients: Expanded cross-cultural orientation and improved organizational development skills. For search firms: The trend towards globalization and outsourcing mandates that search firms must be able to understand cultural issues, assist the client in competency modeling, have skills and ability to integrate managers with varied cultural backgrounds and have the commitment and capacity to recruit at all levels.

DURANT A. (ANDY) HUNTER

Pendleton James Associates, Inc.
One International Place
Suite 2350
Boston, MA 02110
U.S.A.

Telephone: 1 (617) 261-9696
Fax: 1 (617) 261-9697
E-mail: PJAssoc@aol.com

DATE OF BIRTH: November 25, 1948

NATIONALITY: American—Grew up in Williamstown, Massachusetts

EDUCATIONAL BACKGROUND:

University of North Carolina, Chapel Hill, NC, AB, American studies, 1971
George Washington University, Washington, DC, MPA, public administration, 1973

LANGUAGES SPOKEN: English, French (not fluent)

CAREER HIGHLIGHTS: J.P. Morgan, James Hunter Machine Company, and Executive Search since 1985. President and CEO of Pendleton James.

SPECIAL INTERESTS/HOBBIES: Children's organizations, arts, golf, and skiing

GEOGRAPHIC SCOPE OF RECRUITING: Worldwide

SECTOR/INDUSTRY SPECIALIZATION: Financial Services, Private Equity, and Portfolio Companies

FAVORITE HISTORICAL FIGURE/MODEL/MENTOR: Abraham Lincoln

SINGLE MOST IMPORTANT ISSUE IN CONDUCTING A HIGH LEVEL SEARCH: Credibility with the client and candidates. Credibility is earned by expressing good judgment, discretion, professionalism, intelligence as well as by clear communications and a sense of urgency.

BIGGEST COMPETITOR: Big "name firms"

MOST SIGNIFICANT OTHER ASPECT OF PERSONAL OR PROFESSIONAL LIFE: Large family

WHAT IS THE BEST PREPARATION FOR BEING A SUCCESSFUL RECRUITER? It is a combination of being line manager who has hired people and one who has operated in a service/consulting business. Being able to put yourself in the client's shoes, yet having the listening skills and project orientation is very useful.

WHAT WOULD YOU BE DOING IF YOU WERE NOT AN EXECUTIVE RECRUITER? I would be either a private equity investor in companies or an equity portfolio manager. Both these professions require an understanding of people and you place "bets" on these people.

WHAT ARE THE CHARACTERISTICS OF A GREAT CLIENT? A great client has a successful business in an attractive location. They have unquestionable integrity and a sense of urgency. Finally, they pay their bills.

WHAT CHALLENGES DO YOU SEE AHEAD IN THE GLOBAL MARKETPLACE? The greatest challenge is to find real leaders, not just competent practitioners to plan and execute global plans. There is a shortage of people who are willing to step forward and accept the responsibilities and challenges.

THEODORE JADICK

Heidrick & Struggles, Inc.
245 Park Avenue
New York, NY 10167
U.S.A.

Telephone: 1 (212) 867-9876
Fax: 1 (212) 682-5430
E-mail: tnj@h-s.com
Company Website: http://www.h-s.com

DATE OF BIRTH: July 13, 1939

NATIONALITY: American—Grew up in Scranton, Pennsylvania, U.S.A.

EDUCATIONAL BACKGROUND: University of Scranton, B.S., 1961

LANGUAGES SPOKEN: English

CAREER HIGHLIGHTS: Arthur Young & Co., Haskins & Sells, CPA; Managing Partner, New York Office, Heidrick & Struggles; Former H&S Executive Committee Member; Current Member, H&S Management Committee; Managing Partner, North America Board of Directors Practice, H&S.

SPECIAL INTERESTS/HOBBIES: Tennis, golf, squash

GEOGRAPHIC SCOPE OF RECRUITING: Global

SECTOR/INDUSTRY SPECIALIZATION: Board of Directors, CEOs, CFOs

FAVORITE HISTORICAL FIGURE/MODEL/MENTOR: (role models) George Fisher, CEO, Kodak; Stan Gault, CEO, Goodyear; John L. Weinberg, Senior Chairman, Goldman, Sachs & Co.

SINGLE MOST IMPORTANT ISSUE IN CONDUCTING A HIGH LEVEL SEARCH: Integrity—with Board of Directors as well as senior level candidates, it is imperative that they believe in you and trust you with one of the most crucial decisions in their careers.

BIGGEST COMPETITOR: Spencer Stuart

MOST SIGNIFICANT OTHER ASPECT OF PERSONAL OR PROFESSIONAL LIFE: Health care and cancer care. Board of Directors, Calvary Hospital Fund, Bronx, New York—advanced cancer care facility

WHAT IS THE BEST PREPARATION FOR BEING A SUCCESSFUL RECRUITER? I believe the best preparation for a successful recruiter is to develop extraordinary people sensitivities, as we are dealing with clients and potential candidates at a stressful or even critical part of their lives. Keeping this in the forefront of our thinking throughout the entire search process is incredibly important to win and, more important, to maintain their confidence.

WHAT WOULD YOU BE DOING IF YOU WERE NOT AN EXECUTIVE RECRUITER? If I were not an executive recruiter, I would like to be a history teacher and an athletic coach at a prep school.

WHAT ARE THE CHARACTERISTICS OF A GREAT CLIENT? Characteristics of a great client include being totally open with his own and his organization's positives and negatives; strategic vision and focus as to where the organization is going; an impeccable value system; and the ability to articulate his or her vision and to rapidly win the respect and confidence of potential candidates.

WHAT CHALLENGES DO YOU SEE AHEAD IN THE GLOBAL MARKETPLACE? The challenges ahead in the global marketplace are to develop a state-of-the-art information capability on this business which is truly information division and data being gathered around the world by our professionals. Additionally, there would be a challenge to develop a global standard in recruiting analogous to standards developed by the accounting and legal professions.

ARTHUR JANTA-POLCZYNSKI

Russell Reynolds Associates
Boulevard Saint Michel 27
1040 Brussels
Belgium

Telephone: 32-3-743 1220
Fax: 32-2-736 1335
E-mail: arthurjanta@russreyn.com
Company Website: http://www.russreyn.com

DATE OF BIRTH: December 2, 1949

NATIONALITY: Belgian—Grew up in Belgium

EDUCATIONAL BACKGROUND:
  MBA, Harvard Business School (1978)
  Ingenieur Commercial, Ecole de Commerce Solvay (U.L.B.) (1972)

LANGUAGES SPOKEN: English, French, Dutch, Polish, German

CAREER HIGHLIGHTS: 15 years of search experience, 4 years in industry in general management functions

SPECIAL INTERESTS/HOBBIES: Modern art, poetry, golf

GEOGRAPHIC SCOPE OF RECRUITING: Europe

SECTOR/INDUSTRY SPECIALIZATION: Generalist

SINGLE MOST IMPORTANT ISSUE IN CONDUCTING A HIGH LEVEL SEARCH: Creative vision

MOST SIGNIFICANT OTHER ASPECT OF PERSONAL OR PROFESSIONAL LIFE: Have faith

WHAT IS THE BEST PREPARATION FOR BEING A SUCCESSFUL RECRUITER? A combination of experience acquired with a professional service firm (consulting, law, advertising) and of exposure gained as a corporate executive (preferably in line or general management).

WHAT WOULD YOU BE DOING IF YOU WERE NOT AN EXECUTIVE RECRUITER? Managing a business or running a corporation.

WHAT ARE THE CHARACTERISTICS OF A GREAT CLIENT? A great client has a long term vision for the position to be filled and can adapt his/her organization to be able to attract the best talent possible.

WHAT CHALLENGES DO YOU SEE AHEAD IN THE GLOBAL MARKETPLACE? For societies and economies the biggest challenge is to generate enough leaders capable of coping with the technological shifts, and the managerial and social issues linked with these shifts.

BJØRN JOHANSSON

Dr. Bjørn Johansson Associates Inc.
Utoquai 29
CH-8008 Zurich
Switzerland

Telephone: 41-1-262 02 20
Fax: 41-1-262 02 21
E-mail: BJA@BJA.ch
Company Website: http://www.BJA.ch

DATE OF BIRTH: October 15, 1947

NATIONALITY: Norwegian—Grew up in Kristiansand, Norway

EDUCATIONAL BACKGROUND:

1997	Harvard Business School, U.S.A., Owners President Program (OPM)
1978	University of St. Gallen, Switzerland, Dr.oec.HSG degree (Ph.D.)
1973–75	Postgraduate Studies in the U.S.A.
1973	University of St. Gallen, Switzerland, lic.oec.HSG degree (MBA)

LANGUAGES SPOKEN: Norwegian, German, English, Danish, Swedish

CAREER HIGHLIGHTS:

since 1993	Dr. Bjørn Johansson Associates Inc., Zurich
1991–93	President International, Paul Ray & Carré Orban International, Zurich
1985–91	Founding Country Manager Switzerland, Senior Officer and later Managing Director International Board Services, Korn/Ferry International, Zurich
1980–85	Vice President, Spencer Stuart Management Consultants, Zurich

SPECIAL INTERESTS/HOBBIES: People, business and economics, sports, traveling

GEOGRAPHIC SCOPE OF RECRUITING: Worldwide, with a main focus on Europe and North America

SECTOR/INDUSTRY SPECIALIZATION: Industry generalist, focusing on the national and transnational search of Presidents, CEOs and Board Members

FAVORITE HISTORICAL FIGURE/MODEL/MENTOR: Executive Search: Gerard R. Roche and Thomas J. Neff; Global Business Leaders: Percy Barnevik, Chairman ABB; Helmut Maucher, Chairman Nestlé; John F. Welch, Chairman General Electric Corp.; Political Leaders: Margaret Thatcher, Helmut Kohl, Gro Harlem Brundtland

SINGLE MOST IMPORTANT ISSUE IN CONDUCTING A HIGH LEVEL SEARCH: The search must be a complete process: understand my client's strategic need, take a global approach, apply creativity and "out of the box" solutions whenever possible, make sure that the placed top executive fulfills my client's expectations in creating shareholder value.

MOST SIGNIFICANT OTHER ASPECT OF PERSONAL OR PROFESSIONAL LIFE: Today, I have the freedom to determine the success of my own Firm, including turning down assignments whenever appropriate.

WHAT IS THE BEST PREPARATION FOR BEING A SUCCESSFUL RECRUITER? Curiosity and communication skills

WHAT WOULD YOU BE DOING IF YOU WERE NOT AN EXECUTIVE RECRUITER? Invent Executive Search

WHAT ARE THE CHARACTERISTICS OF BEING A GREAT CLIENT? Trust and confidence in my work

WHAT CHALLENGES DO YOU SEE AHEAD IN THE GLOBAL MARKETPLACE? How to overcome the increasing lack of real top global executives

HAROLD E. JOHNSON

LAI Ward Howell
200 Park Avenue
New York, NY 10166
U.S.A

Telephone: 1 (212) 973-7500
Fax: 1 (212) 297-9100
E-mail: Johnshar@lai.usa.com
Company Website: http://www.laix.com

DATE OF BIRTH: July 11, 1939

NATIONALITY: American—Grew up in Lincoln, Nebraska

EDUCATIONAL BACKGROUND:
B.S., Business Administration, University of Nebraska, Lincoln, Nebraska

LANGUAGES SPOKEN: English, some French

CAREER HIGHLIGHTS: 16 years as Head of Human Resources for three of America's largest corporations

SPECIAL INTERESTS/HOBBIES: Golf, theatre

GEOGRAPHIC SCOPE OF RECRUITING: Worldwide

SECTOR/INDUSTRY SPECIALIZATION: Human Resources and all other corporate functions

FAVORITE HISTORICAL FIGURE/MODEL/MENTOR: Churchill

SINGLE MOST IMPORTANT ISSUE IN CONDUCTING A HIGH LEVEL SEARCH: In addition to finding people who have a thorough understanding of the position and the tools to do it, the most important thing a headhunter needs to fully and completely understand is the culture and value system that exists in the client company. Ultimately, the skill mix is easy—but finding the people who have to lead or skillfully change an existing culture is paramount.

MOST SIGNIFICANT OTHER ASPECT OF PERSONAL OR PROFESSIONAL LIFE: I've been fortunate to have been surrounded by exceptional people with whom I've grown, and my business has flourished as, I am happy to say, has theirs.

WHAT IS THE BEST PREPARATION FOR BEING A SUCCESSFUL RECRUITER?
- Policy level experience in industry
- Head of HR of major company
- Conducted numerous searches as a client

WHAT WOULD YOU BE DOING IF YOU WERE NOT AN EXECUTIVE RECRUITER? I would still be in corporate life.

WHAT ARE THE CHARACTERISTICS OF A GREAT CLIENT?
- High standards-consistently
- Understands the search process

WHAT CHALLENGES DO YOU SEE AHEAD IN THE GLOBAL MARKETPLACE? The "demand for talent" will intensify.

JOHN F. JOHNSON

LAI Ward Howell
Key Tower, 127 Public Square
Cleveland, OH 44114-1216
U.S.A.

Telephone: 1 (216) 694-3000
Fax: 1 (216) 694-3052
E-mail: johnsjoh@lai.usa.com
Company Website: http://www.laix.com

DATE OF BIRTH: April 23, 1942

NATIONALITY: American—Grew up in Brooklyn, New York

EDUCATIONAL BACKGROUND:
Tufts University, B.A., economics, 1963
Columbia University, M.B.A., industrial relations, 1964

LANGUAGES SPOKEN: English/Finnish

CAREER HIGHLIGHTS: Leading Amrop International during a three years period of significant growth and development.

SPECIAL INTERESTS/HOBBIES: Wine collecting, big-game fishing, thoroughbred racing, golfing, and traveling.

GEOGRAPHIC SCOPE OF RECRUITING: Primarily North America. Globally through Amrop International.

SECTOR/INDUSTRY SPECIALIZATION: Automotive, metals, paper, rubber, plastics and consumer products focusing on board of directors, CEOs, Presidents, General Managers, CFOs and Human Resources Executives.

FAVORITE HISTORICAL FIGURE/MODEL/MENTOR: F. George Scott, my boss at General Electric, who taught me the value of patience.

SINGLE MOST IMPORTANT ISSUE IN CONDUCTING A HIGH LEVEL SEARCH: Total trust and honesty with clients and candidates. Only in an environment of complete openness can you make the right match.

BIGGEST COMPETITOR: The other top 10 search consultants in America.

MOST SIGNIFICANT OTHER ASPECT OF PERSONAL OR PROFESSIONAL LIFE: Having a wife, Jinny, who loves the search business as much as I do.

WHAT IS THE BEST PREPARATION FOR BEING A SUCCESSFUL RECRUITER? A successful recruiter needs raw intelligence to deal effectively with top management. You need to quickly understand their business problems and issues. Experience in dealing with senior management is essential. Consultants need to sense and understand the pressures at the top levels of business and need to have the courage of their convictions and the willingness to live by them.

WHAT WOULD YOU BE DOING IF YOU WERE NOT AN EXECUTIVE RECRUITER? If after 21 years of recruiting experience I were not recruiting, I would likely develop a consulting practice around organization strategy, design and executive counseling. I would focus on a client base of global US corporations where my international experience could bring value-added contribution.

WHAT ARE THE CHARACTERISTICS OF A GREAT CLIENT? A great client enters the search process as a partner to the consultant. This means the open and honest sharing of information, a sense of time urgency, and the establishment of search completion as a high priority. When these ideas are embraced, cycle times are dramatically reduced and the quality of the finalist candidates will be higher. In a recent search we were able to identify and recruit a million-dollar executive in a total time span of seventeen days.

WHAT CHALLENGES DO YOU SEE AHEAD IN THE GLOBAL MARKETPLACE? First, is global management-overseeing and coordinating operations that span continents. Second is global product development. Third is global training, marketing and manufacturing. Successful globalization requires considerable flexibility in product design and marketing to accommodate local tastes and needs that can't be so easily standardized. A close look at the most successful global corporate strategies reveals a careful balance in product development and marketing between worldwide standardization and local diversification. To compete in the global economy, companies will have to develop a coherent plan for recruiting and developing executives with global awareness and global reach.

DAVID S. JOYS

Heidrick & Struggles, Inc.
245 Park Avenue
New York, NY 10167-0152
U.S.A.

Telephone: 1 (212) 551-0507
Fax: 1 (212) 867-3254
E-mail: djs@h-s.com
Company Website: http://www.h-s.com

DATE OF BIRTH: July 17, 1943

NATIONALITY: American—Grew up in Wisconsin

EDUCATIONAL BACKGROUND:
B.A. (Economics & Psychology), 1965, Amherst College
M.B.A. (Finance & Marketing), 1967, Columbia University Graduate School of Business

LANGUAGES SPOKEN: English, French

CAREER HIGHLIGHTS: Ever expanding record of major CEO recruitments to organizations where new, high impact leadership has dramatically increased shareholder value.

1992–present	Partner, Director, and Member of Executive Committee, Heidrick & Struggles, Inc.
1986–1992	Founder and Managing Director, Higdon, Joys & Mingle, Inc.
1974–1986	Executive Vice President, Russell Reynolds Associates, Inc.
1972–1974	Vice President-Marketing Operations and Services, The Hertz Corporation
1967–1972	Assistant Vice President-General Sales, American Airlines, Inc.

SPECIAL INTERESTS/HOBBIES: Hunting/shooting; fly fishing; golf; squash; Impressionist and post-Impressionist art; antiques

GEOGRAPHIC SCOPE OF RECRUITING: North America, Europe, and Pacific Rim

SECTOR/INDUSTRY SPECIALIZATION: Consumer products and services, financial services, industrial products and services; Board of Director searches

FAVORITE HISTORICAL FIGURE/MODEL/MENTOR: Winston Churchill/Jack Welch/my father

SINGLE MOST IMPORTANT ISSUE IN CONDUCTING A HIGH LEVEL SEARCH: Seize leadership of the process and take full responsibility for its successful resolution.

BIGGEST COMPETITOR: Tom Neff (Spencer Stuart)

MOST SIGNIFICANT OTHER ASPECT OF PERSONAL OR PROFESSIONAL LIFE: Deriving personal and professional satisfaction from "making a difference" and "adding value" while retaining a sense of humor and balance in life. Married; two grown sons.

WHAT IS THE BEST PREPARATION FOR BEING A SUCCESSFUL RECRUITER? Strong business background and broad exposure to various industries . . . or to various sectors within an industry . . . depending on the degree of specialization desired. Experience in an environment characterized by commitment to quality, problem solving, client service, and relationship building.

WHAT WOULD YOU BE DOING IF YOU WERE NOT AN EXECUTIVE RECRUITER? I'd either be running a company which provides "business-to-business" services or I'd be in the financial services world as a senior M&A/LBO player.

WHAT ARE THE CHARACTERISTICS OF A GREAT CLIENT? A great client has:

- a well articulated vision and strategy
- a commitment to success
- high quality standards
- a commitment to extensive, objective communication and feedback
- the good judgment to trust my advice!

WHAT CHALLENGES DO YOU SEE AHEAD IN THE GLOBAL MARKETPLACE?

- Searches at the top are increasingly more global which taxes research resources and places a premium on global communications.
- Downsizing over more than a decade coupled with "Baby Boom demographics" has created a high-end executive supply/demand imbalance. The short-term positives for the search industry may well mask longer term performance/execution shortfalls.

DAVID KEITH

Boyden International Pte Ltd
7 Temasek Boulevard
#31-03 Suntec Tower One
Singapore 038987

Telephone: 65 3389119
Fax: 65 3387117
E-mail: search@boyden.com.sg
Company Website: http://www.yellowpages.com.sg

DATE OF BIRTH: 11-9-1937

NATIONALITY: British—Grew up in U.K.

EDUCATIONAL BACKGROUND:
U.K. public school, university college London, Columbia Graduate School of Business, NY

LANGUAGES SPOKEN: English, French, Malay/Indonesian

CAREER HIGHLIGHTS: Have worked in every country in the Asia Pacific Region

SPECIAL INTERESTS/HOBBIES: Golf, Asian antiques, trekking

GEOGRAPHIC SCOPE OF RECRUITING: Asia Pacific-focus on ASEAN

SECTOR/INDUSTRY SPECIALIZATION: Health care, FMCG, industrial

FAVORITE HISTORICAL FIGURE/MODEL/MENTOR: T. E. Lawrence

SINGLE MOST IMPORTANT ISSUE IN CONDUCTING A HIGH LEVEL SEARCH: Absolute discretion and confidentiality

BIGGEST COMPETITOR: Amrop

WHAT IS THE BEST PREPARATION FOR BEING A SUCCESSFUL RECRUITER?
- Extensive international work experience with MNCs
- Strong sales and marketing capabilities

WHAT WOULD YOU BE DOING IF YOU WERE NOT AN EXECUTIVE RECRUITER? Consulting on Asian market business development opportunities for MNCs

WHAT ARE THE CHARACTERISTICS OF A GREAT CLIENT?
- Realistic expectations
- An open minded attitude
- Patience
- A good understanding of the role of a search consultant

WHAT CHALLENGES DO YOU SEE AHEAD IN THE GLOBAL MARKETPLACE?
- Surviving the Asia Pacific region economic downturn
- Search practice specialization to meet client needs

EDWARD W. KELLEY

Korn/Ferry International
252 Regent Street
London W1R 5DA

Telephone: 44 171 312 3100
Fax: 44 171 312 3130
E-mail: Ed.Kelley@kornferry.com
Company Website: http://www.kornferry.com

[handwritten: no longer @ kornferry]

[handwritten: salary expectation financial services]

[handwritten: candidates - london @ kornferry.u.n]

DATE OF BIRTH: December 18, 1937

NATIONALITY: British/American—Grew up in Oregon, British Columbia, California

EDUCATIONAL BACKGROUND:

BA History, Masters Degree, University of Southern California
Concluded basic course work required for PhD concentrating on Finance and Organisation Development

LANGUAGES SPOKEN: English

CAREER HIGHLIGHTS: The turnaround of a number of companies and leading several significant acquisitions and joint venture agreements for clients. Planning the two Saudi industrial cities Jubail and Yanbu.

SPECIAL INTERESTS/HOBBIES: Skiing, tennis, photography, bicycling, hiking, travel, archaeology, anthropology

GEOGRAPHIC SCOPE OF RECRUITING: Globally

SECTOR/INDUSTRY SPECIALIZATION: Financial Services positions at CEO and Non-Executive level

SINGLE MOST IMPORTANT ISSUE IN CONDUCTING A HIGH LEVEL SEARCH: Lateral thinking

MOST SIGNIFICANT OTHER ASPECT OF PERSONAL OR PROFESSIONAL LIFE: Wife and family

WHAT IS THE BEST PREPARATION FOR BEING A SUCCESSFUL RECRUITER? Someone who has had a broad career background in several industries and functions, with more than one employer. Someone who is self-motivated and good at managing their own priorities, and has the ability to quickly understand the strengths and weaknesses of a company. They must have an embedded sense of quality and service, and interested in working with people.

WHAT WOULD YOU BE DOING IF YOU WERE NOT AN EXECUTIVE RECRUITER? Starting up my own business in a completely different field, not in a services industry.

WHAT ARE THE CHARACTERISTICS OF A GREAT CLIENT? Someone who takes personal ownership of the search and does not delegate it well down the organisation. A person who stays involved and is willing to be challenged and to challenge the consultant.

WHAT CHALLENGES DO YOU SEE AHEAD IN THE GLOBAL MARKETPLACE? I would predict a general consolidation in the search industry with only two or three real global firms surviving out of the present grouping. However, beyond that I think the real challenge is going to come from new entrants into the arena, most likely from technology-based companies. The ultimate threat here is not that one of the existing firms will get far ahead of the others, but that one or two new entrants (again likely technology-based) will knock all of the others out of the box.

ROGER M. KENNY

Boardroom Consultants/Kenny Kindler Tholke
530 Fifth Avenue
Suite 2100
New York, NY 10036
U.S.A.

Telephone: 1 (212) 328-0440
Fax: 1 (212) 328-0441
E-mail: boardroom@board-search.com
Company Website: under construction

DATE OF BIRTH: October 3, 1938

NATIONALITY: American—Grew up in New York City

EDUCATIONAL BACKGROUND:
New York University, MBA, 1961
Manhattan College, BBA, 1959

LANGUAGES SPOKEN: English

CAREER HIGHLIGHTS:
1982–Present Boardroom Consultants/Kenny Kindler Tholke-Managing Partner
1967–1982 SpencerStuart-Senior Vice President and Partner, Head of West Coast Operations, international liaison
1959–1967 Line management and planning positions in The Port of New York/New Jersey Authority

SPECIAL INTERESTS/HOBBIES: Hiking, scuba diving, historical novels

GEOGRAPHIC SCOPE OF RECRUITING: Americas, Europe, Far East/Middle East

SECTOR/INDUSTRY SPECIALIZATION: Sectors: Board Director, CEO Succession, CFO, Chief Marketing and Operating Officers

INDUSTRY SPECIALIZATION: Pharmaceutical/Healthcare, Heavy Manufacturing, Consumer, High Technology

FAVORITE HISTORICAL FIGURE/MODEL/MENTOR:
- Father: taught the importance of relationships and entrepreneurship
- Ronald Reagan: persisted in bringing down the Berlin Wall
- Benjamin Franklin: shared his passion for experimentation

SINGLE MOST IMPORTANT ISSUE IN CONDUCTING A HIGH LEVEL SEARCH: Respect of the board which helps manage the process.

BIGGEST COMPETITOR: The Top 4. We are the option.

MOST SIGNIFICANT OTHER ASPECT OF PERSONAL OR PROFESSIONAL LIFE: Successful marriage and partnership (truly a partnership).

WHAT IS THE BEST PREPARATION FOR BEING A SUCCESSFUL RECRUITER? Successful line management experience, perhaps, public service also.

WHAT WOULD YOU BE DOING IF YOU WERE NOT AN EXECUTIVE RECRUITER? Public service

WHAT ARE THE CHARACTERISTICS OF A GREAT CLIENT? Open communication, listens well, challenges candidates. Excited about the company's future.

WHAT CHALLENGES DO YOU SEE AHEAD IN THE GLOBAL MARKETPLACE? Euro-strategy, "sea change" since the rules have changed, being flexible and nimble, focus on growth and branding.

MICHAEL C. KIEFFER

The Kieffer Group
270 W. Diehl Road, Suite 100
Naperville, IL 60563
\U.S.A.

Telephone: 1 (630) 428-2500
Fax: 1 (630) 428-4050
E-mail: MikeK@TKG.com
Company Website: http://www.TKG.com

DATE OF BIRTH: December 23, 1942

NATIONALITY: U.S.A.-American—Grew up in U.S.A.

EDUCATIONAL BACKGROUND:
Masters in Management-Central Michigan Univ.
B.A. Liberal Arts/Philosophy-Marist College

LANGUAGES SPOKEN: English, Russian

CAREER HIGHLIGHTS: Building largest specialty firm in U.S. (Witt/Kieffer), before again starting own firm.

SPECIAL INTERESTS/HOBBIES: Golf, skiing, theater, teaching

GEOGRAPHIC SCOPE OF RECRUITING: U.S.A.

SECTOR/INDUSTRY SPECIALIZATION: Health Care

FAVORITE HISTORICAL FIGURE/MODEL/MENTOR: Churchill

SINGLE MOST IMPORTANT ISSUE IN CONDUCTING A HIGH LEVEL SEARCH: Fully understand the organization's complexity, tradition, personality and culture. Pro-actively and professionally challenge the client to modify aspects of the position which need to be exposed to attract superior talent.

MOST SIGNIFICANT OTHER ASPECT OF PERSONAL OR PROFESSIONAL LIFE: Taking the time to give something back: very active on volunteer boards and teaching in 4 colleges.

WHAT IS THE BEST PREPARATION FOR BEING A SUCCESSFUL RECRUITER?
- Liberal Arts undergrad degree
- Graduate degree in specialized area
- Leadership position in area of specialty prior to search career.

WHAT WOULD YOU BE DOING IF YOU WERE NOT AN EXECUTIVE RECRUITER?
- Teaching
- Consulting in one form or another

WHAT ARE THE CHARACTERISTICS OF A GREAT CLIENT?
- Open minded
- Willing to take advice
- Treat consultant as partner in the search vs. a hired hand.

RICHARD KING

Cordiner King Hever
Level 44, Rialto
525 Collins Street
Melbourne 3000
Victoria
Australia

Telephone: 61 3-9629 4862
Fax: 61 3-9614 6484
E-mail: ckhmelb@onaustralia.com.au
Company Website: We don't have our own website but
                information on the Hever Group can be obtained
                from http://www.sbpsearch.com

DATE OF BIRTH: August 21, 1938

NATIONALITY: Australian—Grew up in China, England, Australia

EDUCATIONAL BACKGROUND:
Melbourne University: Bachelor of Arts-BA
Bachelor of Laws-LLB
Master of Business Administration-MBA

LANGUAGES SPOKEN: English

CAREER HIGHLIGHTS: Working at board and senior management level in BHP. Being a founding partner of CKH. Helping with the appointment of several very successful CEOs.

SPECIAL INTERESTS/HOBBIES: Family, building, gardening, farming, current affairs and politics.

GEOGRAPHIC SCOPE OF RECRUITING: Worldwide if necessary, mainly Australasia and South-east Asia.

SECTOR/INDUSTRY SPECIALIZATION: We can still be generalists. I worked a lot in resources, higher education, manufacturing industry, public sector; 50 percent of my work is at CEO level.

FAVORITE HISTORICAL FIGURE/MODEL/MENTOR: Nelson Mandela, Capability Brown, Lord Denning, my father.

SINGLE MOST IMPORTANT ISSUE IN CONDUCTING A HIGH LEVEL SEARCH: Thoroughly understand the brief which includes the industry, the company, the role and the expectations of stakeholders. Identify appropriate people and develop their interest in a way which gives them confidence in our professionalism and integrity.

BIGGEST COMPETITOR: Probably Amrop in Australia

MOST SIGNIFICANT OTHER ASPECT OF PERSONAL OR PROFESSIONAL LIFE: Family

WHAT IS THE BEST PREPARATION FOR BEING A SUCCESSFUL RECRUITER? Being qualified in at least two academic disciplines; being broadly experienced by role, industry, geography and organizational size; having a real interest in people and business problems and developing an ability to listen.

WHAT WOULD YOU BE DOING IF YOU WERE NOT AN EXECUTIVE RECRUITER? I used to be a lawyer but having been in executive search for almost 20 years I'm now practically unemployable elsewhere. But it's likely I would be running my own business, probably in the building and construction industry.

WHAT ARE THE CHARACTERISTICS OF A GREAT CLIENT? Great clients are like great friends, they respect your professionalism and trust you implicitly. As a result, it is for them that you do your best work as you will go to any lengths not to let them down.

WHAT CHALLENGES DO YOU SEE AHEAD IN THE GLOBAL MARKETPLACE? I believe more things will remain the same than will be different. Executive searchers will need to master and use the new technologies for greater efficiency and better communication, but most of our business will remain nationally based and the expectations of clients will remain constant.

SCOTT E. KINGDOM

Korn/Ferry International
233 South Wacker Drive
Suite 3300
Chicago, IL 60606
U.S.A.

Telephone: (312) 526-0512
Fax: (312) 559-9026
E-mail: Kingdoms@kornferry.com
Company Website: http://www.kornferry.com

DATE OF BIRTH: June 6, 1959

NATIONALITY: American—Grew up in Minneapolis, Minnesota

EDUCATIONAL BACKGROUND:

University of Colorado, Boulder, Colorado, B.S., Finance

LANGUAGES SPOKEN: English

CAREER HIGHLIGHTS: Advanced from Senior Associate to Partner in Korn/Ferry in Syps. Elected Partner at age 33—youngest in the firm worldwide at time. Promoted to Managing Director of Chicago office at age 35—youngest such position holder worldwide at time. Member of North American Operating Group. Member of North American Finance Committee. Recently nominated to Korn/Ferry Board of Directors.

SPECIAL INTERESTS/HOBBIES: Mountaineering, golf, tennis

GEOGRAPHIC SCOPE OF RECRUITING: U.S. primary, experience in Mexico as well

SECTOR/INDUSTRY SPECIALIZATION: Consumer, Industrial, Technology—Functional Heads + COO, President

FAVORITE HISTORICAL FIGURE/MODEL/MENTOR: Robert Type Jones

SINGLE MOST IMPORTANT ISSUE IN CONDUCTING A HIGH LEVEL SEARCH: The trust between the consultant and the hiring client

MOST SIGNIFICANT OTHER ASPECT OF PERSONAL OR PROFESSIONAL LIFE: Personal: Married 14 years with 4 daughters

WHAT IS THE BEST PREPARATION FOR BEING A SUCCESSFUL RECRUITER? A broad variety of life and professional experiences. Deal orientation matched with relationship management, urgency, and compassion.

WHAT WOULD YOU BE DOING IF YOU WERE NOT AN EXECUTIVE RECRUITER? Financial/portfolio management

WHAT ARE THE CHARACTERISTICS OF A GREAT CLIENT? Clarity of purpose and thought. Consistency of message and desire to win.

WHAT CHALLENGES DO YOU SEE AHEAD IN THE GLOBAL MARKETPLACE? Harnessing of technology for productive use. Regionalism, efficient flow of expertise, resources, and information around the world.

BALDWIN H. KLEP

Heidrick & Struggles
Avenue Louise 81
1050 Brussels, Belgium

Telephone: 32-2-542-0750
Fax: 32-2-542-0752
E-mail: bhk@h-s.com
Company Website: http://www.h-s.com

DATE OF BIRTH: December 23, 1944

NATIONALITY: Dutch—Grew up in the Netherlands

EDUCATIONAL BACKGROUND:
Master in Law, University of Leyden; MBA, Columbia University, NY

LANGUAGES SPOKEN: Dutch, English, and French

CAREER HIGHLIGHTS:
- Brand management at Procter & Gamble, Canada;
- Marketing and sales management at Denby Ltd., U.S.A.;
- General management consulting at Theodore Barry & Associates in Los Angeles;
- Heidrick & Struggles (Los Angeles 1981-1985; Brussels 1985-present).

SPECIAL INTERESTS/HOBBIES: Spotting Euromanagers. Raising two daughters for the twenty-first century. Staying in shape through ice and roller skating, squash, tennis, and golf.

GEOGRAPHIC SCOPE OF RECRUITING: Western Europe

SECTOR/INDUSTRY SPECIALIZATION: Consumer goods, business-to-business services

FAVORITE HISTORICAL FIGURE/MODEL/MENTOR: Napoleon, the consummate European change maker

SINGLE MOST IMPORTANT ISSUE IN CONDUCTING A HIGH LEVEL SEARCH: One must select cross-border specialists who add value by creating the right balance between a European or global strategy and local initiative; and communicate well with the client on progress and problems throughout the search.

BIGGEST COMPETITOR: Euro-pessimism

MOST SIGNIFICANT OTHER ASPECT OF PERSONAL OR PROFESSIONAL LIFE: Bi-continental background offers a cultural bridge between American clients and Europe; author on Euromanagers in several international publications.

WHAT IS THE BEST PREPARATION FOR BEING A SUCCESSFUL RECRUITER? The key is to have a thorough understanding of the client sector through hands-on experience. Other requirements are a genuine interest in people and in organizational dynamics. A successful international recruiter must have studied and/or worked outside of the home country to have gained objectivity on own culture and country, and to understand the subtleties of cross-cultural interaction.

WHAT WOULD YOU BE DOING IF YOU WERE NOT AN EXECUTIVE RECRUITER? I would try to become one.

WHAT ARE THE CHARACTERISTICS OF A GREAT CLIENT? A great client will be decisive, receptive and communicative. A great client will articulate the added value expected from candidates, encourage participation by other client executives in the profile defining exercise, give clear feedback after candidate interviews, be accessible for ongoing communication and for candidate interviewing, and be open-minded about "wild card" candidates.

WHAT CHALLENGES DO YOU SEE AHEAD IN THE GLOBAL MARKET PLACE? My key concern is how executives can physically live up to the challenge of work in global line positions and mentally stay sane in global matrix structures.

KANG-SHIK KOH

Ward Howell International-Seoul
Suite 3501 Korea World Trade Center 159
Samsung-dong, Kangnam-ku, Seoul, Korea

Telephone: 82 2 551 0367 Direct
Fax: 82 2 551 0071 Direct
E-mail: tbcs@nuri.net
      kangshik@unitel.co.kr
Company Website: http://www.headhunter.co.kr

DATE OF BIRTH: July 27, 1953

NATIONALITY: Korean—Grew up in Korea

EDUCATIONAL BACKGROUND:
- B.A. in English Language & Literature, Hankuk University of Foreign Studies, Seoul, Korea
- MBA in Graduate School of International Business of the same univ.
- Government registered management consultant

LANGUAGES SPOKEN: English/Spanish

CAREER HIGHLIGHTS:
- Founded Ward Howell International, Seoul in 1987
- General Manager of Swedish-American joint venture company
- Manager of local commercial bank

SPECIAL INTERESTS/HOBBIES: Pop and classic music, golf, skiing, photographing

GEOGRAPHIC SCOPE OF RECRUITING: Mostly South Korea (Asia sometimes)

SECTOR/INDUSTRY SPECIALIZATION: Semiconductor, Finance, Automotive, Electronics, Telecommunication

FAVORITE HISTORICAL FIGURE/MODEL/MENTOR: Mandela, Martin Luther King

SINGLE MOST IMPORTANT ISSUE IN CONDUCTING A HIGH LEVEL SEARCH: Problems include a frequent lack of multi-national company culture exposure on the candidate side, job security, and the fee structure for Korean companies.

MOST SIGNIFICANT OTHER ASPECT OF PERSONAL OR PROFESSIONAL LIFE: Difficulty in securing professional consultant and researcher due to emerging market

WHAT IS THE BEST PREPARATION FOR BEING A SUCCESSFUL RECRUITER? One must have integrity to gain respect and trust, consistent lifetime self-education for industry knowledge, multi-lingual skills, and sociable and dynamic character.

WHAT WOULD YOU BE DOING IF YOU WERE NOT AN EXECUTIVE RECRUITER? Diplomat or Business leader (entrepreneur or CEO)

WHAT ARE THE CHARACTERISTICS OF A GREAT CLIENT? A great client has good "vision" and management philosophy, a "people first" policy and long-term career, a development and training program, and significant investment on research and development for new product launching.

WHAT CHALLENGES DO YOU SEE AHEAD IN THE GLOBAL MARKETPLACE?
- Search technology innovation through global telecommunication technology advancement
- Increasing demand for global manager to cover the worldwide market
- Mergers and acquisitions among big search firms and small boutique shops

PASI KOIVUSAARI

Boyden International
Eteläranta 4 B
FIN-00130 Helsinki
Finland

Telephone: 358 9 622 6860
Fax: 358 9 6626 8666
E-mail: pasi.koivusaari@boyden.inet.fi
Company Website: http://www.boyden.fi

DATE OF BIRTH: December 17, 1953

NATIONALITY: Finnish—Grew up in Finland

EDUCATIONAL BACKGROUND:
Graduate from Marketing Institute, Finland, 1976
B.Sc. (Econ.), University of Uppsala, Sweden, 1978
Leadership Academy, Finland, 1990–1991
The Boyden Kellogg Advanced Consulting Program, Northwestern University, Evanston, IL, U.S.A., 1997–98

LANGUAGES SPOKEN: Finnish, English, Swedish, (German)

CAREER HIGHLIGHTS: Over 15 years in the business. Assisted in finding the management team for an international Fortune 500 company in Finland, which has grown from a 50 million to 700 million FIM business in a few years.

SPECIAL INTERESTS/HOBBIES: New technologies, photography, literature, music, cycling

GEOGRAPHIC SCOPE OF RECRUITING: Finland, Scandinavia, Europe, Southeast Asia/Pacific, Russia

SECTOR/INDUSTRY SPECIALIZATION: IT/telecom, finance, services, pharmaceuticals

FAVORITE HISTORICAL FIGURE/MODEL/MENTOR: Moses, Churchill, Mannerheim

SINGLE MOST IMPORTANT ISSUE IN CONDUCTING A HIGH LEVEL SEARCH: Thoroughly discussed, thoughtful and written job description (assignment analysis). If this analysis is not right, the search will go wrong.

MOST SIGNIFICANT OTHER ASPECT OF PERSONAL OR PROFESSIONAL LIFE: Lovely wife Anneli, two active and nice children.

WHAT IS THE BEST PREPARATION FOR BEING A SUCCESSFUL RECRUITER? Networking skills are essential. You have to be able to create connections to companies to get assignments and to business community to get candidates. The best preparation is to create the network in some specific business (finance, pharmaceuticals, etc.) by working in the field. This experience is important also to get a view on the organizational behaviour. It is almost a must to have an academical degree from a good university. However, the experience does not have to be from the human resources development sector.

WHAT WOULD YOU BE DOING IF YOU WERE NOT AN EXECUTIVE RECRUITER? I would be (and was) an executive in the IT business. In my dreams, I would like to be a nature photographer or a freelance writer.

WHAT ARE THE CHARACTERISTICS OF A GREAT CLIENT? The great client is the one for whom you are working as a trusted advisor and discussing all kinds of businesses and even personal problems which are not only connected to the searches. Both parties gain more from this kind of relationship.

WHAT CHALLENGES DO YOU SEE AHEAD IN THE GLOBAL MARKETPLACE? The complexity of the problems in executive search is ever growing. This causes a growing global information flow. The challenge is to keep pace by continuously making the process of executive search and information handling faster and more efficient and offering better and better quality to the customers.

R. PAUL KORS

Kors Montgomery International/cFour Partners
1980 Post Oak Boulevard
Suite 2280
Houston, TX 77056
U.S.A.

Telephone: 1 (713) 840-7101
Fax: 1 (713) 840-7260
E-mail: pkors@cfour.com
Company Website: http://www.cfour.com

DATE OF BIRTH: June 12, 1935

NATIONALITY: American—Grew up in Pontiac, Michigan

EDUCATIONAL BACKGROUND:
BBA, University of Michigan, 1958
MBA, University of Southern California, 1965

LANGUAGES SPOKEN: English, Spanish

CAREER HIGHLIGHTS: Every search where the final candidate has made an important difference the client.

SPECIAL INTERESTS/HOBBIES: Skiing, mountain climbing, reading

GEOGRAPHIC SCOPE OF RECRUITING: Global: Half of assignments have an international content.

SECTOR/INDUSTRY SPECIALIZATION: Energy & Technology

FAVORITE HISTORICAL FIGURE/MODEL/MENTOR: Theodore Roosevelt. The story of Teddy Roosevelt transmogrifying from a sickly asthmatic to a high energy outdoorsman, scientist, statesman and eventually the youngest President of the United States was the single most important influence on my life during the formative period of my early teens.

SINGLE MOST IMPORTANT ISSUE IN CONDUCTING A HIGH LEVEL SEARCH: Gaining a thorough understanding of what the client needs and what will be required of the person who fills the position and then translating that into an effective search strategy.

BIGGEST COMPETITOR: Spencer Stuart

MOST SIGNIFICANT OTHER ASPECT OF PERSONAL OR PROFESSIONAL LIFE: Family vacations with my wife and two daughters

WHAT IS THE BEST PREPARATION FOR BEING A SUCCESSFUL RECRUITER? Have the toughest boss in the world in your first position after graduating from college. Survival and eventual triumph with such a leader will begin the process of building the discipline and the sense of mission required to be a high achiever in executive search. Ideally, four to five years in such a role would be followed by two years at the best graduate business school available to you. Your first position as an MBA is most important. Look for a thriving company that is about to undergo a growth spurt. After that, plan on changing employers at least once or twice. Find positions where you and/or your team can be gamebreakers. Enter the executive search field between ages 35-40 with 10-12 years business experience. Find a position working directly for one of the leaders in the search field. Success in this role will provide you with essential paradigms that will enable you to chart your own destiny in the world of executive search.

WHAT WOULD YOU BE DOING IF YOU WERE NOT AN EXECUTIVE RECRUITER? A film producer. Success in feature movie production requires the same skills and abilities as those for a successful executive recruiter. First, you have to enjoy completing difficult projects in a timely manner. Second, you need to be able to deal effectively with dynamic and authoritative people. Third, you must have some strong creative skills. Fourth, you must like managing projects that have a public scorecard. Fifth, and most important, success in film production like achievement in executive recruiting will come only to those who know how to handle their failures.

WHAT ARE THE CHARACTERISTICS OF A GREAT CLIENT?

- Tracks placements and ranks executive recruiters according to how well final candidates perform in their new position.
- Looks for recruiter to provide a coherent but flexible strategy prior to initiating the search and then works with the recruiter to execute the strategy.
- Makes their own choice of the finalist but looks to the recruiter for input and recommendations.

WHAT CHALLENGES DO YOU SEE AHEAD IN THE GLOBAL MARKETPLACE? The biggest challenge facing the global economy is to somehow reverse the widening gap between industrialized nations and countries at the bottom of the economic ladder. These third world countries have wealthy residents. However, the vast majority of their investment capital has been expatriated offshore. The only glimmer of hope for these countries and ultimately for the global market is the development of thriving free-market economies that are sufficient to reverse the flow of capital back into the poorer nations.

MELANIE KUSIN

Heidrick & Struggles
245 Park Avenue
New York, NY 10167
U.S.A.

Telephone: 1 (212) 551-0559
Fax: 1 (212) 370-9035
E-mail: mbk@h-s.com
Company Website: http://www.h-s.com

NATIONALITY: American—Grew up in Texarkana, Texas

EDUCATIONAL BACKGROUND:
Sophie Newcomb College (Tulane University) (BA English Literature)
Tulane University Graduate School of Business (MBA Marketing and Finance)

LANGUAGES SPOKEN: English only

CAREER HIGHLIGHTS:
Getting relevant grounding for recruiting at Oglivy and Mather in account management
Leading the first Ben & Jerry's CEO search
Joining Heidrick & Struggles from Russell Reynolds

SPECIAL INTERESTS/HOBBIES: Skiing, cooking, adventure vacations

GEOGRAPHIC SCOPE OF RECRUITING: Global

SECTOR/INDUSTRY SPECIALIZATION: Retail/fashion/fast food/trend-oriented consumer products & services

FAVORITE HISTORICAL FIGURE/MODEL/MENTOR: Eleanor Roosevelt for her dedication, energy and independence. Virginia Woolf for living an unconventional life.

SINGLE MOST IMPORTANT ISSUE IN CONDUCTING A HIGH LEVEL SEARCH: Focusing Board (or key decision-makers) on capability of candidate relative to critical issues facing a company. Often image of candidate is weighted more than candidate's skills as understood through in-depth references.

MOST SIGNIFICANT OTHER ASPECT OF PERSONAL OR PROFESSIONAL LIFE: Finding renewal each day in my life with my daughter and my husband.

WHAT IS THE BEST PREPARATION FOR BEING A SUCCESSFUL RECRUITER? Best background is any field that tests one's accountability, decisiveness, intuition, intellect, energy and communication skills. Other important characteristics are being a voracious reader of the business press, a natural listener, and reputation as a player in markets one serves.

WHAT WOULD YOU BE DOING IF YOU WERE NOT AN EXECUTIVE RECRUITER? Running another service business.

WHAT ARE THE CHARACTERISTICS OF A GREAT CLIENT? Same as that of a great recruiter: smart, intuitive, supportive, courageous, imaginative, open, decisive.

WHAT CHALLENGES DO YOU SEE AHEAD IN THE GLOBAL MARKETPLACE? Investment in creating leaders: putting priority behind shaping the work environment properly to build best products, processes, people.

MARC G. LAMY

Boyden Global Executive Search
1, Rond Point des Champs Elysées
75008 Paris
France

Telephone: 33 1 44 13 67 00
Fax: 33 1 44 13 67 13
E-mail: 101737.2424@compuserve.com
Company Website: http://www.boyden.fi

DATE OF BIRTH: October 31, 1945

NATIONALITY: French—Grew up in France and U.S.A.

EDUCATIONAL BACKGROUND:

ESCAE-Rouen (French Business School) (June 1970)
MBA-Columbia University (May 1973)

LANGUAGES SPOKEN: Fluent English, fluent French, good Italian, average Spanish

CAREER HIGHLIGHTS:

10 years in banking (8 years in U.S.A.)
14 years in Executive Search (ex Korn/Ferry, ex Heidrick & Struggles); currently Managing Director

SPECIAL INTERESTS/HOBBIES: Human beings in general, my family in particular; collecting banks' umbrellas

GEOGRAPHIC SCOPE OF RECRUITING: Europe

SECTOR/INDUSTRY SPECIALIZATION: Financial Services, CEO and Board Directors, Banking

FAVORITE HISTORICAL FIGURE/MODEL/MENTOR: De Gaulle (since he has combined brain, guts, and . . . heart)

SINGLE MOST IMPORTANT ISSUE IN CONDUCTING A HIGH LEVEL SEARCH: Building trust with candidates and clients. Confidentiality and total dedication to complete. Never take anything for granted. Be serious without taking yourself seriously. Strong overall belief that only best people can be vectors of progress.

MOST SIGNIFICANT OTHER ASPECT OF PERSONAL OR PROFESSIONAL LIFE: The support of an understanding family with whom I share joys and difficulties, good days and bad days, ambitions and doubts. The privilege to be associated daily with a group of outstanding people whom I have recruited for their high ethics and desire to have fun and pursue happiness through a challenging and exciting business life.

WHAT IS THE BEST PREPARATION FOR BEING A SUCCESSFUL RECRUITER? Experience, skills and passion. Experience should include a previous meaningful corporate experience with management responsibilities to understand business and problem solving. Skills are acquired through years and a genuine interest in bringing opportunities to other human beings. Recruiters are like doctors: without passion they cannot be successful.

WHAT WOULD YOU BE DOING IF YOU WERE NOT AN EXECUTIVE RECRUITER? A medical doctor or a priest (or rather a minister because they can get married and have children!)

WHAT ARE THE CHARACTERISTICS OF A GREAT CLIENT? A charismatic leader that has a vision, an ambition and a drive to achieve something big—humanity and a sense of purpose for the benefit of mankind.

WHAT CHALLENGES DO YOU SEE AHEAD IN THE GLOBAL MARKETPLACE? Being global means more complexity and more knowledge to master and integrate in order to make decisions. The best leaders will have to rely more on consensus and team work to collect information and benefit from others' input. Global corporations will need stronger shared values, vision and culture to operate successfully on a worldwide basis.

RICHARD S. LANNAMANN

Russell Reynolds Associates, Inc.
200 Park Avenue
New York, NY 10166
U.S.A.

Telephone: 1 (212) 351-2028
Fax: 1 (212) 370-0896
E-mail: RLANNAMANN@russreyn.com
Company Website: http://www.russreyn.com

DATE OF BIRTH: September 4, 1947

NATIONALITY: American—Grew up in Cincinnati, Ohio

EDUCATIONAL BACKGROUND:
A.B. Economics, Yale University (1969)
M.B.A., Harvard Business School (1973)
Chartered Financial Analyst (1978)

LANGUAGES SPOKEN: English

CAREER HIGHLIGHTS: Joined RRA in 1978; earlier experience as a research analyst and portfolio manager at Smith Barney and U.S. Trust

SPECIAL INTERESTS/HOBBIES: Music, architecture, philanthropy

GEOGRAPHIC SCOPE OF RECRUITING: Worldwide

SECTOR/INDUSTRY SPECIALIZATION: Investment Management

FAVORITE HISTORICAL FIGURE/MODEL/MENTOR: Thomas Jefferson

SINGLE MOST IMPORTANT ISSUE IN CONDUCTING A HIGH LEVEL SEARCH: Identifying and attracting the best candidate

MOST SIGNIFICANT OTHER ASPECT OF PERSONAL OR PROFESSIONAL LIFE: My family and my colleagues

BENGT LEJSVED

Heidrick & Struggles
Kungsgatan 32
S-11135 Stockholm
Sweden

Telephone: 46-8-4021900
Fax: 46-8-4021919
E-mail: ble@h-s.com
Company Website: http://www.h-s.com

DATE OF BIRTH: December 17, 1944

NATIONALITY: Swede—Grew up in Sweden

EDUCATIONAL BACKGROUND:
College-Joint Defence Military Academy-University degree (BA) Human Behaviour

LANGUAGES SPOKEN: English

CAREER HIGHLIGHTS: Built a strong Nordic Region with offices in all four countries

SPECIAL INTERESTS/HOBBIES: History, old cultures, opera

GEOGRAPHIC SCOPE OF RECRUITING: Scandinavia and Northern Europe

SECTOR/INDUSTRY SPECIALIZATION: Industry and Boards

SINGLE MOST IMPORTANT ISSUE IN CONDUCTING A HIGH LEVEL SEARCH: Understanding of clients need and open, honest frequent communication

WHAT IS THE BEST PREPARATION FOR BEING A SUCCESSFUL RECRUITER? Result and service oriented in a nice balance. Interested in learning the business and not only maximize compensation.

WHAT WOULD YOU BE DOING IF YOU WERE NOT AN EXECUTIVE RECRUITER? Line manager-CEO

WHAT CHALLENGES DO YOU SEE AHEAD IN THE GLOBAL MARKETPLACE? More and more globalization of management teams and boards

BRIGITTE LEMERCIER-SALTIEL

Russell Reynolds Associates
7, place Vendôme
75007 Paris
France

Telephone: 33-1-01 49 26 13 10
Fax: 33-1-01 42 60 03 85
E-mail: blemercier-saltiel@russreyn.com
Company Website: http://www.russreyn.com

DATE OF BIRTH: March 10, 1951

NATIONALITY: French—Grew up in France, U.S.A., Vietnam

EDUCATIONAL BACKGROUND:
- Degree from the French Political Science School
- Degree in Communication from the Institut Français de Presse

LANGUAGES SPOKEN: French, English, Spanish

CAREER HIGHLIGHTS:

1988 to date	Country Manager for France
1992-1997	Chairperson for the Professional Development Committee
1993-1995	Member of the Executive Committee
1997-2000	Member of the Executive Committee

SPECIAL INTERESTS/HOBBIES: Contemporary art, Opera, Yoga

GEOGRAPHIC SCOPE OF RECRUITING: International

SECTOR/INDUSTRY SPECIALIZATION: Financial Services-French CEOs and COOs

SINGLE MOST IMPORTANT ISSUE IN CONDUCTING A HIGH LEVEL SEARCH: Trust, courage

MOST SIGNIFICANT OTHER ASPECT OF PERSONAL OR PROFESSIONAL LIFE: Married, two children

WHAT IS THE BEST PREPARATION FOR BEING A SUCCESSFUL RECRUITER? Have a good mentor

WHAT WOULD YOU BE DOING IF YOU WERE NOT AN EXECUTIVE RECRUITER? Managing a service company or a cultural foundation

WHAT ARE THE CHARACTERISTICS OF A GREAT CLIENT? Transparent communication and trust

WHAT CHALLENGES DO YOU SEE AHEAD IN THE GLOBAL MARKETPLACE? Building and keeping relationships

KARL-GUNNAR LINDQUIST

Boyden
Kungsgatan 4 A,
S-111 43 Stockholm
Sweden

Telephone: 46 8 440 41 80, +46 8 440 41 81 (dir.)
Fax: 46 8 440 41 99
Company Website: http://www.boyden.com

DATE OF BIRTH: June 27, 1931

NATIONALITY: Swedish—Grew up in Stockholm, Sweden

EDUCATIONAL BACKGROUND:
MBA-Marketing/Advertising
University studies in sociology, statistics, psychology
Unilever-Internal Management programs

LANGUAGES SPOKEN: Swedish, Scandinavia (except Finnish), English, German, French (conversation)

CAREER HIGHLIGHTS: Unilever career Lintas Adv. Ag., Man. Dir. Scandinavia FCB Foote Cone Belding, built Boyden in Nordic from scratch in 1985. Board member, ESK, the Swedish Assn. for Executive Search Consultants.

SPECIAL INTERESTS/HOBBIES: Sailing, skiing, golf, tennis, bridge, and music

GEOGRAPHIC SCOPE OF RECRUITING: Nordic countries plus major part of Europe

SECTOR/INDUSTRY SPECIALIZATION: FMCG, Health Care/Pharmaceutical/Service sector

FAVORITE HISTORICAL FIGURE/MODEL/MENTOR: Churchill, Margaret Mead, Hans Rausing

SINGLE MOST IMPORTANT ISSUE IN CONDUCTING A HIGH LEVEL SEARCH: To match the company's culture, values and leadership style with that of potential candidates and the demands/expectations.

MOST SIGNIFICANT OTHER ASPECT OF PERSONAL OR PROFESSIONAL LIFE: To let your ethical values guide your professional life.

WHAT IS THE BEST PREPARATION FOR BEING A SUCCESSFUL RECRUITER? Line responsibility. Exp. from various company cultures and ethnic cultures.

WHAT WOULD YOU BE DOING IF YOU WERE NOT AN EXECUTIVE RECRUITER? Still in advertising (global) and communication

WHAT ARE THE CHARACTERISTICS OF A GREAT CLIENT? Professional, demanding, however understanding that a search is a process. Clear in explaining expectations.

WHAT CHALLENGES DO YOU SEE AHEAD IN THE GLOBAL MARKETPLACE? A deeper understanding of fitting in with company culture than the importance of industry experience.

HENRY LING

LTA & Company
20 Raffles Place
#14-02 Ocean Towers
Singapore 048620

Telephone: 65 534-3368
Fax: 65 534-1088
E-mail: ltasg@pacific.net.sg
Company Website: in development

DATE OF BIRTH: March 28, 1951

NATIONALITY: Canadian—Grew up in Hong Kong

EDUCATIONAL BACKGROUND:

M.B.A. University of Southern California
B.Sc. (Management Science) California State University

LANGUAGES SPOKEN: English, Chinese (Mandarin, Shanghainese, Cantonese)

CAREER HIGHLIGHTS:

- Co-founded and established LTA & Company as an independent regional retainer firm in Asia.
- Consultant to two premier global companies on over 150 searches throughout Asia in the past 7 years.

SPECIAL INTERESTS/HOBBIES: Contemporary Chinese oil painting

GEOGRAPHIC SCOPE OF RECRUITING: Southeast Asia, Greater China

SECTOR/INDUSTRY SPECIALIZATION: Financial Services, Consumer Products. Conglomerates.

FAVORITE HISTORICAL FIGURE/MODEL/MENTOR: Ronald Reagan

SINGLE MOST IMPORTANT ISSUE IN CONDUCTING A HIGH LEVEL SEARCH: The consultant's ability to act as advisor to the client and career counsellor to the candidates.

BIGGEST COMPETITOR: As an independent firm, all international firms are biggest competitors.

MOST SIGNIFICANT OTHER ASPECT OF PERSONAL OR PROFESSIONAL LIFE: "Cowboy" to some. "Consultant" to those who know.

WHAT IS THE BEST PREPARATION FOR BEING A SUCCESSFUL RECRUITER? To be a successful search consultant in Asia, one should have experience in blue-chip corporations, business acumen, ability to advise clients/senior executives, ability to convince and negotiate, and a multicultural perspective.

WHAT WOULD YOU BE DOING IF YOU WERE NOT AN EXECUTIVE RECRUITER? Career advisor/counsellor to senior management executives

WHAT ARE THE CHARACTERISTICS OF A GREAT CLIENT? Great clients know what they want, let the consultants do their job, are willing to take advice, and are decisive.

WHAT CHALLENGES DO YOU SEE AHEAD IN THE GLOBAL MARKETPLACE? The businesses of most of the largest corporations are already global. When will the make-up of their top management ranks/Board of Directors reflect this global nature?

CARLOS A. ROJAS MAGNON

Amrop International (Mexico)
Jaime Balmes #11 - Torre A - P.H.
Colonia Los Morales-Polanco
11510 Mexico, D. F.

Telephone: 52 5 557-5642/52 5 557-9403
Fax: 52 5 395-6677
E-mail: 100765.1453@compuserve.com
Company Website: http://www.amrop.com

DATE OF BIRTH: January 11, 1941

NATIONALITY: Mexican—Grew up in Mexico

EDUCATIONAL BACKGROUND:
  Chemical Engineer-Universidad Nacional Autonoma de Mexico, 1963

LANGUAGES SPOKEN: Spanish, English, and Portuguese

CAREER HIGHLIGHTS: Korn/Ferry/Hazzard y Asociados, 1969, Executive V.P.; Korn Ferry Hazzard (1976-1983); Delano Magnon & Associates (1983-1985); Cofounder of Amrop International, Mexico

SPECIAL INTERESTS/HOBBIES: Classical music, scuba diving, and tennis

GEOGRAPHIC SCOPE OF RECRUITING: Mexico

SECTOR/INDUSTRY SPECIALIZATION: Financial services

FAVORITE HISTORICAL FIGURE/MODEL/MENTOR: Winston Churchill

SINGLE MOST IMPORTANT ISSUE IN CONDUCTING A HIGH LEVEL SEARCH: Integrity

MOST SIGNIFICANT OTHER ASPECT OF PERSONAL OR PROFESSIONAL LIFE: Married, two daughters, three grandchildren

WHAT IS THE BEST PREPARATION FOR BEING A SUCCESSFUL RECRUITER? Technical undergraduate degree followed by master's degree in business administration, preferably from a U.S. university. Five to ten years of experience in a major consulting firm or ten to fifteen years of experience in a particular industry, i.e., financial services.

WHAT WOULD YOU BE DOING IF YOU WERE NOT AN EXECUTIVE RECRUITER? Managing my own business probably related to scuba-diving/underwater photography.

WHAT ARE THE CHARACTERISTICS OF A GREAT CLIENT? Rapidly growing organization. The client understands the need for recruiting talent and pays well. Client understands its requirements, can explain them clearly and is quite demanding. The client is always available for rapid communication and it is absolutely honest.

WHAT CHALLENGES DO YOU SEE AHEAD IN THE GLOBAL MARKET PLACE? Search work involving more than one country. Accelerated development of preferred supplier agreements. More and more specialized practice groups.

PHILIP MARSDEN

H. Neumann International
Old London House
32 St. James's Square
London SW1Y 4JR U.K.

Telephone: 44 171 930 5100
Fax: 44 171 930 7470.
E-mail: PMarsden@gkrgroup.com
Company Website: http://www.gkrgroup.com

DATE OF BIRTH: April 18, 1956

NATIONALITY: British—Grew up in U.K., Northern England and Scotland

EDUCATIONAL BACKGROUND:
Ampleforth College, 1969–74
St. Andrews University, 1975–79, M.A. (Hons), History

LANGUAGES SPOKEN: English, French

CAREER HIGHLIGHTS: Head of M&A, Natwest Markets, 1986–91

SPECIAL INTERESTS/HOBBIES: Fishing, golf, rugby (all sports), travel, opera, Scotland, family

GEOGRAPHIC SCOPE OF RECRUITING: Global

SECTOR/INDUSTRY SPECIALIZATION: Financial Services, especially Investment Banking and Asset Management

SINGLE MOST IMPORTANT ISSUE IN CONDUCTING A HIGH LEVEL SEARCH: Quality of the briefing, quality of the client.

BIGGEST COMPETITOR: Spencer Stuart

MOST SIGNIFICANT OTHER ASPECT OF PERSONAL OR PROFESSIONAL LIFE: My family: wife and two sons (10 and 8) and daughter (6) and friends.

WHAT IS THE BEST PREPARATION FOR BEING A SUCCESSFUL RECRUITER? A senior career in the functional specialty of your choice as a headhunter.

WHAT WOULD YOU BE DOING IF YOU WERE NOT AN EXECUTIVE RECRUITER? Following an entrepreneurial career in an alternative industry.

WHAT ARE THE CHARACTERISTICS OF A GREAT CLIENT?
• The ability to listen
• Someone who is passionate about the business they are in
• Someone who is able to make themselves available for closing

WHAT CHALLENGES DO YOU SEE AHEAD IN THE GLOBAL MARKETPLACE? Financial services—higher and higher standards are required in an increasingly competitive marketplace in order to maintain market position.

IGNACIO MARSEILLAN

Spencer Stuart
Paraguay 577, 10th floor
Buenos Aires (1057)
Argentina

Telephone: 54 1 313-2233
Fax: 54 1 313-2299
E-mail: imarseillan@spencerstuart.com.ar
Company Website: http://www.spencerstuart.com

DATE OF BIRTH: January 31, 1962

NATIONALITY: Argentine—Grew up in Argentina

EDUCATIONAL BACKGROUND:
Civil Engineer, University of Buenos Aires
Master in Public Administration, Harvard University

LANGUAGES SPOKEN: Spanish, English, French

CAREER HIGHLIGHTS: JP Morgan, Corporate Finance, New York and Buenos Aires
Bemberg Group, Financial Manager

SPECIAL INTERESTS/HOBBIES: Golf, taekwondo and four children

GEOGRAPHIC SCOPE OF RECRUITING: Argentina and Chile

SECTOR/INDUSTRY SPECIALIZATION: Financial Services, Energy, Consumer

FAVORITE HISTORICAL FIGURE/MODEL/MENTOR: Jesus

SINGLE MOST IMPORTANT ISSUE IN CONDUCTING A HIGH LEVEL SEARCH: Honesty and proactivity

BIGGEST COMPETITOR: Egon Zehnder

MOST SIGNIFICANT OTHER ASPECT OF PERSONAL OR PROFESSIONAL LIFE: I love what I do and I can continue doing it for the rest of my days (which I hope are far away from now). Charity work and helping others.

WHAT IS THE BEST PREPARATION FOR BEING A SUCCESSFUL RECRUITER? Line experience in a company reputable for its excellency. Team sports.

WHAT WOULD YOU BE DOING IF YOU WERE NOT AN EXECUTIVE RECRUITER? I have not found yet any other position that can attract me more than this one.

WHAT ARE THE CHARACTERISTICS OF A GREAT CLIENT?
- Transparency
- Good humor
- Self-confident and seriousness

WHAT CHALLENGES DO YOU SEE AHEAD IN THE GLOBAL MARKETPLACE? Maintaining excellent quality in a market where clients will need new types of profiles. Introducing new products and services without losing focus.

WILLIAM H. (MO) MARUMOTO

Boyden Global Executive Search
2445 M Street, N.W.
Suite 250
Washington, D.C. 20037-1435
U.S.A.

Telephone: 1 (202) 342-7200
Fax: 1 (202) 342-7221
E-mail: Boydendc@aol.com
Company Website: http://www.boyden.com

DATE OF BIRTH: December 16, 1934

NATIONALITY: Japanese American—Grew up in Santa Ana, California

EDUCATIONAL BACKGROUND:
Bachelor of Arts, 1957, Whittier College, Whittier, California
Graduate Studies, 1957-1958, University of Oregon, Eugene, Oregon

LANGUAGES SPOKEN: English, Japanese, and Spanish

SPECIAL INTERESTS/HOBBIES: Gardening, fishing, reading, music and collecting Americana antiques and contemporary art

GEOGRAPHIC SCOPE OF RECRUITING: Primarily domestic

SECTOR/INDUSTRY SPECIALIZATION: Consumer Package Goods, Energy, Manufacturing, Associations, Non-Profit

FAVORITE HISTORICAL FIGURE/MODEL/MENTOR: SirWinston Churchill

SINGLE MOST IMPORTANT ISSUE IN CONDUCTING A HIGH LEVEL SEARCH: Thoroughly understand special needs, expectations, accountability, industry and client's environment and culture.

WHAT IS THE BEST PREPARATION FOR BEING A SUCCESSFUL RECRUITER? Have a solid education and a thorough understanding of business. Thoroughly understand the fundamentals of the search process; be a good listener; think out-of-the-box; pay attention to details, think strategically and be willing to be a partner with your client.

WHAT WOULD YOU BE DOING IF YOU WERE NOT AN EXECUTIVE RECRUITER? Serving as a General Manager of a professional football team.

WHAT ARE THE CHARACTERISTICS OF A GREAT CLIENT? Strategically and carefully thinking through one's specific needs and criteria, and properly articulating this information to the recruiter. Providing detailed information and materials and being responsive to your recruiter and candidates in the search process.

WHAT CHALLENGES DO YOU SEE AHEAD IN THE GLOBAL MARKETPLACE? More use of preferred provider concept with multi-national corporations and globalization of executive search firms coordinating search assignments through a project manager and generating competitive fee arrangements.

RANJAN MARWAH

Executive Access Limited
25/F, Penthouse, Prince's Building
Central
Hong Kong

Telephone: 852 2842-7157
Fax: 852 2877-5334
E-mail: rmarwah@access-asia.com
Company Website: http://www.hk.net/eal

DATE OF BIRTH: November 10, 1948

NATIONALITY: Indian—Grew up in New Delhi

EDUCATIONAL BACKGROUND:
Attended the National Defence Academy (India's West Point) from 1964 to 1967.
Liberal Arts Degree from the University of Delhi.

LANGUAGES SPOKEN: English, Hindi, Urdu

SPECIAL INTERESTS/HOBBIES: Tennis, golf, reading, child care in Hong Kong and China

GEOGRAPHIC SCOPE OF RECRUITING: Asia

SECTOR/INDUSTRY SPECIALIZATION: General

FAVORITE HISTORICAL FIGURE/MODEL/MENTOR: Walt Disney

SINGLE MOST IMPORTANT ISSUE IN CONDUCTING A HIGH LEVEL SEARCH: Benchmarking the best regardless of their presumed availability

BIGGEST COMPETITOR: Old boy network

MOST SIGNIFICANT OTHER ASPECT OF PERSONAL OR PROFESSIONAL LIFE: My own family (7 children) and working with orphans in HK and China

WHAT IS THE BEST PREPARATION FOR BEING A SUCCESSFUL RECRUITER? To be an information professional, researcher, journalist, reporter, investigator, etc.

WHAT WOULD YOU BE DOING IF YOU WERE NOT AN EXECUTIVE RECRUITER? A venture capitalist helping individuals fulfill their potential with capital and mentoring.

WHAT ARE THE CHARACTERISTICS OF A GREAT CLIENT? The capacity to understand his own need, his potential and his ability to trust his search partner completely.

WHAT CHALLENGES DO YOU SEE AHEAD IN THE GLOBAL MARKETPLACE? The best moments are coming where the individuals who make significant change and contribution will become even more important than entire corporations.

NEAL L. MASLAN

LAI Ward Howell
16255 Ventura Blvd., Suite 400
Encino, CA 91436
U.S.A.

Telephone: 1 (818) 905-6010
Fax: 1 (818) 905-3330
E-mail: neal_maslan@compuserve.com
Company Website: http://www.laix.com

DATE OF BIRTH: September 22, 1940

NATIONALITY: American—Grew up in Richmond, Virginia

EDUCATIONAL BACKGROUND:
BA, University of Virginia
MPH, Yale University School of Medicine

LANGUAGES SPOKEN: English; some Spanish

CAREER HIGHLIGHTS: Counseling two clients to consider (and eventually hire) "off-spec" candidates for CEO and CFO; both respectively, had major positive impacts on the company's performance and stock price/IPO.

SPECIAL INTERESTS/HOBBIES: Tennis, community board service, grandchildren

GEOGRAPHIC SCOPE OF RECRUITING: National (U.S.A.)

SECTOR/INDUSTRY SPECIALIZATION: Healthcare services; development stage/pre-IPO and publicly-held managed care; venture capital

FAVORITE HISTORICAL FIGURE/MODEL/MENTOR: My father taught that a man's word is his bond and that ethics beyond reproach and balance in one's life for family, work, and community service is the mark of success.

SINGLE MOST IMPORTANT ISSUE IN CONDUCTING A HIGH LEVEL SEARCH: Ascertaining those who consistently outperformed their industry sectors over time, who were successful when there was not a rising tide; referencing, referencing, referencing; to hear that which is not spoken; to determine corporate culture fit and/or ability to change culture.

MOST SIGNIFICANT OTHER ASPECT OF PERSONAL OR PROFESSIONAL LIFE: Need to deserve and maintain the trust and confidence clients place in me to far exceed, not just meet, their expectations. Success in executive search is measured by client management and service, value added to the search, not just a successful hire.

WHAT IS THE BEST PREPARATION FOR BEING A SUCCESSFUL RECRUITER? A senior general management career, perhaps via a sales/marketing track, in an industry similar to that of clients served; alternative, senior level strategy consulting where consulting and client service and management have been mastered.

WHAT WOULD YOU BE DOING IF YOU WERE NOT AN EXECUTIVE RECRUITER? Either venture capital or CEO of an early/development stage healthcare company.

WHAT ARE THE CHARACTERISTICS OF A GREAT CLIENT? Clear communication/timely feedback; values and listens to consultant for creative suggestions and advice (doesn't view consultant as "order-taker/transactionist"); demanding and insistent about "A" candidates; intimately involved in the search process throughout; decisive.

WHAT CHALLENGES DO YOU SEE AHEAD IN THE GLOBAL MARKETPLACE? From a client perspective, attracting executives who have an understanding of and ability to lead a multicultural workforce and to tailor products and services and marketing to the local market. From a search perspective, a seamless client service capability through a client manager to provide quality results and reasonable cycle time worldwide.

JONATHAN E. McBRIDE

McBride Associates, Inc.
1511 K Street NW
Suite 819
Washington, DC 20005-1497
U.S.A.

Telephone: 1 (202) 638-1150
E-mail: hearthunt@aol.com

DATE OF BIRTH: June 16, 1942

NATIONALITY: American—Grew up in Washington, D.C.

EDUCATIONAL BACKGROUND:
Yale University, BA, 1964

LANGUAGES SPOKEN: English, Spanish

CAREER HIGHLIGHTS: 4 years U.S. Navy, Vietnam & Hollywood; 8 years Merrill Lynch & Co.; 22 years in executive search consulting, the last 19 years as a sole practitioner

SPECIAL INTERESTS/HOBBIES: Squash; close harmony a capella singing; backgammon

GEOGRAPHIC SCOPE OF RECRUITING: North America

SECTOR/INDUSTRY SPECIALIZATION: Classic Generalist

FAVORITE HISTORICAL FIGURE/MODEL/MENTOR:[DELETE ME]

SINGLE MOST IMPORTANT ISSUE IN CONDUCTING A HIGH LEVEL SEARCH: Integrity, as in "wholeness"

MOST SIGNIFICANT OTHER ASPECT OF PERSONAL OR PROFESSIONAL LIFE: I think of myself as a "hearthunter" rather than a "headhunter." I seek personal as well as professional commitment—a synthesis of emotional and rational considerations—in favor of my clients' needs. I also seek integrity—not just "honesty," but a sense of "wholeness"—in those candidates I elect to pursue for clients.

WHAT IS THE BEST PREPARATION FOR BEING A SUCCESSFUL RECRUITER? Doing sufficient "personal homework" that you wind up comfortable enough with who you yourself are that you can listen to and hear what your clients and candidates are actually saying without your own internal "chatter" getting in the way.

WHAT WOULD YOU BE DOING IF YOU WERE NOT AN EXECUTIVE RECRUITER? A professional member of corporate boards of directors.

WHAT ARE THE CHARACTERISTICS OF A GREAT CLIENT? Candor with self, search consultant and candidates; willing to tell the truth about both the possibilities and the pitfalls around the problem/position being addressed; aware that 2 of the 4 highest stress points in life are moving and changing jobs; as a result understands that time is our worst enemy once we get a highly desirable candidate engaged in the process; therefore willing to respond promptly as well take the appropriate initiative to get done what needs get done.

WHAT CHALLENGES DO YOU SEE AHEAD IN THE GLOBAL MARKETPLACE? Not letting clients or candidates get so caught up with the worldwide web and Internet stuff that they forget that relationship and "chemistry" are in fact more important than "information" and/or sophisticated electronic communications capabilities.

HORACIO J. McCOY

Korn/Ferry International, Inc.
Montes Urales No. 505 - Piso 3
Lomas de Chapultepec
México, D. F. 11000
México

Telephone: 52 5 201-5400
Fax: 52 5 202-4469
E-mail: horacio.mccoy@kornferry.com
Company Website: http://www.kornferry.com

DATE OF BIRTH: January 4, 1939

NATIONALITY: Mexican—Grew up in Mexico, Venezuela, Colombia and the U.S.A.

EDUCATIONAL BACKGROUND: University of Southern California, Bachelor of Science degree, Business Administration, 1961, Summa Cum Laude honors

LANGUAGES SPOKEN: Spanish and English

CAREER HIGHLIGHTS: Placement of Latin America CEO for AT&T (Mr. Rodrigo Guerra) as well as various other CEOs for Latin America and Mexico

SPECIAL INTERESTS/HOBBIES: Bible studying, golf, opera

GEOGRAPHIC SCOPE OF RECRUITING: Latin America and North America

SECTOR/INDUSTRY SPECIALIZATION: Consumer Products, Financial Services, and Advanced Technology

FAVORITE HISTORICAL FIGURE/MODEL/MENTOR: John F. Kennedy

SINGLE MOST IMPORTANT ISSUE IN CONDUCTING A HIGH LEVEL SEARCH: Cultural fit with client and chemistry match. Other important issues are: demonstrated ability as change agent, proven leadership skills and team work building, as well as overall business vision.

MOST SIGNIFICANT OTHER ASPECT OF PERSONAL OR PROFESSIONAL LIFE: Continued spiritual development and growth

WHAT IS THE BEST PREPARATION FOR BEING A SUCCESSFUL RECRUITER? A successful recruiter should ideally have spent several meaningful years of his professional career on the client side. The most successful recruiters have had actual management experience or line responsibilities, not limited to Human Resources.

WHAT WOULD YOU BE DOING IF YOU WERE NOT AN EXECUTIVE RECRUITER? Although I have developed a very successful executive recruiter career for the last twenty-two years, my path would probably have taken me to line management at the Senior level, possibly on a regional or global basis.

WHAT ARE THE CHARACTERISTICS OF A GREAT CLIENT? A truly great client provides the executive recruiter with comprehensive profile and job specifications as well as a clear description of the company's culture and chemistry requirements. Also, a great client provides the recruiter with meaningful feedback and responds as quickly as possible to move the recruiting process along in an efficient manner.

WHAT CHALLENGES DO YOU SEE AHEAD IN THE GLOBAL MARKETPLACE? The executive recruiting profession is being heavily impacted on a positive way by globalization and specialization. The leading large global firms now have a definitive advantage and competitive edge in serving clients anywhere in the world with uniform quality. Also, recruiters now have to specialize in order to satisfy client demands.

MILLINGTON F. McCOY

Gould, McCoy & Chadick, Inc.
300 Park Avenue, 20th Floor
New York, NY 10022
U.S.A.

Telephone: 1 (212) 688-8671
Fax: 1 (212) 308-4510
E-mail: GM&C@gouldmccoychadick.com
Company Website: http://www.gouldmccoychadick.com

DATE OF BIRTH: January 22, 1941

NATIONALITY: American—Grew up in Missouri

EDUCATIONAL BACKGROUND:

Harvard Radcliffe Graduate School of Business Administration (HRBPA),
    certificate in Business Administration, 1963
University of Missouri, B.A. with distinction, 1962, Phi Beta Kappa

LANGUAGES SPOKEN: English

CAREER HIGHLIGHTS: Founding/Charter member of the Committee of 200. Profiled in *The New Career Makers* as one of the top ten recruiters of corporate directors, serves on panel of experts of Boardroom Reports, and the Dean's Council for the Harvard Divinity School.

SPECIAL INTERESTS/HOBBIES: Dressage, study of Enneagram

GEOGRAPHIC SCOPE OF RECRUITING: North America, Europe

SECTOR/INDUSTRY SPECIALIZATION: Financial services, high technology, industrial, consumer packaged goods

FAVORITE HISTORICAL FIGURE/MODEL/MENTOR: Historical figure: Margaret Thatcher. Role model: my great aunt, Dr. Anita Bohnsack, the first woman doctor in my hometown. At the turn of century, she went by horse and buggy to deliver babies.

SINGLE MOST IMPORTANT ISSUE IN CONDUCTING A HIGH LEVEL SEARCH: The most important issue is to develop trust between the search consultant and the board, search committee and/or CEO. If the parties have built rapport and trust, any unexpected twists the search journey can be opportunities to learn. Without trust, the process itself is in danger. Trust takes time to develop and is essential in ensuring a successful search process. The search professional must be taken into the confidence of senior management to learn the issues of the business and of the position and to be given time and access to learn the culture of the organization. Without understanding the culture, the search professional cannot make a good fit.

BIGGEST COMPETITOR: Spencer Stuart

MOST SIGNIFICANT OTHER ASPECT OF PERSONAL OR PROFESSIONAL LIFE: Striving to keep a balance between my profession, my family, and my passion for dressage, along with keeping fit and growing personally; giving back and keeping up with friends are my challenge. Without the balance I am not successful on any dimension. "To thine own self be true, or thou canst not be true to any man" guides me.

WHAT IS THE BEST PREPARATION FOR BEING A SUCCESSFUL RECRUITER? Minimum 10 years of business management experience, MBA, the ability to sell, well-developed assessment skills, and understudying a top search professional for several years.

WHAT WOULD YOU BE DOING IF YOU WERE NOT AN EXECUTIVE RECRUITER? I would spend more time with my horses, and use my skills to "give back" to a non-profit or a counseling activity. Earlier, I would have run another kind of business.

WHAT ARE THE CHARACTERISTICS OF A GREAT CLIENT? Active involvement in the search process; good communicator, responsiveness, trust, the ability to attract the best people-and to cut through bureaucracy.

WHAT CHALLENGES DO YOU SEE AHEAD IN THE GLOBAL MARKETPLACE? Shortage of leaders to guide global enterprises.

HERBERT T. MINES

Herbert Mines Associates, Inc.
375 Park Avenue, 3rd Floor
New York, NY 10152
U.S.A.

Telephone: 1 (212) 355-0909
Fax: 1 (212) 223-2186
E-mail: fbtjl@aol.com

DATE OF BIRTH: January 30, 1929

NATIONALITY: American—Grew up in Northeastern U.S.A.

EDUCATIONAL BACKGROUND:
B.A. Economics-Babson College
Masters Degree-Industrial & Labor Relations-Cornell University

LANGUAGES SPOKEN: English

CAREER HIGHLIGHTS: Long time CEO of the most prominent search firm specializing in retail, apparel mfg., textiles, direct marketing, etc. Well known for placing CEO's in those industries.

SPECIAL INTERESTS/HOBBIES: Tennis, sailing, reading, education.

GEOGRAPHIC SCOPE OF RECRUITING: U.S., Canada, U.K., Western Europe, Far East

SECTOR/INDUSTRY SPECIALIZATION: Retail, apparel and home furnishings manufacturing, textiles, direct marketing, cosmetics

FAVORITE HISTORICAL FIGURE/MODEL/MENTOR: Franklin D. Roosevelt

SINGLE MOST IMPORTANT ISSUE IN CONDUCTING A HIGH LEVEL SEARCH: Varies by company and company needs. Learning those requirements is the first step, taking the necessary time, meeting the key players and educating the client on what is do-able at what compensation level. Then the skill is judging the talent.

MOST SIGNIFICANT OTHER ASPECT OF PERSONAL OR PROFESSIONAL LIFE: Spend a great deal of time in non-profit and pro-bono activities. Believe strongly in being active in the broader community.

WHAT IS THE BEST PREPARATION FOR BEING A SUCCESSFUL RECRUITER? There is no single best preparation as good recruiters come from a broad range of disciplines and experiences. Certainly a college education, the ability to communicate orally and in writing, some actual operating experience in business prior to becoming a consultant, the development of wonderful interactive skills which make it possible to deal effectively with a wide range of people (both candidates and clients), the ability to work independently and fine character and integrity, all are important ingredients to be a successful recruiter.

WHAT WOULD YOU BE DOING IF YOU WERE NOT AN EXECUTIVE RECRUITER? Probably an attorney.

WHAT ARE THE CHARACTERISTICS OF A GREAT CLIENT? One who communicates fully on their needs and requirements. One who is flexible in evaluating candidates and very responsive to communications from the search firm. A great client sets realistic parameters for the recruitment process, accepts the search professional's advice and consultation and is realistic about the compensation that will be necessary to attract the preferred candidate.

WHAT CHALLENGES DO YOU SEE AHEAD IN THE GLOBAL MARKETPLACE? The biggest challenge is finding ways to have multiple search firms focus effectively on a single search. This may result in different ways of billing clients and different compensation arrangements for those who participate in a global search.

KYLE R. MITCHELL

Ray & Berndtson/Tanton Mitchell
710-1050 West Pender Street
Vancouver, B.C.
Canada
V6E 3S7

Telephone: 1 (604) 685-0261
Fax: 1 (604) 684-7988
E-mail: kyle_mitchell@ray-berndtson.ca
Company Website: http://www.prb.com

DATE OF BIRTH: June 26, 1941

NATIONALITY: Canadian—Grew up in Vancouver, Canada

EDUCATIONAL BACKGROUND:
B.Comm. UBC
LL.B. UBC

LANGUAGES SPOKEN: English

CAREER HIGHLIGHTS: Senior human resources roles in Montreal and New York before returning to Vancouver to join John Tanton in developing our firm. Eight years ago, we established a Canadian search group that is now one of the two major players in this market. Four years ago we joined with others to form Ray & Berndtson.

SPECIAL INTERESTS/HOBBIES: Photography, cooking

GEOGRAPHIC SCOPE OF RECRUITING: Canada wide searches for B.C. based organizations.

SECTOR/INDUSTRY SPECIALIZATION: Generalist

FAVORITE HISTORICAL FIGURE/MODEL/MENTOR: My earliest mentor was my father, who was an executive in a large department store chain. While he retired early due to ill health, and died very young, I carry to this day some things I learned from him. I have vivid memories of visiting him, when I was a teenager, in the main store of the chain where the head office was located. Walking through the store with him on the way to lunch, he regularly stopped and re-arranged a display of merchandise. In doing so, he impressed upon me the importance of seeing things from a customer perspective. He was clearly customer driven. Moreover, he took a very energetic approach to life. He was very committed to his community and he worked very hard to be the best at what he did.

Our former Prime Minister, Pierre Trudeau, had a tremendous impact on our country and myself. I had the opportunity to see him first hand as I served for five years as a nationally elected officer of the political party that Trudeau represented. He was visionary, always looking for new solutions, not bound by tradition, had a logic that at times was overpowering and his ability to inspire others was, at times, quite remarkable.

My uncle Ted McBride, was a senior human resources executive with a number of major Canadian enterprises. He was a constant point of reference for me during my early career, especially after my father passed away when I was relatively young.

Finally, my partner, John Tanton. We started in business twenty-seven years ago and have been successful in building our business because we bring complementary skills and experience to the table. From day one in our partnership, we have valued what the other brings. Indeed, we have mentored each other over the years; this cross mentorship has been a key ingredient in our success.

continues ▶

SINGLE MOST IMPORTANT ISSUE IN CONDUCTING A HIGH LEVEL SEARCH: Culture fit—establishing objective qualifications—is relatively straight forward. Ensuring a candidate's ability to be effective in a client's current or desired culture is more challenging and critical to success.

BIGGEST COMPETITOR: Caldwell Partners

MOST SIGNIFICANT OTHER ASPECT OF PERSONAL OR PROFESSIONAL LIFE: Family—wife and four wonderful children.

WHAT ARE THE CHARACTERISTICS OF A GREAT CLIENT? First and foremost, they are very open with us. They hold nothing back in giving us a picture of the uniqueness of their organization and the opportunities and challenges facing the individual that is being recruited. This is fundamental to the success of a search. In addition, a great client is one who makes themselves available as required at key stages of the search to help maintain momentum.

WHAT IS THE BEST PREPARATION FOR BEING A SUCCESSFUL RECRUITER? There is no one best preparation. In our office we have people who have been senior executives, who have come from other recruiting firms, who have been in other elements of management consulting and who have been human resource executives.

WHAT WOULD YOU BE DOING IF YOU WERE NOT AN EXECUTIVE RECRUITER? This is a really good question!! Over the many years I have been an executive recruiter, I have had the opportunity to learn about a wide range of executive opportunities. Few have even sparked an interest. I love this profession and the work I do. If I was not in search, I might want to do something completely different, like building on my hobby of photography.

WHAT CHALLENGES DO YOU SEE AHEAD IN THE GLOBAL MARKETPLACE? Organizations are consolidating in almost every industry. Industries are becoming more international. Our clients are evolving from regional to national to international. We have to evolve to meet the changing needs of our clients. So we have to position ourselves to effectively meet their need for talent wherever that need exists. As an example, we, in Vancouver, are currently working with a U.S. based client in conducting searches for people in eastern Canada, the U.S. and China. This is becoming a commonplace experience in executive search.

JÜRGEN B. MÜLDER

Heidrick & Struggles-Mülder & Partner
Frankfurt Airport Center I, Hugo-Eckener-Ring
D-60549 Frankfurt/Main
Germany
Telephone: 49-69-4970020
Fax: 49-69-694134
Company Website: http://www.h-s.com

DATE OF BIRTH: September 14, 1937

NATIONALITY: German—Grew up in Celle, Northern Germany

EDUCATIONAL BACKGROUND:
Master of Engineering Sciences (Diplom-Ingenieur) from Clausthal University, Germany
Ph.D. in comparative law (same university)
MBA from INSEAD, Fontainebleau, France

LANGUAGES SPOKEN: German, English, French, Spanish

CAREER HIGHLIGHTS: Post university experience in mining, petroleum industry and research in Germany, Great Britain, U.S.A., Belgium. Global Chairman and Regional Chairman Europe; successful involvement in expanding the global partnership
1968–1977   Spencer Stuart & Associates, Switzerland, Benelux, Germany; MD and Managing Partner
1978–1997   Amrop International Mülder & Partner, Frankfurt/Germany

SPECIAL INTERESTS/HOBBIES: Sports and traveling, involvement in charity projects
Board Member Council of Christian Entrepreneurs (Wirtschaftsrat der C.D.U.e.V.)
Chairman of Association of German Executive Search Consultants (VDESB) until Nov. 1997
Nominated Chairman of European Advisors to AESC

GEOGRAPHIC SCOPE OF RECRUITING: Germany, Europe, and worldwide

SECTOR/INDUSTRY SPECIALIZATION: CEO, CFO searches; increasing recruitment of Non-Executive Directors in Germany and abroad

FAVORITE HISTORICAL FIGURE/MODEL/MENTOR: Homer, Adenauer/DeGaulle, Mr. Spencer Stuart; Jack Welsh

SINGLE MOST IMPORTANT ISSUE IN CONDUCTING A HIGH LEVEL SEARCH: To understand the hidden agendas within the hiring committee

BIGGEST COMPETITOR: Two individuals in domestic German market

MOST SIGNIFICANT OTHER ASPECT OF PERSONAL OR PROFESSIONAL LIFE: To serve the community and act as an intermediary between business and politics

WHAT ARE THE CHARACTERISTICS OF A GREAT CLIENT? A great client is one with whom you are able to maintain deep rooted relations. He involves you in all his major questions as far as corporate governance and top management compensation is concerned as well as all senior searches in the homeland and abroad. A great client relates his major concerns to you much as you relate your specific market intelligence to him. It is a relationship of mutual trust and candid openness. For such clients you may have cooperated on 50 or more assignments over a decade. A great client tends to accept creative solutions to senior recruitments leaving the traditional patterns of narrow functional or sector background preferences.

GERNOT MÜLLER

Ray & Berndtson
Olof-Palme-Strasse 35
D-60322 Frankfurt am Main
Federal Republic of Germany

Telephone: 49-69-95777-506
Fax: 49-69-95777-901
E-mail: gm@ray-berndtson.de
Company Website: http://www.prb.com

DATE OF BIRTH: January 14, 1943

NATIONALITY: German—Grew up in Munich

EDUCATIONAL BACKGROUND:
Diploma in Business Administration, University of Munich
Ph.D. in Economics, University of Munich

LANGUAGES SPOKEN: German (mother tongue), English (fluent)

CAREER HIGHLIGHTS: Personnel Manager ITT, 25 years of professional experience in executive search with Ray & Berndtson; currently Managing Partner

SPECIAL INTERESTS/HOBBIES: History/political discourse/athletics

GEOGRAPHIC SCOPE OF RECRUITING: National and international clients within Germany

SECTOR/INDUSTRY SPECIALIZATION: General management with a certain emphasis on consumer goods, ind./trade and media

FAVORITE HISTORICAL FIGURE/MODEL/MENTOR: Immanuel Kant, German philosopher; Walther Rathenau, German statesman

SINGLE MOST IMPORTANT ISSUE IN CONDUCTING A HIGH LEVEL SEARCH: Needed are leadership capabilities/charisma, social intelligence, cultural fit, and capacity of mobilizing people, discover their skills and to push their creativeness

MOST SIGNIFICANT OTHER ASPECT OF PERSONAL OR PROFESSIONAL LIFE: Partnership of the global Ray & Berndtson network of 44 offices

WHAT IS THE BEST PREPARATION FOR BEING A SUCCESSFUL RECRUITER?
- High-quality education/comprehensive interests
- Professional experience/managerial background
- In-depth knowledge of a certain branch of industry/focus
- High-level social competence/intelligence, liking people
- International orientation/cosmopolitical approach

WHAT WOULD YOU BE DOING IF YOU WERE NOT AN EXECUTIVE RECRUITER? I would be pursuing professional engagements within the personnel management of a strong internationally oriented industrial firm and cultivating the relevance of human capital as the basis of entrepreneurial success.

WHAT ARE THE CHARACTERISTICS OF A GREAT CLIENT? A great client has long-term cooperation with an executive search firm, high-quality personnel department as the recruiter's partner, professional/efficient handling of search projects and candidates, and decisiveness.

WHAT CHALLENGES DO YOU SEE AHEAD IN THE GLOBAL MARKETPLACE? Organizing a productive competition between the different economic centers (East Asia/Europe/North America); developing the countries of other regions/continents into productive, sound competitors; and implementing a global environmental protection system.

CAROLINE W. NAHAS

Korn/Ferry International
1800 Century Park East #900
Los Angeles, CA 90067
U.S.A.

Telephone: 1 (310) 843-4142
Fax: 1 (310) 553-6452
E-mail: nahass@kornferry.com
Company Website: http://www.kornferry.com

DATE OF BIRTH: June 21, 1948

NATIONALITY: American—Grew up in Los Angeles

EDUCATIONAL BACKGROUND:

BA-UCLA

LANGUAGES SPOKEN: English

CAREER HIGHLIGHTS: First woman partner K/F; managing dir/Southern California Century City office, one of firm's largest regions, Executive Committee, Career Maker's; Board of Directors IHOP, public co.

GEOGRAPHIC SCOPE OF RECRUITING: National and global

SECTOR/INDUSTRY SPECIALIZATION: General practice-senior executives and board directors; several global relationships

FAVORITE HISTORICAL FIGURE/MODEL/MENTOR: Harry Truman; mother; Richard Ferry

SINGLE MOST IMPORTANT ISSUE IN CONDUCTING A HIGH LEVEL SEARCH: Identifying and attracting executives who can make a difference

MOST SIGNIFICANT OTHER ASPECT OF PERSONAL OR PROFESSIONAL LIFE: Personal and professional relationships

WHAT IS THE BEST PREPARATION FOR BEING A SUCCESSFUL RECRUITER?
- Consulting
- Customer/client service experience
- Analyzing business problems
- Sales

WHAT WOULD YOU BE DOING IF YOU WERE NOT AN EXECUTIVE RECRUITER? Lawyer (corporate or trial)

WHAT ARE THE CHARACTERISTICS OF A GREAT CLIENT? Personally engaged in and committed to talent acquisition. Knowledge and strategic vision about their business. Views consultant as partner

WHAT CHALLENGES DO YOU SEE AHEAD IN THE GLOBAL MARKETPLACE? Highly matrixed management structure. Continued demand for high caliber talent complexity. Explosion of demand in emerging countries like India—blending Western and local talent

THOMAS J. NEFF

Spencer Stuart U.S.
277 Park Avenue, 29th floor
New York, NY 10172
U.S.A.

Telephone: 1 (212) 336-0202
Fax: 1 (212) 336-0299
E-mail: tneff@spencerstuart.com
Company Website: http://www.spencerstuart.com

DATE OF BIRTH: October 2, 1937

NATIONALITY: U.S. Citizen—Grew up in Easton, PA

EDUCATIONAL BACKGROUND:
Lehigh University, M.B.A., Marketing and Finance, 1961
Lafayette College, B.S., Industrial Engineering, 1959

LANGUAGES SPOKEN: English

CAREER HIGHLIGHTS:
Spencer Stuart (1976 to Present); currently Chairman
Booz·Allen Hamilton (1974–76)
Entrepreneur (1969–74)
TWA (1966–69)
McKinsey & Company (1963–66)

SPECIAL INTERESTS/HOBBIES: Golf, tennis, jogging, reading periodicals

GEOGRAPHIC SCOPE OF RECRUITING: North America primarily; increasingly global on CEO and Board assignments

SECTOR/INDUSTRY SPECIALIZATION: Generalist at CEO/COO level with multiple industry experience. Also, specialist in Board of Director recruiting and consulting.

SINGLE MOST IMPORTANT ISSUE IN CONDUCTING A HIGH LEVEL SEARCH: Credibility with client earned by reputation, track record, and quality of communications and advice.

MOST SIGNIFICANT OTHER ASPECT OF PERSONAL OR PROFESSIONAL LIFE: Active in not-for-profit world through board service: university, hospital, boys' secondary school.

WHAT IS THE BEST PREPARATION FOR BEING A SUCCESSFUL RECRUITER? Earlier in one's career, several years with a leading management consulting firm coupled with corporate experience, including some general management. After joining a search firm, total focus on learning the art and science of search for the first one to two years with a firm that values quality and client satisfaction more than business development for its newcomers.

WHAT WOULD YOU BE DOING IF YOU WERE NOT AN EXECUTIVE RECRUITER? Principal investing with a buyout firm coupled with serving on several Boards.

WHAT ARE THE CHARACTERISTICS OF A GREAT CLIENT? A client with mutual trust and respect who wants a working partnership, values your opinions, is responsive, and fun to work with.

WHAT CHALLENGES DO YOU SEE AHEAD IN THE GLOBAL MARKETPLACE? Serving global clients on multi-country searches in a reasonable timeframe at a fee that makes sense for both parties.

RAIMONDO NIDER

Korn Ferry International
Sala dei Longobardi 2
20121 Milan
Italy

Telephone: 39 2 72022550
Fax: 39 2 72022611
E-mail: nider@kornferry.com
Company Website: http://www.kornferry.com

DATE OF BIRTH: January 7, 1941

NATIONALITY: Italian—Grew up in Italy

EDUCATIONAL BACKGROUND:
University of Rome, Italy: Political Science
Gonzaga University, Spokane, Wash.: Doctorate work at Department of International Studies

LANGUAGES SPOKEN: Italian, English, Spanish

CAREER HIGHLIGHTS:
Olivetti: Sales, Marketing, Training and Personnel
Egon Zehnder International: Managing Partner, Italy

SPECIAL INTERESTS/HOBBIES: Agriculture (producing wine in Tuscany), music, and gastronomy

GEOGRAPHIC SCOPE OF RECRUITING: Southern Europe, mainly Italy and Greece

SECTOR/INDUSTRY SPECIALIZATION: Generalist, FMCG, Telecommunication and Fashion

FAVORITE HISTORICAL FIGURE/MODEL/MENTOR: Socrates for his sense of ethics/Epicurus for his sense of life

SINGLE MOST IMPORTANT ISSUE IN CONDUCTING A HIGH LEVEL SEARCH: Cultural fit of candidate to mission and new environment

WHAT IS THE BEST PREPARATION FOR BEING A SUCCESSFUL RECRUITER? Professionally, corporate experience in management roles (as senior as possible, size is not too important). A second choice is management consulting background. Personality: great interest in people and cultural diversity, vision and ethics.

WHAT WOULD YOU BE DOING IF YOU WERE NOT AN EXECUTIVE RECRUITER? I would be a gentleman-farmer.

WHAT ARE THE CHARACTERISTICS OF A GREAT CLIENT?
- Open and direct
- Intellectually challenging
- Ethical

WHAT CHALLENGES DO YOU SEE AHEAD IN THE GLOBAL MARKETPLACE? Being able to provide true added value to clients in a world where information and technology will be accessible commodities

PRI NOTOWIDIGDO

Profesindo Reksa Indonesia (PRI) pt/Amrop International
Bapindo Plaza II, 14th Floor
Jl Jend Sudirman Kav 54-55
Jakarta 12190, Indonesia

Telephone: 62 21 526-7072, (62-81) 680-7211 (cellular)
Fax: 62 21 526-7074
E-mail: prijkt@ibm.net
Company Website: http://www.amrop.com

DATE OF BIRTH: May 14, 1947

NATIONALITY: Indonesian—Grew up in Indonesia

EDUCATIONAL BACKGROUND:
Hons BA in Political Science & Psychology (Carleton University, 1974)
MA in International Development (Carleton University, 1975)

LANGUAGES SPOKEN: Indonesian, Javanese, English, and French

CAREER HIGHLIGHTS: Opened AMROP office in Indonesia (1996); opened TASA office in Indonesia (1994); Partner-in-Charge of Human Resources Consulting for KPMG Peat Marwick in Indonesia (1987-1994); Manager of Human Resources Consulting for Price Waterhouse Indonesia (1984-1987); Planner and Project Manager for the Indonesia Desk of the Bilateral Programme for the Canadian International Development Agency (CIDA) in Ottawa, Canada (1977-1984); Education Programme Officer for Canadian University Service Overseas (CUSO) in Ottawa, Canada (1975-1977); and Private Consultant in Cross-Cultural Research and Training in Ottawa, Canada (1972-1984).

SPECIAL INTERESTS/HOBBIES: Music, reading, swimming, and tennis

GEOGRAPHIC SCOPE OF RECRUITING: Indonesia

SECTOR/INDUSTRY SPECIALIZATION: Financial services and professional services

FAVORITE HISTORICAL FIGURE/MODEL/MENTOR: Gandhi—Indians revered him as a saint and began to call him "Mahatma"—which means "great soul" in Sanskrit—a title reserved for the greatest sages. I chose Gandhi because of the great impact he had as a human being as well as an Indian nationalist leader.

SINGLE MOST IMPORTANT ISSUE IN CONDUCTING A HIGH LEVEL SEARCH: Clear communication and understanding with the client

BIGGEST COMPETITOR: Korn/Ferry International

MOST SIGNIFICANT OTHER ASPECT OF PERSONAL OR PROFESSIONAL LIFE: Going home to Indonesia after having spent 30 years overseas.

WHAT IS THE BEST PREPARATION FOR BEING A SUCCESSFUL RECRUITER? Key factors for success are having a passion for your work; building, managing and repairing relationships; having persistence; providing a unique service to your client; understanding your client and his business; and having a business sense for your client as well as for yourself.

continues ▶

WHAT WOULD YOU BE DOING IF YOU WERE NOT AN EXECUTIVE RECRUITER? It's hard to imagine because I love what I'm doing. I could see myself being a writer, as I am now contributing to newspapers and business publications as well as having a monthly column in a business magazine.

WHAT ARE THE CHARACTERISTICS OF A GOOD CLIENT? A good client is someone who has a broad vision, whose values I share or respect, who communicates clearly, and who demonstrates respect for others. Leadership and significant life experience giving the person qualities I respect and can learn from are important.

WHAT CHALLENGES DO YOU SEE AHEAD IN THE GLOBAL MARKETPLACE? Regionalism, communicating effectively with people of other cultures, increasing foreign investment in emerging countries, continued high demand for local executives coupled with relatively low supply of local qualified executives, return of experienced executives to their home countries, strategic alliances, and increasing entrepreneurial activities.

DAYTON OGDEN

Spencer Stuart
277 Park Avenue
New York, N.Y. 10172
U.S.A.

695 E. Main Street
Stamford, CT 06901
U.S.A

Telephone: 1 (203) 326-3715
Fax: 1 (203) 326-3757
E-mail: dogden@spencerstuart.com
Company Website: http://www.spencerstuart.com

DATE OF BIRTH: January 11, 1945

NATIONALITY: American—Grew up in Connecticut

EDUCATIONAL BACKGROUND:
  Yale University, B.A. American Studies, 1967, Dean's List; President, DKE Fraternity
  Hotchkiss School, 1963; 3-letter man; Vice President Student Council; Honor Roll

LANGUAGES SPOKEN: English

CAREER HIGHLIGHTS:
  CEO, Spencer Stuart, 1987–1996
  Board Member—Advanced Tissue Sciences, Project Hope, American Business Conference

SPECIAL INTERESTS/HOBBIES: Tuna fishing; boating; military history; international travel

GEOGRAPHIC SCOPE OF RECRUITING: Worldwide

SECTOR/INDUSTRY SPECIALIZATION: CEOs and Board of Directors

FAVORITE HISTORICAL FIGURE/MODEL/MENTOR: Winston Churchill

SINGLE MOST IMPORTANT ISSUE IN CONDUCTING A HIGH LEVEL SEARCH: Determining the right fit.
  Exhaustive reference checking is the primary tool in determining whether a candidate's track record and personal
  style fits your client's requirement. Once fit has been determined, then attraction becomes key.

BIGGEST COMPETITOR: Varies by region

MOST SIGNIFICANT OTHER ASPECT OF PERSONAL OR PROFESSIONAL LIFE: The most significant
  chapters/experiences in my life have been military experience (Vietnam), leadership of Spencer Stuart, and family.

WHAT IS THE BEST PREPARATION FOR BEING A SUCCESSFUL RECRUITER? There is no set path except that all
  executive recruiters who are successful are students of business. They love companies and are fascinated by how
  they work, how they are organized, and how they are led.

WHAT WOULD YOU BE DOING IF YOU WERE NOT AN EXECUTIVE RECRUITER? I would have enjoyed the
  M&A advisor business. There are many analogies to executive recruiting and the basic descriptions are similar.

WHAT ARE THE CHARACTERISTICS OF A GREAT CLIENT? A great client has high standards, a rigorous process
  and an open communication style. A great client understands the enormous value and competitive advantage of
  partnership with a top executive recruiter and is not excessively price sensitive and is willing to pay for value.

WHAT CHALLENGES DO YOU SEE AHEAD IN THE GLOBAL MARKETPLACE? The biggest challenge is the
  enormous wave of consolidation that is hitting many industries that have been the heaviest users of search. The pace
  of search is at an all time high and solid client relationships can be threatened by unforeseen and unpredictable
  occurrences.

LYNN B. OGDEN

Korn/Ferry International (HK) Ltd.
Rm. 2104-2106 Gloucester Tower
The Landmark
Hong Kong

Telephone: 852 2971-2723
Fax: 852 2810-1632
E-mail: Lynn.Ogden@kornferry.com
Company Website: http://www.kornferry.com

DATE OF BIRTH: April 13, 1961

NATIONALITY: American—Born in New York City, raised in Ohio

EDUCATIONAL BACKGROUND:
  1984   Wesleyan University, BA in East Asian Studies with Honors
  1984   Beijing University, advanced Mandarin

LANGUAGES SPOKEN: French, Mandarin

CAREER HIGHLIGHTS: Joined KFI and making partnership at 32 years of age

GEOGRAPHIC SCOPE OF RECRUITING: Asia with focus on regional searches and country manager assignments in Thailand, Taiwan, Philippines, Korea, and Hong Kong/PRC

SECTOR/INDUSTRY SPECIALIZATION: Consumer Products, Fashion/Retail, Entertainment and Energy

FAVORITE HISTORICAL FIGURE/MODEL/MENTOR: All women who strive for excellence in both career and family; my parents who taught me that I could achieve anything and everything that I put my mind to doing.

SINGLE MOST IMPORTANT ISSUE IN CONDUCTING A HIGH LEVEL SEARCH:
  • Direct contact with decision maker.
  • Frequent communication with client.

BIGGEST COMPETITOR: Myself

MOST SIGNIFICANT OTHER ASPECT OF PERSONAL OR PROFESSIONAL LIFE: Raising two beautiful and intelligent daughters in a bilingual/bicultural environment.

WHAT IS THE BEST PREPARATION FOR BEING A SUCCESSFUL RECRUITER? Tenacity and persistence combined with strong account management tools.

WHAT WOULD YOU BE DOING IF YOU WERE NOT AN EXECUTIVE RECRUITER? Management consultant or career counsellor at a college/university.

WHAT ARE THE CHARACTERISTICS OF A GREAT CLIENT? One that treats the search consultant as a true partner in achieving positive change/results for the firm through successful placements. Responsive and receptive to ideas.

WHAT CHALLENGES DO YOU SEE AHEAD IN THE GLOBAL MARKETPLACE? Management of information resources and potential overload as a result. The need for search individuals to remain focused and provide value-added consultancy and not cookie cutter responses. Defining global leadership to handle those challenges in the 21st Century.

TED A. ORNER

Russell Reynolds Associates
Suite 4800
First Interstate Bank Plaza
1000 Louisiana Street
Houston, TX 77002-5095
U.S.A.

Telephone: 1 (713) 658-1776
Fax: 1 (713) 658-9461
Company Website: http://www.russreyn.com

DATE OF BIRTH: August 18, 1942

NATIONALITY: U.S. citizen—Grew up in Northeastern United States

EDUCATIONAL BACKGROUND:
  B.S. in Civil Engineering (1964), M.S. in Business Management (1965), Lehigh University

LANGUAGES SPOKEN: English

CAREER HIGHLIGHTS: Fifteen years with Shell Oil before joining Russell Reynolds Associates in 1980

SPECIAL INTERESTS/HOBBIES: Reading, traveling, sports, community/church leadership

GEOGRAPHIC SCOPE OF RECRUITING: Worldwide but chiefly North America

SECTOR/INDUSTRY SPECIALIZATION: Natural Resources/Oil & Gas

FAVORITE HISTORICAL FIGURE/MODEL/MENTOR: Abraham Lincoln and King David

SINGLE MOST IMPORTANT ISSUE IN CONDUCTING A HIGH LEVEL SEARCH: Open communication—with
  clients, candidates, and associates; focus; and organization. All three contribute to quality which is what the client
  desires.

BIGGEST COMPETITOR: Time!!

MOST SIGNIFICANT OTHER ASPECT OF PERSONAL OR PROFESSIONAL LIFE: Married to my wife for 34 years!

LUIZ ALBERTO PANELLI

PMC Amrop International
Rua do Rocio 220, 8ᵉ andar
04552-000 São Paulo, SP
Brazil
Telephone: 55 11 822-9077
Fax: 55 11 822-0781
E-mail: pmcamrop@amcham.com.br
Company Website: http://www.amrop.com

DATE OF BIRTH: August 27, 1942

NATIONALITY: Brazilian—Grew up in Brazil

EDUCATIONAL BACKGROUND:
Graduate, São Paulo School of Business Administration, Getulio Vargas Foundation
Extension course, Graduate School of Business, University of Southern California

LANGUAGES SPOKEN: Portuguese, English, Spanish

CAREER HIGHLIGHTS: In executive search since 1968

SPECIAL INTERESTS/HOBBIES: Spectator sports (soccer, car racing, tennis, etc.), walking

GEOGRAPHIC SCOPE OF RECRUITING: Brazil

SECTOR/INDUSTRY SPECIALIZATION: Top management-all sectors

MOST SIGNIFICANT OTHER ASPECT OF PERSONAL OR PROFESSIONAL LIFE: Professional-founding partner of PMC Amrop International, in 1975, and Board Member of Amrop International from 1981 to 1990

WHAT IS THE BEST PREPARATION FOR BEING A SUCCESSFUL RECRUITER? A solid academic background. At least in Brazil, it is necessary for a successful recruiter to speak more than one language: besides Portuguese, English is a must, and Spanish very important. Further, a strong career which leads to strategic positions, and several years acting as an executive recruiter who really likes what he/she does, completes the profile.

WHAT WOULD YOU BE DOING IF YOU WERE NOT AN EXECUTIVE RECRUITER? Probably my preferences would be concentrated in another service firm as a partner or top executive.

WHAT ARE THE CHARACTERISTICS OF A GREAT CLIENT?
- Recognizes the importance of the search firm, and who works in partnership with it;
- Knows what it wants, and clearly defines what it is seeking;
- Does not compete with the search firm; and
- Recognizes the value of the services rendered based upon the results obtained.

WHAT CHALLENGES DO YOU SEE AHEAD IN THE GLOBAL MARKETPLACE? Demonstrating the capacity to assist a global client in an integrated and efficient manner, understanding its culture and requirements. Showing the ability to assist global clients within the search firm's geographical territory in accordance with the rules of the game, and with the same index of success as the other partners in the network.

MANUEL PAPAYANOPULOS

Korn/Ferry International
Montes Urales 505-Piso 3
Lomas de Chapultepec
11000 - Mexico, D.F.
Mexico

Telephone: 52 5 201-5400/19
Fax: 52 5 202-4469
E-mail: E-manuel.papayanopulos@kornferry.com
Company Website: http://www.kornferry.com

DATE OF BIRTH: February 21, 1945

NATIONALITY: Mexican—Grew up in Mexico City

EDUCATIONAL BACKGROUND:
 Industrial Relations, Iberoamericana University, 1969

LANGUAGES SPOKEN: Spanish/English

CAREER HIGHLIGHTS: 22 years in executive search in 2 dominant firms in Latin America

SPECIAL INTERESTS/HOBBIES: Art, water ski, chess

GEOGRAPHIC SCOPE OF RECRUITING: Mexico

SECTOR/INDUSTRY SPECIALIZATION: Health Care/Advanced Technology/General Practice

FAVORITE HISTORICAL FIGURE/MODEL/MENTOR: Armando C. Papayanopulos (father)

SINGLE MOST IMPORTANT ISSUE IN CONDUCTING A HIGH LEVEL SEARCH: Trust. My most successful
 placements have been those in which my client and I have shared common trust and respect. It is a win/win situation
 when you and your client sit on the same side of the table.

BIGGEST COMPETITOR: I have high respect for all my competition in Mexico. Egon Zehnder might be my biggest
 competitor.

MOST SIGNIFICANT OTHER ASPECT OF PERSONAL OR PROFESSIONAL LIFE: Family

WHAT IS THE BEST PREPARATION FOR BEING A SUCCESSFUL RECRUITER? Ideally a successful recruiter should
 have some business background complemented with experience in the service or consulting practice industries; as
 the profession evolves and prospers we will see more of the prototype of the big consulting firms: bright, young,
 energetic MBAs.

WHAT WOULD YOU BE DOING IF YOU WERE NOT AN EXECUTIVE RECRUITER? I love business. I would
 definitely be a General Manager and/or have a business of my own.

WHAT ARE THE CHARACTERISTICS OF A GREAT CLIENT? Usually we all have the perception that a great client is
 a prestigious, sophisticated, visible, respected and leading organization; however my own experience shows that
 strong and visionary CEOs make the real difference to attract the best quality of executives to an organization.

WHAT CHALLENGES DO YOU SEE AHEAD IN THE GLOBAL MARKETPLACE? Technology is the biggest challenge.
 I have heard of some colleagues who, for example, view Internet as a threat to our profession, but the fact is that
 technology can be one of the biggest allies for those who react promptly and efficiently in this area. Global search
 firms will need stronger local practices to truly serve clients on a global basis.

ROBERT L. PEARSON

LAI Ward Howell
1601 Elm Street, Suite 4150
Dallas, TX 75201
U.S.A.

Telephone: 1 (214) 754-0019
Fax: 1 (214) 754-8017
E-mail: pearsrob@lai.usa.com
Company Website: http://www.laix.com

DATE OF BIRTH: April 19, 1939

NATIONALITY: U.S.—Grew up in Chicago, Illinois

EDUCATIONAL BACKGROUND:
 B.S.E.E., Michigan State University, 1961
 M.S., Industrial Management, Massachusetts Inst. of Technology, 1963

LANGUAGES SPOKEN: English

CAREER HIGHLIGHTS: Managing Partner, President and Chief Executive Officer, Lamalie Amrop International (1984)-Present); Executive Director, Russell Reynolds Associates Inc. (1982-1984); President, Pearson Inc. (1971-1982); Vice President, Corporate Finance, R. J. Financial Corporation (1968-1971); Senior Engagement Manager, McKinsey & Company, Inc. (1964-1968); Management Trainee, RCA Missile and Surface Radar Division (1963-1964).

SPECIAL INTERESTS/HOBBIES: Long-distance running, hunting, fishing

GEOGRAPHIC SCOPE OF RECRUITING: International

SECTOR/INDUSTRY SPECIALIZATION: Information Technology, Telecommunications, Manufacturing/Distribution/Logistics, General Management

FAVORITE HISTORICAL FIGURE/MODEL/MENTOR: John Kennedy and Martin Luther King

SINGLE MOST IMPORTANT ISSUE IN CONDUCTING A HIGH LEVEL SEARCH: Completing it satisfactorily

BIGGEST COMPETITOR: Time

MOST SIGNIFICANT OTHER ASPECT OF PERSONAL OR PROFESSIONAL LIFE: Not enough time

WHAT IS THE BEST PREPARATION FOR BEING A SUCCESSFUL RECRUITER? A professional services/consulting background.

WHAT WOULD YOU BE DOING IF YOU WERE NOT AN EXECUTIVE RECRUITER? Fishing

WHAT ARE THE CHARACTERISTICS OF A GREAT CLIENT? Puts true value on the recruiting process and results.

WHAT CHALLENGES DO YOU SEE AHEAD IN THE GLOBAL MARKETPLACE? Key trends: technology, globalization, consolidation

PATRICK S. PITTARD

Heidrick & Struggles
303 Peachtree Street, Suite 4280
Atlanta, GA 30308
U.S.A.

Telephone: 1 (404) 572-0010
Fax: 1 (404) 572-0022
E-mail: psp@h-s.com
Company Website: http://www.h-s.com

DATE OF BIRTH: November 24, 1945

NATIONALITY: American—Grew up in Atlanta, Georgia and Columbus, Ohio

EDUCATIONAL BACKGROUND:

BBA-University of Georgia
Pursued graduate studies at Georgia State University

LANGUAGES SPOKEN: English

CAREER HIGHLIGHTS: Joined H&S in 1983; became Managing Partner of the Atlanta office and built the Southeast Practice. In 1994 became Managing Partner of North America. In 1997 became the Firm's President and CEO. Previously he held management and human resources positions at Citizens and Southern National Bank and Texas Commerce Bank and was a consultant at Kurt Salmon Associates. Before working in corporate America, taught sociology and coached the basketball and football teams at an Atlanta high school.

SPECIAL INTERESTS/HOBBIES: Playing full-court basketball, fly fishing, golf, and collecting carved bears.

GEOGRAPHIC SCOPE OF RECRUITING: National and International

SECTOR/INDUSTRY SPECIALIZATION: Specialization in General Management searches, i.e., CEO/COO

FAVORITE HISTORICAL FIGURE/MODEL/MENTOR: The golfer Bobby Jones, who is the epitome of professionalism, excellence, and integrity.

SINGLE MOST IMPORTANT ISSUE IN CONDUCTING A HIGH LEVEL SEARCH: Being credible at the highest levels, i.e., the candidates and the client. They are placing the future of their company and/or their careers in your hands. Gaining their confidence, and in many cases their friendship, and feeling in every sense a fiduciary to their future. Once both parties gain that level of confidence, the engagement can complete successfully.

MOST SIGNIFICANT OTHER ASPECT OF PERSONAL OR PROFESSIONAL LIFE: A wonderful support mechanism at home, in my office, and within the firm makes an all consuming business do-able and fun.

WHAT IS THE BEST PREPARATION FOR BEING A SUCCESSFUL RECRUITER? Having made a significant number of executive hiring decisions, or coming from a client service business, such as consulting. Our business is changing from a recruiting business to a value-added executive consultancy business.

WHAT WOULD YOU BE DOING IF YOU WERE NOT AN EXECUTIVE RECRUITER? I would probably be still a partner with a consulting firm. I was very happy there when Heidrick & Struggles called fourteen years ago.

continues ▶

WHAT ARE THE CHARACTERISTICS OF A GREAT CLIENT? A great client would be defined as honest, consistent, secure, decisive, and able to give non-judgmental course corrections.

WHAT CHALLENGES DO YOU SEE AHEAD IN THE GLOBAL MARKETPLACE? The great challenge is an expectation of executive talent availability versus reality. There are two few companies developing people and too many that need people. The talent pool is not growing as fast as the world economy. This is evident in compensation escalation. If a significant correction in the economy does not occur, a collision will occur as business vision exceeds the demand for business leaders.

CHARLES A. POLACHI, JR.

Fenwick Partners/Heidrick & Struggles
57 Bedford St.
Suite 101
Lexington, MA 01770
U.S.A.

Telephone: 1 (781) 676-1900
Fax: 1 (781) 861-7546
E-mail: cpolachi@fenwickpartners.com
Company Website: http://www.fenwickpartners.com

DATE OF BIRTH: July 18, 1953

NATIONALITY: American—Grew up in Pelham, N.Y.

EDUCATIONAL BACKGROUND:
BA, Holy Cross College, 1975
MBA, Boston College, 1982

LANGUAGES SPOKEN: Spanish

CAREER HIGHLIGHTS:
1975–1978: Data General
1978–present: Search; co-founded Fenwick 1983

SPECIAL INTERESTS/HOBBIES: Not-for-profit organizations; Board member, Wang Center

GEOGRAPHIC SCOPE OF RECRUITING: National and international

SECTOR/INDUSTRY SPECIALIZATION: Information Technology, Venture Capital

FAVORITE HISTORICAL FIGURE/MODEL/MENTOR: My dad

SINGLE MOST IMPORTANT ISSUE IN CONDUCTING A HIGH LEVEL SEARCH: Clear, concise profile of person sought with specific, measurable performance criteria

MOST SIGNIFICANT OTHER ASPECT OF PERSONAL OR PROFESSIONAL LIFE: My family

WHAT IS THE BEST PREPARATION FOR BEING A SUCCESSFUL RECRUITER?
- Broad liberal arts education with MBA
- High growth experience with early employers

WHAT WOULD YOU BE DOING IF YOU WERE NOT AN EXECUTIVE RECRUITER? Farmer

WHAT ARE THE CHARACTERISTICS OF A GREAT CLIENT? Accessible, open, frequent communication

WHAT CHALLENGES DO YOU SEE AHEAD IN THE GLOBAL MARKETPLACE? Competition for talented multinational executives

STEVEN B. POTTER

Highland Search Group, L.L.C.
565 Fifth Avenue
New York, NY 10017
U.S.A.

Telephone: Work: 1 (212) 328-1109
　　　　　 Fax: 1 (212) 328-1198
E-mail: steve.potter@searchers.com
Company Website: http://www.searchers.com

DATE OF BIRTH: December 31, 1954

NATIONALITY: American—Grew up in Woodbury, Connecticut

EDUCATIONAL BACKGROUND:
Taft School 1969–1973
Yale University 1973–1977-BA Major in History, Varsity Hockey, Varsity Lacrosse

LANGUAGES SPOKEN: English

CAREER HIGHLIGHTS: At 32 years old, one of the youngest managing directors at Russell Reynolds Associates 1987. Made member of the Executive Committee at 39 and ran Asia and Global Investment Banking practice. On cover of *Institutional Investor*, May 1984.

SPECIAL INTERESTS/HOBBIES: Mountain climbing (Everest 1991), ice hockey, seaplane pilot, reading, politics

GEOGRAPHIC SCOPE OF RECRUITING: International

SECTOR/INDUSTRY SPECIALIZATION: Financial services, investment banking, merchant banking & direct investment, senior management

FAVORITE HISTORICAL FIGURE/MODEL/MENTOR: Thomas Jefferson

SINGLE MOST IMPORTANT ISSUE IN CONDUCTING A HIGH LEVEL SEARCH: Trust by candidates and clients

BIGGEST COMPETITOR: The sum of the boutiques

MOST SIGNIFICANT OTHER ASPECT OF PERSONAL OR PROFESSIONAL LIFE: Starting the Highland Search Group in September 1995, with Georges Holzberger and Jim Phillips. Firm ranked in top 10 in the US in terms of revenue in its first year in business; #1 in terms of revenues per recruiter, per partner and per professional. In 1997, Highland has grown 60% in second full year in business to about $19.5 million in revenues and has six partners. Unique "Goldman like" approach gives us a completion rate that is substantially higher than our competitors particularly the large firms.

　　I spend time with my lovely wife, Jody, and three wonderful children. I love to fly seaplanes and climb mountains—organized a 1991 Everest North Face Expedition that summited ten climbers (out of 30) with no deaths or injuries.

WHAT IS THE BEST PREPARATION FOR BEING A SUCCESSFUL RECRUITER? There is no "best" preparation— anything that prepares one for a role that demands a tremendous amount of empathy, integrity, a sense of urgency, hard work, and judgment.

WHAT WOULD YOU BE DOING IF YOU WERE NOT AN EXECUTIVE RECRUITER? Probably climbing mountains or bush flying in Alaska.

WHAT ARE THE CHARACTERISTICS OF A GREAT CLIENT? Leadership, vision, a sense of urgency, an interesting multidimensional person.

WHAT CHALLENGES DO YOU SEE AHEAD IN THE GLOBAL MARKETPLACE? Increased competition, consolidation of service firms, more time demands on recruiters, a need for more complete, cheaper, in-depth information on people and companies in a shorter time frame.

WINDLE B. PRIEM

Korn/Ferry International
200 Park Avenue, 37th Floor
New York, NY 10166
U.S.A.

Telephone: 1 (212) 687-1834
Fax: 1 (212) 687-2637
Company Website: http://www.kornferry.com

DATE OF BIRTH: October 17, 1937

NATIONALITY: American—Grew up in Boston, Massachusetts

EDUCATIONAL BACKGROUND:
  Worcester Polytechnic Institute, BSME, 1959
  Babson College, MBA, 1964
  Harvard Business School, PMD, 1975

LANGUAGES SPOKEN: English

CAREER HIGHLIGHTS:
  Recruited more than 100 Presidents or Chairmen for financial institutions during the last 22 years.

GEOGRAPHIC SCOPE OF RECRUITING: Mainly U.S.A.

SECTOR/INDUSTRY SPECIALIZATION: Financial Services

SINGLE MOST IMPORTANT ISSUE IN CONDUCTING A HIGH LEVEL SEARCH: Recruit an executive who can really make a difference.

BIGGEST COMPETITOR: Roche and Neff

WHAT CHALLENGES DO YOU SEE AHEAD IN THE GLOBAL MARKETPLACE? In the future, clients will want more service on a cost effective and timely basis.

MARYLIN L. PRINCE

Higdon Prince Inc.
230 Park Avenue, Suite 1455
New York, New York 10169
U.S.A.

Telephone: 1 (212) 986-4662
Fax: 1 (212) 986-5002

DATE OF BIRTH: August 10, 1953

NATIONALITY: U.S. citizen—Grew up in Pennsylvania

EDUCATIONAL BACKGROUND:

1975   B.A. Degree, Psychology, Elmira College
1977   M.A. Degree, Counseling, Hunter College

LANGUAGES SPOKEN: English

CAREER HIGHLIGHTS:

1976-1977   ITT Education Services (New York): Director of Counseling
1977-1979   Citibank N.A. (New York): Recruiting Manager
1979-1983   Bank of America (Los Angeles): Director of Management Development/Sales Training
1983-1986   Russell Reynolds Associates (New York): Associate, Financial Services Practice
1986-1992   Higdon, Joys & Mingle, Inc. (New York: Executive Director
1992-Present   Higdon Prince Inc. (New York): President and Managing Director

SPECIAL INTERESTS/HOBBIES: Bicycling; exercise; antiquing; reading; theater; Co-Chair, Annual Fund of Friends Seminary; Board Member, Center for Family Connections

GEOGRAPHIC SCOPE OF RECRUITING: North America and Europe

SECTOR/INDUSTRY SPECIALIZATION: Financial services with major expertise in all aspects of global investment management.

FAVORITE HISTORICAL FIGURE/ROLE MODEL/MENTOR: Golda Meier, an admired woman and respected leader of the free world, for her character and courage in holding together a nation under fire.

SINGLE MOST IMPORTANT ISSUE IN CONDUCTING A HIGH LEVEL SEARCH: The ability to assess a suitable match between a candidate's personal and professional characteristics against the position requirements and cultural aspects of a client organization.

MOST SIGNIFICANT OTHER ASPECT OF PERSONAL OR PROFESSIONAL LIFE: My husband and I are dual-career parents of a 12-year-old son and together we strive to achieve the highest level of happiness and success throughout our personal and professional lives.

WHAT IS THE BEST PREPARATION FOR BEING A SUCCESSFUL RECRUITER? What is unique about the executive search profession is that typically people do not grow up with their sights set on becoming an executive recruiter. It is a career that is usually discovered after having had experience in another industry or discipline. There is no one best way to prepare; however, there are certain characteristics that successful people share. For executive search, these include intelligence, inquisitiveness, intuition, selling skills, strong interpersonal skills and individual

continues ▶

initiative. Previous work experience in an industry for which you want to recruit can be very helpful in launching a recruiting career. In the end, success is determined by one's ability to relate to clients as well as prospective candidates and to be able to assess a company's needs and successfully satisfy those requirements.

WHAT WOULD YOU BE DOING IF YOU WERE NOT AN EXECUTIVE RECRUITER? I would either be an owner of a vineyard, or the President of a not-for-profit organization.

WHAT ARE THE CHARACTERISTICS OF A GREAT CLIENT? A great client views his/her recruiter as an extension or representative of their organization. A client should work together as a "partner" with the recruiter to accomplish their collective goal, which is to identify and attract the best candidate for the requirement. Clients should see recruiters not as "vendors" but rather as providers of a service which will prove to be critical to the success of the organization. Prospective candidates need to be viewed as "candidates" and not "applicants" and should feel appreciated for having an interest in exploring the opportunity. Honest feedback, both positive and negative, and open lines of communication with the executive recruiter, are critical to the success of the search. Together with the recruiter, the client should consider any problem which arises with the search as one which should be solved together. A great client is a good listener, has a sense of humor, and allows his/her personality to come through during the course of an assignment to both the recruiter and the candidates. Responsiveness and a sense of urgency on the part of the client is also of importance. Finally, a great client is one who will compliment the recruiter when a job has been well done, and will provide further opportunity to continue the professional relationship when additional search needs arise.

WHAT CHALLENGES DO YOU SEE AHEAD IN THE GLOBAL MARKETPLACE? Integration of differences from the most obvious things such as peoples and time zones to technologies, ethical and cultural approaches to business and risk tolerances.

FINN KROGH RANTS

Amrop International
Christians Brygge 24
1559 Copenhagen V
Denmark

Telephone: 45 33 14 01 55
Fax: 45 33 14 41 55
E-mail: Finn.Rants@amrop.com
Company Website: http://www.amrop.com

DATE OF BIRTH: 02.10.53

NATIONALITY: Danish—Grew up in Copenhagen

EDUCATIONAL BACKGROUND:
   1981: Chartered Accountant
   1978: Bachelor of Commerce

LANGUAGES SPOKEN: Danish, English

CAREER HIGHLIGHTS: Established Amrop International in Denmark as market leader

SPECIAL INTERESTS/HOBBIES: Tennis and sailing

GEOGRAPHIC SCOPE OF RECRUITING: Mainly Scandinavia, Russia, also global

SECTOR/INDUSTRY SPECIALIZATION: Consumer, Industry

BIGGEST COMPETITOR: Our biggest competitor is our ability to continuously be the prime mover in the market, who puts up standards for the search business regarding ethics, quality, creativity and speed. This means teaching the customers and potential customers what good quality is in co-operation with a search company.

WHAT IS THE BEST PREPARATION FOR BEING A SUCCESSFUL RECRUITER? The best preparation for being a successful recruiter is the ability to understand the company's strategy and define the demands of the person(s) who is to be hired, in order that the total human resource in the company is optimized.

WHAT WOULD YOU BE DOING IF YOU WERE NOT AN EXECUTIVE RECRUITER? If I was not a successful recruiter, I would be working in a big international service company, probably as a Sales and Marketing Director, Finance or Human Resource Director.

WHAT ARE THE CHARACTERISTICS OF A GREAT CLIENT? The characteristics of a great client is a client with whom the search consultant can have an open, honest and confidential dialogue. Furthermore, it is very important that the client uses the executive search as a natural part of the company's strategical development and to optimize the goal achievement.

WHAT CHALLENGES DO YOU SEE AHEAD IN THE GLOBAL MARKETPLACE? The challenge is getting the clients to co-operate with the executive recruiter on a more strategical level and not primarily use executive search in connection with "fire extinguishing."

PAUL RICHARD RAY, JR.

Ray & Berndtson
301 Commerce St., Suite 2300
Fort Worth, TX 76102
U.S.A.

Telephone: 1 (817) 334-0500
Fax: 1 (817) 334-0779
Company Website: http://www.prb.com

DATE OF BIRTH: November 6, 1943

NATIONALITY: American—Grew up in Fort Worth, Texas

EDUCATIONAL BACKGROUND:
University of Arkansas, BSBA, University of Texas, JD

LANGUAGES SPOKEN: English

CAREER HIGHLIGHTS:
- Outstanding student, one of 35 at the University of Texas—1969
- Who's Who in American Colleges and Universities, 1966
- President, student body, University of Texas School of Law
- Director of marketing for major consumer products company at age 30
- Selected as member of Young Presidents Organization (must be president of company before age 40)
- Chairman, Association of Executive Search Consultants, 1995 to present
- President & CEO, Ray & Berndtson, 1986 to present
- First recipient of The Eleanor Raynolds Award for combining excellence in search with a commitment to volunteerism, 1993
- Gardner Heidrick award for outstanding contribution to the executive search consulting profession, 1997

SPECIAL INTERESTS/HOBBIES: Running, hunting, fishing, horseback riding

GEOGRAPHIC SCOPE OF RECRUITING: Global

SECTOR/INDUSTRY SPECIALIZATION: Top management, consumer products, and professional services

FAVORITE HISTORICAL FIGURE/MODEL/MENTOR: Historical Figure: Mohandas Ghandi. Mentor: Hudnell Christopher, R.J. Reynolds Industries, to whom I reported to Hudnell Christopher when I was a marketing manager at RJR. He taught me the importance of listening to other people, leading by example and setting a course that others could understand and follow. Essentially, he taught me the fundamentals of leadership. Role Model: Colin Stokes, former chairman, R.J. Reynolds Industries, who taught me that the head of a multi-billion corporation could lead with real humanity. He set a clear vision and operated with the utmost integrity, all the time conveying a warmth that endeared you to him and engendered great confidence.

SINGLE MOST IMPORTANT ISSUE IN CONDUCTING A HIGH LEVEL SEARCH: Chemistry and culture fit (most senior level searches fail for these reasons, not qualification), sense of humor

MOST SIGNIFICANT OTHER ASPECT OF PERSONAL OR PROFESSIONAL LIFE: My immediate (wife and 3 children) and extended (parents, nine brothers and sisters) family.

WHAT IS THE BEST PREPARATION FOR BEING A SUCCESSFUL RECRUITER? In today's environment, very specific industry experience provides the best foundation for a successful career as a recruiter. The science of recruiting can be taught. But extensive knowledge about a particular industry segment enables a recruiter to truly add value to his or her clients and effectively assess talent for their organizations.

WHAT WOULD YOU DO IF YOU WERE NOT AN EXECUTIVE RECRUITER? Had I not entered the executive search profession, I would have probably started my own business developing and manufacturing a consumer product of some type. Assuming success, my goal would have been to take the company public or sell it to a larger company.

WHAT ARE THE CHARACTERISTICS OF A GREAT CLIENT? A great client recognizes the value of establishing a deep and committed relationship with a top-rate executive search firm. Their willingness to openly share all of the issues affecting the company underscores a commitment to establishing long-term associations and not just conducting transactions. They consider us a partner in helping them build their organizations with talented human capital.

WHAT CHALLENGES DO YOU SEE AHEAD IN THE GLOBAL MARKETPLACE? Everyone in search faces the same challenge: the ability to deliver truly seamless service to organizations separated by not only geography, but culture. The advances in technology will be important in overcoming the geographic challenges, and developing capabilities in the most important markets of the world will enable recruiters to deliver service globally with local expertise.

JOHANN REDEHLINGHUYS

Amrop International
Suite 702, Nedbank Gardens
33 Bath Avenue
Rosebank, JHB
South Africa

P.O. Box 52858
Saxonwold, 2132

Telephone: 27 21 880-5910
Fax: 27 21 880-5145
E-mail: amropmjr@iafrica.com
Company Website: http://www.amrop.co.za

DATE OF BIRTH: 11/12/1941

NATIONALITY: South African—Grew up in Capetown, South Africa

EDUCATIONAL BACKGROUND:
  Honours degree in psychology from Rhodes University

LANGUAGES SPOKEN: English and Afrikaans

CAREER HIGHLIGHTS: Started business in 1970. Invited to become Amrop representative in S.A. 1983.

SPECIAL INTERESTS/HOBBIES: Politics, current affairs, art, skiing, diving

GEOGRAPHIC SCOPE OF RECRUITING: Southern Africa and Indian Ocean Rim

SECTOR/INDUSTRY SPECIALIZATION: Financial Services, Hospitality Industry

FAVORITE HISTORICAL FIGURE/MODEL/MENTOR: All successful entrepreneurs

SINGLE MOST IMPORTANT ISSUE IN CONDUCTING A HIGH LEVEL SEARCH: Managing the expectations of your client, the candidate, and yourself. Understanding the real needs and meeting them.

BIGGEST COMPETITOR: Spencer Stuart

MOST SIGNIFICANT OTHER ASPECT OF PERSONAL OR PROFESSIONAL LIFE: Being the head of the family is more important than being the head of a business.

WHAT IS THE BEST PREPARATION FOR BEING A SUCCESSFUL RECRUITER? A good academic training to develop the mind-not in any particular field-followed by some solid experience in almost any part of a well run business. Otherwise any experience that would develop self-reliance, strong networking capabilities, coaching skills and the ability to negotiate successfully.

WHAT WOULD YOU BE DOING IF YOU WERE NOT AN EXECUTIVE RECRUITER? I used to think that it might have been architecture, but these days a more exciting option would be investment banking, stockbroking or something in financial services.

WHAT ARE THE CHARACTERISTICS OF A GREAT CLIENT? Decisiveness and someone who understands his own needs. A great client is open, understands his own agendas and allows the development of a trusting relationship.

WHAT CHALLENGES DO YOU SEE AHEAD IN THE GLOBAL MARKETPLACE? A considerable change in the way senior executives work and view their careers, redefining our lives in the wake of dramatic technological change.

GARY T. REIDY

Amrop International
Level 9
155 George Street
Sydney NSW 2000
Australia

Telephone: 61 2 9252 3500
Fax: 61 2 9247 2757
E-mail: gary.reidy@amrop.com
Company Website: http://www.amrop.com

DATE OF BIRTH: January 6, 1945

NATIONALITY: Australian—Grew up in Australia

EDUCATIONAL BACKGROUND:
Barrister-at-Law (Sydney University)

LANGUAGES SPOKEN: English

CAREER HIGHLIGHTS:

- Graduate-Officer Training Unit (R.A.R.)
- Awarded Military Cross (SVN)
- Admission to the Bar, NSW and Old Supreme Courts
- Appointed Managing Director, ACI Building Products Group
- Partner, Amrop International (since 1989)
- Managing Partner, Amrop International (since 1995)
- Acquisition of an unlisted public company

SPECIAL INTERESTS/HOBBIES: Breeding stud cattle, agriculture, food, wine

GEOGRAPHIC SCOPE OF RECRUITING: Global

SECTOR/INDUSTRY SPECIALIZATION: Senior executive and non-executive director level searches in resources/mining, manufacturing, infrastructure, banking and finance, technology, health; senior executive team assessments

FAVORITE HISTORICAL FIGURE/MODEL/MENTOR: Sir Winston Churchill

SINGLE MOST IMPORTANT ISSUE IN CONDUCTING A HIGH LEVEL SEARCH: Establishing/maintaining business partnership with clients; sharing confidences. Mutual understanding of strategic intent, needs and expectations.

BIGGEST COMPETITOR: Other international senior executive, retained executive search firms

MOST SIGNIFICANT OTHER ASPECT OF PERSONAL OR PROFESSIONAL LIFE: Integrity and mutual respect

WHAT IS THE BEST PREPARATION FOR BEING A SUCCESSFUL RECRUITER? Discipline of mind and diverse experience

WHAT WOULD YOU BE DOING IF YOU WERE NOT AN EXECUTIVE RECRUITER? I would be a senior executive role in a publicly listed company or a Barrister-at-Law.

continues ▶

WHAT ARE THE CHARACTERISTICS OF A GREAT CLIENT? Willingness to enter into a strong business partnership; sharing confidences with the search professional and providing comprehensive briefings on requirements in terms of strategic intent and organisational design and culture.

WHAT CHALLENGES DO YOU SEE AHEAD IN THE GLOBAL MARKETPLACE? In an environment of globalisation, coupled with local downsizing and the contraction of middle-management levels in many companies, corporate success will be defined by the ability to attract, develop and retain the global executive who is capable of filling roles which require management of diversity and complexity.

WOLFGANG REINERMANN

H. Neumann International Management Consultants
Cecilienallee 59
D-40474 Düsseldorf
Germany
Telephone: 49 211-454890
Fax: 49 211-4541767
Company Website: http://www.neumann-inter.com

DATE OF BIRTH: November 4, 1938

NATIONALITY: German—Grew up in Salzburg, Austria

EDUCATIONAL BACKGROUND: Educated by Jesuits; MBA from a prestigious German University

LANGUAGES SPOKEN: German, English

CAREER HIGHLIGHTS: Head of Personnel Services Division PA Worldwide; Board Member of H. Neumann International

SPECIAL INTERESTS/HOBBIES: Classic music, mountain hiking, golf

GEOGRAPHIC SCOPE OF RECRUITING: Worldwide

SECTOR/INDUSTRY SPECIALIZATION: Consumer goods, capital goods, retail, textile/apparel, financial services, search of supervisory board members

FAVORITE HISTORICAL FIGURE/MODEL/MENTOR: Alexander the Great

SINGLE MOST IMPORTANT ISSUE IN CONDUCTING A HIGH LEVEL SEARCH: Confidence of client based on experience, competence and personality of consultant

BIGGEST COMPETITOR: Mülder/Heidrick & Struggles

MOST SIGNIFICANT OTHER ASPECT OF PERSONAL OR PROFESSIONAL LIFE: Family and job enrichment

WHAT IS THE BEST PREPARATION FOR BEING A SUCCESSFUL RECRUITER?
- Exceptional competence in certain industry sectors
- Dedication and commitment to clients
- Ability to deliver solutions and solve problems
- Being a change agent

WHAT WOULD YOU BE DOING IF YOU WERE NOT AN EXECUTIVE RECRUITER? A sports TV reporter or a mountain guide

WHAT ARE THE CHARACTERISTICS OF A GREAT CLIENT? A great client exhibits frankness and loyalty, confidence in the recruiter's competence, willingness to build a lasting partnership, and leadership and successful track record.

WHAT CHALLENGES DO YOU SEE AHEAD IN THE GLOBAL MARKETPLACE?
- Multicultural approach in the search for top managers
- Globalization requires international management ability
- Frontierless presence of executive search firms as a "mirror" of multinational corporations

MARIA DA GLORIA RIBEIRO

Amrop International Portugal
Av. António Augusto de Aguiar
1050 Lisboa
Portugal
Telephone: 351.1.357 3677
Fax: 351.1.352 0457
E-mail: lisbon@amrop.com
Company Website: http://www.amrop.com

DATE OF BIRTH: September 30, 1956

NATIONALITY: Portuguese—Grew up in Portugal

EDUCATIONAL BACKGROUND:
 Master Degree in Psychology from Faculdade de Psicologia e Ciências da Educacão (Porto University) in 1980

LANGUAGES SPOKEN: Portuguese, English, French, Spanish

CAREER HIGHLIGHTS: To achieve the global quality (strategic intelligence, research, management)

SPECIAL INTERESTS/HOBBIES: Reading, travel

GEOGRAPHIC SCOPE OF RECRUITING: Worldwide

SECTOR/INDUSTRY SPECIALIZATION: Finance, consumer goods, automotive

SINGLE MOST IMPORTANT ISSUE IN CONDUCTING A HIGH LEVEL SEARCH: To be able to understand the client's business, the cultural values and strategies in order to feel 100% inside the company and to influence, through the recruitment, the best way to achieve the goals.

MOST SIGNIFICANT OTHER ASPECT OF PERSONAL OR PROFESSIONAL LIFE: Being a mother

WHAT IS THE BEST PREPARATION FOR BEING A SUCCESSFUL RECRUITER? Degree in Psychology (Organizational Behavior area) + MBA

WHAT WOULD YOU BE DOING IF YOU WERE NOT AN EXECUTIVE RECRUITER? Due to my background, Marketing Director. However, in my dreams, I would have been a Choreographer (classic) or a writer (poetry).

WHAT ARE THE CHARACTERISTICS OF A GREAT CLIENT? Someone intelligent, who is willing to create a partnership with us and to take advantage of all our potentialities as Executive Search consultants.

WHAT CHALLENGES DO YOU SEE AHEAD IN THE GLOBAL MARKETPLACE? International searches (cross border searches); development of specialized Practice Groups.

GERARD R. ROCHE

Heidrick & Struggles
245 Park Avenue, 43rd Floor
New York, NY 10167
U.S.A.

Telephone: 1 (212) 551-0505
Fax: 1 (212) 867-3254
E-mail: grr@h-s.com
Company Website: http://www.h-s.com

DATE OF BIRTH: July 27, 1931

NATIONALITY: American—Grew up in Scranton, PA

EDUCATIONAL BACKGROUND:
New York University, MBA, 1958
University of Scranton, BS (Accounting), 1953

LANGUAGES SPOKEN: English

CAREER HIGHLIGHTS:
1964 to present: Heidrick & Struggles (Chairman since 1981)
Earlier Marketing & Account Management roles with Kordite (Mobil Oil), ABC, AT&T

SPECIAL INTERESTS/HOBBIES: Golf, walking, reading, friendly debate

GEOGRAPHIC SCOPE OF RECRUITING: International

SECTOR/INDUSTRY SPECIALIZATION: Generalist with strong emphasis on high level corporate general management searches in a variety of industries.

FAVORITE HISTORICAL FIGURE/MODEL/MENTOR: Vaclav Havel (most admired), Gardner Heidrick (mentor)

SINGLE MOST IMPORTANT ISSUE IN CONDUCTING A HIGH LEVEL SEARCH: Client communication and management

BIGGEST COMPETITOR: Spencer Stuart/Tom Neff

MOST SIGNIFICANT OTHER ASPECT OF PERSONAL OR PROFESSIONAL LIFE: Faith

WHAT IS THE BEST PREPARATION FOR BEING A SUCCESSFUL RECRUITER? Make sure you're born right . . . good early environment . . . lots of human contact . . . warm both hands before the fire of life.

WHAT WOULD YOU BE DOING IF YOU WERE NOT AN EXECUTIVE RECRUITER? God only knows, but I certainly wouldn't have gotten this far.

WHAT ARE THE CHARACTERISTICS OF A GREAT CLIENT? Human understanding, decisiveness, patience, values, communicator, big thinker, out of box thinker, sense of humor.

WHAT CHALLENGES DO YOU SEE AHEAD IN THE GLOBAL MARKETPLACE? Depersonalization of the business, need to run big organizations like small ones, more global outlook, less parochialism.

ROBERT S. ROLLO

R. Rollo Associates
725 South Figueroa Street, Suite 3230
Los Angeles, CA 90017
U.S.A.

Telephone: 1 (213) 688-9444
Fax: 1 (213) 688-8358
E-mail: rrollo@mindspring.com

DATE OF BIRTH: April 4, 1947

NATIONALITY: American—Grew up in Long Beach, California

EDUCATIONAL BACKGROUND:
University of Southern California, Los Angeles, California
1969 Bachelor of Science-Business Administration
1970 Master of Business Administration-International Business

LANGUAGES SPOKEN: English, Spanish

CAREER HIGHLIGHTS:

1992-Present	Managing Partner, R. Rollo Associates, Los Angeles, California
1981-1992	Managing Partner, Korn/Ferry International, Los Angeles, California
1978-1981	Manager, Strategic Planning/Vice President Marketing, AM International, Los Angeles, California
1973-1978	Vice President, Union Bank, Los Angeles, California
1970-1973	Lt. jg., U.S. Navy

SPECIAL INTERESTS/HOBBIES: Exotic travel, outdoor sports, boating, model railroading

GEOGRAPHIC SCOPE OF RECRUITING: Worldwide, with a main focus on the Western United States

SECTOR/INDUSTRY SPECIALIZATION: Industry generalist, with a specialty in financial services, investment management, packaged goods, and energy. All searches at the senior level, including presidents, chief executive officers, managing directors, and board members.

FAVORITE HISTORICAL FIGURE/MODEL/MENTOR:
- Merriweather Lewis (Lewis & Clark); Thomas Jefferson; John Paul Jones
- David Packard, Founder, Hewlett Packard; Walter Cronkite, Journalist; Chuck Yeager, test pilot
- Roy Ash, Founder, Litton Industries; Richard Ferry, Founder, Korn/Ferry International; Robert Dockson, Dean, USC School of Business

SINGLE MOST IMPORTANT ISSUE IN CONDUCTING A HIGH LEVEL SEARCH: Grasping the key elements of a situation which will lead to the client being totally comfortable with the final candidate selection, and then designing a search that will successfully meet those needs.

BIGGEST COMPETITOR: The untapped market of companies that have not yet used the services of a top quality executive search firm.

MOST SIGNIFICANT OTHER ASPECT OF PERSONAL OR PROFESSIONAL LIFE: Active involvement with my wife and the exciting lives of our four children with significant community service.

WHAT IS THE BEST PREPARATION FOR BEING A SUCCESSFUL RECRUITER? Good, broad education. Practical business management experience. International exposure. Working closely for/with successful leaders.

WHAT WOULD YOU BE DOING IF YOU WERE NOT AN EXECUTIVE RECRUITER? An athletic coach or an organizer of unusual adventure trips.

WHAT ARE THE CHARACTERISTICS OF A GREAT CLIENT?

- Well founded understanding of what the client is looking for.
- Invites the recruiter to be part of the client's team while conducting the search.
- Is enthusiastic and positive about the company, the position, and recruiting an outstanding executive into the business.

WHAT CHALLENGES DO YOU SEE AHEAD IN THE GLOBAL MARKETPLACE?

- Continued consolidation of companies in most major industries.
- Financial inter-dependence of the global market.
- Intelligently filtering the most appropriate information available to make sound decisions.

PHILIPPA ROSE

The Rose Partnership
12 Copthall Avenue
London EC2R 7DH, U.K.
Telephone: 44 171 466 6000
E-mail: general@the.rosepartnership.wo.uk

DATE OF BIRTH: December 18, 1958

NATIONALITY: British—Grew up in Paris, then Essex

EDUCATIONAL BACKGROUND:
- New Hall School, Boreham, Chelmsford, Essex
- Did not go to university
- Associate of the London College of Music (ALCM)

LANGUAGES SPOKEN: French and Italian

SPECIAL INTERESTS/HOBBIES: Interior design, 17th century English country furniture, Indian cooking, hiking, rock and roll dancing, holistic medicine

GEOGRAPHIC SCOPE OF RECRUITING: U.K. and continental Europe

SECTOR/INDUSTRY SPECIALIZATION: Corporate Finance

FAVORITE HISTORICAL FIGURE/MODEL/MENTOR: Empress Josephine

SINGLE MOST IMPORTANT ISSUE IN CONDUCTING A HIGH LEVEL SEARCH: Understanding your client and the job

BIGGEST COMPETITOR: Julian Sainty

MOST SIGNIFICANT OTHER ASPECT OF PERSONAL OR PROFESSIONAL LIFE: Four children under age 9

WHAT IS THE BEST PREPARATION FOR BEING A SUCCESSFUL RECRUITER? My preference is to hire people with at least two years' experience in the area, discipline, or product in which they are to recruit. I also look for experience of something totally different; for experience of recruiting is not essential and can be a disadvantage.

WHAT WOULD YOU BE DOING IF YOU WERE NOT AN EXECUTIVE RECRUITER? I would be running my own business in one of the following lines: Country House hotels, possibly with a "retreat" theme; or some business which aimed to educate the business community and the city in holistic medicine. It might be possible to combine the two.

WHAT ARE THE CHARACTERISTICS OF A GREAT CLIENT?
- Total openness. Mutual trust. One who treats his search consultant as a trusted advisor.
- Gives efficient and speedy feedback post candidate meetings.
- Good judge of character. Confident enough to hire unusual/imaginative profiles. Puts calibre before experience.
- Pays fees without argument or negotiation.
- Sense of humor. Fun to work with.

WHAT CHALLENGES DO YOU SEE AHEAD IN THE GLOBAL MARKETPLACE? The challenge is to deal with the logistics of covering the globe thoroughly while maintaining consistent standards, perfect coordination and integration of the project, and a seamless front to the client. It is just about achievable within a region, but globally it is certainly testing.

LOUISA WONG ROUSSEAU

Bó Lè Associates
15/F., Onfem Tower, No. 29, Wyndham Street, Central,
Hong Kong
Telephone: 852-2525-4339
Fax: 852-2525-7153 (F)
E-mail: lwr@asiaonline.net

NATIONALITY: American—Grew up in Hong Kong

EDUCATIONAL BACKGROUND:
B.Sc., University of Toronto
MBA, Harvard Business School

LANGUAGES SPOKEN: Cantonese, Mandarin, and English

CAREER HIGHLIGHTS:
JP Morgan, 1981–1982
Alexander Department Store, 1982–1987
Russell Reynolds Associates, HK, 1987–1996
Bó Lè Associates, 1996–Present

GEOGRAPHIC SCOPE OF RECRUITING: Asia

SECTOR/INDUSTRY SPECIALIZATION: Financial Services, Consumer Products and Services

SINGLE MOST IMPORTANT ISSUE IN CONDUCTING A HIGH LEVEL SEARCH:
- Absolute partnership with client, must have clear understanding of all issues and dynamics related to the search
- Straight and direct communication with the client

WHAT IS THE BEST PREPARATION FOR BEING A SUCCESSFUL RECRUITER? A successful recruiter is on-the-ground, with at least 5 years work experience so that he/she can develop broad business sense. He/she should have a clear mind set, be very open-minded, and extremely flexible. He/she must be prepared to observe, listen and learn from the others as well as work very hard. He/she should be willing to "mump" into the business, which is about managing changes and influencing events.

WHAT WOULD YOU BE DOING IF YOU WERE NOT AN EXECUTIVE RECRUITER? I might retire, travel all over the world, do some teaching or consulting works.

WHAT ARE THE CHARACTERISTICS OF A GREAT CLIENT? A great client is a "partner" who is responsible, equally responsive, very demanding, a good communicator with the ability and authority to make decisions. Open communication is extremely important. He/she should ideally adopt a "give and take" approach as the recruiter is expected to do all the time. We are expected to "earn" the respect from our clients whom we hope will also respect our time and effort, and manage the various recruiting firms on an open and fair basis.

WHAT CHALLENGES DO YOU SEE AHEAD IN THE GLOBAL MARKETPLACE? The rapid change of technology and its impact on all businesses including executive search.

GLENDON ROWELL

Boyden International Limited
8 Queens' Road, 12th Floor
Hong Kong

Telephone: 852-2868 3882
Fax: 852-2810 6198
E-mail: GRowell@boyden.com.hk
Company Website: http://www.boyden.com

DATE OF BIRTH: April 29, 1936

NATIONALITY: American—Grew up in U.S.A.

EDUCATIONAL BACKGROUND:

- BA, Psychology, Brown University, Providence, Rhode Island, U.S.A.
- MBA, University of Connecticut, U.S.A.
- PhD, University of California, Los Angeles, U.S.A.

LANGUAGES SPOKEN: English, Spanish, some Tagalog, Cantonese

CAREER HIGHLIGHTS: Becoming a managing director/president at age 34, then president of Avon Philippines and Asia regional director, Avon.

SPECIAL INTERESTS/HOBBIES: Tennis, scuba, writing (articles and children's stories)

GEOGRAPHIC SCOPE OF RECRUITING: China, Hong Kong, Philippines

SECTOR/INDUSTRY SPECIALIZATION: I try to do the very best for every client, regardless of industry.

FAVORITE HISTORICAL FIGURE/MODEL/MENTOR: Winston Churchill

SINGLE MOST IMPORTANT ISSUE IN CONDUCTING A HIGH LEVEL SEARCH: Presenting candidates whose goals, aspirations, and—most importantly—personal "chemistry" match those of the client. Very often, new executives from outside the company must be agents-of-change so it is imperative that they be effective immediately in their new corporate management culture.

WHAT IS THE BEST PREPARATION FOR BEING A SUCCESSFUL RECRUITER? To have had executive general management experience.

WHAT WOULD YOU BE DOING IF YOU WERE NOT AN EXECUTIVE RECRUITER? Buying, rebuilding, and selling troubled companies.

WHAT ARE THE CHARACTERISTICS OF A GREAT CLIENT? Someone who knows fairly precisely what he wants and yet will allow his recruiter the latitude to present creative solutions.

WHAT CHALLENGES DO YOU SEE AHEAD IN THE GLOBAL MARKETPLACE? More "in-house" recruiters and more boutiques.

ROGER RYTZ

Spencer Stuart
Hottingerstrasse 21
ZH - 8032 Zürich, Switzerland

Telephone: 41-1-252 11 11
Fax: 41-1-252 13 12
E-mail: rrytz@spencerstuart.com
Company Website: http://www.spencerstuart.com

DATE OF BIRTH: February 13, 1941

NATIONALITY: Swiss—Grew up in Bern (Switzerland)

EDUCATIONAL BACKGROUND:

Masters degree in Electronic Engineering from the Federal Institute of Technology in Zürich (Dipl. El.-Ing. ETHZ). Post graduate degree in Industrial Engineering from the FIT. PhD in Operations Research.

LANGUAGES SPOKEN: German, English, French, Italian

CAREER HIGHLIGHTS:

Since 1981 Consultant with Spencer Stuart, since 1989 Managing Director Switzerland.
1978–1981 General Manager Marketing and Technology for SIHI-Halberg, an international pump manufacturer.
1970–1978 McKinsey & Company, Zürich, Munich, Milan and Paris.

SPECIAL INTERESTS/HOBBIES: People and their personal development; performing arts; piloting aircraft and paragliders, and other outdoor sports.

GEOGRAPHIC SCOPE OF RECRUITING: Worldwide, with emphasis on Europe

SECTOR/INDUSTRY SPECIALIZATION: Research-based industries like high-tech, pharmaceuticals and chemicals, industrial goods. Board Director searches and consulting.

FAVORITE HISTORICAL FIGURE/MODEL/MENTOR: Outstanding leaders in industry and management, science, psychology and organizational development.

SINGLE MOST IMPORTANT ISSUE IN CONDUCTING A HIGH LEVEL SEARCH: Commitment and ability to understand the client's real needs, together with the access to a qualified international network of key executives.

MOST SIGNIFICANT OTHER ASPECT OF PERSONAL OR PROFESSIONAL LIFE: Personal development in most relevant dimensions of life.

WHAT IS THE BEST PREPARATION FOR BEING A SUCCESSFUL RECRUITER? A successful career in management and/or consulting together with a genuine interest in people and strong skills in relationship management.

WHAT WOULD YOU BE DOING IF YOU WERE NOT AN EXECUTIVE RECRUITER? A management consultant, or a personal coach for top managers.

WHAT ARE THE CHARACTERISTICS OF A GREAT CLIENT? A great client is a smart, strong, self-confident leader who knows what he wants; is fast in his thinking and decisive; trusts you but challenges your work and has high, but realistic expectations.

WHAT CHALLENGES DO YOU SEE AHEAD IN THE GLOBAL MARKETPLACE? The strategic challenges for executive search are the choices of geographical markets, the size of your practices in each market and industry, and the clients you want to work for. Operationally an executive search firm has to establish a global network of offices adhering to world-wide quality standards, establish and efficiently exploit a world-wide database, and correctly assess managers from different cultures for top positions in countries other than their home country.

ERIC J. SALMON

Eric Salmon & Partners
95 avenue des Champs-Elysées
75008 Paris
France

Telephone: 33 1 53 23 88 88
Fax: 33 1 53 23 88 80
E-mail: salmon.esppa@integra.fr
Company Website: http://www.integra.fr/salmon.partners

DATE OF BIRTH: 6-1-1938

NATIONALITY: French—Grew up in France

EDUCATIONAL BACKGROUND:
- Degree in Electrical Engineering Institut Electrotechnique de Grenoble (France).
- Master of Science University of Grenoble (France).

LANGUAGES SPOKEN: French (mother tongue), English, Italian, Spanish

CAREER HIGHLIGHTS:
- 1965–1970   Degremont, water and waste treatment.
- 1970–1990   Egon Zehnder International, Partner in charge France, Great Britain, Italy, Spain, Portugal.
- 1990 to date   Founder Eric Salmon & Partners

SPECIAL INTERESTS/HOBBIES: Reading: history and philosophy. Traveling in Asia. Mountain climbing.

GEOGRAPHIC SCOPE OF RECRUITING: Europe and North America

SECTOR/INDUSTRY SPECIALIZATION: Industry, Consumer and Services

FAVORITE HISTORICAL FIGURE/MODEL/MENTOR: Napoleon, deGaulle

SINGLE MOST IMPORTANT ISSUE IN CONDUCTING A HIGH LEVEL SEARCH:
- Being perceived as problem solver and trustworthy.
- Inspire confidence to both clients and candidates.
- Highest confidentiality and ethics.
- Negotiation ability.
- Creative thinking.
- International competence.

ANTHONY SAXTON

Saxton Bampfylde International
35 Old Queen Street
London SW1H 9JA
England

Telephone: 44 171 799 1433
Fax: 44 171 222 0489
E-mail: anthony@saxbam.co.uk.

DATE OF BIRTH: July 23, 1934

NATIONALITY: British—Grew up in England, Malta, Scotland, and India

EDUCATIONAL BACKGROUND:
Harrow School; studied Russian in Naval Intelligence
Worked as a dustman (refuse collector) in Kensington, London

LANGUAGES SPOKEN: English, French, and lapsed Russian

CAREER HIGHLIGHTS: Involvement in the appointment of some astonishingly effective chief executives

SPECIAL INTERESTS/HOBBIES: Church of England and the Benadictines, European Union, windsurfing, and water skiing

SECTOR/INDUSTRY SPECIALIZATION: International general management; major experience in retailing and international consumer goods

SINGLE MOST IMPORTANT ISSUE IN CONDUCTING A HIGH LEVEL SEARCH: Understanding what are the issues and problems the client organisation will face and finding someone relevant to those, rather than just to the here and now

BIGGEST COMPETITOR: Egon Zehnder

MOST SIGNIFICANT OTHER ASPECT OF PERSONAL OR PROFESSIONAL LIFE: Being a Benadictine oblate, a part-time monk at Alton Abbey

WHAT IS THE BEST PREPARATION FOR BEING A SUCCESSFUL RECRUITER? The best preparation is to be a line hiring manager in an international company. That way you know what it really feels like.

WHAT WOULD YOU BE DOING IF YOU WERE NOT AN EXECUTIVE RECRUITER? I would either be a Priest within the Church of England or a Corporate Finance guy with an excellent investment bank like Goldman Sachs.

WHAT ARE THE CHARACTERISTICS OF A GREAT CLIENT? The characteristics of a great client are that they share the problem with you; they treat you like a partner-and therefore always get the best out of you.

WHAT CHALLENGES DO YOU SEE AHEAD IN THE GLOBAL MARKETPLACE? The marketplace is global and therefore, however well organised you are internationally, you still have to catch too many aeroplanes.

JOSETTE SAYERS

Jouve & Associes
54 avenue Marceau
75008 Paris
France

Telephone: 33 1 40 70 90 00
Fax: 33 1 47 20 55 56
E-mail: jsayers@dialup.iway.fr
Company Website: A 1998 project

DATE OF BIRTH: September 2, 1949

NATIONALITY: American and Irish—Grew up in Europe (U.K., Germany, Italy, Netherlands) and U.S.A.

EDUCATIONAL BACKGROUND: Attended international schools in Europe throughout secondary education. Graduated with honors in Romance Languages from Wesleyan University in 1971 (one of first women graduates), followed by Business Degree in France from "Centre de Perfectionnement aux Affaires" (CPA-Paris) in 1985.

LANGUAGES SPOKEN: Bilingual English-French. Knowledge of Italian, some Dutch.

CAREER HIGHLIGHTS: Have worked from French base since 1972 with and on behalf of Euro-American business ventures, initially with an electronics and telecom company, then in executive search (15 years) including as a founding member and Partner of Jouve & Associes, created in 1986. President of Jouve & Associes Board as of Spring 1996.

SPECIAL INTERESTS/HOBBIES: Glass stemware collecting, travel, jazz music

GEOGRAPHIC SCOPE OF RECRUITING: France, U.K., Benelux, Germany and U.S.A.

SECTOR/INDUSTRY SPECIALIZATION: High technology and telecommunications, consumer goods, leisure and media, legal and tax specialists. Primary focus over last 15 years: cross-culture, Euro-American recruitments.

FAVORITE HISTORICAL FIGURE/MODEL/MENTOR: Marie Curie for her contribution to humanity.

SINGLE MOST IMPORTANT ISSUE IN CONDUCTING A HIGH LEVEL SEARCH: Ability to listen and interpret creatively what the client/decision-maker truly wants!

BIGGEST COMPETITOR: Time

MOST SIGNIFICANT OTHER ASPECT OF PERSONAL OR PROFESSIONAL LIFE: Living in and enjoying Paris, particularly my extraordinary new home on the Place des Vosges in the Marais.

WHAT IS THE BEST PREPARATION FOR BEING A SUCCESSFUL RECRUITER? In today's and tomorrow's marketplace, the best preparation combines excellent educational credentials (including an MBA) and previous corporate experience acquired within a major player in its industry. Particular functional expertise is not a key factor although previous experience in an advisory role to demanding clients, both internal and external, would be a distinct asset when joining a service business. International exposure is a must for the future.

WHAT WOULD YOU BE DOING IF YOU WERE NOT AN EXECUTIVE RECRUITER? Working to promote a non-profit international organization that helps underprivileged children obtain an education would please me immensely. I would also travel extensively.

WHAT ARE THE CHARACTERISTICS OF A GREAT CLIENT? A great client is a professional who perceives the executive recruiter as his or her business partner in solving complex business and people problems. A great client enjoys sharing the search process and the challenge of coopting the best man or woman for the job.

WHAT CHALLENGES DO YOU SEE AHEAD IN THE GLOBAL MARKETPLACE? I see the challenges as dual-fold:

As an industry, a major challenge is how to use advanced technologies and new communications vehicles (the Internet for example) in an optimal way relative to executive search while maintaining the right balance in a people-driven business where qualitative issues and personalized services are key success factors. Search is a people-driven business going far beyond the frontiers of geography, nationality and culture in a technology-driven era. Reconciling these issues in a progressive, creative fashion is a big challenge.

For executive recruiters as individuals, the challenge is to learn to "think global" and not simply be a member of a global network or a company that is "going global." "Think different" is easier said than done and requires time, energy, personal resourcefulness and a commitment to learning new things.

RAE SEDEL

Russell Reynolds Associates
24 St. James's Square
London SW1Y 4HZ, England

Telephone: 44-171-839-7788
Fax: 44-171-839-9395
E-mail: rsedel@russreyn.com
Company Website: http://www.russreyn.com

DATE OF BIRTH: March 1, 1949

NATIONALITY: American

EDUCATIONAL BACKGROUND:

BA in Economics (Phi Beta Kappa, 1970), University of California, Los Angeles
M.B.A. (1971), University of California, Los Angeles.

LANGUAGES SPOKEN: English

CAREER HIGHLIGHTS: Prior to Russell Reynolds Associates, worked for Pacific Telesis as Vice President-Consumer Markets, with a staff of 13,000 and more than 1 billion customer transactions annually. Earlier, held positions in general management, sales, marketing, planning and operations.

GEOGRAPHIC SCOPE OF RECRUITING: Global, with particular focus on European assignments

SECTOR/INDUSTRY SPECIALIZATION: Technology/Telecommunications

SINGLE MOST IMPORTANT ISSUE IN CONDUCTING A HIGH LEVEL SEARCH: Ongoing, open and shared communication through all phases of the search process.

WHAT IS THE BEST PREPARATION FOR BEING A SUCCESSFUL RECRUITER? Knowing your industry and being a quick, smart problem solver. Using your intuition, but backing it up with due diligence, such as thoroughly conducting references for a potential candidate. Moxie is key to completing a search to a client's satisfaction. Also, it is helpful to come from the industry you are serving and have held positions similar to the ones for which you are recruiting.

WHAT WOULD YOU BE DOING IF YOU WERE NOT AN EXECUTIVE RECRUITER? I would probably be running a large-scale business, or perhaps raising guide dogs.

WHAT ARE THE CHARACTERISTICS OF A GREAT CLIENT? A great client knows his business and the problems he is trying to solve; he knows himself, his strengths and weaknesses. He is ready to hire the person who can solve his business problems. The ideal client has the good sense to demand and allow the recruiting partner to find the right solution and will do what it takes to attract the best—both in terms of personal time, attention, and money.

WHAT CHALLENGES DO YOU SEE AHEAD IN THE GLOBAL MARKETPLACE? Because today's marketplace is global, it requires a change in the way we all do business. It also requires a different kind of preparation for top executives as far as mobility and perspective. There is far greater demand than there is talent, and companies will take greater risks in order to attract "high flyers." The person who is prepared, multi-faceted, multi-functional, multi-cultural, and mobile will succeed. In addition, there is now a mix of opportunity—with both the traditional large multi-nationals and the entrepreneurial start-up. Thus, the opportunities have doubled but the number of qualified executives has not. This will be an issue going forward for candidates, clients, and executive recruiters.

GERARDO SEELIGER

Seeliger y Condé/Amrop International
Velazquez, 18
28001 Madrid
Spain

Telephone: 91-577-9977
Fax: 91-577-4124
E-mail: SEELIGER.CONDE@mad.servicom.es
Company Website: http://www.amrop.com

DATE OF BIRTH: 1947

NATIONALITY: Spanish—Grew up in Spain, Germany, U.K.

EDUCATIONAL BACKGROUND:
Degree in Economics, University of Freiburg, Germany

LANGUAGES SPOKEN: Spanish, English, German, French

CAREER HIGHLIGHTS: Olympic athlete; ran RRA office in Madrid and Los Angeles; founder of own firm, GM Bankers Trust Spain; GM Adiden Holding, Switzerland

SPECIAL INTERESTS/HOBBIES: Sailing, classical music, adventure travel, archeology

GEOGRAPHIC SCOPE OF RECRUITING: U.S.A., Europe, Latin America

SECTOR/INDUSTRY SPECIALIZATION: Finance, entertainment and sports, fast moving consumer goods

FAVORITE HISTORICAL FIGURE/MODEL/MENTOR: Columbus

SINGLE MOST IMPORTANT ISSUE IN CONDUCTING A HIGH LEVEL SEARCH: Trust of client

BIGGEST COMPETITOR: Heidrick & Struggles, Egon Zehneter Inernational, Spencer Stuart

MOST SIGNIFICANT OTHER ASPECT OF PERSONAL OR PROFESSIONAL LIFE: Involved in sports for over 40 years competitively. Extensive theme-traveling: archeology, adventure.

WHAT IS THE BEST PREPARATION FOR BEING A SUCCESSFUL RECRUITER? First class academic background. 10 years experience within industry (Banking, IT, Consumer) in a multinational, aggressive environment managing, hiring and firing people.

WHAT WOULD YOU BE DOING IF YOU WERE NOT AN EXECUTIVE RECRUITER? An adventurer, working for National Geographic or a senior member of the International Olympic Committee, or writing a book on 17 years experience in executive search.

WHAT ARE THE CHARACTERISTICS OF A GREAT CLIENT? Impatience, spontaneous transparency, strategic thinker, excellence in communicating his concerns, enthusiastic, sensitive interviewer engaging personal warmth, generous in fees.

WHAT CHALLENGES DO YOU SEE AHEAD IN THE GLOBAL MARKETPLACE?
- Attracting strong global clients
- Building a strong network of global practices
- Attracting the best recruiting professionals
- Making the career of a recruiter attractive to university graduates

HERMANN SENDELE

Spencer Stuart & Associates GmbH
Prinzregentenstrasse 61
81675 Munich, Germany

Telephone: 089-455553-0
Fax: 089-455553-33
E-mail: HSendele@spencerstuart.com
Company Website: http://www.spencerstuart.com

DATE OF BIRTH: April 26, 1941

NATIONALITY: German—Grew up in Germany and U.S.A.

EDUCATIONAL BACKGROUND:
BBA Economics (U.S.A.) + MBA Finance (U.S.A.) + PhD Marketing (Germany)

LANGUAGES SPOKEN: German + English

CAREER HIGHLIGHTS: Management experience in the U.S.A. and in Europe in the Chemical Industry, Information Technology and Consumer Products Industry; currently managing director of Spencer Stuart, Germany.

SPECIAL INTERESTS/HOBBIES: Hiking, mountain climbing, active politically on a local level

GEOGRAPHIC SCOPE OF RECRUITING: Europe, with a prime focus on Central and Eastern Europe, Europe-U.S.A., Europe-Asia

SECTOR/INDUSTRY SPECIALIZATION: I consider myself a true generalist with particular experience in Automotive, Consumer products, IT/Telecom, Financial Services, Non-exec. Director searches

FAVORITE HISTORICAL FIGURE/MODEL/MENTOR: Many

SINGLE MOST IMPORTANT ISSUE IN CONDUCTING A HIGH LEVEL SEARCH: Client dedication and, on an equal basis, candidate dedication

BIGGEST COMPETITOR: Myself, if I deviate from the above

MOST SIGNIFICANT OTHER ASPECT OF PERSONAL OR PROFESSIONAL LIFE: Genuine interest in changes affecting client industries on a national and international level.

WHAT IS THE BEST PREPARATION FOR BEING A SUCCESSFUL RECRUITER? Minimum of 10 years of management experience, ideally in more than one company and in different areas of management.

WHAT WOULD YOU BE DOING IF YOU WERE NOT AN EXECUTIVE RECRUITER? Hold a position in the top management of an international company (ideally automotive or telecommunication industry).

WHAT ARE THE CHARACTERISTICS OF A GREAT CLIENT? A person/company which appreciates the consultant as somebody who is there to help him solve an important recruiting problem and therefore communicates with him openly.

WHAT CHALLENGES DO YOU SEE AHEAD IN THE GLOBAL MARKETPLACE? Clients are refocusing and restructuring their companies on a continuous basis. This leads to an ever increasing demand for outside talents, since clients demand the best available managers to manage their companies. While I assist my clients in "finding the best," I have to cope with the social and ethical question of how the search industry can best help those who have been replaced.

SUN KOO SHIM

Amrop International (SKS Consultants Inc.)
14th Floor, Dong-A Ilbo Building
#145-1, Chungjungro 3-Ka
Seodaemoon-ku, Seoul 120-013
Republic of Korea

Telephone: 82 2 393-1810
Fax: 82 2 393-1811
E-mail: skshim@amrop.co.kr
Company Website: http://www.amrop.co.kr

DATE OF BIRTH: February 18, 1933

NATIONALITY: Korean—Grew up in Republic of Korea and United States (13 years in Nashville, Chicago, St. Louis and New York)

EDUCATIONAL BACKGROUND:

B.S. degree, Accounting, George Peabody College, Vanderbilt University, Nashville, Tennessee
M.B.A. degree, Finance, Graduate School of Business Administration, Northwestern University, Chicago, Illinois

LANGUAGES SPOKEN: English, Korean, and Japanese

CAREER HIGHLIGHTS:

1965–67	Auditor, Arthur Young & Company, NY
1967–86	Managing Partner, Arthur Young, Seoul Office
1986–88	Chairman, Young Wha Accounting Corporation, Seoul, Korea
1988–94	Managing Partner, Ernst & Young Consulting Corporation, Seoul, Korea
1994–Present	Managing Partner, Amrop International, Seoul
1997–Present	Chairman, Asia Pacific Region, Amrop International

SPECIAL INTERESTS/HOBBIES: Reading history, golf

GEOGRAPHIC SCOPE OF RECRUITING: Concentrated in the Republic of Korea and West Coast of the U.S.A.

SECTOR/INDUSTRY SPECIALIZATION: Information Technology; Health Care; Manufacturing (automotives and high tech products); Consumer

FAVORITE HISTORICAL FIGURE/MODEL/MENTOR: General Douglas MacArthur, for strategy and thought; Mario Formerchella, a former partner of Ernst & Young, as a mentor in practicing consultancy

SINGLE MOST IMPORTANT ISSUE IN CONDUCTING A HIGH LEVEL SEARCH: Searching a master of strategy and leadership with a deep cross cultural understanding and experience

BIGGEST COMPETITOR: Korn/Ferry International

MOST SIGNIFICANT OTHER ASPECT OF PERSONAL OR PROFESSIONAL LIFE: Enjoyment with personal and professional accomplishment

WHAT IS THE BEST PREPARATION FOR BEING A SUCCESSFUL RECRUITER? Study of business administration with an emphasis on industrial and business organization, personnel and psychology; experience in a large business organization with good training and education systems; and analytical experience.

continues ▶

WHAT WOULD YOU BE DOING IF YOU WERE NOT AN EXECUTIVE RECRUITER? I would be a business organization and restructuring consultant.

WHAT ARE THE CHARACTERISTICS OF A GREAT CLIENT? A great client has a good understanding of search practices; works closely with a search consultant; provides full information regarding the organization, business, situation in which the search need arose, detailed job description; makes themselves available on a timely basis for continuous consultation through the search process.

WHAT CHALLENGES DO YOU SEE AHEAD IN THE GLOBAL MARKETPLACE? Challenges include the requirement for international experience with a good cross cultural understanding, emphasis on communication skills and team work, and mobility-and willingness to travel and work abroad.

WILLIAM D. SIMON

Korn/Ferry International
1800 Century Park East, Suite 900
Los Angeles, CA 90067
U.S.A.

Telephone: 1 (310) 843-4102
Fax: 1 (310) 553-6452
E-mail: William.Simon@kornferry.com
Company Website: http://www.kornferry.com

DATE OF BIRTH: September 11, 1954

NATIONALITY: American—Grew up in Los Angeles, California

EDUCATIONAL BACKGROUND:
B.A., Political Science; University of California, Berkeley

LANGUAGES SPOKEN: English

CAREER HIGHLIGHTS: Head of Korn/Ferry's Media and Entertainment practice worldwide

SPECIAL INTERESTS/HOBBIES: Tennis, jazz music, gardening, reading, travel

GEOGRAPHIC SCOPE OF RECRUITING: Worldwide

SECTOR/INDUSTRY SPECIALIZATION: Entertainment, Media, Communications

FAVORITE HISTORICAL FIGURE/MODEL/MENTOR: Jimmy Carter

SINGLE MOST IMPORTANT ISSUE IN CONDUCTING A HIGH LEVEL SEARCH: Thorough knowledge and understanding of the client company, its needs, its place in the market, its competition, its management style and the various factors influencing the company.

MOST SIGNIFICANT OTHER ASPECT OF PERSONAL OR PROFESSIONAL LIFE: Family

WHAT IS THE BEST PREPARATION FOR BEING A SUCCESSFUL RECRUITER? A successful track record in specific industry experience. Also, one must have the ability to understand multiple levels of issues; must have a good perception of people and an ability to "close" complex matters; must have excellent listening skills and thorough understanding of the client company competition and strategic issues.

WHAT WOULD YOU BE DOING IF YOU WERE NOT AN EXECUTIVE RECRUITER? Running a mid-size entertainment/media company or an investment/merchant banker in the entertainment/media business.

WHAT ARE THE CHARACTERISTICS OF A GREAT CLIENT? One who understands his/her strengths and weaknesses, one who knows how to make decisions; one who is comfortable with his/her own instincts; one who sees the impact of people on an organization; and one who has a strategy for hiring an executive, what the executive can do and how he/she will impact the company.

WHAT CHALLENGES DO YOU SEE AHEAD IN THE GLOBAL MARKETPLACE? Increased competition, strengthening of global brands; enhanced technology; international and local offices working together; increasing demand for expert executives.

DOUGLAS M. SMITH

LAI Ward Howell
1300 Grove Avenue, Suite 100
Barrington, Illinois 60010
U.S.A.

Telephone: (847) 382-2206
Fax: (847) 382-2247
E-mail: WHI-APG@compuserve.com
Company Website: http://www.laix.com

DATE OF BIRTH: April 23, 1956

NATIONALITY: Canadian—Grew up in Canada

EDUCATIONAL BACKGROUND:
Masters of Industrial Relations degree—1984, Wayne State University
Honors Bachelors degree in Business Administration—1980, University of Windsor

LANGUAGES SPOKEN: English, French (partial)

CAREER HIGHLIGHTS:
Youngest Vice President of Human Resources of $4 billion Canadian company at age 29.
Chosen as 1 of 50 business people around the world by the Japanese court to be a part of unique business project.

SPECIAL INTERESTS/HOBBIES: Outdoor activities and environmental issues.

GEOGRAPHIC SCOPE OF RECRUITING: Global-including Far East, Europe, North and South America.

SECTOR/INDUSTRY SPECIALIZATION: Manufacturing sector, automotive industry

FAVORITE HISTORICAL FIGURE/MODEL/MENTOR: Jacques Cousteau

SINGLE MOST IMPORTANT ISSUE IN CONDUCTING A HIGH LEVEL SEARCH: Clear and in-depth understanding of the client organization including the dynamics of their business and the scope of the role.

MOST SIGNIFICANT OTHER ASPECT OF PERSONAL OR PROFESSIONAL LIFE: Recognition by the marketplace for my industrial knowledge, expertise, and "value-added" client support.

WHAT IS THE BEST PREPARATION FOR BEING A SUCCESSFUL RECRUITER? Be able to truly understand the client's needs and the dynamics of their business. Be understanding of the needs of the candidates and have the ability to balance the two. If you can deliver on one-half of what you promise a client in getting the search, you are already ahead of one-half your competition.

WHAT WOULD YOU BE DOING IF YOU WERE NOT AN EXECUTIVE RECRUITER? Two very different roles: University Professor or an Operations Director of a manufacturing activity.

WHAT ARE THE CHARACTERISTICS OF A GREAT CLIENT? Appreciation of the value-added strategic partnership with the right search firm and a willingness to be an "active partner" in their business.

WHAT CHALLENGES DO YOU SEE AHEAD IN THE GLOBAL MARKETPLACE? In response to the melding of individual national markets into one global market, there is a need to adopt and adjust local market successes to the uniqueness of the international marketplace.

JOHN E. SMITH, JR.

Smith Search, S.C.
Barranca del Muerto 472
Col. Alpes
Mexico, D.F. 01010
Mexico

Telephone: 52 5 593 8766; 52 5 651 6912
Fax: 52 5 593 8969
E-mail: smith@mail.internet.com.mx
Company Website: http://www.smithsearch.com.mx

DATE OF BIRTH: December 22, 1933

NATIONALITY: American—Grew up in U.S.A. (East Greenwich, Rhode Island)

EDUCATIONAL BACKGROUND:
School of Foreign Service, Georgetown University, 1957

LANGUAGES SPOKEN: English, Spanish

CAREER HIGHLIGHTS: Director, Noble & Assoc., Latin America's largest ad agency. Consistently most important independent recruiter, Mexico.

SPECIAL INTERESTS/HOBBIES: Skiing, biking, writing

GEOGRAPHIC SCOPE OF RECRUITING: Mexico, North and South America

SECTOR/INDUSTRY SPECIALIZATION: Generalist

FAVORITE HISTORICAL FIGURE/MODEL/MENTOR: Abraham Lincoln

SINGLE MOST IMPORTANT ISSUE IN CONDUCTING A HIGH LEVEL SEARCH: Intellectual integrity, candidate evaluations and client relations

BIGGEST COMPETITOR: Korn/Ferry

MOST SIGNIFICANT OTHER ASPECT OF PERSONAL OR PROFESSIONAL LIFE: Author, speaker, founder of a clan numbering 42

WHAT IS THE BEST PREPARATION FOR BEING A SUCCESSFUL RECRUITER? A Liberal Arts education preferably complemented by Master's level studies; a clearly successful business career, having risen to the top of one's chosen industry or profession wherein analysis and articulation are central to success; extensive travel; reasonably high and varied intellectual curiosity particularly with respect to unfolding challenges as they might relate to past experiences.

WHAT WOULD YOU BE DOING IF YOU WERE NOT AN EXECUTIVE RECRUITER? Journalism and/or politics.

WHAT ARE THE CHARACTERISTICS OF A GREAT CLIENT? A sense of mission, a clear definition of needs, the ability to motivate the executive recruiter on the basis of trust and teamwork, to allow the recruiter the same privilege the client allows for himself; i.e., to err without demolishing the client/recruiter relationship.

WHAT CHALLENGES DO YOU SEE AHEAD IN THE GLOBAL MARKETPLACE? Increased necessity of understanding and respecting other cultures, greater linguistic abilities, promoting generally accepted global standards of excellence while not impinging upon the indispensable, entrepreneurial sector. To frown upon policies aimed at fomenting and prolonging unacceptable standards of living on some peoples and countries so that others' economic conditions may be inequitably advantageous.

LAURI STÅHLBERG

Amrop International/Ståhlberg & Ahtikari Oy
Bulevardi 2 A
00120 Helsinki
Finland

Telephone: +358 9 660 466
Fax: +358 9 611 910
E-mail: lauri.stahlberg@amrop-fi.com
Company Website: http://www.amrop.com

DATE OF BIRTH: April 4, 1943

NATIONALITY: Finnish—Grew up in Finland

EDUCATIONAL BACKGROUND:
Master of Laws, University of Helsinki

LANGUAGES SPOKEN: Finnish, Swedish, English, German

CAREER HIGHLIGHTS: Developing a successful executive search operation of four offices (Helsinki, St. Petersburg, Tallinn, and Riga), covering Finland and the emerging markets in Russia and the Baltic States

SPECIAL INTERESTS/HOBBIES: Literature, golf, hunting

GEOGRAPHIC SCOPE OF RECRUITING: Local and international clients served in Finland, Russia and the Baltic States. Multicountry searches.

SECTOR/INDUSTRY SPECIALIZATION: Manufacturing, financial services and telecommunications

FAVORITE HISTORICAL FIGURE/MODEL/MENTOR: Galileo Galilei

SINGLE MOST IMPORTANT ISSUE IN CONDUCTING A HIGH LEVEL SEARCH: Search is about solving the client's problem. Sensitivity to the client's needs, understanding the problem and its background is crucial. The search process and quality must be consistent both in old and the emerging markets.

WHAT IS THE BEST PREPARATION FOR BEING A SUCCESSFUL RECRUITER? Business background with lifelong interest in people and organisations.

WHAT WOULD YOU BE DOING IF YOU WERE NOT AN EXECUTIVE RECRUITER? A business executive in a large corporation.

WHAT ARE THE CHARACTERISTICS OF A GREAT CLIENT? Result oriented professional approach to using the service.

WHAT CHALLENGES DO YOU SEE AHEAD IN THE GLOBAL MARKETPLACE? The tendency towards strategic global or regional partnerships in using executive search is a challenge and an opportunity.

GILBERT R. STENHOLM, JR.

Spencer Stuart
401 North Michigan Avenue
Suite 3400
Chicago, IL 60611
U.S.A.

Telephone: 1 (312) 321-8338
Fax: 1 (312) 822-0116
Company Website: http://www.spencerstuart.com

DATE OF BIRTH: February 2, 1946

NATIONALITY: Swedish descent; American citizen—Grew up in South Carolina

EDUCATIONAL BACKGROUND:
B.A. Business Administration, Bob Jones University

LANGUAGES SPOKEN: English; limited Spanish

CAREER HIGHLIGHTS: 17 years at Spencer Stuart; currently co-managing director of Consumer Goods Practice; 5 years at Booz, Allen & Hamilton, and earlier with General Foods and Baxter International

SPECIAL INTERESTS/HOBBIES: Golf, politics, and traveling

GEOGRAPHIC SCOPE OF RECRUITING: Primarily in North America and some focus in Europe

SECTOR/INDUSTRY SPECIALIZATION: Consumer Goods & Services Practice Leader; CEO and Board work across all businesses

FAVORITE HISTORICAL FIGURE/MODEL/MENTOR: Dwight D. Eisenhower

SINGLE MOST IMPORTANT ISSUE IN CONDUCTING A HIGH LEVEL SEARCH: Judgment, which relates to thoroughly reading client needs, matching their needs with the culture/chemistry, business dynamics and providing client/candidate with value and insight.

MOST SIGNIFICANT OTHER ASPECT OF PERSONAL OR PROFESSIONAL LIFE: Gaining client's respect and confidence, balancing family and firm commitments, and remembering to have fun and enjoy our short time on this earth.

WHAT IS THE BEST PREPARATION FOR BEING A SUCCESSFUL RECRUITER? Develop functional and industry expertise, earlier from a Fortune 500 co.mpany role and later through search with clients.

WHAT WOULD YOU BE DOING IF YOU WERE NOT AN EXECUTIVE RECRUITER? Pro golfer or in the health care products industry.

WHAT ARE THE CHARACTERISTICS OF A GREAT CLIENT? Responsive, open-minded, sell the positives. Willing to adapt to client needs.

WHAT CHALLENGES DO YOU SEE AHEAD IN THE GLOBAL MARKETPLACE? Local and regional marketing to adapt to local customers and consumers: what's good for France and China is not necessarily a fit in U.S.A. and vice versa.

BRIAN M. SULLIVAN

Sullivan & Company
40 Wall Street
New York, NY 10005
U.S.A.

Telephone: 1 (212) 442-3000
Fax: 1 (212) 422-9100

DATE OF BIRTH: March 13, 1953

NATIONALITY: American—Grew up in Braintree, Massachusetts

EDUCATIONAL BACKGROUND:
Lehigh University, Bachelor of Science, Finance, 1975
Denver University, Master of Business Administration, Finance, 1976

LANGUAGES SPOKEN: English

CAREER HIGHLIGHTS: Successfully completed the following global assignments for:
Bankers Trust Company, Hong Kong office, recruited Head of Asian Project Finance.
Chase Manhattan Bank, recruited Head of U.S. Securities Division.
Putnam Investments, recruited Chief Financial Officer.
Putnam Investments, recruited the Head of Emerging Markets Debt Portfolio Management.

SPECIAL INTERESTS/HOBBIES: Active participation in The Economic Club of New York, and The Association of Executive Search Consultants as a Board of Directors member. Hobbies include golf, cigars, wine, and travel.

GEOGRAPHIC SCOPE OF RECRUITING: The world's financial centers.

SECTOR/INDUSTRY SPECIALIZATION: Financial services industries, including investment banking, commercial banking, asset management and hedge funds; also, consulting organizations serving the financial services industries.

FAVORITE HISTORICAL FIGURE/MODEL/MENTOR: Ronald Reagan, who demonstrated keen leadership skills and an unwavering dedication to a set of core values. In doing so, he helped restore confidence in the people he led as President. As a role model for good management, Reagan helped me understand the value of setting clear objectives, recruiting good supporting people and delegating the authority and responsibility for meeting those objectives. As a role model for an executive search consultant, he taught me that being direct and honest yet compassionate was the key to being held in high esteem by both clients and candidates. In turn, this has enabled me to become a strategic advisor to clients and a confidant and sounding board to candidates.

SINGLE MOST IMPORTANT ISSUE IN CONDUCTING A HIGH LEVEL SEARCH: Trust. As an intermediary between candidate and client, gaining the trust of both parties enables me to facilitate the conversations and sometimes delicate negotiations on a timetable that suits both parties and their different sensitivities.

Because of the nature of senior level searches, there is a delicate balance of business negotiation and personal emotion throughout the process. By establishing trust, the executive search consultant can manage the process so that the most important result occurs; the arrival of a top caliber candidate into the inner sanctum of a client organization with both parties feeling positive about the process, as well as the result.

BIGGEST COMPETITOR: Time

MOST SIGNIFICANT OTHER ASPECT OF PERSONAL OR PROFESSIONAL LIFE: Aside from my marriage and the close relationships I have developed with my partners and certain clients (all because of shared goals and values), the most meaningful and rewarding aspect of my life has been the relationship that I developed with the Chege family of Kikuyu, Kenya. This began in 1988 when I sponsored a young boy, Gikaru, with school fees and other necessities of life. Three years later my wife, Pam and I visited Africa and met with the Chege family. As a result of that encounter and the understanding we developed, she and I, our parents and some friends now sponsor 10 children in the village and have purchased a plot of land for the Chege family to farm. We correspond frequently and are pleased to learn that our sponsorship is making a difference in many lives of the families in the Kikuyu village.

WHAT IS THE BEST PREPARATION FOR BEING A SUCCESSFUL RECRUITER? Sales and consulting. Good recruiters are constantly selling their clients' opportunities to prospective candidates. Success depends upon making the other party understand and get excited about your opportunity. Salesmanship requires dogged persistence and so does recruiting. Good salespeople and good recruiters have to be able to rebound from persistent rejection and go on to make the next sales call. Successful recruiters do more than place bodies in chairs. They serve as strategic advisors to their clients and educate them as to the realities of the marketplace. Experience as a Management Consultant sharpens your analytical and problem-solving skills. Successful recruiters are salespeople, consultants and strategic advisors.

WHAT WOULD YOU BE DOING IF YOU WERE NOT AN EXECUTIVE RECRUITER? If I were not a recruiter, I would be working on Wall Street—that's where all the action is. I love the thrill of the deal, so I might be a capital markets salesperson. I am also interested in advising clients and solving problems while building and creating something of lasting value. So I might, instead, be an investment banker or mergers and acquisitions specialist helping my clients to shape and finance their strategic plans.

WHAT ARE THE CHARACTERISTICS OF A GREAT CLIENT? Great clients work with their recruiters as partners, teaming to get the job done. They understand how the search process works and are willing to put in the time to complete the assignment successfully. Furthermore, great clients regard search as a strategic service (versus a commodity) and listen to the advice and counsel of their recruiters. Most of all, a great client is willing to put forth the same amount of effort of effort as I do to complete the search.

WHAT CHALLENGES DO YOU SEE AHEAD IN THE GLOBAL MARKETPLACE? The biggest threat to the search industry comes from firms that are more interested in size and scale than in quality. We are just now beginning to see an emerging trend towards consolidation. Many firms will go along with the trend for fear of being left by the wayside. As firms merge, we will see a blend and homogenization of cultures. Entrepreneurship may give way to "corporate" behavior. People forget that it is the cultures that made firms successful in the first place.

The same thing happened on Wall Street 20 years ago and it is happening again on a global scale. Old style partnerships-in which everyone feels that they own a stake and, therefore, act as owners of the business—are being replaced by huge businesses with huge infrastructures. Those infrastructures can be supported as long as the market is strong; when the market weakens, firms may be tempted to take on the wrong clients or wrong assignments in order to maintain revenues flows; they may also be tempted to cut corners in order to maintain margins.

The biggest challenge, then, will be to maintain quality and best practices in an industry that is going through a significant transformation.

TAN SOO JIN

Amrop International/Gattie-Tan Soo Jin Management
Consultants Pte Ltd

3 Shenton Way
Shenton House #11-08
Singapore 068805

Telephone: 65-225 3188
Fax: 65-224 7585
E-mail: tsj2709@singnet.com.sg
Company Website: http://www.amrop.com

DATE OF BIRTH: September 27, 1945

NATIONALITY: Malaysian—Grew up in Batu Pahat, Johor, Malaysia

EDUCATIONAL BACKGROUND:

B. Econs (Monash University, Australia)

MBA (University of New South Wales, Australia)

FMIS (Fellow of the Marketing Institute of Singapore)

LANGUAGES SPOKEN: English, Hokkien

CAREER HIGHLIGHTS: Special Projects, Shell Sydney; Lecturer in Business Administration, University of Singapore; Marketing Manager, Smith & Nephew; Senior Consultant, Korn/Ferry; Principal, Egon Zehnder; Founding Partner, Gattie-Tan Soo Jin Consultants.

SPECIAL INTERESTS/HOBBIES: Reading, music, philatelic and other collectibles

GEOGRAPHIC SCOPE OF RECRUITING: Singapore, Malaysia, Indonesia

SECTOR/INDUSTRY SPECIALIZATION: Banking & Finance, Consumer Marketing, Automotive, Health Care

FAVORITE HISTORICAL FIGURE/MODEL/MENTOR: The Lord Jesus Christ

SINGLE MOST IMPORTANT ISSUE IN CONDUCTING A HIGH LEVEL SEARCH: Integrity and honesty in dealing with client and candidates

BIGGEST COMPETITOR: Korn/Ferry

MOST SIGNIFICANT OTHER ASPECT OF PERSONAL OR PROFESSIONAL LIFE: First local to join an Executive Search company in 1977. Started own company in 1984 and became the first Asian Partner Firm of Amrop International in 1984.

WHAT IS THE BEST PREPARATION FOR BEING A SUCCESSFUL RECRUITER? Experience in industry covering general management/marketing and finance. Interest in meeting people and an analytical, problem solving mind.

WHAT WOULD YOU BE DOING IF YOU WERE NOT AN EXECUTIVE RECRUITER? A general manager in a fast moving consumer goods company or a university professor.

WHAT ARE THE CHARACTERISTICS OF A GREAT CLIENT? One who takes ownership of the assignment, able to share his vision for the company and willing to recruit the best.

WHAT CHALLENGES DO YOU SEE AHEAD IN THE GLOBAL MARKETPLACE? Finding managers who can make a difference in the companies they work in. Able to face unexpected change, courageous enough to make difficult decisions.

MARTIN Y. TANG

Spencer Stuart & Associates (HK) Ltd.
17/F Bank of East Asia Building
10 Dès Voeux Road Central
Hong Kong

Telephone: 852 2521-8373
Fax: 852 2810-5246
E-mail: mtang@spencerstuart.com
Company Website: http://www.spencerstuart.com

DATE OF BIRTH: July 6, 1949

NATIONALITY: Irish—Grew up in Hong Kong, U.S.A.

EDUCATIONAL BACKGROUND:
1970, Cornell University, BS (Electrical Engineering)
1972, Massachusetts Institute of Technology, MS (Sloan School of Management)

LANGUAGES SPOKEN: English, Cantonese, Mandarin, and French

CAREER HIGHLIGHTS: Bank of America (1973–1977); South Sea Textile Mfg. Co. (1977–1986); Techno-Ventures (HK) Ltd. (1986–1988); Norman Broadbent HK Ltd. (1988–1992); Spencer Stuart (1992–present)

SPECIAL INTERESTS/HOBBIES: Trustee of Cornell University; Council Member of the HK University of Science & Technology.

GEOGRAPHIC SCOPE OF RECRUITING: Asia excluding Japan.

SECTOR/INDUSTRY SPECIALIZATION: Senior level & Chief Executive assignments in the public and private sectors, banking and commerce.

FAVORITE HISTORICAL FIGURE/MODEL/MENTOR: Dayton Ogden, CEO of Spencer Stuart (1987–1996)

SINGLE MOST IMPORTANT ISSUE IN CONDUCTING A HIGH LEVEL SEARCH: Knowing what your client is really looking for.

MOST SIGNIFICANT OTHER ASPECT OF PERSONAL OR PROFESSIONAL LIFE: Family

WHAT IS THE BEST PREPARATION FOR BEING A SUCCESSFUL RECRUITER?
- Learn how to listen
- Keep up with trends in your clients' industries
- Imagine yourself on the other side of the table: as a client, as a candidate

WHAT WOULD YOU BE DOING IF YOU WERE NOT AN EXECUTIVE RECRUITER? Probably retire. Can't imagine anything outside of search that's as exciting and as much fun.

WHAT ARE THE CHARACTERISTICS OF A GREAT CLIENT?
- One who is willing to listen to your advice and build up a relationship based on trust
- Has realistic expectations about candidates and the attractions of the job
- When they say, "We'll pay what it takes," really mean it

WHAT CHALLENGES DO YOU SEE AHEAD IN THE GLOBAL MARKETPLACE? Persuading executives in a two-income family to relocate.

RAYMOND C.P. TANG

Russell Reynolds Associates
Suite 3801-4 Edinburgh Tower
15 Queen's Road Central
The Landmark
Hong Kong, China
Telephone: 852 2523-9123
Fax: 852 2845-9044
E-mail: rtang@russreyn.com
Company Website: http://www.russreyn.com

DATE OF BIRTH: March 17, 1949

NATIONALITY: British citizen—Grew up in Hong Kong

EDUCATIONAL BACKGROUND:

1966   St. Paul's Co-educational College, Hong Kong

1972   Tufts University, Boston

1975   Yale University School of Medicine, New Haven

LANGUAGES SPOKEN: Cantonese, Mandarin, English

CAREER HIGHLIGHTS: 13 years of executive recruiting experience. Previous career with Johnson & Johnson and in healthcare/hospital management.

GEOGRAPHIC SCOPE OF RECRUITING: Greater China and North Asia

SECTOR/INDUSTRY SPECIALIZATION: CEOs and regional senior management

SINGLE MOST IMPORTANT ISSUE IN CONDUCTING A HIGH LEVEL SEARCH: Client management and extensive communication.

MICHAEL A. TAPPAN

LAI Ward Howell
99 Park Avenue
New York, NY 10016
U.S.A.

Telephone: 1 (212) 953-5853
Fax: 1 (212) 697-1398
E-mail: mtappan@lai.usa.com
Company Website: http://www.laix.com

DATE OF BIRTH: January 31, 1939

NATIONALITY: American—Grew up in New York City

EDUCATIONAL BACKGROUND:
Yale University, B.A. English Literature 1960
Harvard Business School, M.B.A. Finance 1962
Chartered Financial Analyst 1968

LANGUAGES SPOKEN: English, French

CAREER HIGHLIGHTS: Creation and management of Ward Howell's company in Russia, 1992–present; founded and managed Russell Reynolds office in Paris, 1977–79.

SPECIAL INTERESTS/HOBBIES: Golf, gardening, cross-country skiing, travel, classical music

GEOGRAPHIC SCOPE OF RECRUITING: North America and Europe for positions in Russia and former Soviet Union.

SECTOR/INDUSTRY SPECIALIZATION: All sectors/industries. Specialization is filling client needs in Russia/FSU.

FAVORITE HISTORICAL FIGURE/MODEL/MENTOR: Sir Winston Churchill and Max Ulrich (Ward Howell founder)

SINGLE MOST IMPORTANT ISSUE IN CONDUCTING A HIGH LEVEL SEARCH: Does the candidate have creative vision, the ability to communicate it to the organization and inspire buy-in, the practical realism to build an effective strategic plan, and the leadership to make it all happen?

MOST SIGNIFICANT OTHER ASPECT OF PERSONAL OR PROFESSIONAL LIFE: Family

WHAT IS THE BEST PREPARATION FOR BEING A SUCCESSFUL RECRUITER? Excellent oral and written communications and strong analytical skills. A graduate education in business that has imparted understanding of how business organizations really work. Business experience that includes contribution to strategic planning, inter-functional involvement, and the achievement of specific business objectives. Ideal exposure would include consulting or another comparable client service role. The ability to listen, dedication to client service, goal-orientation, determination, persistence, teamwork, and the ability to drive a project to completion without supervision.

WHAT WOULD YOU BE DOING IF YOU WERE NOT AN EXECUTIVE RECRUITER? I would still be in the investment management business, which I left 26 years ago to enter recruiting. I would be in an entrepreneurial business, ideally in an international environment, much like what I am doing today. Without question, I would be in business, which I believe to be one of the best ways to combine personal creativity, action in the real world, and achievement of worthwhile goals for oneself and for others.

continues ▶

WHAT ARE THE CHARACTERISTICS OF A GREAT CLIENT? First and foremost, a great client teams with the recruiter to get the job done. This means honest and open communications, accessibility, quick response time, instant feedback, reasonable flexibility, realism, and focus on getting the project completed.

WHAT CHALLENGES DO YOU SEE AHEAD IN THE GLOBAL MARKETPLACE? The great challenge ahead is the imbalance in the emerging markets between available trained and experienced executive talent and the enormous and rapidly growing need for such talent. Finding people willing and able to accept this challenge, to work in often very difficult environments, and to build businesses will be the most difficult task facing the recruiting industry during the first decade of the twenty-first century.

REINHARD G. THIEL

Heidrick & Struggles
Am Seestern 8
40547 Düsseldorf
Germany

Telephone: 0211-5 21 36-0
Fax: 0211-59 16 27
E-mail: 106314.3063compuserve.com
Company Website: http://www.h-s.com

DATE OF BIRTH: December 31, 1945

NATIONALITY: German—Grew up in Austria, Germany, Africa

EDUCATIONAL BACKGROUND:
University Degrees in Civil Engineering (M.Sc.) and Business Administration (MBA)

LANGUAGES SPOKEN: German, English, (French)

CAREER HIGHLIGHTS:
Managing Director (Medical Supply)
Shareholder (from 1978–1997) and Managing Partner, Amrop International Germany
Board Member Amrop International
Partner and Director (from 10/97) Heidrick & Struggles International, Germany

SPECIAL INTERESTS/HOBBIES: Golf, concerts (classic and jazz), squash/badminton, lions

GEOGRAPHIC SCOPE OF RECRUITING: Mainly Germany (and worldwide in cooperation with H&S partners).

SECTOR/INDUSTRY SPECIALIZATION: Insurance and Banking, Retail, Real Estate and Construction, Mechanical

MOST IMPORTANT ISSUES IN CONDUCTING A HIGH LEVEL SEARCH:
- Industry knowledge and experience at the appropriate functional and Board level
- Personal handling of the assignment
- Top research capacity and close involvement of the researcher with the client
- Specific interview techniques
- Reference checks, conducted personally on top level
- Strictl obedience to the off-limits policy

MOST SIGNIFICANT OTHER ASPECT OF PERSONAL OR PROFESSIONAL LIFE: Having achieved the number one position in Germany with my German partners

WHAT IS THE BEST PREPARATION FOR BEING A SUCCESSFUL RECRUITER? Excellent, international education and studies (preferably in more than one discipline), some industry experience and further training (research, interviewing and sales) in one of the top five executive search companies.

WHAT WOULD YOU BE DOING IF YOU WERE NOT AN EXECUTIVE RECRUITER? Probably high-level manager in the real estate or construction industries

WHAT ARE THE CHARACTERISTICS OF A GREAT CLIENT? A great client is demanding, but fair ; exhibits personal leadership and charisma; and is a top motivator.

WHAT CHALLENGES DO YOU SEE AHEAD IN THE GLOBAL MARKETPLACE?
- High professional coverage of the most important area within each practice.
- Being among the 3–4 top recruiters in each country.

JOHN T. THOMPSON

Heidrick & Struggles
1740 Sand Hill Road
Menlo Park, California 94025-7096
U.S.A.

Telephone: 1 (650) 234-1520
Fax: 1 (650) 854-2932
E-mail: jtt@ix.netcom.com
Company Website: http://www.h-s.com

DATE OF BIRTH: January 11, 1948

NATIONALITY: American—Grew up in small town in Virginia
and South Boston

LANGUAGES SPOKEN: English

CAREER HIGHLIGHTS:
Co-founder of the technology practice for Heidrick & Struggles
Most influential job in career: Director of Organizational Development with The Williams Companies. Built this practice to be number one worldwide.

SPECIAL INTERESTS/HOBBIES: Audiophile and golf

GEOGRAPHIC SCOPE OF RECRUITING: North America

SECTOR/INDUSTRY SPECIALIZATION: CEO searches across industry sectors

FAVORITE HISTORICAL FIGURE/MODEL/MENTOR: Thomas Jefferson

SINGLE MOST IMPORTANT ISSUE IN CONDUCTING A HIGH LEVEL SEARCH: Ability to add value and credibility to the board of directors on CEO searches and serve as a consultant to the board

MOST SIGNIFICANT OTHER ASPECT OF PERSONAL OR PROFESSIONAL LIFE: My wife Phyllis and two children

WHAT IS THE BEST PREPARATION FOR BEING A SUCCESSFUL RECRUITER? Organizational consulting, plus successful corporate experience

WHAT WOULD YOU BE DOING IF YOU WERE NOT AN EXECUTIVE RECRUITER? Organizational development consulting

WHAT ARE THE CHARACTERISTICS OF A GREAT CLIENT? Open, responsive, timely, decisive, and willing to be bold. Also willing to think about the unconventional candidate.

WHAT CHALLENGES DO YOU SEE AHEAD IN THE GLOBAL MARKETPLACE? Continued rapid change, higher demand for executive search services

HEINER THORBORG

Heiner Thorborg GmbH & Co. KG
Opernplatz 4
D - 60313 Frankfurt am Main
Germany

Telephone: 49 (69) 92 07 45 -0
Fax: 49 (69) 92 07 45 50

DATE OF BIRTH: August 8, 1944

NATIONALITY: German—Grew up in Hamburg, Germany

EDUCATIONAL BACKGROUND:
1969   M.A. in Business Economics, University of Hamburg
1979   Senior Managers Program (SMP), Harvard Graduate School of Business

LANGUAGES SPOKEN: German, English, French

CAREER HIGHLIGHTS: Managing Director at the age of 30 (South Africa), Managing Partner with Egon Zehnder Int. until 1989

SPECIAL INTERESTS/HOBBIES: Music, literature, skiing

GEOGRAPHIC SCOPE OF RECRUITING: International with German focus

SECTOR/INDUSTRY SPECIALIZATION: None

FAVORITE HISTORICAL FIGURE/MODEL/MENTOR: Historical figure: J. F. Kennedy; Mentor: Egon Zehnder

SINGLE MOST IMPORTANT ISSUE IN CONDUCTING A HIGH LEVEL SEARCH: Personal relationship between consultant, client and candidate based on trust and confidence.

MOST SIGNIFICANT OTHER ASPECT OF PERSONAL OR PROFESSIONAL LIFE: Success

WHAT IS THE BEST PREPARATION FOR BEING A SUCCESSFUL RECRUITER? Excellent education, successful track record in management, last but not least several years of training with a leading consulting firm.

WHAT WOULD YOU BE DOING IF YOU WERE NOT AN EXECUTIVE RECRUITER? I would either be in top management or run my own business outside management consulting.

WHAT ARE THE CHARACTERISTICS OF A GREAT CLIENT? A great client must have excellent people skills, entrepreneurial talent and must have a clearly defined strategy and/or vision. He should have good people judgment and regard executive search as a fine art, which is crucial to anybody's business.

WHAT CHALLENGES DO YOU SEE AHEAD IN THE GLOBAL MARKETPLACE? Everybody is talking about globalization and the need for creating globally operating companies. One of the most important challenges will be to find a sound balance between globalization and focus on local needs and demands.

MITSUHARU TOMIZAWA

Heidrick & Struggles
Kasumigaseki Building, 31F
3-2-5, Kasumigaseki
Chiyoda-ku, Tokyo 100-6031
Japan
Telephone: 81-3-3500-5310
Fax: 81-3-3500-5350
E-mail: mxt@h-s-japan.com
Company Website: http://www.h-s.com

DATE OF BIRTH: March 16, 1949

NATIONALITY: Japanese—Grew up in Japan

EDUCATIONAL BACKGROUND:
California State University, Los Angeles, Master's degree in Economics, 1975
International Christian University, Tokyo, Bachelor's degree in Social Science, 1971

LANGUAGES SPOKEN: Japanese (native) and English (fluent)

CAREER HIGHLIGHTS:
- Partner of Heidrick & Struggles (Tokyo: 1997–Present)
- Chairman/Managing Director of Spencer Stuart Japan (Tokyo: 1988–1996)
- Vice President of Bank of America NT & SA (Japan and California: 1978–1988)
- Mitsui Bank (presently known as Sakura Bank) (Tokyo: 1971–1973)

SPECIAL INTERESTS/HOBBIES: Listening to music/jogging

GEOGRAPHIC SCOPE OF RECRUITING: Japan

SECTOR/INDUSTRY SPECIALIZATION: Consumer goods (durable and non-durable), Industrial Products, Financial Services, Information Technology

FAVORITE HISTORICAL FIGURE/MODEL/MENTOR: Mr. Kaii Higashiyama (a distinguished contemporary Nihon-ga painter)

SINGLE MOST IMPORTANT ISSUE IN CONDUCTING A HIGH LEVEL SEARCH: In-depth understanding of corporate vision

MOST SIGNIFICANT OTHER ASPECT OF PERSONAL OR PROFESSIONAL LIFE: Family and children

WHAT IS THE BEST PREPARATION FOR BEING A SUCCESSFUL RECRUITER? Nurture the ability to take failure as a way to success

WHAT WOULD YOU BE DOING IF YOU WERE NOT AN EXECUTIVE RECRUITER? Either a medical doctor or a lawyer

WHAT ARE THE CHARACTERISTICS OF A GREAT CLIENT? Board minded, with the ability to articulate corporate needs effectively. Participating in the search process with a sense of urgency

WHAT CHALLENGES DO YOU SEE AHEAD IN THE GLOBAL MARKETPLACE? To identify business executives who belong to the top echelon in their specialty in order to meet growing needs of clients

TAMAS TOTH

H. Neumann International
1090 Vienna   1122 Budapest
Günthergasse 3   Rath GY. u. 54
Austria   Hungary
Telephone: 43-1-40140313
Fax: (in Budapest): 36-1-2144000
E-mail: ttoth@hneumann.hu
Company Website: http://www.hneumann-inter.com

DATE OF BIRTH: August 19, 1947

NATIONALITY: Hungarian—Grew up in Hungary

EDUCATIONAL BACKGROUND:
  Electrical Engineer, Technical University of Budapest
  Postgraduate studies in Economics
  Ph.D., Information Technology

LANGUAGES SPOKEN: English, German, Russian

CAREER HIGHLIGHTS:
  15 years with IBM (Hungary and CEE responsibilities)
  H. Neumann International since 1989

SPECIAL INTERESTS/HOBBIES: Tennis; to study, to write articles and to give lectures on "Manager as Public Figure"

GEOGRAPHIC SCOPE OF RECRUITING: Central and Eastern Europe, Europe

SECTOR/INDUSTRY SPECIALIZATION: Banking/Financial Services, Nonexecutive Directors

FAVORITE HISTORICAL FIGURE/MODEL/MENTOR: Dr. Helmut Neumann

SINGLE MOST IMPORTANT ISSUE IN CONDUCTING A HIGH LEVEL SEARCH: Act as a "proactive bridge" between the Western and Eastern social/intellectual and management cultures and to contribute to the integration of managers/leaders into the unified Europe.

MOST SIGNIFICANT OTHER ASPECT OF PERSONAL OR PROFESSIONAL LIFE: Csaba and Marton, my sons

WHAT IS THE BEST PREPARATION FOR BEING A SUCCESSFUL RECRUITER? Management experience of many years with special focus on organisational development, business development and people management. In this context. It is also worth establishing an individual approach to managing the problems and tasks from a strategic and a complex point of view. Finally, a communication culture must be developed in a target oriented way that is proactive and always aimed at establishing mutual trust.

WHAT WOULD YOU BE DOING IF YOU WERE NOT AN EXECUTIVE CONSULTANT? I would be acting as a Strategic Consultant or as an M&A Investment Banker.

WHAT ARE THE CHARACTERISTICS OF A GREAT CLIENT? A great client considers the executive recruiter as a strategic consultant in leadership, management, and human resource fields; and is open and ready to develop and maintain a relationship-type of approach.

WHAT CHALLENGES DO YOU SEE AHEAD IN THE GLOBAL MARKETPLACE? The marketplace will become more and more global, but the "local" cultural and intellectual components will have a major influence. Leadership and management rapidly shift from a geographical orientation to a global industry practice and product group oriented tendency. Emerging management structures will be faced by the increase of cross-cultural and cross-intellectual challenges. The effective and successful Executive Recruiter plays a proactive role in this process.

JOHN W. TOWNSEND

Gardiner, Townsend & Associates
101 East 52nd Street
New York, NY 10022
U.S.A.

Telephone: 1 (212) 230-1889
Fax: 1 (212) 838-0424

DATE OF BIRTH: September 17, 1944

NATIONALITY: American—Grew up in Baltimore, Maryland

EDUCATIONAL BACKGROUND:
  University of Pennsylvania, B.A., Latin American Studies, 1966
  University of Pennsylvania (Wharton), M.B.A., 1972

LANGUAGES SPOKEN: English, Spanish, and Modern Greek

CAREER HIGHLIGHTS:
  1985–90   Head of Investment Banking, UBS (New York)
  1978–85   Vice President in International Corporate Finance: Goldman Sachs & Co. (New York)

SPECIAL INTERESTS/HOBBIES: Windsurfing, Choral Singing, Language Study, Independent School Education (on Board and Governance Committee of New York State Association of Independent Schools)

GEOGRAPHIC SCOPE OF RECRUITING: U.S., Latin America, and Europe

SECTOR/INDUSTRY SPECIALIZATION: Finance

FAVORITE HISTORICAL FIGURE/MODEL/MENTOR: Thomas Cope (19th century American merchant and civic leader). Benedict Arnold (one of the most misunderstood figures in American history).

SINGLE MOST IMPORTANT ISSUE IN CONDUCTING A HIGH LEVEL SEARCH: Matching client expectations with true, perhaps unrevealed, candidate aspirations

MOST SIGNIFICANT OTHER ASPECT OF PERSONAL OR PROFESSIONAL LIFE: Active involvement in New York City philanthropy and charity (Trustee and Head of Finance Committee, Altman Foundation; Member of the Executive Committee and Board of Directors of City Harvest)

CHRISTOPHER TRAUB

Traub and Associates, Ltd./Ward Howell International
Suite 504
No. 207, Tun Hwa North Road
Taipei, Taiwan, R.O.C.

Telephone: 886-2-514-0443
Fax: 886-2-719-8124
E-mail: ctraub@whi.com.tw
Company Website: http://www.laix.com

DATE OF BIRTH: November 20, 1962

NATIONALITY: American—Grew up in U.S.A.

EDUCATIONAL BACKGROUND:
  BA, Anthropology, East Asian Studies, Oberlin College, Ohio, U.S.A.

LANGUAGES SPOKEN: English, Mandarin

CAREER HIGHLIGHTS: Executive search consultant, 1988–present; Value-added network service sales management, Taiwan, 1987; Market research consulting, 1986

SPECIAL INTERESTS/HOBBIES: Adventure sports, management development, multimedia production, music

GEOGRAPHIC SCOPE OF RECRUITING: Greater China

SECTOR/INDUSTRY SPECIALIZATION: Technology (telecoms, semiconductors, computer systems), financial services, consumer

FAVORITE HISTORICAL FIGURE/MODEL/MENTOR: Marco Polo, Christopher Columbus

SINGLE MOST IMPORTANT ISSUE IN CONDUCTING A HIGH LEVEL SEARCH: Adopting a balanced, responsible and ethical approach to achieve clarity and alignment between candidates and clients. Exhaustive coverage of the market is critical.

MOST SIGNIFICANT OTHER ASPECT OF PERSONAL OR PROFESSIONAL LIFE: Achieving a sense of balance between a demanding professional life and personal goals.

WHAT IS THE BEST PREPARATION FOR BEING A SUCCESSFUL RECRUITER? Conceptual broad-based educational background, emphasizing learning ability; and extensive exposure to interpersonal communication and assessment

WHAT WOULD YOU BE DOING IF YOU WERE NOT AN EXECUTIVE RECRUITER? Operating a leadership and teambuilding consultancy focused on emerging markets (China, India, Indonesia, etc.) in a challenging outdoor setting.

WHAT ARE THE CHARACTERISTICS OF A GREAT CLIENT? Clear understanding of his/her company's strengths, weaknesses, vision, and current needs. Moves quickly through evaluation and negotiation process. Sensitive to cultural issues.

WHAT CHALLENGES DO YOU SEE AHEAD IN THE GLOBAL MARKETPLACE? In Asia, continued shortfall of capable management talent; in search, the combination of megafirms consolidating, and small, price and contingency driven firms entering the marketplace.

ANDREW P.Y. TSUI

Korn/Ferry International (HK) Ltd.
Room 2104-2106 Gloucester Tower
The Landmark, Central
Hong Kong

Telephone: 852 2971-2735 (direct)/(852) 2521-5457 (main)
Fax: 852 2810-1632
E-mail: tsui@kornferry.com
Company Website: http://www.kornferry.com

DATE OF BIRTH: April 17, 1952

NATIONALITY: Canadian—Grew up in Hong Kong

EDUCATIONAL BACKGROUND:
Bachelor of Social Sciences, Hong Kong University (1975)

LANGUAGES SPOKEN: English, Mandarin, Cantonese

CAREER HIGHLIGHTS:
1986–96 Russell Reynolds Associates
1983–85 Irving Trust, now known as Bank of New York
1979–83 Sun Hung Kai Securities
1978–79 Price Waterhouse

SPECIAL INTERESTS/HOBBIES: Boating, karaoke, gym workout

GEOGRAPHIC SCOPE OF RECRUITING: Around the world as well as Asia Pacific

SECTOR/INDUSTRY SPECIALIZATION: Financial Services, CEO Practice, Non-Profit Organizations

FAVORITE HISTORICAL FIGURE/MODEL/MENTOR: My late father, Paul

SINGLE MOST IMPORTANT ISSUE IN CONDUCTING A HIGH LEVEL SEARCH: Positioning the client and the candidate; knowing them well

MOST SIGNIFICANT OTHER ASPECT OF PERSONAL OR PROFESSIONAL LIFE: Enjoy organizing parties and fund raising events

WHAT IS THE BEST PREPARATION FOR BEING A SUCCESSFUL RECRUITER?
- Being a natural in remembering people
- Being an enthusiastic match-maker
- Being an approachable and service oriented person
- Being great in one-on-one meetings

WHAT WOULD YOU BE DOING IF YOU WERE NOT AN EXECUTIVE RECRUITER? In the Corporate Communications/Investor Communications/Financial Communications area helping Asian companies bridge the cultural gap with US/Western investors.

WHAT ARE THE CHARACTERISTICS OF A GREAT CLIENT?
A great client takes you in as a trusted advisor and sees the search consultant as a partner.

WHAT CHALLENGES DO YOU SEE AHEAD IN THE GLOBAL MARKETPLACE? Asia in the next 12–24 months getting back to normalcy after currency and stock market turmoil which has led to corporate bankruptcies and lay-offs.

ROBERTO VALAGUSSA

Search Partners International
24 rue Clément Marot
75008 Paris
France
Telephone: 33 1 47.23.74.81
Fax: 33 1 47.23.05.86

DATE OF BIRTH: November 14, 1952

NATIONALITY: Italian—Grew up in Italy

EDUCATIONAL BACKGROUND:
Istituto Leone XIII, Milan
Universita L. Bocconi, Milan

LANGUAGES SPOKEN: Italian, English, French, Spanish

CAREER HIGHLIGHTS:
Co-founder Search Partners International
International General Manager—Gruppo Editoriale Fabbri-(Mondedori)
Senior Partner—H. Neumann International in Paris and Milan

SPECIAL INTERESTS/HOBBIES: Traveling, reading, sports; escaping to my home in Southhampton (New York)

GEOGRAPHIC SCOPE OF RECRUITING: Worldwide

SECTOR/INDUSTRY SPECIALIZATION: Industry, Consumer Goods, Media/entertainment/publishing

FAVORITE HISTORICAL FIGURE/MODEL/MENTOR: Giulio Cesare, Christoforo Colombo

SINGLE MOST IMPORTANT ISSUE IN CONDUCTING A HIGH LEVEL SEARCH: Total availability; creativity

BIGGEST COMPETITOR: Heidricks & Struggles

MOST SIGNIFICANT OTHER ASPECT OF PERSONAL OR PROFESSIONAL LIFE: Aiming to be as close as possible to the client, traveling.

WHAT IS THE BEST PREPARATION FOR BEING A SUCCESSFUL RECRUITER? Having had a successful general management position in the past.

WHAT WOULD YOU BE DOING IF YOU WERE NOT AN EXECUTIVE RECRUITER? Publisher or a professional in the field of sports (player or journalist).

WHAT ARE THE CHARACTERISTICS OF A GREAT CLIENT? Development on an international scale.

WHAT CHALLENGES DO YOU SEE AHEAD IN THE GLOBAL MARKETPLACE? Finding top quality managers; the challenges and opportunities of advanced technology

MARIA ELENA VALDEZ

Korn/Ferry International
Montes Urales 505 Piso 3
Lomas de Chapultepec
Mexico, D.F. 11000

Telephone: 52 5 202 5900
Fax: 52 5 202 4469
E-mail: MValdes@KFerry.attmail.com
Company Website: http://www.kornferry.com

DATE OF BIRTH: January 27, 1955

NATIONALITY: Mexican—Grew up in the U.S. and in Mexico

EDUCATIONAL BACKGROUND:
 MBA University of Denver
 MA University of Denver
 BA University of Denver

LANGUAGES SPOKEN: English and Spanish

CAREER HIGHLIGHTS: Having taken away a major search from the competition and being able to successfully fill the job in 2 months.

SPECIAL INTERESTS/HOBBIES: Reading, travel, and music

GEOGRAPHIC SCOPE OF RECRUITING: Mexico, Puerto Rico, Miami, U.S. Hispanic market

SECTOR/INDUSTRY SPECIALIZATION: Consumer

FAVORITE HISTORICAL FIGURE/MODEL/MENTOR: Golda Meir

SINGLE MOST IMPORTANT ISSUE IN CONDUCTING A HIGH LEVEL SEARCH: Once one has understood the client's business, culture and needs, assuming one is providing the client FAST, HIGH QUALITY SERVICE and that one is innovative and willing to go the extra mile, the most important issue is TRUST and INTEGRITY and being able to add extra value to every search.

MOST SIGNIFICANT OTHER ASPECT OF PERSONAL OR PROFESSIONAL LIFE: Family and friends

WHAT IS THE BEST PREPARATION FOR BEING A SUCCESSFUL RECRUITER? A successful recruiter should be able to really understand the business world, and know what client service is really all about.

WHAT WOULD YOU BE DOING IF YOU WERE NOT AN EXECUTIVE RECRUITER? I would be back in a Human Resources role, or working in a service organization.

WHAT ARE THE CHARACTERISTICS OF A GREAT CLIENT? Someone who works with you, who really knows what he wants, yet at the same time can be flexible. Someone who has a global vision and strategy and with an excellent reputation in the market.

WHAT CHALLENGES DO YOU SEE AHEAD IN THE GLOBAL MARKETPLACE? Technology for one, as well as being able to grow as fast as the market demands.

JEAN-MARIE VAN DEN BORRE

Korn/Ferry International
Avenue Louise 523
Louizalaan 523
B-1050 Brussels
Belgium

Telephone: 32-2-640.32.40
Fax: 32-2-640.83.82
E-mail: Jean-Marie.vandenborre@kornferry.com
Company Website: http://www.kornferry.com

DATE OF BIRTH: July 17, 1942

NATIONALITY: Belgian—Grew up in Ghent, Belgium

EDUCATIONAL BACKGROUND:
1966   Doctor of Laws degree, Ghent State University
1966   License in Notaryship
1968   Postgraduate license in European Law
1980   Business Administration Certificate from Cepac (Solvay Business School)

LANGUAGES SPOKEN: Dutch, French, English, German, Rumanian; good notions of Italian, Spanish, Russian

CAREER HIGHLIGHTS: Legal Counsel Europe, Africa, the Middle East of Holiday Inns (1971–1974); Partner and Senior Vice President of Spencer Stuart (1974–1984); Partner, former Board Director, Senior Officer, Managing Partner Benelux of Korn/Ferry International (1984–present) and Chairman of the worldwide Human Resources & Development Committee (Promotions Committee) (as of 1997)

SPECIAL INTERESTS/HOBBIES: Tennis (president of Knokke Tennis Club), international politics, photography, video

GEOGRAPHIC SCOPE OF RECRUITING: Europe/North America

SECTOR/INDUSTRY SPECIALIZATION: Generalist with strong experience in industry and energy

FAVORITE HISTORICAL FIGURE/MODEL/MENTOR: John Kennedy/Albert Frere/Michael Boxberger

SINGLE MOST IMPORTANT ISSUE IN CONDUCTING A HIGH LEVEL SEARCH: Client satisfaction: understand and represent accurately the client, his objectives and his needs and make sure they are met fully

WHAT IS THE BEST PREPARATION FOR BEING A SUCCESSFUL RECRUITER? Having had a very varied career in terms of management positions, business sectors and international experience. Management positions should ideally include commercial and human resources posts.

WHAT WOULD YOU BE DOING IF YOU WERE NOT AN EXECUTIVE RECRUITER? Hold a top management position in a medium-sized dynamic international company.

WHAT ARE THE CHARACTERISTICS OF A GREAT CLIENT? A real professional who is demanding but reasonable and realistic in his expectations (mainly in terms of speed), who also understands that we cannot create candidates who do not exist and that some searches will take more time than expected. Further a person who interacts regularly with us and who can recognize (relating to our profession) good performance.

WHAT CHALLENGES DO YOU SEE AHEAD IN THE GLOBAL MARKETPLACE? Challenges include maintaining consistent quality of work, the influence of the Internet, finding quality global top managers, meeting faster delivery requirements, and sustaining real and permanent international cooperation within executive search firms.

GERARD L. VAN DEN BROEK

Spencer Stuart
Gabriel Metsustraat 9
1071 D2 Amsterdam
Holland

Telephone: 31-20-6646566
Fax: 31-20-6620632
E-mail: gvandenbroek@spencerstuart.com
Company Website: http://www.spencerstuart.com

DATE OF BIRTH: May 5, 1941

NATIONALITY: Dutch—Grew up in Holland

EDUCATIONAL BACKGROUND:
Rotterdam University, Business law degree, 1969

LANGUAGES SPOKEN: Dutch, English, German

CAREER HIGHLIGHTS: 10 years management of Spencer Stuart Amsterdam; startup of 2 successful diversification

SPECIAL INTERESTS/HOBBIES: Sailing

GEOGRAPHIC SCOPE OF RECRUITING: Holland

SECTOR/INDUSTRY SPECIALIZATION: Board searches/Financial Services industry

FAVORITE HISTORICAL FIGURE/MODEL/MENTOR: Julius Caesar

SINGLE MOST IMPORTANT ISSUE IN CONDUCTING A HIGH LEVEL SEARCH: To be trusted by client and candidates completely

BIGGEST COMPETITOR: Egon Zehnder

MOST SIGNIFICANT OTHER ASPECT OF PERSONAL OR PROFESSIONAL LIFE: To be consulted on other issues than search

WHAT IS THE BEST PREPARATION FOR BEING A SUCCESSFUL RECRUITER? (General) management of a service oriented company.

WHAT WOULD YOU BE DOING IF YOU WERE NOT AN EXECUTIVE RECRUITER? Own and manage a financial services company

WHAT ARE THE CHARACTERISTICS OF A GREAT CLIENT? That he puts his trust in you and asks for personal advice

WHAT CHALLENGES DO YOU SEE AHEAD IN THE GLOBAL MARKETPLACE? Specialization; segmentation

PETER C. VAN DE VELDE

Amrop International
Level 9
155 George Street
Sydney NSW 2000
Australia

Telephone: 61 2 9252 3500
Fax: 61 2 9247 2757
E-mail: Peter.VandeVelde@amrop.optusmsg.net.au
Company Website: http://www.amrop.com

DATE OF BIRTH: January 28, 1940

NATIONALITY: Australian—Grew up in Australia

EDUCATIONAL BACKGROUND:

Melbourne Grammar School (School Captain 1958 - School Centenary Year)
Bachelor of Science, University of Melbourne

LANGUAGES SPOKEN: English

CAREER HIGHLIGHTS:

In Search:

- Managing Partner of Amrop International in Australasia (mid-1980s to mid-1990s), responsible for devising strategies and managing the firm into the position of market leadership.
- International Chairman of the Amrop International Group (1989 to 1991), brought the Group into the top six search practices worldwide by initiating and negotiating the entry into Amrop of Lamalie in the U.S.A., Caldwell Partners in Canada, Whitehead Mann in the U.K., and a number of other search practices in Europe, Latin America and Asia, which gave the the Amrop Group leadership in geographic coverage.
- Developed and implemented the strategy for ensuring the effective conduct of international searches.

Prior to Search:

- Chief Executive Officer of Rank Industries Australia Limited—the Australian subsidiary of the Rank Organisation plc. Previously on the Board and International Advisory Committee of PA Management Consultants and Regional Director for New South Wales.

SPECIAL INTERESTS/HOBBIES: Golf, gardening, chairing a community project on the development of an aged care residential facility. Trustee, Committee for Economic Development of Australia (CEDA). Director, Foodbank NSW Limited. Director, Foodbank Australia Limited. Director, Corporate Recovery Partners Pty Limited.

GEOGRAPHIC SCOPE OF RECRUITING: Australia and New Zealand-some work in the broader Asia Pacific Region and some focused work in North American and the U.K.

SECTOR/INDUSTRY SPECIALIZATION: Broad practice at the top of the Australian market at CEO, CFO, Chairmen and Non-Executive Director level. In industrial, resources, financial services (especially insurance and funds management), and management services (especially law) sectors.

FAVORITE HISTORICAL FIGURE/MODEL/MENTOR: Sir Thomas More

continues ▶

SINGLE MOST IMPORTANT ISSUE IN CONDUCTING A HIGH LEVEL SEARCH: Gaining a comprehensive understanding of the client's business and the key issues with which the newly appointed executive must deal, including understanding the dynamics of the market(s) in which the client operates.

BIGGEST COMPETITOR: In Australia, Chris Thomas of Egon Zehnder and Kerry McInnes (recently retired) of Spencer Stuart.

MOST SIGNIFICANT OTHER ASPECT OF PERSONAL OR PROFESSIONAL LIFE:

Professionally:

- Consistently, in the past seven years, personally billing in excess of US$1 million annually, and, for the past three years, billing in excess of US$1.5 million annually.
- Acting as a pro bono adviser to both the Anglican and Catholic Dioceses of Sydney and some other charities.

Personally:

- Happily married since 1965 with four well educated, high achieving children.

WHAT IS THE BEST PREPARATION FOR BEING A SUCCESSFUL RECRUITER? Possessing a lively and contemporary understanding of the dynamics of business and of organisation structures. To be able to combine successful senior line management experience (i.e., to have been in a role requiring the management of people and issues resulting in the successful delivery of shareholder value) with the sensitivity and perception derived from effective experience as an adviser/consultant (i.e., to be an effective persuader, seller of concepts, agent of change).

WHAT WOULD YOU BE DOING IF YOU WERE NOT AN EXECUTIVE RECRUITER? At this stage of my career, I would expect to be on a number of Boards as an independent non-executive director and/or acting as an adviser to Boards on strategic issues.

WHAT ARE THE CHARACTERISTICS OF A GREAT CLIENT? An organisation with a very clear view of its own market positioning, with strong and effective internal communication and a clear and well communicated understanding of short and long term business objectives.

WHAT CHALLENGES DO YOU SEE AHEAD IN THE GLOBAL MARKETPLACE? A growing requirement for increasing levels of genuine specialisation. A growing requirement for improved speed of response. Rapidly escalating technological advances impacting on the execution of search assignments.

KARIN VASSILOPOULOS

H. Neumann International
Günthergasse 3
1090 Vienna
Austria

Telephone: 43-1-40 140-310
Fax: 43-1-40 140-5274
E-mail: k.vass@magnet.at
Company Website: http://www.hneumann-inter.com

DATE OF BIRTH: March 14, 1945

NATIONALITY: Austria—Grew up in Vienna, Austria

EDUCATIONAL BACKGROUND:
B.A. International Studies
M.A. International Marketing

LANGUAGES SPOKEN: German, English, French, Greek (fluent), Italian, Russian (basic)

SPECIAL INTERESTS/HOBBIES: The study of cultural differences, nature and outdoor life, fine arts, antiques

GEOGRAPHIC SCOPE OF RECRUITING: Fformer Soviet Union (globally in international searches)

SECTOR/INDUSTRY SPECIALIZATION: Wide experience in various sectors

FAVORITE HISTORICAL FIGURE/MODEL/MENTOR: Heinrich Schliemann

SINGLE MOST IMPORTANT ISSUE IN CONDUCTING A HIGH LEVEL SEARCH: To understand in depth not only the client's needs but also the corporate culture and organisational environment to find the best possible match for any given position.

MOST SIGNIFICANT OTHER ASPECT OF PERSONAL OR PROFESSIONAL LIFE:
- Honesty and integrity
- Full identification with any given task

WHAT IS THE BEST PREPARATION FOR BEING A SUCCESSFUL RECRUITER? In addition to a good business education a preparedness for continuous learning and an extensive problem solving orientation must prevail.

WHAT WOULD YOU BE DOING IF YOU WERE NOT AN EXECUTIVE RECRUITER? I would be a manager and organiser of cultural events, mainly of fine arts exhibitions and projects.

WHAT ARE THE CHARACTERISTICS OF A GREAT CLIENT? A great client is a person who understands the importance of the human resource who in the end manages and controls all other resources, i.e., capital, equipment, technology in any given organisation.

WHAT CHALLENGES DO YOU SEE AHEAD IN THE GLOBAL MARKETPLACE? The biggest challenge is to bridge the cultural gaps in a global environment. Only those search consultants will succeed who have a deep multi-cultural understanding and who will achieve in optimally integrating a candidate in a client company.

GAIL H. VERGARA

Spencer Stuart
401 N. Michigan Avenue
Chicago, IL 60611
U.S.A.

Telephone: 1 (312) 321-8342
Fax: 1 (312) 822-0116
E-mail: gvergara@spencerstuart.com
Company Website: http://www.spencerstuart.com

DATE OF BIRTH: January 6, 1948

NATIONALITY: American—Grew up in Chicago

EDUCATIONAL BACKGROUND:
Master's, Social Work, University of Illinois
Bachelor's, Sociology, University of Colorado

LANGUAGES SPOKEN: English and Spanish (un poco)

CAREER HIGHLIGHTS:

1973–80	Administrator, Mercy Hospital, Chicago, IL
1980–91	Witt Associates (now Witt, Kieffer, Ford, Hadelman & Lloyd)
1987–91	Executive Vice President
1991–Present	Spencer Stuart
1997–Present	Managing Director-Chicago
1996–97	Global Life Sciences Practice Leader
1991–95	Senior Director

SPECIAL INTERESTS/HOBBIES: Antiques, jogging, golf

GEOGRAPHIC SCOPE OF RECRUITING: National and international

SECTOR/INDUSTRY SPECIALIZATION: Life Sciences including healthcare systems, hospitals, managed care, pharmaceuticals, insurance

FAVORITE HISTORICAL FIGURE/MODEL/MENTOR: Historical: Mother Theresa;
Role Model: Lou Hamity—my father

SINGLE MOST IMPORTANT ISSUE IN CONDUCTING A HIGH LEVEL SEARCH: Integrity

MOST SIGNIFICANT OTHER ASPECT OF PERSONAL OR PROFESSIONAL LIFE: Persistence

WHAT IS THE BEST PREPARATION FOR BEING A SUCCESSFUL RECRUITER? Studying personality and behavior

WHAT WOULD YOU BE DOING IF YOU WERE NOT AN EXECUTIVE RECRUITER? Running an adoption agency, or if I won the lottery, be a great philanthropist.

WHAT ARE THE CHARACTERISTICS OF A GREAT CLIENT? Open and frequent communication

WHAT CHALLENGES DO YOU SEE AHEAD IN THE GLOBAL MARKETPLACE? The merging of cultural differences in an effort to truly become global businesses.

TIM VIGNOLES

Garner International
6 Derby Street
Mayfair
London W1Y 7HD

Telephone: 44 171 629 8822
Fax: 44 171 629 8833
E-mail: garner.int@btinternet.com
Company Website: http://www.garnerinternational.co.uk

DATE OF BIRTH: June 7, 1940

NATIONALITY: British—Grew up in England-Ireland

EDUCATIONAL BACKGROUND:

Sedbergh School, Cumbria, England
Trinity College, Dublin, Ireland

LANGUAGES SPOKEN: English and French (basic)

CAREER HIGHLIGHTS:

- Setting up and heading, for seven years, the European office of the Global Entertainment and Media Practice of Korn/Ferry International.
- Vice President heading European Production and Distribution for Columbia Pictures Television and establishing them as the leading exponent of Co-Production in Europe.
- Heading the European Operations as Vice President of Production and Distribution for MCA Television and pioneering the early days of U.K./U.S.A. Co-Production.
- Early training at BBC Television and in the theatre in Ireland and U.K.

SPECIAL INTERESTS/HOBBIES: Art and artists, books and writers, theatre, cinema, music and horse racing.

GEOGRAPHIC SCOPE OF RECRUITING: U.K., U.S.A., Europe, Central Europe, Middle East, Australia, the Far East.

SECTOR/INDUSTRY SPECIALIZATION: Entertainment and Media

FAVORITE HISTORICAL FIGURE/MODEL/MENTOR: Historic Figure: Sir Winston Churchill; Mentors: William Macquitty ,(Former Chairman of Ulster TV,. Photographer,. Author,. Film Producer, and Buddhist), Brian Brolly, (Founder and former CEO of The Really Useful Co. MD at MCA Television), and Sir Paul Fox, (Former MD of BBC Television and Yorkshire Television, Former Chairman of The Racecourses Association)

SINGLE MOST IMPORTANT ISSUE IN CONDUCTING A HIGH LEVEL SEARCH: Understanding fully all aspects of the client's brief, mutually with the client before commencing the search.

MOST SIGNIFICANT OTHER ASPECT OF PERSONAL OR PROFESSIONAL LIFE: My Family and Ireland.

WHAT IS THE BEST PREPARATION FOR BEING A SUCCESSFUL RECRUITER? Hands on actual management experience in the industry sectors in which one specialises.

WHAT WOULD YOU BE DOING IF YOU WERE NOT AN EXECUTIVE RECRUITER? Running my own Art Gallery and Bookshop!

WHAT ARE THE CHARACTERISTICS OF A GREAT CLIENT? A great client understands the search process fully,.acts as a communicative full partner in the process, has courage, trust, and is decisive.

WHAT CHALLENGES DO YOU SEE AHEAD IN THE GLOBAL MARKETPLACE? A much more personal service and a concentration in specialisation in specific sectors, as general headhunting and recruitment goes increasingly to electronic communication and electronic database solutions.

JEAN-DOMINIQUE VIRCHAUX

Heidrick & Struggles
5201 Blue Lagoon Drive, Suite 795
Miami, FL 33126
U.S.A.

Telephone: 1 (305) 262-2606
Fax: 1 (305) 262-6697
E-mail: vir@h-s.com
Company Website: http://www.h-s.com

DATE OF BIRTH: September 25, 1953

NATIONALITY: Swiss—Grew up in Switzerland

EDUCATIONAL BACKGROUND:
Certified Public Accountant, 1982
The University of the State of New York
Commercial Science, 1975
Fribourg, Switzerland

LANGUAGES SPOKEN: English, French, Spanish

CAREER HIGHLIGHTS:
1996–Present	Heidrick & Struggles Inc., Managing Partner of the Latin America Regional Office, Miami, Florida
1984–1996	Tasa International A.G.: Caracas, Venezuela (1984–93); Santiago, Chile (1994–96)
1990–1996	President of Latin America, Member of the Executive Committee and the Board of Directors of TASA International.
1978–1984	Price Waterhouse, New York City, New York and Caracas, Venezuela
1975–1978	Societe Fiduciere Suisse, Geneva, Switzerland

SPECIAL INTERESTS/HOBBIES: Skiing

GEOGRAPHIC SCOPE OF RECRUITING: Latin America and southeastern U.S.A., especially southern Florida

SECTOR/INDUSTRY SPECIALIZATION: General Practice, Financial Services, Consumer Goods

WHAT IS THE BEST PREPARATION FOR BEING A SUCCESSFUL RECRUITER? Management consultant and/or General Manager at a young age. Multicultural and international exposure.

WHAT WOULD YOU BE DOING IF YOU WERE NOT AN EXECUTIVE RECRUITER? In search since 1984 when I was 31 years old. However to pick an activity I would say Private Banker.

WHAT ARE THE CHARACTERISTICS OF A GREAT CLIENT? Work as a team with the search consultant. Think out of the box in terms of profile of candidates.

WHAT CHALLENGES DO YOU SEE AHEAD IN THE GLOBAL MARKETPLACE?
- Going from a transaction relationship to an information relationship.
- Seamless execute searches on a global basis.

JUDITH M. VON SELDENECK

Diversified Search Inc.
2005 Market Street
Suite 3300
Philadelphia, PA 19103
U.S.A.

Telephone: 1 (800) 432-3932
Fax: 1 (215) 568-8399

DATE OF BIRTH: June 6, 1940

NATIONALITY: American—Grew up in North Carolina

EDUCATIONAL BACKGROUND:
B.A. Political Science, University of North Carolina, Chapel Hill, North Carolina
American University College of Law, Washington, D.C.: Evening School, no degree

LANGUAGES SPOKEN: English

CAREER HIGHLIGHTS:
- Executive Assistant to Senator Walter Mondale
- Founded Diversified Search Companies in 1973
- Appointed to numerous Boards of Directors, including CoreStates Financial Corp., Tasty Baking Company, AAA Mid Atlantic, Keystone Insurance, Greater Philadelphia Chamber of Commerce, Association of Executive Search Consultants
- Founding member of the Committee of 200 (the top 200 business women in the country)

SPECIAL INTERESTS/HOBBIES: Golf, fishing

GEOGRAPHIC SCOPE OF RECRUITING: U.S.A., Nationwide

SECTOR/INDUSTRY SPECIALIZATION: General Corporate, Healthcare, Financial Services, Boards of Directors, Not-for-Profit, Education

FAVORITE HISTORICAL FIGURE/MODEL/MENTOR: Walter Mondale, John F. Kennedy

SINGLE MOST IMPORTANT ISSUE IN CONDUCTING A HIGH LEVEL SEARCH: Negotiating complex compensation packages and bringing searches to successful closure on a timely basis.

MOST SIGNIFICANT OTHER ASPECT OF PERSONAL OR PROFESSIONAL LIFE: Husband and two sons

WHAT IS THE BEST PREPARATION FOR BEING A SUCCESSFUL RECRUITER? There is no single route. It's a question of personality and ability to relate to all kinds of people. You have to be able to provide service to multiple constituencies with tight deadlines for results.

WHAT WOULD YOU BE DOING IF YOU WERE NOT AN EXECUTIVE RECRUITER? I would be a lawyer-litigator or out trying to start another business. I'd always be working for myself.

WHAT ARE THE CHARACTERISTICS OF A GREAT CLIENT? One that confides in you, sees search as a top priority in their universe and wants to enjoy the process and participate.

WHAT CHALLENGES DO YOU SEE AHEAD IN THE GLOBAL MARKETPLACE? Search organizations must be able to provide global coverage for clients who require it. The difference between cultures—for example in the methods and process by which candidates are evaluated—requires sensitive, informed, and highly competent consultant teams.

SERGEI I. VOROBIEV

Ward Howell International Holdings Ltd.
15 Bolshoi Tryokhgorny per.
123022 Moscow
Russia

Telephone: 7 (095) 956-68-45
Fax: 7 (095) 252-19-82
E-mail: info@whru.com
Company Website: http://www.laix.com

DATE OF BIRTH: September 19, 1964

NATIONALITY: Russian—Grew up in St. Petersburg, Russia

EDUCATIONAL BACKGROUND:

St. Petersburg State Technical University, MSc Physics, 1987

L'Agence pour la Cooperation Technique, Industrielle et Economique, Paris and St. Petersburg Engineering-Economics Institute; Joint Courses in Business Admin.; Diploma 1991–1992

LANGUAGES SPOKEN: Russian, English

CAREER HIGHLIGHTS:

1990–1992   Founding Partner and General Director of Baltic Consulting Group (leading local search company)

1993–present   Founding Partner and General Director of Ward Howell, Russia

SPECIAL INTERESTS/HOBBIES: The art of public speaking, drama, tennis

GEOGRAPHIC SCOPE OF RECRUITING: Russia and the rest of the world, wherever the right candidate might be

SECTOR/INDUSTRY SPECIALIZATION: Financial services, consulting, heavy industry

FAVORITE HISTORICAL FIGURE/MODEL/MENTOR: Winston Churchill/Peter the Great

SINGLE MOST IMPORTANT ISSUE IN CONDUCTING A HIGH LEVEL SEARCH: If at the certain stage a candidate continues to ask too many questions, he/she is bound to be a wrong one.

MOST SIGNIFICANT OTHER ASPECT OF PERSONAL OR PROFESSIONAL LIFE: Intellectual curiosity, commitment to continual growth and new challenges

WHAT IS THE BEST PREPARATION FOR BEING A SUCCESSFUL RECRUITER? First hand experience of senior management. This allows the recruiter to find a common language with both clients and candidates and gives him the opportunity to provide "value added consultancy." In addition, he should have had a sophisticated education, making it easier to adapt to the problems of diversified clients and identify ways of solving them. Of course, a good consultant should also have rich personal and professional life experience.

WHAT WOULD YOU BE DOING IF YOU WERE NOT AN EXECUTIVE RECRUITER? Most probably, a general manager of a large company. However, in a better world I could see myself as a politician or public speaker.

WHAT ARE THE CHARACTERISTICS OF A GREAT CLIENT? A great client has to be represented by an outstanding individual. The client has to be demanding and want a lot from you. Be ready to listen and learn

WHAT CHALLENGES DO YOU SEE AHEAD IN THE GLOBAL MARKETPLACE? If the industry continues to grow rapidly, too many professionals will be looking for other professionals. This will lead to tough competition both on a personal (consultant vs. consultant) and corporate (company vs. company) level. Companies will have to work as effective machines and will be headed by capable and talented executives, comparable to those at the forefront of the clients' industries.

DIDIER VUCHOT

Vuchot Ward Howell
11 avenue Myron T. Herrick
75008 Paris
France

Telephone: 33 1 42 56 29 57
Fax: 33 1 42 25 13 23
E-mail: 106202.324@compuserve.com
Company Website: http://www.laix.com

DATE OF BIRTH: November 10, 1944

NATIONALITY: French—Grew up in France

LANGUAGES SPOKEN: French and English

CAREER HIGHLIGHTS:
- For eighteen years in the profession as Founding Partner of Vuchot Ward Howell in Paris
- Prior to VWH, founding CEO of a temporary work company sold to the European market leader
- Started career in advertising with Publicis as Account Manager. Member of the AESC European Advisory Committee, formerly President of APROCERD
- Member of Ward Howell's International Council. Teacher at HEC, France.

SPECIAL INTERESTS/HOBBIES: Wine, golf, literature

GEOGRAPHIC SCOPE OF RECRUITING: Worldwide expertise in luxury goods

SECTOR/INDUSTRY SPECIALIZATION: Premium brand industries, Professional services, Financial services

SINGLE MOST IMPORTANT ISSUE IN CONDUCTING A HIGH LEVEL SEARCH: Discernment, determination

WHAT IS THE BEST PREPARATION FOR BEING A SUCCESSFUL RECRUITER? Having been faced with corporate strategic issues and people career management.

WHAT WOULD YOU BE DOING IF YOU WERE NOT AN EXECUTIVE RECRUITER? Investment banker/venture capitalist

WHAT ARE THE CHARACTERISTICS OF A GREAT CLIENT? Demonstrate long-term relationship

WHAT CHALLENGES DO YOU SEE AHEAD IN THE GLOBAL MARKETPLACE? The need to internationalize one's capability to help people to work together more effectively.

FREDERICK W. WACKERLE

Fred Wackerle, Inc.
20 N. Wacker Drive, Suite 3310
Chicago, IL 60606
U.S.A.

Telephone: 1 (312) 641-2977
Fax: 1 (312) 641-2367

DATE OF BIRTH: June 25, 1939

NATIONALITY: American—Grew up in Chicago, Illinois

EDUCATIONAL BACKGROUND:
BS, Monmouth College

LANGUAGES SPOKEN: English, German (spoken)

CAREER HIGHLIGHTS:
1997–present	Fred Wackerle, Inc.
1970–97	McFeely Wackerle Shulman
1968–70	Vice President, R.M. Schmitz
1966–68	Partner, Berry Henderson & Aberlin
1964–66	Associate, A.T. Kearney Search
1962–64	Assistant Personnel Director, Stewart Warner Corp.
1961–62	Operations Manager, Ball Brothers Co.

SPECIAL INTERESTS/HOBBIES: Modern art/Trustee, Monmouth College

GEOGRAPHIC SCOPE OF RECRUITING: North America

SECTOR/INDUSTRY SPECIALIZATION: CEO or CEO successor *only*; positions compensating more than $800k annually; minimum professional fee $250k.

FAVORITE HISTORICAL FIGURE/MODEL/MENTOR: Gandhi

SINGLE MOST IMPORTANT ISSUE IN CONDUCTING A HIGH LEVEL SEARCH: A complete understanding among all parties: client, search consultant, and candidate regarding the mission, scope, and candidate profile being sought to fulfill.

BIGGEST COMPETITOR: Messrs. Roche, Neff, Johnson, James and certain partners of large firms.

MOST SIGNIFICANT OTHER ASPECT OF PERSONAL OR PROFESSIONAL LIFE: My not-for-profit activities and taking time to counsel out-of-work executives.

WHAT IS THE BEST PREPARATION FOR BEING A SUCCESSFUL RECRUITER? Some experience in a large, international (global) corporation, giving exposure to functional and organizational matrices.

WHAT WOULD YOU BE DOING IF YOU WERE NOT AN EXECUTIVE RECRUITER? Teaching business policy/ethics/career planning in graduate business school and playing tuba in a dixieland band.

WHAT ARE THE CHARACTERISTICS OF A GREAT CLIENT? Total partnership/openness with the consultant, responsive communications, and understanding of the search and recruitment process.

WHAT CHALLENGES DO YOU SEE AHEAD IN THE GLOBAL MARKETPLACE? Challenges include a shrinking talent pool, too few search consultants, and client blockages.

RICHARD A. WALL III

Heidrick & Struggles International
100 Piccadilly
London
W1V 9FN
U.K.

Telephone: 44 171 491 3124 5831
Fax: 44 171 491 5877
Company Website: http://www.h-s.com

DATE OF BIRTH: December 22, 1952

NATIONALITY: American—Grew up in New York area

EDUCATIONAL BACKGROUND:
B.S. B.A., Georgetown University, 1970–1974
MBA, Boston College, 1975–1977

LANGUAGES SPOKEN: English

CAREER HIGHLIGHTS: Having the privilege and pleasure of working in the U.K. for the past 15 years

SPECIAL INTERESTS/HOBBIES: Escaping to my house on the far away island Nantucket

GEOGRAPHIC SCOPE OF RECRUITING: Majority of work conducted in Europe, some U.S. and Asian searches

SECTOR/INDUSTRY SPECIALIZATION: Financial services-specifically senior investment banking appointment

FAVORITE HISTORICAL FIGURE/MODEL/MENTOR: Role model/mentor: Richard A. Wall Jr.—my father

SINGLE MOST IMPORTANT ISSUE IN CONDUCTING A HIGH LEVEL SEARCH: Managing the expectations of our clients and candidates and delivery of an outstanding result on a timely basis

BIGGEST COMPETITOR: Consolidation/mergers in industry

MOST SIGNIFICANT OTHER ASPECT OF PERSONAL OR PROFESSIONAL LIFE: Personal: 6-year-old daughter; Professional: partner and friend Isabelle Martin

WHAT IS THE BEST PREPARATION FOR BEING A SUCCESSFUL RECRUITER? Relevant business skills in specific sectors (banking, technology, industry), superior education, international experience, good writing and communication skills

WHAT WOULD YOU BE DOING IF YOU WERE NOT AN EXECUTIVE RECRUITER? Working in a senior administrative role in banking

WHAT ARE THE CHARACTERISTICS OF A GREAT CLIENT? Responsiveness, openness, relationship oriented, and fun to work for and with

WHAT CHALLENGES DO YOU SEE AHEAD IN THE GLOBAL MARKETPLACE? Improving on looking in other markets on an efficient manner and to be lateral thinkers

ANDREW E. WEIDENER

Ray & Berndtson
191 Peachtree Street, N.E., Suite 3800
Atlanta, GA 30303
U.S.A.

Telephone: 1 (404) 215-4600
Fax: 1 (404) 215-4620
E-mail: Aweidener@rayberndtson.com
Company Website: http://www.rayberndtson.com

DATE OF BIRTH: May 19, 1943

NATIONALITY: American—Grew up in Philadelphia, Pennsylvania

EDUCATIONAL BACKGROUND:
  MBA, Marketing, Temple University, 1968
  B.S., Economics, University of Pennsylvania-Wharton School, 1965

LANGUAGES SPOKEN: English

CAREER HIGHLIGHTS:
  1983–85   Sara Lee Corporation: Senior Vice President, Group Officer
  1981–83   Shasta Beverages: President and Chief Executive Officer (1981–83); Vice President, Sales and Marketing
            (1979–81)
  1977–79   H.J. Heinz: General Manager, Sales (1977–79); Regional Sales Manager (1974–77)

SPECIAL INTERESTS/HOBBIES: Sports, reading, and travel

GEOGRAPHIC SCOPE OF RECRUITING: National

SECTOR/INDUSTRY SPECIALIZATION: Consumer Products

FAVORITE HISTORICAL FIGURE/MODEL/MENTOR: Benjamin Franklin

SINGLE MOST IMPORTANT ISSUE IN CONDUCTING A HIGH LEVEL SEARCH: Culture fit

MOST SIGNIFICANT OTHER ASPECT OF PERSONAL OR PROFESSIONAL LIFE: My family

WHAT IS THE BEST PREPARATION FOR BEING A SUCCESSFUL RECRUITER? Having held an upper level
  management position in corporate America

WHAT WOULD YOU BE DOING IF YOU WERE NOT AN EXECUTIVE RECRUITER? Upper level management-
  general management

WHAT ARE THE CHARACTERISTICS OF A GREAT CLIENT? Culture consistency, vision, constantly striving to
  change to improve regardless of success in a given year

WHAT CHALLENGES DO YOU SEE AHEAD IN THE GLOBAL MARKETPLACE? Consistency of operation and
  service needed worldwide

TERJE WIIG

Korn/Ferry International
Haakon VII's gt. 2
0161 Oslo
Norway

Telephone: 47 22 83 96 00
Fax: 47 22 83 96 01
E-mail: wiig@kornferry.com
Company Website: http://www.kornferry.com

DATE OF BIRTH: March 13, 1947

NATIONALITY: Norwegian—Grew up in Oslo

EDUCATIONAL BACKGROUND:
1971   Norwegian School of Management
1977   University of Wisconsin, U.S.A., Master of Business Administration

LANGUAGES SPOKEN: English

CAREER HIGHLIGHTS: Established my own local company, Search Partner, with no experience in recruitment

SPECIAL INTERESTS/HOBBIES: Skiing crosscountry/downhill, mountain hiking

GEOGRAPHIC SCOPE OF RECRUITING: Europe

SECTOR/INDUSTRY SPECIALIZATION: General/Consumer-High level

SINGLE MOST IMPORTANT ISSUE IN CONDUCTING A HIGH LEVEL SEARCH: Honesty

WHAT IS THE BEST PREPARATION FOR BEING A SUCCESSFUL RECRUITER? Know the main challenges and show interest for the client's business. Be honest. Be prepared to say "yes" and "no." Be relaxed, make a good atmosphere and listen.

WHAT WOULD YOU BE DOING IF YOU WERE NOT AN EXECUTIVE RECRUITER? Manage a small international business in my local market.

WHAT ARE THE CHARACTERISTICS OF A GREAT CLIENT? Trust. A great client gives you some freedom and is open, available, and understand and accepts the complexity of our business. Wants to build a long-term relationship with you that can help him to be successful.

WHAT CHALLENGES DO YOU SEE AHEAD IN THE GLOBAL MARKETPLACE? Larger international partner-owned structures in the search business that can handle the growing global reach. National borders will be less important in successful recruitment-successful managers are more flexible. However, a two-career family would be a challenge. Small local search firms will survive in their local market.

GERD WILHELM

Hager, Wilhelm & Partner/Amrop International
Heiligenstädter Str. 51
A-1190 Vienna, Austria

Telephone: 43-1-3688700 or mobile 43-664-1001920
Fax: 43-1-3688777
E-mail: Gerd.wilhelm@amrop.com
       Gerd.wilhelm@hwp.at (private)
Company Website: http://www.amrop.com

DATE OF BIRTH: April 19, 1951

NATIONALITY: Austrian—Grew up in Salzburg

EDUCATIONAL BACKGROUND:
Magister (Mag. rev.soc.oec) equivalent to MBA, Wirtschafisuniveritat Wien (Business University of Economics)

LANGUAGES SPOKEN: German, English

CAREER HIGHLIGHTS:
- Managing Partner, H. Neumann, Austria
- Responsible for Amrop's central and eastern European operations

SPECIAL INTERESTS/HOBBIES: Sailing, golf

GEOGRAPHIC SCOPE OF RECRUITING: Austria, central and eastern Europe

SECTOR/INDUSTRY SPECIALIZATION: FMCG/telecom industry

FAVORITE HISTORICAL FIGURE/MODEL/MENTOR: Mozart

SINGLE MOST IMPORTANT ISSUE IN CONDUCTING A HIGH LEVEL SEARCH: Top quality sourcing

BIGGEST COMPETITOR: E. Zehnder, Neumann, Korn/Ferry

WHAT IS THE BEST PREPARATION FOR BEING A SUCCESSFUL RECRUITER? Thousands of interviews, time spent in research, and experience

WHAT WOULD YOU BE DOING IF YOU WERE NOT AN EXECUTIVE RECRUITER? I would be in the film/TV/entertainment business, write books, and sail the world!

WHAT ARE THE CHARACTERISTICS OF A GREAT CLIENT?
- Clear understanding of search objectives
- Flexibility in the process
- Trust
- Time, when time is needed in the process

WHAT CHALLENGES DO YOU SEE AHEAD IN THE GLOBAL MARKETPLACE?
- The big firms will get really big!
- "Strong locals" will face severe problems through "globalization" of major clients/businesses
- New industries

WALTER E. WILLIAMS

LAI Ward Howell
99 High St., 27th Floor
Boston, MA 02110-2320
U.S.A.

Telephone: 1 (617) 292-6242
Fax: 1 (617) 292-6247
E-mail: williwal@lai.usa.com
Company Website: http://www.laix.com

DATE OF BIRTH: March 15, 1946

NATIONALITY: American—Grew up in Michigan

EDUCATIONAL BACKGROUND:
1968   B.S., Yale University
1974   M.B.A., Harvard Business School

LANGUAGES SPOKEN: English, Spanish (limited)

CAREER HIGHLIGHTS:
1981–93   Managing Director, Russell Reynolds Associates
1993–96   SVP & Director, Canny, Bowen Inc.

SPECIAL INTERESTS/HOBBIES: Sailboat racing, tennis, art history

GEOGRAPHIC SCOPE OF RECRUITING: U.S.A. and U.K.

SECTOR/INDUSTRY SPECIALIZATION: Investment Management, Real Estate, Insurance Industry

FAVORITE HISTORICAL FIGURE/MODEL/MENTOR: Benjamin Franklin

SINGLE MOST IMPORTANT ISSUE IN CONDUCTING A HIGH LEVEL SEARCH: Personal and professional credibility of the search consultant.

MOST SIGNIFICANT OTHER ASPECT OF PERSONAL OR PROFESSIONAL LIFE: Past President, Harvard Business School Association of Boston

WHAT IS THE BEST PREPARATION FOR BEING A SUCCESSFUL RECRUITER? An MBA degree, combined with 5–10 years of experience in a client-oriented environment (consulting, commercial banking, investment banking, etc.)

WHAT WOULD YOU BE DOING IF YOU WERE NOT AN EXECUTIVE RECRUITER? Management consultant or venture capitalist

WHAT ARE THE CHARACTERISTICS OF A GREAT CLIENT? An attitude of "partnership" with a search firm; a willingness to listen; responsiveness and selling skills.

WHAT CHALLENGES DO YOU SEE AHEAD IN THE GLOBAL MARKETPLACE? A lack of truly multinational executives; increased functional specialization vs. general management experience; the continued rise in two-career families limiting geographic mobility.

DAVID L. WITTE

LAI Ward Howell
1000 Louisiana, Suite 3150
Houston, Texas 77002
U.S.A.

Telephone: 1 (713) 655-1805
Fax: 1 (713) 655-7854
E-mail: wittedav@lai.usa.com
Company Website: http://www.laix.com

DATE OF BIRTH: January 29, 1942

NATIONALITY: American—Grew up in Texas

EDUCATIONAL BACKGROUND:
B.S., Michigan State University, 1964

LANGUAGES SPOKEN: English and German

CAREER HIGHLIGHTS:

3/98–Present	Executive Vice President, Specialty Practice Group Development, LAI Ward Howell
8/96–3/98	CEO, Ward Howell International
7/87–3/98	Managing Director, Ward Howell

SPECIAL INTERESTS/HOBBIES: Sailing, family travel

SECTOR/INDUSTRY SPECIALIZATION: Chemical/Energy

MOST SIGNIFICANT OTHER ASPECT OF PERSONAL OR PROFESSIONAL LIFE: Serving global clients

WHAT IS THE BEST PREPARATION FOR BEING A SUCCESSFUL RECRUITER? Successful business career

WHAT WOULD YOU BE DOING IF YOU WERE NOT AN EXECUTIVE RECRUITER? CEO of service company

WHAT ARE THE CHARACTERISTICS OF A GREAT CLIENT? Empower your team to win by obtaining the best talent

WHAT CHALLENGES DO YOU SEE AHEAD IN THE GLOBAL MARKETPLACE? War for global managers

ROBERT WONG

Korn/Ferry International
Rua Verbo Divino, 1488 - 5th floor - Unit 51 A
São Paulo, SP 04719-904
Brazil

Telephone: 55 11 5181-9200
Fax: 55 11 5181-6050
E-mail: robert.wong@kornferry.com
Company Website: http://www.kornferry.com

DATE OF BIRTH: March 3, 1948

NATIONALITY: Brazilian—Grew up in São Paulo, Brazil

EDUCATIONAL BACKGROUND:
Chapel American High School, São Paulo, 1966
B.Sc, Escola Politécnica of the University of São Paulo, 1972
CBI-Confederation of British Industry Scholar, London, 1979
Executive Education Program, Harvard Business School, Boston, 1995

LANGUAGES SPOKEN: English, Portuguese, Chinese

CAREER HIGHLIGHTS: Regional V. President, Managing Dir., Member of Exec. Committee, Co-Chairman of Operating Committee

SPECIAL INTERESTS/HOBBIES: Tennis, photography, traveling, seminar speaking, little league coaching

GEOGRAPHIC SCOPE OF RECRUITING: Latin America, with focus on Brazil

SECTOR/INDUSTRY SPECIALIZATION: Banking, High Tech, Telecom, Consumer Products, Entertainment

FAVORITE HISTORICAL FIGURE/MODEL/MENTOR: Abraham Lincoln/my dad/Horacio McCoy

SINGLE MOST IMPORTANT ISSUE IN CONDUCTING A HIGH LEVEL SEARCH: Completely understanding a client's needs. This means grasping the company's culture and also the hiring executive's personality, likes and dislikes. I have, on occasion, worked inside the client's company to observe day-to-day operations.

MOST SIGNIFICANT OTHER ASPECT OF PERSONAL OR PROFESSIONAL LIFE: Committed and not merely involved, tri-cultural (Chinese/American/Brazilian), regard executive search as a profession, and not only as a business.

WHAT IS THE BEST PREPARATION FOR BEING A SUCCESSFUL RECRUITER?
- Have a genuine interest in people.
- Acquire in-depth "know-how" of the industry, but most importantly the "know-who."
- Regard your work as a profession, and not simply as a business.

WHAT WOULD YOU BE DOING IF YOU WERE NOT AN EXECUTIVE RECRUITER? I would most probably be a medical doctor or psychologist.

WHAT ARE THE CHARACTERISTICS OF A GREAT CLIENT? A great client knows what they want and how to verbalize it, regards you as a partner in the search process, and respects the participants in the process.

WHAT CHALLENGES DO YOU SEE AHEAD IN THE GLOBAL MARKETPLACE? Challenges include the widening gap between the developed countries and the developing ones, and the harnessing of Information Technology for the benefit of mankind as a whole.

TREVOR LAURENCE WOODBURN

Woodburn Mann (Pty) Ltd/Ward Howell International
102A Albertyn Avenue   P.O. Box 783683
Wierda Valley   Sandton 2146
Sandton, South Africa   South Africa

Telephone: 27 11 883 3197
Fax: 27 11 783 0229
E-mail: woodburnmann@compuserve.com
Company Website: [Currently under development]

DATE OF BIRTH: September 12, 1940

NATIONALITY: South African—Grew up in Pretoria, South Africa.

Twenty years in various senior executive positions in the telecommunications, electrical engineering and electronic industries in South Africa culminating in the position of Chief Executive of the South African subsidiary of a major electrical engineering multi-national corporation.

EDUCATIONAL BACKGROUND:

Bachelor of Science in Electrical Engineering: B.Sc. (Eng) (Natal)
Master of Science in Engineering (Computer Science): M.Sc. (Eng) (Wits)
Master of Business Administration: M.B.A. (Cape Town)
Doctor of Philosophy in Commerce: Ph.D. (Comm) (Wits)

LANGUAGES SPOKEN: English, Afrikaans

CAREER HIGHLIGHTS: Twenty years in various senior executive positions in the telecommunications, electrical engineering and electronic industries in South Africa culminating in the position of Chief Executive of the South African subsidiary of a major electrical engineering multi-national corporation.

Appointed Managing Director of a GEC Subsidiary at the age of 36. Established and grew Woodburn Mann (Pty) Ltd, an Executive Search Consultancy, from one person and one company, to a group of seven companies and 40 people over the past 15 years.

SPECIAL INTERESTS/HOBBIES: Non-executive chairmen and directors, telecommunications / scuba diving, photography, wild life.

GEOGRAPHIC SCOPE OF RECRUITING: Entire African continent, including Indian Ocean islands

SECTOR/INDUSTRY SPECIALIZATION: Top executives and nonexecutive chairmen/directors across all sectors

FAVORITE HISTORICAL FIGURE/MODEL/MENTOR:

- Sir Winston Churchill, a great leader, statesman and brilliant orator.
- Albert Einstein, a brilliant lateral thinker and formulator of the theory of relativity.
- Jan Smuts, a great leader, statesman with vision, a brilliant scholar and formulator of the concept of holism.
- Dr. Anna Mann, an inspirational pioneer of third generation research based executive search and the doyen of search for non-executive chairmen and directors.

SINGLE MOST IMPORTANT ISSUE IN CONDUCTING A HIGH LEVEL SEARCH: Quality and depth of research to identify the best available candidates locally, regionally, nationally and internationally against a well constructed, comprehensive specification

BIGGEST COMPETITORS: Amrop, TASA

MOST SIGNIFICANT OTHER ASPECT OF PERSONAL OR PROFESSIONAL LIFE: An achieving, well-educated family (wife and two grown sons). Having established and built up a major executive search practice, and a significant synergistic human resources consulting group of companies in South Africa.

WHAT IS THE BEST PREPARATION FOR BEING A SUCCESSFUL RECRUITER?

- At least five years general management line experience with "bottom-line" responsibility and a marketing orientation.
- An outgoing, extrovert personality with sensitivity and empathy with people.
- An innovative, creative mind and an exposure to, or understanding of research methodology.

WHAT WOULD YOU BE DOING IF YOU WERE NOT AN EXECUTIVE RECRUITER? Chief Executive of a large group of industrial companies, probably in the electrical, telecommunications or information technology fields.

WHAT ARE THE CHARACTERISTICS OF A GREAT CLIENT? Great clients are those with whom one is able to establish a close working relationship and rapport, who are supportive, committed to finding the best candidate, and who participate closely as project members.

WHAT CHALLENGES DO YOU SEE AHEAD IN THE GLOBAL MARKETPLACE? A need to quickly identify and assess the best possible and most suitable candidates locally, nationally and internationally. This could be achieved by using sophisticated technology, including satellite tracking of executives and the application of virtual reality in combination with video conferencing to interview candidates live and in three dimensions, simultaneously, anywhere on earth.

MATTHEW WRIGHT

Russell Reynolds
26 St. James Square
London SW1Y 4HZ
U.K.

Telephone: 44 171 830-8050
Fax: 44 171 873-0389
E-mail: mwright@russreyn.com
Company Website: http://www.russreyn.com

DATE OF BIRTH: 4-2-1963

NATIONALITY: British—Grew up in U.K., London and Surrey

EDUCATIONAL BACKGROUND:
Epsom College, 10 0' levels, 3 A' levels
Hull University, Law degree, LLB Hons

LANGUAGES SPOKEN: English

CAREER HIGHLIGHTS:
- Russell Reynolds: Head of European Operations and Financial Services
- Korn/Ferry International: U.K. and European Financial Services

SPECIAL INTERESTS/HOBBIES: Family, rugby, cricket

GEOGRAPHIC SCOPE OF RECRUITING: Global—60 percent of my searches are global

SECTOR/INDUSTRY SPECIALIZATION: Financial services

SINGLE MOST IMPORTANT ISSUE IN CONDUCTING A HIGH LEVEL SEARCH: Integrity and honesty in communicating with the client and candidate

WHAT IS THE BEST PREPARATION FOR BEING A SUCCESSFUL RECRUITER? Successful recruiters can be successful from a variety of backgrounds: there is no one proven route to success. However, the best possible preparation is clearly an active exposure at management level to your "industry" specialization.

WHAT ARE THE CHARACTERISTICS OF A GREAT CLIENT?
- Commitment
- Partnership
- Ability to think laterally and take a risk
- Clarity of thought

WHAT CHALLENGES DO YOU SEE AHEAD IN THE GLOBAL MARKETPLACE?
- Continued "consolidation" within several sectors
- Continued "requirements" for truly global managers with experience of leading multi-cultural and multi-products

KYUNG H. YOON

Heidrick & Struggles
9 Temasek Boulevard, Suite 32-02, Suntec City Tower Two
Singapore 038989

Telephone: 65 332-5001
Fax: 65 338-1260
E-mail: khy@h-s.com
Company Website: http://www.h-s.com

DATE OF BIRTH: November 3, 1954

NATIONALITY: American—Grew up in U.S.A., France, Korea

EDUCATIONAL BACKGROUND:
  MBA, University of Chicago
  BA, Goucher College
  Educated in Seoul, Paris, Washington, D.C., Chicago

LANGUAGES SPOKEN: English, French, Korean, Chinese, Japanese

CAREER HIGHLIGHTS: Successfully started up 3 businesses including Heidrick & Struggles Singapore operations.

SPECIAL INTERESTS/HOBBIES: Painting, arts, travel

GEOGRAPHIC SCOPE OF RECRUITING: Worldwide

SECTOR/INDUSTRY SPECIALIZATION: Technology, Professional Services, Financial Services

FAVORITE HISTORICAL FIGURE/MODEL/MENTOR: Mother Theresa

SINGLE MOST IMPORTANT ISSUE IN CONDUCTING A HIGH LEVEL SEARCH: Understanding the culture of the client and the chemistry between the candidate and top management.

WHAT IS THE BEST PREPARATION FOR BEING A SUCCESSFUL RECRUITER? The best preparation for being a successful recruiter is experience at senior-level management and industry knowledge. Extensive high-level contacts with key people is also important.

WHAT WOULD YOU BE DOING IF YOU WERE NOT AN EXECUTIVE RECRUITER? I would be an entrepreneur, setting up new businesses in the U.S.A. and Asia.

WHAT ARE THE CHARACTERISTICS OF BEING A GREAT CLIENT? A great client has the desire and ability to communicate clearly.

WHAT CHALLENGES DO YOU SEE AHEAD IN THE GLOBAL MARKETPLACE? Truly global execution capabilities are rare. The challenges will be to effectively utilize technology and to build excellent global partnerships.

LI HSIAO YUAN

Strategic Executive Search Pte Ltd/Ward Howell International
7 Temasek Boulevard #43-02
Suntec Tower One
Singapore 038987

Telephone: 65 334-3855
Fax: 65 334-3955
E-mail: hyli@whises.com.sg
Company Website: http://www.laix.com

DATE OF BIRTH: October 18, 1948

NATIONALITY: Singapore citizen—Grew up in Singapore

EDUCATIONAL BACKGROUND:
  Bachelor of Arts (Honours), University of Singapore
  Master of Social Science, University of Singapore

LANGUAGES SPOKEN: English and Mandarin

CAREER HIGHLIGHTS: 17 years in Executive Search, 8 years in Human Resources, Marketing & Planning

SPECIAL INTERESTS/HOBBIES: Music, reading and sports

GEOGRAPHIC SCOPE OF RECRUITING: Southeast Asia

SECTOR/INDUSTRY SPECIALIZATION: High-tech, fast moving consumer goods, IT

FAVORITE HISTORICAL FIGURE/MODEL/MENTOR: General Douglas MacArthur

SINGLE MOST IMPORTANT ISSUE IN CONDUCTING A HIGH LEVEL SEARCH: Extra tenacity

WHAT IS THE BEST PREPARATION FOR BEING A SUCCESSFUL RECRUITER? Perceptive listener and communicator, strong interpersonal skills, highly detail-oriented, know company and culture, know industry, ability to influence and persuade at senior level, must like the profession.

WHAT WOULD YOU BE DOING IF YOU WERE NOT AN EXECUTIVE RECRUITER? HR management consultant

WHAT ARE THE CHARACTERISTICS OF A GREAT CLIENT? Consultative, one who listens, shares information honestly, willing to accept consultant's advice, decisive, realistic expectations, familiar with search process and pays bills punctually when happy with service.

WHAT CHALLENGES DO YOU SEE AHEAD IN THE GLOBAL MARKETPLACE? Due to economic downturn in regional/international economy, clients are increasingly cautious about using search. Also, clients are adopting shorter-term measures—using recruitment agencies, contract workers, downsizing, etc.

Top Global Firms

The first half of 1998 has been extremely volatile for the executive search profession. The top global firms are getting bigger while the smaller, niche firms are becoming better positioned. Many of the medium-sized firms are finding it difficult to compete. Several of the larger firms are attempting to acquire specialist and smaller, well-positioned firms around the world to enhance their geographic breadth or their sector strength. These firms are making public offerings to finance their growth. Still other firms are carefully assessing whether to go public. This general volatility in the marketplace has made it most difficult to provide a standard ranking of the key firms on a global basis, since many of the member firms of big networks are changing their alliances (or thinking about doing so). That said, I provide brief snapshots of what I have recently considered to be the top global firms. I offer this information by way of overview and to help familiarize the reader with these firms. In addition to giving insight into the top firms, the information will help the reader in evaluating other firms by noting what aspects of ownership and organization may be especially relevant.

THE TOP FIRMS

The top firms do an increasing amount of senior level, CEO, board and nonexecutive director assignments. They are well-known "brand names" around the world. The top four global firms, in net revenue, are American (see Table 1). They are

Table 1 Top global executive search firms by net revenue, 1995–1997

Firm	Revenue ($ millions)			% change 1996 to 1997	Number of offices in 1997
	1995	1996	1997		
Korn/Ferry International	248	270	301	12	71
Heidrick & Struggles	161	199	277	39	50
Spencer Stuart	147	185	229	24	42
Russell Reynolds	132	147	184	25	33
Amrop International	126	153	182	18	94
Egon Zehnder International	146	164	182	11	48
Ray Berndtson	90	108	117	9	44
Ward Howell International	73	89	105	18	50
H. Neumann International	72	68	82	21	43
Transearch International	50	56	68	21	64
A. T. Kearney	31	38	53	40	32
Hever Group	45	48	54	12	27
Norman Broadbent	58	49	53	10	18
Horton International	31	41	51	25	39
Boyden	40	48	50	5	65

Source: "Executive Search in Asia & Australasia—1997," EIU/Economist Intelligence Unit, London

wholly owned, integrated organizations, as distinct from affiliations of independent, locally owned groups.

1. Korn/Ferry International (Los Angeles based), is the world's largest firm with revenue estimated at $316 million for fiscal year 1998. It is well known for its broad geographic scope (its 71 offices are spread across 36 countries), its specialty practice groups, innovative Internet ventures, and other technology. Korn/Ferry is highly regarded for its global entertainment practice and its market leadership in Asia and Los Angeles. Recent additions of senior partners (Kenneth MacLannan and Barry Gould in financial services and Dick Buschmann in FMCG) to the London office complement the existing strong team.

2. Heidrick & Struggles is ranked second in revenue ($277 million in 1997) and is quickly approaching first place. It is well regarded for its speciality practice groups, especially its advanced technology group based in Menlo Park. Its recent acquisition of Fenwick Partners (a specialist technology firm near Boston) complements its strength in the information technology sector and gives Heidrick & Struggles a dominant position in technology around the world. Also, its recent acquisition of Mülder, the top ranked firm in Germany, raises its visibility and prestige.

3. Spencer Stuart ($229 million in fiscal year 1997) is third. Under the capable direction of chairman David Kimbell, it is highly regarded, particularly for its board director, CEO, nonexecutive assignments in the U.S.A. and Europe.

4. Russell Reynolds ($184 million at the end of fiscal year 1997), another American firm, is especially well regarded in financial services, telecommunications, and consumer goods.

5. Amrop International, the fifth-ranked firm, is a network organization of independent member firms. Originally founded in Paris, it is a non-integrated association of independent locally owned firms with equity. Its revenue in 1997 was $182 million. Amrop has been quite a trendsetter recently as two of its major partner firms—Lamalie Amrop (U.S.A.) and Whitehead Mann (U.K.)—had successful public offerings in 1997. Amrop's U.S.A. member firm also acquired Ward Howell (ranked eighth worldwide) in the U.S.A. in early 1998.

The next four firms that round out the top ten are all quite different in organization type, nationality, and services offered.

6. Egon Zehnder International (EZI), ranked first in Europe with revenue in 1997 of $182 million, was founded in Zurich, Switzerland by Dr. Egon Zehnder (formerly of Spencer Stuart). EZI is well known for its geographic scope, its strong MBA-type analytic culture, and its management assessment services.

7. Ray Berndtson (net revenue of $117 million in 1997) consists of two firms in joint venture: Ray Berndtson in the U.S.A. (founded by Paul Ray Sr. and run by Paul Ray Jr.) is Houston-based; Berndtson Ray is an association of independent firms in Europe. Of these, Berndtson International, is one of the top three firms in Germany.

8. Ward Howell (net revenue of approximately $105 million in 1997) is a non-integrated association of independent firms with equity. The group has regional heads similar to Amrop International.

9. H. Neumann was (until late 1997) a joint venture conglomerate of many firms including: GKR (U.K. based), H. Neumann International, (Austrian based), Morgan & Banks in Asia and MRI (Management Recruiters International,) in the U.S.A. (Cleveland-based). In November 1997 its U.K. arm (GKR) severed its relationship with H. Neumann to form an allegiance with Pendleton James, a smaller, high-end New York firm.

The remaining top firms are also undergoing change.

10. Transearch is run by Alain Tanugi in Paris. The group had revenue of $68 million in 1997.

11. A. T. Kearney (Chicago based, 1997 revenue of approximately $53 million) is the only firm in the top fifteen associated with a management consulting firm (A. T. Kearney Consulting). It was acquired in 1996 by EDS. Although well

known in the U.S.A., it has not established a visible presence in Europe, where it is run by Frank Schroder out of London.

12. The Hever Group ($54 million in revenue in 1997) is a loose association of well-regarded, high-end firms including Saxton Bampfylde in the U.K., Delta Group in Germany, Kenny Kindler in the U.S.A. (New York), and Cordiner King in Australia.

13. Norman Broadbent was originally founded by two partners, Miles Broadbent and David Norman (both ex-Russell Reynolds), in the U.K.. They split up in early 1997 in a rather controversial and heated divorce. Now there are three off-shoot firms: The Miles Partnership (general management); Norman Broadbent Intl, run by Gary Luddington (search/selection); and Sainty Beatson Hird (financial services). NBI had approximately $53 million in revenue in 1997.

14. Horton was founded by Robert Horton, a search professional in Avon, Connecticut. The firm focuses on "entry strategy" for global clients in developing markets and, with revenues of $51 million in 1997, had one of the highest growth rates in 1997.

15. Boyden had $50 million in revenue in 1997 with 65 offices worldwide. It has recently elected a new global chairman (Sheila Avrin McLean) and is slowly trying to rebuild its image as an outstanding worldwide firm.

Other global firms include associations such as IIC Partners, TASA, the Accord Group, Inesa, and KPMG Foster Associates. There are also numerous highly respected smaller, boutique firms, many of which concentrate in one sector. For instance, Highland Partners, Sullivan & Company, the Rose Partnership, and Baines Gwinner are all well known in the United Kingdom for financial services. Many of the smaller firms are being aggressively pursued by the global ones at this time.

As reflected in the top fifteen and on into other lower ranked firms, the market is undergoing much change and consolidation—and that is expected to continue throughout the year. There is no consistent organization or ownership structure format for the search firms. Many hybrid types exist to serve multinational clients. The trend is towards more integration and closer cooperation to better serve more sophisticated and demanding clients on a global (or regional) basis. The wholly owned, integrated firms seem to offer the most efficient way to provide global service to clients. The more loosely structured associations have an increasingly difficult time serving global clients when it comes to global communication, investment in advanced technology, agreement on brand name, and so on. This is an important issue and a question to be addressed in the years ahead. How can the more loosely structured firms compete with the wholly owned integrated ones in serving clients on a worldwide basis?

As discussed in Chapter Two, it is important to understand how individual consultants are compensated, for this will tell you a great deal about their level of motivation to conduct your assignment. For example, if the consultants are compensated only for work done in their own geographic market (and for their own clients), then they will not be highly motivated to assist their colleagues with cross-border, multi-country projects (which are increasingly the norm). Many search firms are revising their compensation systems to motivate or provide an incentive for multi-country work.

Similarly, revenue per consultant shows at what overall level of management the firm works; it typically reflects higher level searches. Spencer Stuart, Heidrick & Struggles, and Russell Reynolds have the highest overall revenue per consultant on a global basis.

SUMMARY AND ASSESSMENT OF TOP GLOBAL FIRMS

To complete this directory, I provide a short summary of each of the top fifteen global firms, including the headquarter's address, senior management, and services provided. I also include my brief assessment of each firm's current direction.

1. Korn/Ferry International

1800 Century Park East Suite 900
Los Angeles, CA 90067, U.S.A.
Telephone: 1 (310) 552-1834
Fax: 1 (310) 553-8640
Company website: http://www.kornferry.com

Integrated firm

Senior management:
Richard Ferry, chairman, Los Angeles
Michael Boxberger, president and CEO, Los Angeles
Edward Kelley, president, Europe, London
Peter L Dunn, vice-chairman, management services, Los Angeles
Windle Priem, president, North America, New York

Total offices worldwide: 71
Services provided: executive search, management audit, selection

Assessment: Moving forward

Number one firm worldwide. Also number one in Asia and Latin America where its largest recent growth has occurred. The firm has good geographic balance and breadth, shows aggressive global leadership, and is good at global client relationships. Innovative in advanced technology: first to experiment with cyberspace headhunting via Internet. Getting stronger in specialty practice groups (especially media and entertainment, health care, consumer goods) and in serving global clients. Needs to do more CEO/board level work and get stronger in Europe.

2. Heidrick & Struggles

Sears Tower, Suite 4200
233 South Wacker Drive
Chicago, Illinois 60606, U.S.A.
Telephone 1 (312) 496-1200
Fax: 1 (312) 469-1295
Company website: http://www.h-s.com

Integrated firm

Senior management:
Gerard Clery-Melin, CEO, Europe, Paris
Thomas Friel, managing partner, Asia Pacific, Menlo Park, CA
Thomas Mitchell, managing partner, Latin America, Los Angeles
Patrick Pittard, managing partner, North America, Atlanta
Richard Nelson, chief financial and administrative officer and global counsel,
                Americas and Asia Pacific, Chicago
Michel Vignan, chief financial and administrative officer, Europe, Paris

Total offices wordwide: 50
Services provided: executive search, board director search

Assessment: Moving forward

Number two firm worldwide, quickly moving toward number one. The firm grew 39 percent in 1997, with the brilliant acquisition of Mülder & Partners (a top German firm) and Fenwick Partners (a technology firm near Boston). The strong likelihood of a public offering is extremely positive. Aggressive worldwide hiring of outstanding consultants with proven track records. Leaders in advanced technology, CEO/nonexecutives and general industry search. Strong culture of specialty practice groups. Getting much stronger in Latin America and Asia (where it grew 74 percent in 1997). One of the top two firms in Europe.

3. Spencer Stuart

277 Park Avenue
New York, NY 10172, U.S.A.
Telephone: 1 (212) 336-0200
Fax: 1 (212) 336-0296
Company website: http://www.spencerstuart.com

Integrated firm

Senior management:
David Kimbell, chairman worldwide, London
Joe Griesedieck, CEO, worldwide, San Francisco
Piers Marmion, COO, worldwide, London
Rich Kurkowski, CFO, Chicago

Total offices worldwide: 42
Services provided: executive search, board director search, management audit,
management selection, remuneration advice

Assessment: Moving forward

One of the top three firms worldwide. Leader in CEO/board/nonexecutive director searches, especially in the U.S.A. and U.K.. During 1997, the firm had particularly strong growth in financial services and board practice. Especially strong teams in Europe and Latin America, with aggressive hiring in continental Europe. Focus on high quality work. Local office profit centers are key.

4. Russell Reynolds
200 Park Avenue
New York, NY 10166, U.S.A.
Telephone: 1 (212) 351-2000
Fax: 1 (212) 370-0896
Company website: http://www.russreyn.com

Integrated firm

Senior management:
Hobson Brown Jr, president and CEO, New York
Matthew Wright, managing director, Europe, New York
Joseph Spence and Gordon Grand, managing directors, Americas, Atlanta, New York
Stephen Scroggins, managing director, Asia, New York
Rae Sedel, managing director, sector management, London
Kate Bryant, VP, corporate communications, New York
Albert Morris, CFO, New York

International executive committee:
Hobson Brown Jr, Henry de Montebello, Jane Kingsley, Richard Lannamann, Anthony Price, Joseph Spence, Annie Wee, Matthew Wright, Andrea Redmond, Peter Drummond-Hay, Arthur Janta-Polczynski, Brigitte LeMercier-Saltiel, Rae Sedel, Stephen Scroggins, Raymond Tang.

Total offices worldwide: 33
Services provided: executive search, board director search

Assessment: Moving forward

Fourth largest global firm with strong presence in financial services, biotech, and telecommunications. Focus on high quality, global cross-border work. Strong teams in the U.K., France, Benelux, and getting stronger in Los Angeles and Asia. Matthew Wright (popular and proven in financial services) is the firm's new managing director in Europe. One of the issues is how large the firm needs to be to compete effectively with the top five. Russell Reynolds has 33 offices, whereas Korn/Ferry has 71 worldwide. In 1997, it grew 25 percent, with the highest growth in Europe and Latin America. It opened offices in Buenos Aires, São Paulo, Copenhagen, and Amsterdam; it acquired KPMG selection in Toronto.

5. Amrop International

200 Park Avenue Suite 3100
New York, NY 10166, U.S.A.
Telephone: 1 (212) 953-7900
Fax: 1 (212) 837-3535
Company website: http://www.amrop.com

Close association

Senior management:
Daniel Gauchat, chairman, Sydney
Jose Carillo, regional chairman, Americas, Monterey
Gerardo Seeliger, regional chairman, Europe, Madrid
Hideaki Furuta, regional chairman, Asia, Tokyo
Michael Ascot, executive member, Bangkok
Simon Bartholomew, member, London
Douglas Caldwell, member, Toronto
Roddy Gow, executive member, New York
Gerd Krampe, member, Frankfurt

Total offices worldwide: 94
Services provided: executive search, board director search, management audit and assessment, selection, interim management

Assessment: On hold

Already strong in automotive, consumer goods, and financial services, Amrop's recent acquisition of Ward Howell in the U.S.A. will greatly strengthen its U.S.

presence in many sectors, including health care, insurance, and automotive. High quality teams in the U.K., Australia, Scandinavia/Finland, South Africa, Brazil, Singapore, and many other markets. Public offerings in U.S.A., Canada, and U.K. have been well received. Branding and integration issues exist worldwide.

6. Egon Zehnder International

350 Park Avenue
New York, NY 10022, U.S.A.
Telephone: 1 (212) 519-6000
Fax: 1 (212) 519-6060
Company website: http://www.zehnder.com

Integrated firm

Senior management:
Egon Zehnder, chairman, Zurich
Daniel Meiland, CEO, New York

Board of directors and executive committee:
Wilhelm Friz Boyens, John Grumbar, Victor Loewenstein, Daniel Meiland, Joost Nanninga, Gabriel Sanchez-Zinny, Nils Sjogren, Egon Zehnder

Total offices worldwide: 48
Services provided: executive search, board director search, management appraisal

Assessment: Moving forward

Sixth largest firm worldwide. One of the top two in Europe and high quality presence in both Latin America and Asia. Its global growth in 1997 was approximately 11 percent; yet in the United States alone, it had 21 percent growth. The firm opened new offices in Menlo Park, California, Kuala Lampur, and New Delhi. Strong analytical culture with many McKinsey alumni on board. Heavy emphasis on training and partnership spirit. Compensation based on worldwide profits of the firm (only global firm with this policy). Outstanding in Argentina, many emerging markets (India, Malaysia). Very good practice in management appraisal (assessment of senior executives, especially in joint venture or merger situations).

7. Ray Berndtson

301 Commerce Street, Suite 2300
Fort Worth, Texas 76102, U.S.A.
Telephone: 1 (817) 334-0500
Fax: 1 (817) 334-0779
Company website: http://www.prb.com

Strategic alliance

Global executive board:
Theo Gehlen and Paul Ray Jr, (co-chairs), Craig Dudley, W. Carl Lovas, David Love, Gernot Müller, David Radden, Finn Werdi, Geoffrey Forester, Roger J. Marshall, Jimmy Lo (ex-officio), Clarence Lobo (ex-officio)

Total offices worldwide: 44
Services provided: executive search, board director search, management audit

Assessment: Moving forward

Seventh largest firm worldwide. Strong presence in the U.S.A., Canada, France, and Germany. U.S. leader Paul Ray Jr. is well-respected and charismatic. However, organizational ownership structure of the group in Europe and Asia is independent and does not encourage cross-border work efforts.

8. Ward Howell International

44 N. Virginia Street, Suite 3B
Crystal Lake, Illinois 60014-4016, U.S.A.
Telephone: 1 (815) 479-9415
Fax: 1 (815) 479-9320
Company website: http://www.laix.com

Locally owned association

Senior management:
Bernt Prasuhn, speaker, Europe/Africa, Düsseldorf
Maurice Ellett, speaker, Asia-Pacific, Auckland

Total offices worldwide: 50
Services provided: executive search, board director search, interim management (Germany), strategic consulting (U.K.), management audit and assessment

Assessment: On hold

Was the eighth largest firm worldwide until its U.S. group was acquired by Amrop International in December 1997. The group needs to find a new U.S. partner. Many strong partner firms exist in Europe and Asia and their future will be resolved this year. Very strong teams in South Africa, France, Russia, eastern Europe and Asia. Wait and see.

9. H. Neumann International

Gunthergasse 3
1090 Vienna, Austria
Telephone: 43 (1) 401-400
Fax: 43 (1) 401-4077
Company website: http://www.neumann-inter.com

Combination—integrated and joint venture

Senior management:
Helmut Neumann, founder and chairman, H. Neumann Int'l
Holger Frenzel, board member, Vienna
Daniel Grenon, board member, Paris
Wolfgang Reinermann, board member, Frankfurt
Tamas Toth, board member, Vienna and Budapest

Total offices worldwide: 43
Services provided: executive search, selection, management audit, human
                   resources consulting and management contracting

Assessment: Moving forward cautiously

GKR (U.K.) and Neumann (Austria, Europe) had an informal association until
November 1997 when they officially separated. H. Neumann is now associated
with Pendleton James in the U.S. and seeking to develop other partners in Europe
and Asia. They are well respected in the U.K. and especially strong in financial services, media, and industry. N. H. Newman Intl, a Vienna based firm that is known
in Eastern Europe, will try to find another U.K. partner.

10. Transearch International

160 av de Versailles
75016 Paris, France
Telephone: 33 (1) 40 50-3480
Fax: 33 (1) 40 50-3242
Company website: http://www.transearch.com

Locally owned association

Senior management:
Alain Tanugi, President, Paris
Ewaldo Endler, VP, Latin America, São Paulo

Michael Chipps, VP Europe, London
George Lim, VP Asia, Hong Kong
Steven Pegim, VP North America, Chicago

Total offices worldwide: 64
Services provided: executive search, management audit and assessment, selection

Assessment: Moving forward

Tenth largest firm worldwide, headquartered in Paris. Some interesting member firms in Asia/Australasia, India, Kuwait, South Africa. One of its biggest challenges is effective cross-border client service.

11. A. T. Kearney

22 West Adams Street
Chicago, Illinois 60606, U.S.A
Telephone: 1 (312) 648-0111
Fax: 1 (312) 223-6369
Company website: http://www.atkearney.com

Combination—integrated and joint venture

Senior management:
Charles W. Sweet, president, Chicago
Frank Schroeder, managing director, Europe, London
Stephen G. Fischer, managing director, Asia, Hong Kong
Jack Groban, Managing director, North America

Total offices worldwide: 32
Services provided: executive search, management audit, human resource
                        consulting

Assessment: Moving forward cautiously

Growing stronger around the world especially in Chicago, Hong Kong, and London. However its ownership structure is still an issue long term. It is associated with A. T. Kearney Consulting and owned by EDS.

12. Hever Group

Saxton Bampfylfde Intl.
35 Old Queen St
London SW1H 9JA, England
Telephone: 44 171 799-1433
Fax: 44 171 222-0489
Company website: http://www.sbpsearch.com/intlnet.htm

Locally owned association

Senior management:
Anthony Saxton, Saxton Bampfylde, vice chairman, London
Axel Hampe, chairman, Delta Group, Munich
Simon Laver, secretariat, London

Total offices worldwide: 27
Services provided: executive search, board director search

Assessment: Moving forward

A closely linked network of well-established firms including Kenny Kindler (New York), Saxton Bampfylde (U.K.), Cordiner King (Australia) and Delta Group (Germany). Cordiner King is well known for its public sector and board of director work in Australia. Delta is one of the top three search firms in Germany.

13. Norman Broadbent International

65 Curzon St.
London W1Y 8NA, England
Telephone: 44 171 629-9626
Fax: 44 171 629-9900

Combination—integrated and joint venture

Senior management:
Gary Luddington, managing director, London

Total offices worldwide: 18
Services provided: executive search, chairman and board director search, management assessment

Assessment: On hold

One of the finest global firms until 1996 when founders David Norman and Miles Broadbent split up; Miles Broadbent now has his own small, upscale firm in London (The Miles Partnership) as does Julian Sainty in financial services (Sainty Beatson Hird). Former partner Barry Gould has joined Korn/Ferry. Gary Luddington is trying hard to reestablish what was once a very fine firm.

14. Horton International

420 Lexington Avenue, Suite 810
New York, NY 10170, U.S.A.
Telephone: 1 (212) 973-3780
Fax: 1 (212) 973-3798
Company website: http://www.horton-intl.com

Combination: integrated and joint venture

Senior management:
Robert H Horton, chairman and CEO, president, Americas, New York
Michael Baak, regional coordinator, Europe, Frankfurt
Jim Hayman, regional coordinator, Asia Pacific, Melbourne

Global executive board:
Michael Baak, Gerad Dietrich, Jim Hayman, Robert Horton, Joe Keiser, Helga
Long, Arlinot Marin, Luigi Rossi, Alfred Stum

Total offices worldwide: 39
Services provided: executive search, management audit, organization development
and transformation consulting, sourcing strategic alliances

Assessment: Moving forward

Strong, consistent growth worldwide, especially in the U.S. and Asia. Special strategy is to assist clients moving into foreign markets by finding joint venture partners and providing organization transformation assistance; especially good in emerging markets. The group has several large clients in the power, telecommunication and infrastructure fields in eastern Europe and China.

15. Boyden

364 Elwood Avenue
Hawthorne, NY 10531, U.S.A.
Telephone: 1 (914) 747-0093
Fax: 1 (914) 747-0108
Company website: http://www.boyden.com

Locally owned network with equity

Global executive board:
Sheila Avrin McLean, chairman, New York
Georgiana Kolenaty, director Asia Pacific, Taiwan
Marc Lamy, director Europe, Paris

Karl Lange, director Europe, Frankfurt
Richard McAllister, director North America, Chicago
John Murray, director Latin America, São Paulo
David Keith, director Asia Pacific, Singapore

Total offices worldwide: 65
Services provided: executive search, human resource consulting, interim management, management audit and assessment, selection

Assessment: Moving forward

Fifteenth largest firm. Its new chairman, Sheila McLean, is the ex-head of AESC, the professional association of search firms. The group has been expanding its presence in Europe and Asia and now needs to strengthen its U.S. team.

Global 200 Consultants by Sector/Industry

In this appendix, the top consultants are listed by their area of specialization, as defined by the following sector/industry categories:

- CEO/Board of Directors
- Automotive
- Consulting and Professional Services
- Consumer Financial Services
- Education, Nonprofit Organizations, Associations and Foundations
- Fashion, Luxury, and Retail
- Fast Moving Consumer Goods
- Financial Services
- General Management
- Industry, Manufacturing, and Construction
- Information Technology
- Insurance
- International, Cross-Border Specialists
- Investment Banking and Trading
- Media, Entertainment, and Publishing
- Natural Resources

- Pharmaceutical/Health Care
- Real Estate
- Sports, Recreation, Leisure, and Hospitality
- Telecommunications
- Venture Capital and Start up Companies

Cross references for categories covering a number of fields are included. Note that a new breed of consultants, those who specialize in cross-border and often cross-sector searches are included in the heading of international, cross-border specialists. As the most significant aspect of executive search, the category of CEO/Board of Directors is listed here first.

CEO/Board of Directors

Appointments at board level are increasingly the result of strategic planning as companies merge, acquire, and take on new directions. Business leaders must now operate within an environment of ongoing restructuring of industries, rapid technological change, evolving strategic alliances, and emerging markets. Thus, there is increasing demand for executive directors with multinational experience. Firms are looking for nonexecutive directors to help manage their new-found independence; chairs are interested in finding suitable candidates for their smooth succession.

The leading firm at the main board level, particularly in the U.S.A. and the U.K., is Spencer Stuart. Heidrick & Struggles also does significant work in this growing field, especially in the U.S.A. and Germany. The following individuals are well established and highly visible, veteran search consultants who focus on the hiring of very senior CEO and board director assignments. For additional listings, please see the category of General Management.

Name	Firm	Primary Location
Javier Anitua	Russell Reynolds	Madrid
Stephen Bampfylde	Saxton Bampfylde	London
Michael Boxberger	Korn/Ferry International	Los Angeles
Miles Broadbent	The Miles Partnership-	London
Hobson Brown, Jr.	Russell Reynolds	New York
Paul Buchanan-Barrow	Korn/Ferry International	London
Skott Burkland	Skott/Edwards Consultants	Morristown, New Jersey
Dennis Carey	Spencer/Stuart	Philadelphia
James Carpenter	Russell Reynolds	New York
Jeffrey Christian	Christian & Timbers	Cleveland, Ohio
Bruno Colombo	Spencer Stuart	Milan
Ian Cordiner	Cordiner King Hever	Melbourne

Peter Crist	Crist Partners, Ltd.	Chicago
Guilherme Dale	Spencer Stuart	São Paulo
Gianni Dell'Orto	Heidrick & Struggles	Milan
David DeWilde	Chartwell Partners Int'l, Inc.	San Francisco
H. Bruce Dingman	Robert W. Dingman Company, Inc.	Westlake Village, Calif.
Maurice Ellett	Ward Howell International	Auckland, New Zealand
Leon Farley	Leon A. Farley Associates	San Francisco
Richard Ferry	Korn/Ferry International	Los Angeles
Thomas Friel	Heidrick & Struggles	Menlo Park, California
R. William Funk	Korn/Ferry International	Dallas
Francisco Gasset	Spencer Stuart	Madrid
William Gould	Gould, McCoy & Chadick	New York
Joseph Griesedieck, Jr	Spencer Stuart	San Francisco
John T. W. Hawkins	Russell Reynolds	Washington, D.C.
Jonathan Holman	The Holman Group	San Francisco
Theodore Jadick	Heidrick & Struggles	New York
Bjørn Johansson	Bjørn Johansson Associates Inc.	Zurich
John Johnson	LAI Ward Howell	Cleveland, Ohio
David Joys	Heidrick & Struggles	New York
Edward Kelley	Korn/Ferry International	London
Roger Kenny	Boardroom Consultants/ Kenny Kindler Tholke	New York
Richard King	Cordiner King Hever	Melbourne
Scott Kingdom	Korn/Ferry International	Chicago
Marc Lamy	Boyden Global Executive Search	Paris
Bengt Lejsved	Heidrick & Struggles	Stockholm
Brigitte Lemercier-Saltiel	Russell Reynolds	Paris
Jürgen Mülder	Mülder & Partner/ Heidrick & Struggles	Frankfurt
Caroline Nahas	Korn/Ferry International	Los Angeles
Dayton Ogden	Spencer Stuart	New York
Patrick Pittard	Heidrick & Struggles	Atlanta
Gary Reidy	Amrop International	Sydney
Wolfgang Reinermann	H. Neumann International	Düsseldorf
Robert Rollo	R. Rollo Associates	Los Angeles
Roger Rytz	Spencer Stuart	Zürich
Hermann Sendele	Spencer Stuart & Associates GmbH	Munich
Gilbert Stenholm, Jr	Spencer Stuart	Chicago
Martin Tang	Spencer Stuart	Hong Kong
Raymond Tang	Russell Reynolds	Hong Kong
John Thompson	Heidrick & Struggles	Menlo Park, Calif.
Tamas Toth	H. Neumann International	Vienna and Budapest

Andrew Tsui	Korn/Ferry International	Hong Kong
Gerard L. van den Broek	Spencer Stuart	Amsterdam
Peter Van de Velde	Amrop International	Sydne
Judith von Seldeneck	Diversified Search Inc.	Philadelphia
Frederick Wackerle	Fred Wackerle, Inc	Chicago
Trevor Woodburn	Ward Howell International/ Woodburn Mann (Pty) Ltd.	Sandton, South Africa

Automotive

This sector divides into original equipment (OE) versus suppliers. Therefore, there are specialists such as the OE consultants who know Ford, GM, Chrysler, and Toyota. There are also specialists such as RW, Dana, GKN, and other parts makers who supply the big automakers. It is important to note that the automotive industry is changing, for example, GM is creating its own suppliers with Delphi and Ford is following suit.

Name	**Firm**	**Primary Location**
John Brock	Korn/Ferry International	Houston
Nanno de Vries	Amrop International	Zurich
Axel Hampe	Delta Management Consultants GmbH	Munich
Friedbert Herbold	Amrop/Hofmann Herbold & Partner	Köenigstein, Germany
John Johnson	LAI Ward Howell	Cleveland, Ohio
Kang-Shik Koh	Ward Howell International	Seoul
Maria da Gloria Ribeiro	Amrop International	Lisbon
Hermann Sendele	Spencer Stuart & Associates GmbH	Munich
Sun Koo Shim	Amrop International	Seoul
Douglas Smith	LAI Ward Howell	Barrington, Illinois
Tan Soo Jin	Amrop International/ Gattie-Tan Soo Jin Management Consultants Pte Ltd.	Singapore

Consulting and Professional Services

The consulting and professional services sector, a field of growing importance, includes accounting, human resources, law, professional services, consulting firms, as well as senior- level functional positions within corporations (that is, General Counsel within an industrial firm). In some search firms, this sector is called the Business Services Practice area.

298

Name	Firm	Primary Location
Juha-Pekka Ahtikari	Amrop International/ Ståhlberg & Ahtikari Oy	Helsinki
Aysegül Aydin	Amrop International	Istanbul
Herbert Bechtel	Heidrick & Struggles/ Mülder & Partner	Frankfurt
Michael Bekins	Korn/Ferry International	Los Angeles
Bruce Beringer	Heidrick & Struggles	London
Irena Brichta	Heidrick & Struggles	Prague
Alex Cirone	Korn/Ferry International	Buenos Aires
Bruno Colombo	Spencer Stuart	Milan
James Drury III	Spencer Stuart	Chicago
Sakie Fukushima	Korn/Ferry International	Tokyo
Daniel Gauchat	Amrop International	Sydney
Anders Gulliksson	Korn/Ferry International	Stockholm
Harold Johnson	LAI Ward Howell	New York
Baldwin Klep	Heidrick & Struggles	Brussels
Pasi Koivusaari	Boyden International	Helsinki
Karl-Gunnar Lindquist	Boyden International	Stockholm
Pri Notowidigdo	Amrop International Profesindo Reksa Indonesia (PRI)	Jakarta
Paul Richard Ray, Jr.	Ray & Berndtson	Fort Worth, Texas
Eric Salmon	Eric Salmon & Partners	Paris
Josette Sayers	Jouve & Associes	Paris
Peter Van de Velde	Amrop International	Sydney
Sergei Vorobiev	Ward Howell International Holdings, Ltd.	Moscow
Didier Vuchot	Vuchot Ward Howell	Paris
Kyung Yoon	Heidrick & Struggles	Singapore

Consumer Financial Services

Financial services has expanded to the extent that many consultants specialize in certain aspects of the field. Those who list their speciality as banking (including commercial banking) follow. A separate category follows later in the directory for investment banking (including investment management) and trading.

Name	Firm	Primary Location
George Abdushelishvili	Ward Howell International Holdings Ltd.	Moscow
Linda Bialecki	Bialecki Inc.	New York
Choon Soo Chew	Russell Reynolds	Singapore
Roderick Gow	LAI Ward Howell	New York

Marc Lamy	Boyden Global Executive Search	Paris
Steven Potter	Highland Search Group	New York
Gary Reidy	Amrop International	Sydney
Brian Sullivan	Sullivan & Company	New York
Martin Tang	Spencer Stuart	Hong Kong
Reinhard Thiel	Heidrick & Struggles	Düsseldorf
Tamas Toth	H. Neumann International	Vienna and Budapest
Richard A. Wall III	Heidrick & Struggles	London
Robert Wong	Korn/Ferry International	São Paulo

Education, Nonprofit Organizations, Associations and Foundations

This sector, currently more established in the U.S.A. than elsewhere, is growing worldwide. Search objectives in this sector include finding senior executives for educational institutions (for example, university presidents), for nonprofit foundations, and for all types of cultural associations, museums and government affairs institutions and charities. In the U.S.A., some firms have also established diversity practice groups that assist clients in addressing the issues of gender, ethnic, and racial diversity in hiring.

Name	Firm	Primary Location
Stephen Bampfylde	Saxton Bampfylde	London
Maurice Ellett	Ward Howell International	Auckland, New Zealand
R. William Funk	Korn/Ferry International	Dallas
Richard King	Cordiner King Hever	Melbourne
William Marumoto	Boyden Global Executive Search	Washington, D.C.
Andrew Tsui	Korn/Ferry International	Hong Kong
Judith von Seldeneck	Diversified Search Inc.	Philadelphia

Fashion, Luxury, and Retail

Together, fashion, luxury goods, and retail constitute an important and growing sector. The search consultants who specialize in this sector tend to be from the field, which is quite broad and ranges from cosmetics to home furnishings. Often they are from large luxury goods firms such as LVMH or from big retailers. However, many luxury goods clients are looking for successful candidates from other fields—often FMCG with classic marketing/distribution skills or from record/video firms for their retail/distribution knowledge. Many also look to headhunters in other disciplines where they tend to follow a wider pool of talent and do not have the off-limits restrictions of a headhunter who already works for many luxury goods clients.

Name	Firm	Primary Location
Aysegül Aydin	Amrop International	Istanbul
Bruno-Luc Banton	Russell Reynolds	Paris
Guilherme Dale	Spencer Stuart	São Paulo

Floriane de Saint Pierre	F.S.P. SA	Paris
Nanno de Vries	Amrop International	Zurich
James Drury III	Spencer Stuart	Chicago
Sakie Fukushima	Korn/Ferry International	Tokyo
Andrew Garner	Garner International Ltd.	London
Daniel Gauchat	Amrop International	Sydney
Jean-Pierre Gouirand	Heidrick & Struggles	Paris
Daniel Grenon	H. Newmann International	Paris
Joseph Griesedieck, Jr	Spencer Stuart	San Francisco
Melanie Kusin	Heidrick & Struggles	New York
Herbert Mines	Herbert Mines Associates, Inc.	New York
Raimondo Nider	Korn/Ferry International	Milan
Lynn Ogden	Korn/Ferry International	Hong Kong
Wolfgang Reinermann	H. Neumann International	Düsseldorf
Anthony Saxton	Saxton Bampfylde International	London
Reinhard Thiel	Heidrick & Struggles	Düsseldorf
Didier Vuchot	Vuchot Ward Howell	Paris

Fast Moving Consumer Goods

The consumer goods field is basically considered fast moving consumer goods (FMCG). It is large, diversified, and crosses many industry/sector/functional boundaries. It includes consumer marketing, consumer packaged goods, consumer products, direct marketing, and even tobacco. Thus it is difficult to form a dedicated consumer goods practice group within a search firm. Search consultants in the consumer goods area tend to be generalists who follow many industry sectors. This specialty includes the large food and consumer electronic groups such as Colgate, P&G, Sony, Guinness Grand Met, and Lesieur.

Name	Firm	Primary Location
George Abdushelishvili	Ward Howell International Holdings Ltd.	Moscow
Juha-Pekka Ahtikari	Amrop International/ Ståhlberg & Ahtikari Oy	Helsinki
Aysegül Aydin	Amrop International	Istanbul
Bruno-Luc Banton	Russell Reynolds	Paris
Michael Bekins	Korn/Ferry International	Los Angeles
Bruce Beringer	Heidrick & Struggles	London
Irena Brichta	Heidrick & Struggles	Prague
Kurt Bruusgaard	Ray & Berndtson	Copenhagen
Dick Buschman	Korn/Ferry International	Amsterdam
James Carpenter	Russell Reynolds	New York
Alex Cirone	Korn/Ferry International	Buenos Aires
Bruno Colombo	Spencer Stuart	Milan

Luis Condé Moller	Seeliger y Condé/Amrop Int'l	Barcelona
Nestor D'Angelo	Heidrick & Struggles	Caracas
Guilherme Dale	Spencer Stuart	São Paulo
Gianni Dell'Orto	Heidrick & Struggles	Milan
Nanno de Vries	Amrop International	Zurich
Lauren Doliva	Heidrick & Struggles	San Francisco
James Drury III	Spencer Stuart	Chicago
Sakie Fukushima	Korn/Ferry International	Tokyo
John Gardner	Heidrick & Struggles	Chicago
Andrew Garner	Garner International Ltd.	London
Francisco Gasset	Spencer Stuart	Madrid
Daniel Gauchat	Amrop International	Sydney
William Gould	Gould, McCoy & Chadick	New York
Richard Glynn	Richard Glynn Consultants Pte Ltd.	Singapore
Joseph Griesedieck, Jr	Spencer Stuart	San Francisco
Anders Gulliksson	Korn/Ferry International	Stockholm
Friedbert Herbold	Hofmann Herbold & Partner/ Amrop International	Köenigstein, Germany
David Joys	Heidrick & Struggles	New York
David Keith	Boyden International	Singapore
Roger Kenny	Boardroom Consultants/ Kenny Kindler Tholke	New York
Scott Kingdom	Korn/Ferry International	Chicago
Baldwin Klep	Heidrick & Struggles	Brussels
Melanie Kusin	Heidrick & Struggles	New York
Karl-Gunnar Lindquist	Boyden International	Stockholm
Henry Ling	LTA & Company	Singapore
Ignacio Marseillan	Spencer Stuart	Buenos Aires
William Marumoto	Boyden Global Executive Search	Washington, D.C.
Horacio McCoy	Korn/Ferry International	Lomas de Chapultepec, Mexico
Millington McCoy	Gould, McCoy & Chadick, Inc.	New York
Herbert Mines	Herbert Mines Associates, Inc.	New York
Henry de Montebello	Russell Reynolds	Paris
Gernot Müller	Ray & Berndtson	Frankfurt
Raimondo Nider	Korn/Ferry International	Milan
Lynn Ogden	Korn/Ferry International	Hong Kong
Finn Krogh Rants	Amrop International	Copenhagen
Paul Richard Ray, Jr.	Ray & Berndtson	Fort Worth, Texas
Maria da Gloria Ribeiro	Amrop	Lisbon
Wolfgang Reinermann	H. Neumann International	Düsseldorf
Robert Rollo	R. Rollo Associates	Los Angeles
Louisa Wong Rousseau	Bó Lè Associates	Hong Kong

Eric Salmon	Eric Salmon & Partners	Paris
Anthony Saxton	Saxton Bampfylde International	London
Josette Sayers	Jouve & Associes	Paris
Gerardo Seeliger	Seeliger y Condé/Amrop Int'l	Madrid
Hermann Sendele	Spencer Stuart & Associates GmbH	Munich
Sun Koo Shim	Amrop International	Seoul
Gilbert Stenholm, Jr	Spencer Stuart	Chicago
Tan Soo Jin	Amrop Int'l/Gattie-Tan Soo Jin Management Consultants Pte Ltd.	Singapore
Mitsuharu Tomizawa	Heidrick & Struggles	Tokyo
Christopher Traub	Ward Howell International/ Traub and Associates,Ltd.	Taipei, Taiwan
Roberto Valagussa	Search Partners International	Paris
Maria Valdez	Korn/Ferry International	Lomas de Chapultepec, Mexico
Jean-Dominique Virchaux	Heidrick & Struggles	Miami
Andrew Weidener	Ray & Berndtson	Atlanta
Terje Wiig	Korn/Ferry International	Oslo
Gerd Wilhelm	Amrop International/ Hager, Wilhelm & Partner	Vienna
Robert Wong	Korn/Ferry International	São Paulo
Li Hsiao Yuan	Strategic Executive Search Pte Ltd./ Ward Howell International	Singapore

Financial Services

A specialty practice group typically absorbs the culture of its industry. The financial services groups are transaction-oriented businesses and tend to be fast turnover and deal-oriented teams. Very often, many of the individuals are formerly from New York City or Wall Street practices. They do pro-active research and focus on market intelligence that is often quite specialized (for example, derivatives experts). They also tend to concentrate on key financial markets such as New York, London, and Hong Kong.

The financial services sector includes many excellent global firms (such as Russell Reynolds and Korn/Ferry); it also has many well established niche boutiques (such as Baines Gwinner, The Highland Group, The Rose Partnership, Armstrong Consulting Group, Whitney Group), which tend to be either London- or New York-based. The larger global firms have established practice groups to compete with these fast moving, highly focused boutique firms. Many consultants work in more than one subsector (for example, asset management and investment banking). This is typically true outside of the U.S.A.. Insurance and real estate sectors tend to have dedicated specialists who came from these industries.

The financial services sector consists of five major subsectors:

- Asset or investment management (that is, the buy side). This subsector includes firms such as Mercury Asset Management and Putnam.

- Consumer financial services. This relates to consumer services and products including credit cards, bank accounts, private banking.

- Insurance. This includes life, property and casualty insurance.

- Investment banking/global banking. This includes private equities and derivatives.

- Real estate.

This directory includes so many highly qualified specialists that four of these sectors—consumer financial services, insurance, investment banking and trading, and real estate—are listed separately under those headings. Those consultants who list their specialty as financial services in general, follow. Some of those listed here also practice within certain areas of financial services. For example, Michel Flasaquier, Hideaki Furuta, Neal Maslan, and Charles Polachi, Jr., specialize in venture capital and startup companies.

Name	Firm	Primary Location
Jacques André	Ray & Berndtson	New York
Aysegül Aydin	Amrop International	Istanbul
Jonathan Baines	Baines Gwinner Ltd.	London
Linda Bialecki	Bialecki Inc.	New York
David Wesley Benn	Korn/Ferry International	Sydney
Robert Benson	Spencer Stuart	Frankfurt and Stamford, Connecticut
Bruce Beringer	Heidrick & Struggles	London
Irena Brichta	Heidrick & Struggles	Prague
Dick Buschman	Korn/Ferry International	Amsterdam
Magnus Carlsson	Amrop International	Stockholm
Choon Soo Chew	Russell Reynolds	Singapore
Luis Condé Moller	Seeliger y Condé/Amrop Int'l	Barcelona
Nestor D'Angelo	Heidrick & Struggles	Caracas
David DeWilde	Chartwell Partners Int'l, Inc.	San Francisco
Leon Farley	Leon A. Farley Associates	San Francisco
Michel Flasaquier	Jouve & Associes	Paris
Hideaki Furuta	Jomon Associates Inc.	Tokyo
Jay Gaines	Jay Gaines & Co.	New York
E. Nicholas Gardiner	Gardiner, Townsend & Associates	New York

Bob Gattie	Amrop International	Singapore
Richard Glynn	Richard Glynn Consultants Pte Ltd.	Singapore
Roderick Gow	LAI Ward Howell	New York
Henry Higdon	Higdon Prince	New York
Lawrence Holmes	Canny Bowen Int'l	Baltimore
Georges Holzberger	Highland Search Group, LLC	New York
W. Michael Honey	Ray & Berndtson	Calgary
Durant Hunter	Pendleton James Associates, Inc.	Boston
David Joys	Heidrick & Struggles	New York
Edward Kelley	Korn/Ferry International	London
Kang-Shik Koh	Ward Howell International	Seoul
Pasi Koivusaari	Boyden International	Helsinki
Marc Lamy	Boyden Global Executive Search	Paris
Brigitte Lemercier-Saltiel	Russell Reynolds	Paris
Henry Ling	LTA & Company	Singapore
Carlos Magnon	Amrop International	Colonia Los Morales, Mexico
Philip Marsden	H. Neumann	London
Ignacio Marseillan	Spencer Stuart	Buenos Aires
Neal Maslan	Ward Howell International	Encino, California
Horacio McCoy	Korn/Ferry International	Lomas de Chapultepec, Mexico
Millington McCoy	Gould, McCoy & Chadick, Inc.	New York
Pri Notowidigdo	Amrop International/Profesindo Reksa Indonesia (PRI)	Jakarta
Charles Polachi, Jr.	Fenwick Partners/H&S	Lexington, Mass.
Steven Potter	Highland Search Group	New York
Windle Priem	Korn/Ferry International	New York
Marylin Prince	Higdon Prince Inc.	New York
Johann Redehlinghuys	Amrop International	Johannesburg South Africa
Wolfgang Reinermann	H. Neumann International	Düsseldorf
Maria da Gloria Ribeiro	Amrop International	Lisbon
Robert Rollo	R. Rollo Associates	Los Angeles
Philippa Rose	The Rose Partnership	London
Louisa Wong Rousseau	Bó Lè Associates	Hong Kong
Gerardo Seeliger	Seeliger y Condé/Amrop Int'l	Madrid
Hermann Sendele	Spencer Stuart & Associates GmbH	Munich
Lauri Ståhlberg	Amrop International/ Ståhlberg & Ahtikari Oy	Helsinki

Brian Sullivan	Sullivan & Company	New York
Tan Soo Jin	Amrop International/ Gattie-Tan Soo Jin Management Consultants Pte Ltd.	Singapore
Mitsuharu Tomizawa	Heidrick & Struggles	Tokyo
Tamas Toth	H. Neumann International	Vienna and Budapest
John Townsend	Gardiner, Townsend & Associates	New York
Christopher Traub	Ward Howell International/ Traub and Associates, Ltd.	Taipei, Taiwan
Andrew Tsui	Korn/Ferry International	Hong Kong
Gerard L. van den Broek	Spencer Stuart	Amsterdam
Judith von Seldeneck	Diversified Search Inc.	Philadelphia
Peter Van de Velde	Amrop International	Sydney
Jean-Dominique Virchaux	Heidrick & Struggles	Miami
Sergei Vorobiev	Ward Howell InternationalHoldings, Ltd.	Moscow
Didier Vuchot	Vuchot Ward Howell	Paris
Richard A. Wall III	Heidrick & Struggles	London
Annie Wee	Russell Reynolds	Singapore
Walter Williams	LAI Ward Howell	Boston
Matthew Wright	Russell Reynolds	London
Kyung Yoon	Heidrick & Struggles	Singapore

General Management

Consultants who described themselves as generalists or listed their speciality as general management are included in the following listing. In addition, please see the category of CEO/Board of Directors.

Name	Firm	Primary Location
Michael Bekins	Korn/Ferry International	Los Angeles
Jean-Marie Van Den Borre	Korn/Ferry International	Brussels
Paul Buchanan-Barrow	Korn/Ferry International	London
Kurt Bruusgaard	Ray & Berndtson	Copenhagen
Skott Burkland	Skott/Edwards Consultants	Morristown, New Jersey
Luiz Cabrera	PMC Amrop Int'l	São Paulo
Alex Cirone	Korn/Ferry International	Buenos Aires
Gerard Clery-Melin	Heidrick & Struggles	Paris
Ian Cordiner	Cordiner King Hever	Melbourne
Anne Fawcett	The Caldwell Partners/ Amrop International	Toronto

Richard Glynn	Richard Glynn Consultants Pte Ltd.	Singapore
John T. W. Hawkins	Russell Reynolds	Washington, D.C.
Arthur Janta- Polczynski	Russell Reynolds Associates	Brussels
Bjørn Johansson	Bjørn Johansson Associates Inc.	Zurich
Richard King	Cordiner King Hever	Melbourne
Ranjan Marwah	Executive Access Limited	Hong Kong
Jonathan McBride	McBride Associates Inc.	Washington, D.C.
Kyle Mitchell	Ray & Berndtson/Tanton Mitchell	Vancouver, B.C.
Gernot Müller	Ray & Berndtson	Frankfurt
Caroline Nahas	Korn/Ferry International	Los Angeles
Raimondo Nider	Korn/Ferry International	Milan
Luiz Alberto Panelli	PMC Amrop International	São Paulo
Manuel Papayanopulos	Korn/Ferry International	Lomas de Chapultepec, Mexico
Robert Pearson	LAI Ward Howell	Dallas
Patrick Pittard	Heidrick & Struggles	Atlanta
Steven Potter	Highland Search Group	New York
Paul Richard Ray, Jr.	Ray & Berndtson	Fort Worth, Texas
Gerard Roche	Heidrick & Struggles	New York
Robert Rollo	R. Rollo Associates	Los Angeles
Glendon Rowell	Boyden International Ltd.	Hong Kong
Anthony Saxton	Saxton Bampfylde International	London
Judith von Seldeneck	Diversified Search Inc.	Philadelphia
Hermann Sendele	Spencer Stuart & Associates GmbH	Munich
John E. Smith, Jr.	Smith Search, SC	Mexico City
Michael Tappan	LAI Ward Howell	New York
Heiner Thorborg	Heiner Thorborg GmbH & Co.	Frankfurt
Peter Van de Velde	Amrop International	Sydney
Karin Vassilopoulos	H. Neumann International	Vienna
Jean-Dominique Virchaux	Heidrick & Struggles	Miami
Terje Wiig	Korn/Ferry International	Oslo

Industry, Manufacturing, and Construction

There is a continual drive among manufacturers for higher quality and lower costs. This leads to sharper focus at the center and often to the outsourcing of noncore operations. The industry, manufacturing, and construction sector includes companies involved in the manufacture of components, parts, and finished goods, and in the fabrication of metals, plastics, other raw materials. It includes companies involved in the manufacture of capital equipment, transportation components, and other durables sold mainly to nonconsumer markets. Also included in this sector are agricultural products, engineering and construction, wholesaling and distribution, paper, and the chemical industries.

Name	Firm	Primary Location
Michael Bekins	Korn/Ferry International	Los Angeles
Robert Benson	Spencer Stuart	Frankfurt and Stamford, Connecticut
Dick Buschman	Korn/Ferry International	Amsterdam
Magnus Carlsson	Amrop International	Stockholm
James Carpenter	Russell Reynolds	New York
Guilherme Dale	Spencer Stuart	São Paulo
Nestor D'Angelo	Heidrick & Struggles	Caracas
David DeWilde	Chartwell Partners International, Inc.	San Francisco
James Drury III	Spencer Stuart	Chicago
Maurice Ellett	Ward Howell International	Auckland, New Zealand
Michel Flasaquier	Jouve & Associes	Paris
E. Nicholas Gardiner	Gardiner, Townsend & Associates	New York
John Gardner	Heidrick & Struggles	Chicago
William Gould	Gould, McCoy & Chadick	New York
Jean-Pierre Gouirand	Heidrick & Struggles	Paris
Joie Gregor	Heidrick & Struggles	New York
Anders Gulliksson	Korn/Ferry International	Stockholm
Friedbert Herbold	Amrop International/ Hofmann Herbold & Partner	Köenigstein, Germany
John Johnson	LAI Ward Howell	Cleveland, Ohio
David Joys	Heidrick & Struggles	New York
David Keith	Boyden International	Singapore
Roger Kenny	Boardroom Consultants/ Kenny Kindler Tholke	New York
Richard King	Cordiner King Hever	Melbourne
Scott Kingdom	Korn/Ferry International	Chicago
Bengt Lejsved	Heidrick & Struggles	Stockholm
Millington McCoy	Gould, McCoy & Chadick, Inc.	New York
William Marumoto	Boyden Global Executive Search	Washington, D.C.
Henry de Montebello	Russell Reynolds Associates	Paris
Gernot Müller	Ray & Berndtson	Frankfurt
Robert Pearson	LAI Ward Howell	Dallas
Finn Krogh Rants	Amrop International	Copenhagen
Gary Reidy	Amrop International	Sydney
Roger Rytz	Spencer Stuart	Zürich

Eric Salmon	Eric Salmon & Partners	Paris
Sun Koo Shim	Amrop International/ SKS Consultants	Seoul
Douglas Smith	LAI Ward Howell	Barrington, Illinois
Lauri Ståhlberg	Amrop International/ Ståhlberg & Ahtikari Oy	Helsinki
Reinhard Thiel	Heidrick & Struggles	Düsseldorf
Mitsuharu Tomizawa	Heidrick & Struggles	Tokyo
Roberto Valagussa	Search Partners International	Paris
Jean-Marie Van Den Borre	Korn/Ferry International	Brussels
Sergei Vorobiev	Ward Howell International Holdings, Ltd.	Moscow

Information Technology

The information technology (IT) sector includes hardware and electronics, information systems, software, internet and new media technologies. Within hardware and electronics, segments include chips, hardware components, networking hardware, personal computers, peripherals and workstations. Software systems include multimedia products, systems integration and systems software.

Two well-established firms in the IT field are Heidrick & Struggles and Russell Reynolds. During the 1980s, Heidrick & Struggles developed one of the first and most outstanding practice groups in the IT field. This group was founded by Tom Friel and John Thompson out of Menlo Park, California. They lead the practice today and are two of the most highly visible and well-respected consultants in IT search worldwide. They have patiently and relentlessly formed their dream team of technology-focused consultants who work together on an ongoing basis for Heidrick & Struggles clients around the world. This practice group has been the most successful one at Heidrick & Struggles. Not surprisingly, Friel has pushed the development of his practice group to markets such as Singapore and Tokyo.

Because of the sheer vibrancy of the technology sector, search consultants find that belonging to a dedicated practice group is quite challenging. Because Silicon Valley firms have an average annual growth rate of 200 percent (firms must grow quickly and globally), the headhunter can, and should be prepared to, play a dynamic role. Thus the specialty practice group concept really makes sense in the IT field. It provides ongoing market intelligence for the client. Well-informed consultants are aware of merger activity, market trends, up-and-coming stars, and so on.

The technology pie is growing. Whereas the technology world used to be simple—hardware/software/telecommunications—the market is much more complicated now. Roles are changing and the need for creative and strategic skills has never been higher. It is important to note that the CIO has become an important partner of the CEO in the drive to help companies maintain a competitive advantage as technology changes. And because talented executives are entering the field from other sectors, the good search consultant must know not only the proven and visible stars in technology, but be aware of other executives from outside the technology field.

Name	Firm	Primary Location
Juha-Pekka Ahtikari	Amrop International/ Ståhlberg & Ahtikari Oy	Helsinki
Jean-Louis Alpeyrie	Heidrick & Struggles	New York
David Anderson	Heidrick & Struggles	Dallas
Akira Arai	Korn/Ferry International	Tokyo
Herbert Bechtel	Heidrick & Struggles/ Mülder & Partner	Frankfurt
Skott Burkland	Skott/Edwards Consultants	Morristown, New Jersey
Alan Choi	Korn/Ferry International	Hong Kong
Michael Christy	Heidrick & Struggles	Vienna, Virginia
Leon Farley	Leon A. Farley Associates	San Francisco
Michel Flasaquier	Jouve & Associes	Paris
Thomas Friel	Heidrick & Struggles	Menlo Park, California
Koichi Fukuda	Heidrick & Struggles	Tokyo
Jay Gaines	Jay Gaines & Co.	New York
Bob Gattie	Amrop International	Singapore
Daniel Gauchat	Amrop International	Sydney
Mike Goldstone	Heidrick & Struggles	Hong Kong
William Gould	Gould, McCoy & Chadick	New York
Mina Gouran	Korn/Ferry International	London
Joie Gregor	Heidrick & Struggles	New York
Axel Hampe	Delta Management Consultants GmbH	Munich
Jonathan Holman	The Holman Group	San Francisco
Lawrence Holmes	Canny Bowen International	Baltimore
Robert Horton	Horton International Inc.	New York
Roger Kenny	Boardroom Consultants/ Kenny Kindler Tholke	New York
Scott Kingdom	Korn/Ferry International	Chicago
Kang-Shik Koh	Ward Howell International	Seoul
Pasi Koivusaari	Boyden International	Helsinki
R. Paul Kors	Kors Montgomery International/ cFour Partners	Houston

Horacio McCoy	Korn/Ferry International	Lomas de Chapultepec, Mexico
Millington McCoy	Gould, McCoy & Chadick, Inc.	New York
Manuel Papayanopulos	Korn/Ferry International	Lomas de Chapultepec, Mexico
Robert Pearson	LAI Ward Howell	Dallas
Charles Polachi, Jr.	Fenwick Partners/H&S	Lexington, Massachusetts
Gary Reidy	Amrop International	Sydney
Roger Rytz	Spencer Stuart	Zürich
Josette Sayers	Jouve & Associes	Paris
Rae Sedel	Russell Reynolds	London
Hermann Sendele	Spencer Stuart & Associates GmbH	Munich
Sun Koo Shim	Amrop International/ SKS Consultants	Seoul
Mitsuharu Tomizawa	Heidrick & Struggles	Tokyo
Christopher Traub	Ward Howell International/ Traub and Associates, Ltd.	Taipei, Taiwan
Robert Wong	Korn/Ferry International	São Paulo
Kyung Yoon	Heidrick & Struggles	Singapore
Li Hsiao Yuan	Strategic Executive Search Pte Ltd./ Ward Howell International/	Singapore

Insurance

Insurance is considered an integral part of the financial services sector. The focus in this sector is in the same key markets (New York, London, Hong Kong) and Switzerland.

Name	Firm	Primary Location
Michael Corey	LAI Ward Howell	Lake Geneva, Wisconsin
Roderick Gow	LAI Ward Howell	New York
Reinhard Thiel	Heidrick & Struggles	Düsseldorf
Walter Williams	LAI Ward Howell	Boston, Massachusetts
Peter Van de Velde	Amrop Intl	Sydney
Gail Vergara	Spencer Stuart	Chicago

International, Cross-Border Specialists

A select group of highly talented, cross-culturally sensitive executive search consultants function across regional boundaries or typically focus on a panregional basis. For the most part, they have grown up, been educated in, or had previous work experience in two or more different markets worldwide and tend to speak different languages and understand their cultures. Consultants in the top firms, notably Egon Zehnder and Korn/Ferry, often fit this "cross-border" mold. Here are a few examples.

- Mike Bekins (Korn/Ferry-Los Angeles,Tokyo) spent 20 years living in Asia for Korn/Ferry (including Tokyo, Sydney, and other Asian locations). He is responsible for global relationships that typically bridge the U.S.A. and Asia, especially Australia/New Zealand, Tokyo and South Korea.
- Young Kuan-Sing (Korn/Ferry-Singapore) is Asian focused and responsible for Southeast Asia and for Asian family groups, a new, emerging practice group for Korn/Ferry. He and his team must constantly maintain focus throughout Asia and also deal effectively with multinational interests in the U.S.A..
- Joost Nanninga (Egon Zehnder International-Amsterdam) develops new business in Europe and especially thoughout the Benelux region. He is equally at home in Amsterdam or Brussels.
- Josette Sayers (Jouve & Associes, Paris), who specializes in Euro-American recruitments, was educated in both the U.S.A. and France. She is fluent in French and resides in Paris; however she is just as home in Silicon Valley or San Francisco.
- Mike Tappan (LAI Ward Howell-New York) focuses on global clients with Russian interests. He has built up one of the most outstanding young consultant teams in Moscow, all of whom were MBA classmates.
- Charles Tseng (Egon Zehnder International-Singapore) runs the EZI offices in Singapore and Malaysia. He is very much at home in any of the Asian markets.

These are but a few examples. Others, firmly grounded in cross-border work, are listed below.

Name	Firm	Primary Location
Jean-Louis Alpeyrie	Heidrick & Struggles	New York
David Anderson	Heidrick & Struggles	Dallas
Stephen Bampfylde	Saxton Bampfylde	London
Bruno-Luc Banton	Russell Reynolds	Paris
Michael Bekins	Korn/Ferry International	Los Angeles
Robert Benson	Spencer Stuart	Frankfurt and Stamford, Connecticut
Bruce Beringer	Heidrick & Struggles	London
Michael Boxberger	Korn/Ferry International	Los Angeles
Miles Broadbent	The Miles Partnership	London
Hobson Brown, Jr.	Russell Reynolds	New York
James Carpenter	Russell Reynolds	New York

James Drury III	Spencer Stuart	Chicago
Leon Farley	Leon A. Farley Associates	San Francisco
Hideaki Furuta	Jomon Associates Inc.	Tokyo
Daniel Gauchat	Amrop International	Sydney
William Gould	Gould, McCoy & Chadick	New York
Roderick Gow	LAI Ward Howell	New York
Jürgen Mülder	Mülder & Partner/ Heidrick & Struggles	Frankfurt
Caroline Nahas	Korn/Ferry International	Los Angeles
Josette Sayers	Jouve & Associes	Paris
Michael Tappan	LAI Ward Howell	New York

Investment Banking and Trading

Financial consultants who list their speciality as investment banking (including investment management) and trading are listed below. For more general banking services, see the listings for consumer financial services and financial services, earlier in this directory.

Name	Firm	Primary Location
Jonathan Baines	Baines Gwinner Ltd.	London
Linda Bialecki	Bialecki Inc.	New York
Magnus Carlsson	Amrop International	Stockholm
Roderick Gow	LAI Ward Howell	New York
Georges Holzberger	Highland Search Group, LLC	New York
Richard Lannamann	Russell Reynolds	New York
Philip Marsden	H. Neumann	London
Steven Potter	Highland Search Group, LLC	New York
Marylin Prince	Higdon Prince Inc.	New York
Brian Sullivan	Sullivan & Company	New York
Richard A. Wall III	Heidrick & Struggles	London
Annie Wee	Russell Reynolds	Singapore

Media, Entertainment, and Publishing

Media, entertainment, and publishing headhunters are often considered to be "entertainment types" who do headhunting on the side. They are at ease among media industry executives. This often means they have a more relaxed look than their counterparts in fields such as financial services; many tend to dress like entertainment or media types and talk their language. They may even come from the entertainment fields of TV, broadcast, or publishing. This sector also includes advertising and communications.

Well-known media/entertainment headhunters in the U.S.A. include Bill Simon and Michelle James, both of Korn/Ferry, and Stephen Unger of Spencer

Stuart. Outside of the U.S.A., they include Ian Ritchie at Russell Reynolds (ex-BBC), Peter Paschek at Delta Management Consultants in Berlin, and Gil Carrick at GKR in London. Another well-known headhunter in this sector is Tim Vignoles (ex-Korn/Ferry media/entertainment practice group in London, and with the BBC before that), who has recently joined a smaller boutique firm (Garner International) because he felt that entertainment clients are better served by a a specialist firm devoted to their industry sector.

Name	Firm	Primary Location
George Abdushelishvili	Ward Howell International Holdings Ltd.	Moscow
Jean-Louis Alpeyrie	Heidrick & Struggles	New York
Aysegül Aydin	Amrop International	Istanbul
Bruno-Luc Banton	Russell Reynolds	Paris
Floriane de Saint Pierre	F.S.P. SA	Paris
Lauren Doliva	Heidrick & Struggles	San Francisco
Jay Gaines	Jay Gaines & Co.	New York
Richard Glynn	Richard Glynn Consultants Pte Ltd.	Singapore
Gernot Müller	Ray & Berndtson	Frankfurt
Lynn Ogden	Korn/Ferry International	Hong Kong
Josette Sayers	Jouve & Associes	Paris
Gerardo Seeliger	Seeliger y Condé/Amrop Int'l	Madrid
William Simon	Korn/Ferry International	Los Angeles
Roberto Valagussa	Search Partners	Paris
Tim Vignoles	Garner International	London
Robert Wong	Korn/Ferry International	São Paulo

Natural Resources

In the natural resources sector, consultants specialize in oil and gas exploration, development and refining, mining and metals explorations and production, utilities and environmental services. This can include chemicals, process industries, and forest products. Assets in many developing nations that were once nationalized have been opened to private investment, widening markets for oil and gas companies and other companies that devevelop natural resources.

Name	Firm	Primary Location
John Brock	Korn/Ferry International	Houston
Guilherme Dale	Spencer Stuart	São Paulo
R. William Funk	Korn/Ferry International	Dallas
W. Michael Honey	Ray & Berndtson	Calgary
Richard King	Cordiner King Hever	Melbourne

R. Paul Kors	Kors Montgomery International/ cFour Partners	Houston
Ignacio Marseillan	Spencer Stuart	Buenos Aires
William Marumoto	Boyden Global Executive Search	Washington, D.C.
Lynn Ogden	Korn/Ferry International	Hong Kong
Ted Orner	Russell Reynolds	Houston
Gary Reidy	Amrop International	Sydney
Robert Rollo	R. Rollo Associates	Los Angeles
Jean-Marie Van Den Borre	Korn/Ferry International	Brussels
David Witte	LAI Ward Howell	Houston

Pharmaceutical/Health Care

The healthcare field is undergoing consolidation and change: the old functional hierarchies are dissolving, the business is getting tougher and more strategic. The quality of relationships and networking is now key. There has been a good deal of merger and consolidation among the big firms. According to Peter Bassett, head of the pharmarceutical practice group at Korn/Ferry, there are more fluid boundaries and access to market intelligence is rising. Many dynamic markets are emerging, including medical devices and diagnostics, healthcare information systems, healthcare services, pharmaceuticals, therapeutics, therametrics, patient care, and of course, the fast growing biotechnology field.

The healthcare executive of today is presented with dramatic change, including the acceleration of the cycle for drug development, new delivery technologies, and more sophisticated management information systems. The sector can include startup firms (for example, early stage medical devices companies) to fully integrated giant global pharmaceutical firms. Two of the leading global search firms in the pharmaceutical field are Korn/Ferry and Egon Zehnder.

Name	Firm	Primary Location
George Abdushelishvili	Ward Howell International Holdings Ltd.	Moscow
Peter Bassett	Korn/Ferry International	London
Irena Brichta	Heidrick & Struggles	Prague
Skott Burkland	Skott/Edwards Consultants	Morristown, New Jersey
Michael Corey	LAI Ward Howell	Lake Geneva, Wisconsin
Gianni Dell'Orto	Heidrick & Struggles	Milan
Michel Flasaquier	Jouve & Associes	Paris
Koichi Fukuda	Heidrick & Struggles Int'l	Tokyo
Francisco Gasset	Spencer Stuart	Madrid
Bob Gattie	Amrop International	Singapore
William Gould	Gould, McCoy & Chadick	New York

David Keith	Boyden International	Singapore
Roger Kenny	Boardroom Consultants/	New York
	Kenny Kindler Tholke	
Pasi Koivusaari	Boyden International	Helsinki
Richard Glynn	Richard Glynn Consultants Pte Ltd.	Singapore
John T. W. Hawkins	Russell Reynolds	Washington, D.C.
Michael Kieffer	The Kieffer Group	Naperville, Illinois
Karl-Gunnar Lindquist	Boyden International	Stockholm
Neal Maslan	LAI Ward Howell	Encino, California
Manuel Papayanopulos	Korn/Ferry International	Lomas de Chapultepec, Mexico
Gary Reidy	Amrop International	Sydney
Roger Rytz	Spencer Stuart	Zürich
Sun Ko Shim	Amrop International/	Seoul
	SKS Consultants	
Tan Soo Jin	Amrop International/	Singapore
	Gattie-Tan Soo Jin Management	
	Consultants Pte Ltd.	
Judith von Seldeneck	Diversified Search Inc.	Philadelphia
Gail Vergara	Spencer Stuart	Chicago

Real Estate

Real Estate, another specialty within financial services, has its own specialists.

Name	Firm	Primary Location
David DeWilde	Chartwell Partners Int'l, Inc.	San Francisco
Reinhard Thiel	Heidrick & Struggles	Düsseldorf
Walter Williams	LAI Ward Howell	Boston

Sports, Recreation, Leisure, Hospitality

Consultants who specialize in leisure activities, including sports and recreation, are included in this sector, as are those who work in hospitality, including the hotel industry.

Name	Firm	Primary Location
Aysegül Aydin	Amrop International	Istanbul
Bruno-Luc Banton	Russell Reynolds	Paris
Henry de Montebello	Russell Reynolds	Paris
Floriane de Saint Pierre	F.S.P. SA	Paris
Johann Redehlinghuys	Amrop International	Johannesburg South Africa
Gerardo Seeliger	Seeliger y Condé/Amrop Int'l	Madrid

Telecommunications

Just as the specialty practice group concept makes sense in the field of information technology, so too does it make sense in the telecommunications field. Specialists in this sector can provide current market intelligence concerning merger activity, market trends, rising stars, and other important factors this fast moving field.

The privatization of telecommunications infrastructures in many developing markets has created a demand for market-driven executives. The good search consultant knows the proven and visible stars in telecommunications, and is aware of other executives from a variety of fields or related disciplines.

Name	Firm	Primary Location
Juha-Pekka Ahtikari	Amrop International/ Ståhlberg & Ahtikari Oy	Helsinki
David Anderson	Heidrick & Struggles	Dallas
Michel Flasaquier	Jouve & Associes	Paris
Andrew Garner	Garner International Ltd.	London
Mike Goldstone	Heidrick & Struggles	Hong Kong
Mina Gouran	Korn/Ferry International	London
Jonathan Holman	The Holman Group	San Francisco
Robert Horton	Horton International Inc.	New York
Kang-Shik Koh	Ward Howell International	Seoul
Pasi Koivusaari	Boyden International	Helsinki
Raimondo Nider	Korn/Ferry International	Milan
Robert Pearson	LAI Ward Howell	Dallas
Josette Sayers	Jouve & Associes	Paris
Rae Sedel	Russell Reynolds	London
Hermann Sendele	Spencer Stuart & Associates GmbH	Munich
Lauri Ståhlberg	Amrop International/ Ståhlberg & Ahtikari Oy	Helsinki
Christopher Traub	Ward Howell International/ Traub and Associates, Ltd.	Taipei, Taiwan
Gerd Wilhelm	Amrop International/ Hager, Wilhelm et Partner	Vienna, Austria
Robert Wong	Korn/Ferry International	São Paulo

Global 200
Consultants by Firm Name

Amrop International (see also The Caldwell Partners; Gattie-Tan Soo Jin Management Consultants Pte; Hager, Wilhelm et Partner; Hofmann Herbold & Partner; PMC Amrop International; Profesindo Reksa Indonesia (PRI); Seeliger y Condé; SKS Consultants Inc.; Ståhlberg & Ahtikari Oy)

Juha-Pekka Ahtikari
Aysegül Aydin
Magnus Carlsson
Luis Condé Moller
Nanno de Vries
Anne Fawcett
Bob Gattie
Daniel Gauchat
Carlos Magnon
Pri Notowidigdo
Luiz Panelli

Finn Krogh Rants
Johann Redehlinghuys
Maria Da Gloria Ribeiro
Gary Reidy
Gerardo Seeliger
Sun Koo Shim
Lauri Ståhlberg
Tan Soo Jin
Peter Van de Velde
Gerd Wilhelm

Baines Gwinner Ltd.
Jonathan Baines

Bialecki Inc.
Linda Bialecki

Boardroom Consultants/Kenny Kindler Tholke
Roger Kenny

Bó Lè Associates
Louisa Wong Rousseau

Boyden Global Executive Search
Marc Lamy
William Marumoto

Boyden International
David Keith
Pasi Koivusaari
Karl-Gunnar Lindquist
Glendon Rowell

The Caldwell Partners/Amrop international
Anne Fawcett

Canny Bowen International
Lawrence Holmes

Chartwell Partners Internatonal, Inc.
David DeWilde

Christian & Timbers
Jeffrey Christian

Cordiner King Hever
Ian Cordiner
Richard King

Crist Partners, Ltd.
Peter Crist

Delta Management Consultants GmbH/Hever
Axel Hampe

Robert W. Dingman Company, Inc.
H. Bruce Dingman

Diversified Search Inc.
Judith Von Seldeneck

Egon Zehnder International
Egon Zehnder, founder and chairman of EZI, preferred that I not profile individual consultants from his firm in *The Global 200*. Yet to leave EZI consultants entirely out of the book would result in an enormous gap. Here then, is a much

abbreviated listing of some of the outstanding consultants in that firm, together with their specialty and primary location. An asterisk (*) by the specialty indicates the practice group leader.

Name	Sector	Location
Wilhelm Boyens	CEO/Board of Directors	Hamburg
Ross Brown	Information Technology*	San Francisco
Claudio Ceper	Fashion	Milan
Gerard Francin	CEO/Board of Directors	Paris
Ignacio Gasset	Financial Services	Madrid
Nicola Gavazzi	Automotive*	Milan
Peter Goyne	Financial Services	New York
John Grumbar	Financial Services	London
Luc Hanssens	Automotive	Brussels
Takashi Kurisaka	Pharmaceuticals/Health Care	Tokyo
Kai Lindholst	Pharmaceuticals/Health Care*	Chicago
Andrew Lowenthal	Financial Services	London
Daniel Meiland	CEO/Board of Directors	New York
Dario Pastrana	Fast Moving Consumer Goods*	Mexico City
Ulf Pueschel	Industry	Düsseldorf
Francesco Queirolo	Natural Resources*	Lyon, France
Robin Roberts	Information Technology	London
David Rogers	Fast Moving Consumer Goods	London
Mark Schappel	Fashion	New York
Nils Sjogren	CEO/Board of Directors	Copenhagen
J. Robert Swidler	CEO/Board of Directors	Montreal
Christopher Thomas	Industry	Melbourne
Charles Tseng	Consulting Services	Kuala Lampur, Malaysia
Rajeev Vasudeva	Industry	New Delhi
Philip Vivian	Information Technology	London
Egon Zehnder	CEO/Board of Directors	Zurich
Gabriel Sanchez Zinny	Consulting Services	Buenos Aires

Executive Access Limited
Ranjan Marwah

F.S.P. SA
Floriane de Saint Pierre

Leon A. Farley Associates
Leon Farley

Fenwick Partners/Heidrick & Struggles
Charles Polachi, Jr.

Jay Gaines & Company
Jay Gaines

Gardiner, Townsend & Associates
E. Nicholas Gardiner

John Townsend

Garner International
Andrew Garner

Tim Vignoles

Gattie-Tan Soo Jin Management Consultants Pte/Amrop International
Bob Gattie

Tan Soo Jin

Richard Glynn Consultants Pte Ltd.
Richard Glynn

Gould, McCoy & Chadick, Inc.
William Gould

Millington McCoy

Hager, Wilhelm et Partner/Amrop International
Gerd Wilhelm

Heidrick & Struggles (see also Fenwick Partners, Mülder & Partner)

Jean-Louis Alpeyrie	Joie Gregor
David Anderson	Theodore Jadick
Herbert Bechtel	David Joys
Bruce Beringer	Baldwin Klep
Irena Brichta	Melanie Kusin
Michael Christy	Bengt Lejsved
Gerard Clery-Melin	Jürgen Mülder
Nestor D'Angelo	Patrick Pittard
Gianni Dell'Orto	Gerard Roche
Lauren Doliva	Reinhard Thiel
Thomas Friel	John Thompson
Koichi Fukuda	Mitsuharu Tomizawa
John Gardner	Jean-Dominique Virchaux
Mike Goldstone	Richard A. Wall III
Jean-Pierre Gouirand	Kyung Yoon

Heiner Thorborg GmbH & Co. KG
Heiner Thorborg

Hever Group (see Delta Management Consultants GmbH)

Higdon Prince Inc.
Henry Higdon
Marylin Prince

Highland Search Group, L.L.C.
Georges Holzberger
Steven Potter

Hofmann Herbold & Partner/Amrop International
Friedbert Herbold

The Holman Group, Inc.
Jonathan Holman

Horton International Inc.
Robert Horton

Bjørn Johansson Associates Inc.
Dr. Bjørn Johansson

Jomon Associates Inc.
Hideaki Furuta

Jouve & Associes
Michel Flasaquier
Josette Sayers

Kenny Kindler Tholke
Roger Kenny

The Kieffer Group
Michael Kieffer

Korn/Ferry International

Akira Arai
Peter Bassett
Michael Bekins
David Wesley Benn
Michael Boxberger
John Brock
Paul Buchanan-Barrow
Dick Buschman
Alan Choi
Alex Cirone
Richard Ferry
Sakie Fukushima
R. William Funk
Mina Gouran
Anders Gulliksson

Edward Kelley
Scott Kingdom
Horacio McCoy
Caroline Nahas
Raimondo Nider
Lynn Ogden
Manuel Papayanopulos
Windle Priem
William Simon
Andrew Tsui
Maria Valdez
Jean-Marie van den Borre
Terje Wiig
Robert Wong

Kors Montgomery International/cFour Partners

R. Paul Kors

LAI Ward Howell

Michael Corey
Roderick Gow
Harold Johnson
John Johnson
Neal Maslan

Robert Pearson
Douglas Smith
Michael Tappan
Walter Williams
David Witte

LTA & Company

Henry Ling

McBride Associates, Inc.

Jonathan McBride

The Miles Partnership

Miles Broadbent

Herbert Mines Associates, Inc.

Herbert Mines

Mülder & Partner/Heidrick & Struggles

Herbert Bechtel
Jürgen Mülder

H. Neumann International

Philip Marsden
Wolfgang Reinermann

Tamas Toth
Karin Vassilopoulos

Pendleton James Associates, Inc.

Durant Hunter

PMC Amrop International

Luiz Carlos De Queirós Cabrera
Luiz Alberto Panelli

Profesindo Reksa Indonesia (PRI)/Amrop international

Pri Notowidigdo

Ray Berndtson (see also Tanton Mitchell)

Jacques André
Kurt Bruusgaard
W. Michael Honey
Kyle Mitchell

Gernot Müller
Paul Ray Jr
Andrew Weidener

R. Rollo Associates

Robert Rollo

The Rose Partnership

Philippa Rose

Russell Reynolds

Javier Anitua
Bruno-Luc Banton
Hobson Brown, Jr.
James Carpenter
Choon Soo Chew
Henry de Montebello
John Hawkins

Arthur Janta-Polczynsk
Richard Lannamanl
Brigitte Lemercier-Saltiel
Ted Orner
Rae Sede
Raymond Tang
Matthew Wright

Eric Salmon & Partners

Eric Salmon

Saxton Bampfylde International

Stephen Bampfylde
Anthony Saxton

Search Partners International
Roberto Valagussa

Seeliger y Condé/Amrop International
Luis Condé Moller
Gerardo Seeliger

Skott/Edwards Consultants
Skott Burkland

SKS Consultants Inc.
Sun Koo Shim

Smith Search, S.C.
John Smith, Jr.

Spencer Stuart

The profiles in Directory One include Spencer Stuart consultants from many countries, but not from the United Kingdom. Piers Marmion, head of Europe for Spencer Stuart (London based), preferred that I not single out consultants from the London/Leeds offices. I respected his wishes and did not include profiles from those people. However, at the end of the following list, you will find the names of several of the most respected consultants from Spencer Stuart's U.K. team. There are many more.

Robert Benson	Thomas Neff
Dennis Carey	Dayton Ogden
Bruno Colombo	Roger Rytz
Guilherme de Noronha Dale	Hermann Sendele
James Drury III	Gilbert Stenholm, Jr.
Francisco Gasset	Martin Tang
Joseph Griesedieck, Jr.	Gerard Van Den Broek
Ignacio Marseillan	Gail Vergara

The following Spencer Stuart consultants practice out of London or Leeds, in the United Kingdom.

Name	Sector
Jason Chauffer	Financial Services
Michael Holford	Industry/Manufacturing
David Kimbell	CEOs /Board of Directors
Lorna Parker	Financial Services
Simon Russell	Pharmaceutical/Health care
Anthony Vardy	Media and Entertainment
Peter Williamson	Financial Services

Ståhlberg & Ahtikari Oy/Amrop International
Juha-Pekka Ahtikari
Lauri Ståhlberg

Strategic Executive Search Pte Ltd.
Li Hsiao Yuan

Sullivan & Company
Brian Sullivan

Tanton Mitchell/Ray Berndtson
Kyle Mitchell

Traub and Associates, Ltd./Ward Howell International
Christopher Traub

Vuchot Ward Howell
Didier Vuchot

Frederick Wackerle, Inc.
Frederick Wackerle

Ward Howell International (see also LAI Ward Howell, Strategic Executive Search Pte Ltd.; Traub and Associates, Ltd.; Vuchot Ward Howell; Woodburn Mann (Pty) Ltd.)

George Abdushelishvili   Sergei Vorobiev
Maurice Ellett   Trevor Woodburn
Kang-Shik Koh   Li Hsiao Yuan
Christopher Traub

Woodburn Mann (Pty) Ltd./Ward Howell International
Trevor Woodburn

Global 200
Consultants by Country

Argentina
Alex Cirone
Ignacio Marseillan

Australia/NSW
David Wesley Benn
Ian Cordiner
Daniel Gauchat
Richard King
Gary Reidy
Peter Van de Velde

Austria
Tamas Toth
Karin Vassilopoulos
Gerd Wilhelm

Belgium
Arthur Janta-Polczynski
Baldwin Klep
Jean-Marie VanDen Borre

Brazil
Luiz Carlos de Queiros Cabrera
Guilherme De Noronha Dale
Luiz Alberto Panelli
Robert Wong

Canada
Anne Fawcett
W. Michael Honey
Kyle Mitchell

Czech Republic/Slovakia
Irena Brichta

Denmark
Kurt Bruusgaard
Finn Krogh Rants

Finland
Juha-Pekka Ahtikari
Pasi Koivusaari
Lauri Ståhlberg

France

Bruno-Luc Banton
Gerard Clery-Melin
Floriane de Saint Pierre
Michel Flasaquier
Jean-Pierre Gouirand
Marc Lamy
Brigitte Lemercier-Saltiel
Henry de Montebello
Eric Salmon
Josette Sayers
Roberto Valagussa
Didier Vuchot

Germany

Herbert Bechtel
Robert Benson
Axel Hampe
Friedbert Herbold
Jürgen Mülder
Gernot Müller
Wolfgang Reinermann
Hermann Sendele
Reinhard Thiel
Heiner Thorborg

Holland/The Netherlands

Dick Buschman
Gerard van den Broek

Hong Kong/China

Alan Choi
Mike Goldstone
Ranjan Marwah
Lynn Ogden
Glendon Rowell
Louisa Wong Rousseau
Martin Tang
Raymond Tang
Andrew Tsui

Hungary

Tamas Toth

Indonesia

PRI Notowidigdo

Italy

Bruno Colombo
Gianni Dell'Orto
Raimondo Nider

Japan

Akira Arai
Koichi Fukuda
Sakie Fukushima
Hideaki Furuta
Mitsuharu Tomizawa

Korea

Kang-Shik Koh
Sun Koo Shim

Mexico

Carlos Magnon
Horacio McCoy
Manuel Papayanopulos
John Smith, Jr.
Maria Valdez

New Zealand

Maurice Ellett

Norway

Terje Wiig

Portugal

Maria Da Gloria Ribeiro

Russia

George Abdushelishvili
Sergei Vorobiev

Singapore

Choon Soo Chew
Bob Gattie
Richard Glynn
David Keith
Henry Ling
Tan Soo Jin
Kyung Yoon
Li Hsiao Yuan

South Africa

Johann Redehlinghuys
Trevor Woodburn

Spain

Javier Anitua
Luis Condé Moller
Francisco Gasset
Gerardo Seeliger

Sweden

Magnus Carlsson
Anders Gulliksson
Bengt Lejsved
Karl-Gunnar Lindquist

Switzerland

Nanno de Vries
Bjørn Johansson
Roger Rytz

Taiwan

Christopher Traub

Turkey

Aysegül Aydin

United Kingdom

Jonathan Baines
Stephen Bampfylde
Peter Bassett
Bruce Beringer
Miles Broadbent
Paul Buchanan-Barrow
Andrew Garner
Mina Gouran
Edward Kelley
Philip Marsden
Philippa Rose
Anthony Saxton
Rae Sedel
Tim Vignoles
Richard A. Wall III
Matthew Wright

United States of America

Jean-Louis Alpeyrie
David Anderson
Jacques André
Linda Bialecki
Michael Bekins
Robert Benson
Michael Boxberger
John Brock
Hobson Brown, Jr.
Skott Burkland
Dennis Carey
James Carpenter
Jeffrey Christian
Michael Christy
Michael Corey
Peter Crist
David DeWilde
H. Bruce Dingman
Lauren Doliva
James Drury III
Leon Farley
Richard Ferry
Thomas Friel
R. William Funk
Jay Gaines

United States of America (*continued*)

E. Nicholas Gardiner
John Gardner
William Gould
Roderick Gow
Joie Gregor
Joseph Griesedieck, Jr.
John Hawkins
Henry Higdon
Jonathan Holman
Lawrence Holmes
Georges Holzberger
Robert Horton
Durant Hunter
Theodore Jadick
Harold Johnson
John Johnson
David Joys
Roger Kenny
Michael Kieffer
Scott Kingdom
R. Paul Kors
Melanie Kusin
Richard Lannamann
William Marumoto
Neal Maslan
Jonathan McBride
Millington McCoy
Herbert Mines

Caroline Nahas
Dayton Ogden
Ted Orner
Robert Pearson
Patrick Pittard
Charles Polachi, Jr.
Steven Potter
Windle Priem
Marylin Prince
Paul Ray Jr.
Robert Rollo
Gerard Roche
Judith Von Seldeneck
William Simon
Douglas Smith
Gilbert Stenholm, Jr.
Brian Sullivan
Michael Tappan
John Thompson
John Townsend
Gail Vergara
Jean-Dominique Virchaux
Frederick Wackerle
Andrew Weidener
Walter Williams
David Witte

Venezuela

Nestor D'Angelo